Beyond Sovereignty
Territory and Political Economy
in the Twenty-First Century

Beyond Sovereignty reveals a vision of the future, now unfolding, in which technological developments, especially in areas of electronics and telecommunications, have shifted the balance away from purely territorial political forms to a greater role for non-territorial organizations and identities. The result of this shift that David Elkins foresees is 'government *à la carte*,' in which there will be greater diversity of governmental forms and a wider range of choice for groups and individuals.

Elkins begins with a brief history of ways in which technological changes contributed to the creation of nation-states as we have known them since the seventeenth century. He also considers some of the ways in which political organization in the past has been non-territorial (for example, the Roman Catholic Church). Though nationalism has been part of non-territorial organization throughout most of human history, it has been embodied in territorial states only for three hundred years at most, and is now finding expression in political units which cannot be territorial in the way most existing states are, as may be inferred from observing most aboriginal nations and the diaspora of many ethnic groups.

Elkins then examines trends which weaken the exclusive and all-purpose nature of the territorial nation-state, such as the globalization of trade, finance, research and development, and marketing, which has created transnational corporations. He then switches his focus to political institutions and instruments of governance, many of which have already been decoupled from their territorial roots. In exploring a non-territorial political future, however, the line between political and social or economic realms has blurred, and thus an inquiry into the state system necessarily leads to a consideration of democracy, community, identity, and postmodern conceptions of individuality, among many other topics.

DAVID J. ELKINS is a professor in the Department of Political Science, University of British Columbia.

DAVID J. ELKINS

Beyond Sovereignty: Territory and Political Economy in the Twenty-First Century

UNIVERSITY OF TORONTO PRESS
Toronto Buffalo London

© University of Toronto Press Incorporated 1995
Toronto Buffalo London
Printed in Canada

ISBN 0-8020-2940-x (cloth)
ISBN 0-8020-7768-4 (paper)

∞

Printed on acid-free paper

Canadian Cataloguing in Publication Data

Elkins, David J.
  Beyond sovereignty : territory and political economy in the twenty-first century

  Includes bibliographical references and index.
  ISBN 0-8020-2940-X (bound) ISBN 0-8020-7768-4 (pbk.)

  1. Twenty-first century – Forecasts.   I. Title.

  CB161.E55 1995   303.49'09'05   C95-930027-9

University of Toronto Press acknowledges
the financial assistance to its publishing program of the
Canada Council and the Ontario Arts Council.

Contents

Preface vii

Introduction 3

1. Is Territory Imperative? 13

2. Technology and Territory 40

3. Economics and Territory 79

4. Functions and Administration 122

5. Non-Territorial Federalism 147

6. A Community of Communities 167

7. Majority Rules 202

8. A Menu for the Twenty-First Century 235

Notes 271

Index 299

Preface

I struggled to avoid writing this book, but it won. Once I became 'possessed,' the rest was fun because everything had some relevance. The daily news, novels, poetry, and scholarly writings seemed to have equal relevance (or irrelevance) to the future, especially when that future can only be understood in the context of medieval European history, environmentalism, aboriginal concepts of property, military technology, bureaucratic reform, the evolution of transnational corporations, deathstar satellites, the organization of restaurants, supercomputers, federalism, economic externalities, cyberspace, mass media, financial markets, international migration, virtual communities, nationalism and the 'construction' of nations, family structure, religious imperialism, and the shifting boundary between public and private domains.

No one can master so many topics, and I admit to expertise in only a few of them. Thus, I have relied on friends and other scholars even more than usual. They made me do it!

Along the way, I have had many opportunities to display my ideas, arguments, and ignorance to individuals and to groups who did not hesitate to question and criticize what I put forward. Especially helpful were seminars at the Centre for Management Development in Ottawa, the University of Ottawa, the University of Toronto, and the University of British Columbia. Even before I decided to write it, the book benefited by my discussions with Sandford Borins, Alan Cairns, Joe Carens, David Hawkes, Thomas Hueglin, Robert H. Jackson, Peter Russell, Sharon Sutherland, and David Welch. The book is now longer and better because of the people who read all or parts of the manuscript in draft: Ron Deibert, Avigail Eisenberg, Noemi Gal-Or, Michael Goldberg, John Helliwell, Robert H. Jackson, Willem Maas, Stephen Milne, Scott Pegg,

Douglas Ross, John Quigley, Mark Zacher, and two reviewers for University of Toronto Press, one of whom (Vincent Ostrom) was kind enough to identify himself.

Some of my audiences or readers needed no convincing, some will never be convinced of the plausibility of my vision, and some claim to have learned a lot about topics of interest to them. Whatever their reaction, these colleagues paid me the high compliment of taking my book seriously and offering honest opinions. Despite their honesty and expertise, I have not had the wit or will to accept all their suggestions; and each reader will no doubt spot some of these lapses on my part. I accept full responsibility for errors and omissions just as I lay claim to any originality readers may find in my vision of the next century.

One of the charming sidelights of eliciting comments from smart people was the humour which often accompanied their insights. I will offer only one example of many. Thomas Hueglin's reaction to an early draft was that my approach amounted to 'anarchy from a rational choice perspective.' This epithet contains enough truth for me to offer it as a talisman for readers lost in the maze of this book, or perhaps for those lost in the future it describes.

Vancouver, June 1994

Beyond Sovereignty
Territory and Political Economy
in the Twenty-First Century

Introduction

I have just returned from a journey into the twenty-first century. This journey was not a prediction but constituted a vision of a world to come, a world incipient in the present but largely invisible. No matter how closely the twenty-first century turns out to resemble my vision, looking back from that vantage point should allow readers to see their immediate world freshly. As Marcel Proust wrote: 'The real voyage of discovery consists not in seeking new lands, but in seeing with new eyes.'[1]

The future must be different from the present, as the present is different from the past. Yet they cannot be too different, since one grows out of the other. And some aspects of history are circular or cyclical or spiralling, repeating or mirroring earlier patterns. Thus, in understanding the dominant features of political authority in the twenty-first century, I will refer frequently to 'the feudal nebula of the Middle Ages' from which condensed the 'planets' we call nation-states.[2] Those nation-states have been evolving and are now declining in hegemony; and understanding their origins will help to envision what may lie 'beyond nations' or 'beyond sovereignty.'

With a time-frame of centuries and a stage that expands from Western Europe to the entire globe, attention to local and temporary details would require many volumes, if not a whole library. Can one small book be of any use? As I will argue, close examination of details often serves to mask or render invisible the broad rhythms of history, the shifting tectonic plates which create the mountains and valleys. 'A microscope would reveal other patterns, but a telescope is appropriate for our purposes.'[3]

This vision reveals a future that is already happening, but virtually no one has noticed because discussion relies on a vocabulary appropriate to the era now ending rather than the one being born or created or constructed. Part of the aim of this book, therefore, involves a challenge to redefine concepts, to question assumptions, to try to force discourse to catch up with reality. The vision I offer – as with any other vision – is contingent; it can be made to happen or it can be prevented; it is neither impossible nor inevitable. If readers look forward to the world described here, they should work for its actualization; if not, they should work to actualize their alternative vision. Either way, their efforts will be futile if they begin from outdated premises and misconstrue the significance of patterns obscured by the lens of common concepts. 'Thought achieves more in the world than practice; for, once the realm of imagination has been revolutionized, reality cannot resist.'[4]

Recent years have seen many predictions or visions about political, military, economic, and social life in the twenty-first century. Many are likely to be accurate, but they lie beyond the limits of this book. To set the stage for my own vision of the global future, let me review a few scenarios briefly and identify some features they share. This should highlight what my book has to offer, how it overlaps with other visions, and why it offers something novel. The review is intended to give a reasonable sample of a vast literature; it is neither complete nor chosen at random. Readers should note that I do not necessarily agree or disagree with these scenarios. I list them as illustrations, not to endorse or attack them.

The first scenario involves the nuclear proliferation which has been evident for some time. Nuclear weapons were not monopolized for very long by the superpowers, and with scientific advances in many countries and with the breakup of the Soviet Union, vastly more countries have gained access to nuclear warheads. Thus, a common prediction foresees regional nuclear wars, although no immediate danger of all-out nuclear war.

Whether involving nuclear weapons or not, the second scenario foretells of wars of redistribution. These are most likely among the nations of the South, but they might involve some aspects of North-South conflict. Such wars would hardly constitute a new type of event, since wars have been fought for booty and access to resources for millennia. As disparities of wealth become more and more evident, and as the bipolar world of the Cold War gives way to a multipolar state system, limited wars may occur more often.

The third type of prediction involves trade wars and increased protectionism. These could take several forms, ranging from selected industries in a few countries through protectionist blocs of countries (the

European Community, North America) to wholesale failure of GATT and massive curtailment of international trade or even collapse of the trading system for a period of time.

The fourth scenario exemplifies another form of protectionism, but of cultures rather than economies. As the tumult of the future world increases, the prediction states that more and more people will try to migrate or will become refugees. And as those numbers escalate, resistance to immigration will also rise in the different parts of the world. Of course, some countries have never been very welcoming of foreigners, but this scenario suggests that even the most open societies like Canada, Australia, and the United States will endeavour to shut their borders.

A fifth scenario finds the vast personnel and expertise of national espionage organizations like the CIA and KGB redirected and refocused on industrial espionage or private surveillance. Some of this has, obviously, occurred even in the Cold War, but this prediction expects an almost total change of focus.

Whether through nuclear wars or conventional wars or just greater industrialization, the sixth set of predictions looks ahead to cataclysmic ecological collapse. For some predictions, this will be the result of global warming, for others the depletion of forests, and for others incremental pollution along current lines.

Economic depression on a global scale – and even more severe than the 1930s – constitutes the seventh scenario. Protectionism, xenophobia, wars, and other factors could trigger the disaster, as could ecological collapse. Some foresee a Malthusian basis for depression, since the poorest areas of the world generally have the highest birthrates while the most affluent areas are basically below replacement rate except for immigration.

An eighth possibility may be a subset of several of the above predictions. Biogenetic engineering seems likely to revolutionize agriculture, enhancing yields and nutritional value and so on. But at least two types of negative consequences could occur. If there is reliance on relatively few strains throughout the world, a threat to these becomes a threat to survival globally. Even if the first threat proves groundless, agricultural productivity will simply make redundant the millions of peasants and labourers in the South. Unlike farmers in Europe and its offshoots, who were drawn to cities in the past century by the lure of manufacturing jobs, the rural poor in less affluent countries do not have the option of higher paid employment elsewhere – unless the elsewhere involves migration.

Related perhaps to the scenario just described, the ninth also involves genetic engineering but in a different form. Here one may instance the dire predictions of a global holocaust which could follow from the accidental or deliberate release of recombinant DNA or organisms modified by such DNA. So far such events occur only in science fiction stories, but many believe it is only a matter of time until this scenario comes true.

Having mentioned science fiction, I must refer to that type known as 'cyberpunk' as the tenth scenario. The pioneer writer, of course, was William Gibson – originally with *Neuromancer* and most recently with *Virtual Light* – whose world of 'cyberspace' consists predominantly of gangs, drugs and drug cartels, predatory multinational corporations, and pervasive violence. Yet oddly enough, it is a world still full of hope and pleasure, especially in *Virtual Light*. I will return at several points in the book to some aspects of 'cyberspace' because my vision of the twenty-first century shares many features with Gibson's.

The eleventh version of the future may be represented by a book which contains most of these other scenarios, Alvin Toffler's *Powershift*. It deserves separate citation for several reasons. It involves more research, I believe, than any other scenario I have read. It is sober and balanced where many other writers are alarmist or fail to consider positive as well as negative features of their scenarios or predictions. It is also one of the few futurist projections which has politics as its primary focus, as does this book. Although I would praise it in most respects, and although it bears more similarities to my vision than most of the ones above, it stops short in my view by failing to outline the radically new 'logic' which will hold together the new political world of the twenty-first century. Naturally, I believe that my book correctly identifies that logic, or at least suggests where it will be found. Readers – especially those yet unborn – will decide if I am correct.

Although this entire book contains my vision, let me offer a synopsis as the twelfth and final scenario in this summary. The rise of the territorial nation-state to its present position as the universal standard of political organization brought many things most current observers view as blessings (including individualism, the concept of personal rights, and economic development) as well as many curses (including totalitarian regimes, colonialism, and destruction or assimilation of a myriad of other political forms). Technological developments – especially in areas of electronics and telecommunications – have shifted the balance away from purely territorial political forms to a greater role for non-territorial organizations and identities. Although these new forms and forces do not preclude any of the other eleven scenarios, they constitute a new 'logic' which opens up possibilities unknown or unimagined or unattainable until now. My vision or scenario, therefore, consists of following the 'logic' of non-territorial political organization to reveal some benefits (and some dangers) which all the other scenarios ignore or play down or evaluate differently. The avenues this logic opens up include new dimensions of democracy and citizenship, enhanced forms of community, a reconciliation between individual and group needs, and more flexible and focused types of government which offer more choices to citizens than simply which elite will govern them.

My book is a work of imaginative non-fiction, which may make it seem like an oxymoron. It is thus not a normal scholarly work, although it draws on a great deal of scholarly evidence. The twenty-first-century world envisioned here is the product of my imagination: it is a vision, a scenario, a schema, a model, an interpretation, but the scholarship, facts, and related material make it non-fiction rather than fiction. At the end, the reader may decide whether it is plausible, possible, a fantasy, a fiction, or an oxymoron.

Described in this way, the book may appear to claim a unique status. This would be an inaccurate deduction. I believe that most of the predictions or scenarios above should be seen as imaginative non-fiction too. They involve predictions or imaginative evocations of one or another aspect of the 1990s, the new millennium, or the twenty-first century, but many are less honest in their self-description. Not all of the authors of such scenarios warn the reader that they are guessing or predicting or envisioning or imagining a world; or, if they do, the warning is disguised as extrapolation or just the logical consequences of current events. Some books speak with authority, and some with humility; and both postures can have the effect of lowering readers' awareness of the author's audacity. This is less true of some authors, and I do not make these statements in order to lay blame. Instead, I offer these observations so that my book may be judged in the same terms – as presenting an imagined world, but on the basis of the most accurate information currently available.

The books containing these scenarios about the future are cited in many places in my book. As they should be, since one can learn from them if one takes them with the proverbial grains of salt. I have not, therefore, listed them all at this point; but I do wish to discuss some features they share.

The most prominent feature shared by the futurist books I have in mind concerns their pessimism. They paint a picture which is usually gloomy, depressing, and even frightening. They emphasize dangers and traps. Friends who have read my book in draft form, by contrast, have generally expressed surprise at how upbeat and optimistic it is. Readers can decide for themselves at the end whether they see more dangers or more hope in the vision I present. The answer does not depend simply on adding up costs or benefits but also on recognizing that what is a benefit in some eyes may be a cost in other eyes, and vice versa.

In my own opinion, my vision seems less gloomy than most others because it tries to highlight positive features that may characterize the twenty-first century, but which are played down or ignored in the other scenarios. But it also can be viewed in another light: that it is equally full of dangers, but ones less obvious or less visible to people who have been numbed by the horrors and atrocities of the twentieth century. Part of the effort required to evaluate these scenarios involves an awareness of how loaded or biased our words and concepts can be. For example, many of the scenarios or predictions above imply a lack of control or a fear that events are moving to a point beyond the control of governments, even if well-intentioned ones. Another way of stating this process, and one developed at great length in the book, involves the observation that 'out of control' can also mean 'not under someone else's control.' If you feel that power is slipping away from your government (as many Americans do, for example) is that because another government (Japan? Europe?) is on the rise, or because governments are yielding some of their sovereignty and military might to other forms of governance? The latter perception constitutes the core of my argument. I believe there are possible benefits from the weakening of central governments, but the dangers depend on who takes up the slack. Whether this view entails hope or gloom will be a judgment each reader should make.

The single most important reason for seeing my scenario as less pessimistic or less dangerous also rests on an illusion of perception or perspective. The goblins in nearly all of the above scenarios are very familiar to anyone aware of the news in recent decades – war, nuclear threats, pollution, over-population, espionage, ecological collapse, and many others. The demons lurking in my scenario are much less familiar, although they may turn out to be as bad or worse than familiar evils – computer viruses, lack of confidentiality of personal data, less rootedness in a place because of opportunities for non-territorial communities, more choices and thus a greater sense of loss at options foregone, and many more.

Readers should also bear in mind that nothing in my scenario forecloses the possibility of occurrence of the other predictions. Every part of my envisioned world could become reality and yet wars, disease, ecological collapse, and deadly recombinant DNA could wreak havoc in the twenty-first century. I believe firmly that some of what is outlined in this book makes some versions of other scenarios less likely, but shifting the probabilities does not preclude rare or calamitous events. I wish it did.

The final feature which all of these dozen scenarios share is their partiality and complementarity. Each foregrounds certain aspects of current events or future trends and obscures or ignores others. These are matters of emphasis based on informed judgments about the relative importance of key variables. Toffler may be an exception because of his effort to be comprehensive historically and to account for all or most social, economic, and political transformations up to the present, or 'waves' as he calls them. My book is also partial to the extent that it abstracts the role of *territoriality* from the network of concepts highlighted by the sum total of these scenarios. Although the book examines many features of the world, it does so by casting the analysis in terms of the historical emphasis up to now on the territorial basis for political authority. This necessarily slights other valuable concepts, but it is justified in my mind by the lack of consideration given to territoriality in the other scenarios.

Part of the argument, therefore, rests on teasing out options, trends, possibilities, and assumptions which have been obscured or masked by the blatant obviousness of many frightening events of our time and by the language analysts use to describe and evaluate what they observe. This book endeavours to make visible the forces and actors now in the background, partly by simply calling attention to them, partly by putting them in a novel and imaginative framework, and partly by redefining some of the concepts which have become commonplace but which no longer reflect as accurately as they once did what occurs in our daily lives. If other people have emphasized the tragedy of *Hamlet*, perhaps there will be relief to focus on the background brought to centre stage in *Rosencrantz and Guildenstern Are Dead*. I must remind readers, however, that the latter play was, despite its comic moments, also a tragedy. One can learn more, I believe, by comparing the above scenarios than from any one of them alone. A couple of previews of what redefinition or pointing to new phenomena can accomplish will serve as prelude to the book and as conclusion to this prelude. How does one make the invisible visible? Ultimately, the book is its own example.

Television has been one of the most visible objects of daily life for many years. Even in remote areas or in less affluent countries, television as machine and television as entertainment have become familiar to global citizens. After all, over 800 million households worldwide now have television reception. And yet there have been absolutely momentous changes behind the familiar facade of the TV screen in terms of delivery, content, and reach.

Broadcasting in the literal sense has become less common, and targeted ('addressable') audiences more so, because of the spread of cable systems, fibre optics, and scrambled satellite transmission. As a result, neighbours may watch entirely different programs; and we rapidly approach an era of interactive TV and multimedia convergence of TV, telephone, and computer in the so-called Information Superhighway. These developments are spelled out in later chapters. Here I wish simply to note that all such changes have been invisible in the literal sense that they have not been portrayed on the screens themselves but are to be found 'behind' them in the new forms of delivery. Nevertheless, because of these technological changes, a new era will become visible very soon. My vision takes account of these hidden developments.

Likewise, what any one person watches may have changed incrementally, but collectively the change has been revolutionary. Three or four networks offering largely the same menu have been supplemented by additional channels and incipient networks with more selective or targeted content, and these will in turn be surpassed before this book appears in print by 'deathstar' satellites with channel capacities in the hundreds.

New means of delivery of vast menus of programming imply, finally, that the inherent *territoriality* of TV in its early years has been replaced almost totally by the absence of territorial limits; and both territoriality and its absence have been in the background. This book puts them in the foreground and explores the vast implications of the metamorphosis from territoriality to non-territorial organization.

Another example involves currency transactions and exchange rates. Doubtless every reader of a book like this has travelled abroad and converted currency, traveller's cheques, or credit card purchases. Over the past few decades, no alteration in the system has been visible, except perhaps a greater volatility of rates for some currencies. Yet the entire purpose of the system has evolved from an adjunct of commercial trade to a self-contained system almost totally divorced from trade.

As trade expands, most people would assume that more currency trading also occurs, and of course that inference has some (albeit a small) basis in fact. But the amount of currency trading so far exceeds the level needed to equalize commercial transactions among nations that for all practical purposes, they are as segregated as the markets for (say) oil and hog futures. In the early 1990s world trade in goods came to about U.S. $700 billion *per year*, whereas by now currency trading averages about U.S. $800–$900 billion *per day*! That is, for every dollar exchanged to satisfy trade needs, there are another three hundred or so dollars exchanged purely for currency speculation. Why?

Several reasons may be adduced, not least of which concerns the ability to conduct currency trades on a twenty-four-hour basis because of advances in telecommunications technology. The reason I want to emphasize here, however, concerns the usefulness of our concept of trade, or more precisely the usefulness of noticing that 'trade' has several new meanings virtually unknown before this generation. First, a majority of the dollar-value of world trade in manufactured goods in recent years involves the movement of semi-finished goods *within a company but between nations*. For example, components of cars or TVs or running shoes may be manufactured in anywhere from two to ten countries and combined only in the country where they are to be marketed. In what useful sense is this series of transactions all called by the same label of 'trade'? Should the repeated 'import' and 'export' of the goods by the same company show up in the trade balances of several countries? Perhaps they should, but if so the implications are quite different than they were when India shipped raw cotton to Britain and purchased cotton cloth and clothing manufactured there.

A second new sense of trade may be confronted with a concrete example. The United States has for years fretted about its balance of payment deficit with Japan, and perhaps it should. But part of the deficit results from categorizing 'imports' on the basis of the physical location of a company's headquarters rather than any of several other indicators. For example, the largest exporter of microchips from Japan to the United States has for several years been Texas Instruments, a company founded in Dallas, Texas, but now manufacturing its microchips in Japan. Is it a U.S. company? A Japanese company? Does it matter? To whom does it matter?

The fact that Texas Instruments' microchips from Japan show up as part of the United States' deficit in balance of payments has been a concern to some people. One may point out, however, that from another perspective the United States does not have a balance of *payments* problem, since it pays in U.S. dollars as do almost all countries. Thus, it does not need to 'earn' hard currency in order to pay for its imports; its own currency *is* the hard currency which the world trade system uses. Only if enough traders think that the American dollar will collapse, and thus refuse to use it, need the American economy generate a surplus of 'exports' over 'imports.' The status of the American dollar may be one of those 'good news–bad news' stories which makes it difficult to decide whether this book is optimistic or pessimistic.

Finally, note the last sense of 'trade' brought to consciousness by these examples. If trade in goods and the payment of the American deficit are largely divorced from currency trading, then currency itself can be traded as a commodity without devastating effects on the trade in goods. Of course, there has always been speculation in currencies. What has become clear recently is that currencies' values today do not depend very much on the goods traded by nations. Instead, nations' political stability and the desires of large capital pools to take advantage of stable or unstable political situations have enhanced the role of currency as a commodity. One final observation about this new system: the large capital pools are not primarily 'capitalist' in the usual sense; but pools of pension funds, mutual funds, daily cash flows of transnational corporations, and cash or bonds of the governments themselves. Because of vast technological networks, the capital markets of the world have become a single capital market. Money, banking, finance, and investment recognize no borders. And thus these realms have been transformed from territorial to non-territorial organizations. So have many other realms, and the implications of that transformation will, I argue here, distinguish the twenty-first-century world from the last few centuries.

This book focuses especially on political institutions and instruments of governance, many of which have already been decoupled from their territorial roots. In exploring our non-territorial political future, however, we will see that the line between political and social or economic realms has blurred, and thus an inquiry into the state system necessarily leads to a consideration of democracy, community, identity, and postmodern conceptions of individuality, among many other topics.

1

Is Territory Imperative?

Is territory imperative? Must nations and provinces rest necessarily on assumptions about territoriality? Historically at least three assumptions underlay our institutional experiments. Indeed, they have formed a deep and unconscious part of the political culture of the Western world and its colonies for over three hundred years. The three assumptions involve:

1. exclusive use of territory
2. continuous territory
3. contiguous territory

Territoriality will be used to mean that all three of these assumptions are assumed as the basis of political authority, especially at the national level. To 'relax' assumptions about territoriality, as I will do throughout ensuing chapters, means to assume that only one or two of the assumptions hold. For example, reserves for Indians are not territorial in the way nations are because they do not presume contiguity of reserves with each other even though the reserves may be for the exclusive use of status Indians. All of the assumptions play a role in our conception of appropriate political units and the exercise of political authority.

The assumption of exclusivity is probably the most important of these. It involves 'monopoly of force' and 'authoritative allocation of values,' but goes beyond those features.[1] We used to assume that religions should have their own territory or 'turf.'[2] As nations replaced universal religions as the sovereign arbiters of life and death, the 'compactness' and 'boundedness' of religion gave way to our now familiar intermingling of believers in the same area. Instead, we refuse to countenance the intermingling of nations, or provinces for that matter, although I believe that this assumption is in process of breaking down.

The difference between continuous and contiguous may not be crucial for many purposes, but the speculations below about other kinds of nations and provinces make it useful to keep them separate. 'Contiguous' means not broken into two or more geographically separate pieces (as in the former East and West Pakistan). 'Continuous' means no unit embedded within another, completely surrounded by it. For present discussion, waters (rivers, bays, straits, etc.) are not deemed to result in non-continuous or non-contiguous territory. Only land occupied exclusively by another province or nation can divide such units into separate parts or can be embedded within them.

All three assumptions have been violated in one place or another. For example, the United States does not seem greatly concerned that its forty-eight mainland states are not contiguous with Alaska (or Hawaii, but again water is not usually seen as a barrier). Embedded units are quite rare, however, unless one counts things like some of the 'homelands' in South Africa. Some countries, such as Switzerland and Paraguay, are landlocked; but they are surrounded by several countries rather than by a single country. Thus, they do not interrupt the continuity of other countries.

The assumption of exclusive use of territory is violated in all federal systems, since two 'sovereign' orders of government share the same territory. This was, of course, one reason why federalism was a novel idea; and it is easy to overlook what we now take for granted.[3] The British colonial office in the 1860s was hesitant to endorse Canadian federal schemes because of this feature; they thought it odd or illogical to divide the sovereignty of the Crown or of Parliament. Nevertheless, it worked well enough that we now forget how tentatively the idea was put forward because of the concern about exclusive use of territory. Other possible examples of non-exclusive use of territory might be joint trusteeship of colonial possessions, as in some South Pacific islands. By and large, as with the other two assumptions, 'violations' are rare and, when they occur, not always noticed because these assumptions are part of the perceptual 'lens' through which we view the institutions of modern government.

To anticipate, I should note that these three assumptions, taken together, lead logically to a fourth condition – congruent territories. That is, administrative units within a nation (or province) have the same boundaries even though they deal with different matters. This point will

Is Territory Imperative? 15

be particularly important in delineating administrative implications of relaxing these three assumptions about territory.

These assumptions are worth questioning, I believe, because they are very recent additions to our political culture. For the first millennium or so of the Christian era, politics was carried out with no belief that a territorial base was essential to the state, even though many rulers coveted territory. Peoples migrated and conquered other peoples.[4] Warriors ruled and were challenged by other warriors. Exclusive use of territory was rarely achieved for long, and continuous and contiguous territories were almost unknown except for some cities or towns.

Market systems, authority or command systems, and persuasive systems are said to constitute the grand categories of political analysis.[5] All have generally been assumed in recent centuries to require, or rest on, a territorial basis. Nations protect 'their' industries; governments exercise coercive force over a territory and enforce the ultimate authoritative allocation of values; and the media of communication (especially radio and television) are deemed to be instruments of indoctrination and control to such an extent that *coup d'état* planners move simultaneously against the seat of government and the headquarters of the national broadcasting system.

But time brings changes. Not only have market systems penetrated all countries – and not just industrialized ones – but international 'globalization' of economic relations has placed many economic functions beyond the control of nations, even rich and powerful ones like the United States or Japan. Likewise, political organizations at the local or regional level and at the supra-national level compete with nations for the allegiance of citizens. And the media of mass communication have changed in several ways: more channels as a result of cable and satellite transmission; fewer newspapers and more competition across media types; more specialized and targeted media formats, advertising, and content; decoupling of broadcasting from territory because of cable and satellite capacities; greater audience fragmentation; greater audience control because of multiplication of options; and the end of 'prime time' because of taping capacities on VCRs. For some people, territory has a temporal quality: for example, Canadian 'snowbirds' who winter in Florida or Arizona, and people who own time-share accommodations.

In short, the territoriality of political, economic, and cultural life has been shattered in recent decades. The particular ways in which most aspects of our lives have been bundled or packaged in containers called nation-states have been increasingly challenged and subtly eroded. The implications of the 'unbundling' of nation-states are probably countless, but some are the focus of this book.

To forestall one particular concern, let me note that geography is not the same as territory, which is not the same as space. Every material object takes up space, and so do organizations. But there are different ways of occupying space; and the forms we call exclusivity, continuity, and contiguity are especially strong and contentious. Geography as a field of study does not presume that exclusive, continuous, and contiguous use of space is common or necessary or desirable. Instead much of the study of geography revolves around density of use, overlapping use, non-congruent boundaries or borders, and linkages across space.

ASSUMPTIONS AND CULTURES

Our lives would be greatly complicated by constant questioning of the institutions and traditions which underlie or constitute our cultures. As we accept and operate an institution, we take it for granted. There is no apparent need to ask each day why we came to rely on that institution rather than another. Such queries arise, however, when alternative visions beckon or when changes in technology or related institutions broaden the range of feasible alternatives or make more costly the pursuit of daily habits. Chapter 2 will outline many technological changes which led us to our current reliance on territorial forms of political organization, and it will emphasize on-going changes in technology which suggest that non-territorial political forms may be more appropriate in the future. Chapter 3 looks at economic changes – and equally crucial, changes in economic *ideas* – which reinforced the previous reliance on territorial politics, as well as the evolution of economic ideas and practices which now favour non-territorial organizations.

The complex and interconnected set of assumptions about appropriate institutions and behavioural modes, and about the range of plausible variations on them, compose what we mean by culture. Not culture in the 'high culture' sense of opera and painting but culture in the sense of a way of life so taken for granted that it seems natural, 'a given,' and the hidden premise on which we can base our arguments and actions.[6]

These assumptions or premises are of a special kind. They consist of largely unconscious restrictions on the range of fundamental aspects of our civilization, and not just of details or speculations. Of course, we make lots of assumptions that do not receive close scrutiny every day of our lives. For example, that stop lights are red rather than green or blue,

Is Territory Imperative? 17

or that black is the colour of mourning (even though in India white is used for that situation). These assumptions are properly part of the culture, but they are less pervasive and less fundamental than some others, such as the territoriality of political organizations – less pervasive because restricted for whatever reason to a particular culture group and less fundamental because one can more readily imagine them changing without disrupting our lives in many other ways.

It may be observed that these pervasive and fundamental assumptions resist change more than the assumptions 'at the surface.' That is partly a tautology since labile assumptions would not be fundamental. But it is not entirely a tautology because one sign of something's fundamental nature concerns how difficult it is to remember that it is actually an assumption, that is, to imagine that the world could be different or perhaps has been different in the past or may even be different elsewhere today. That is why I stated above that we question assumptions when an alternative vision beckons. Such deep-rooted assumptions which evade most people's notice that they are assumptions I will refer to as *tectonic* assumptions. Tectonic changes occur rarely, but they render problematic many aspects of our lives. They call into question the very grounds of our arguments. They are debated and eventually a new assumption or set of assumptions comes to seem natural or even inevitable. Why did we not think of this sooner? How could we previously have believed that silly idea?

A VISION OF TECTONIC CHANGE

We are now in the midst of a tectonic change in several areas of our lives. One in particular will receive most of the attention in this book, but its ramifications will require that a few words be recorded about other tectonic changes.[7] Territoriality is thus the centrepiece, the keystone, the first among many changes in this exploration of the past and the future. Uncovering the ramifications of territoriality will lead to several observations about the meaning of individuality, types of community, mass society, democracy, and citizenship.

To highlight the taken-for-granted nature of territoriality, I offer a vision of another world premised on the relaxation of assumptions about territoriality. This vision may or may not turn out to be accurate as a detailed prediction about the world in the twenty-first or later centuries. Prediction is not my goal. Instead I want to corrode the presumptiveness of the set of assumptions about territoriality which have served as the unspoken framework of European political thought for about three centuries and the framework for every part of the inhabited areas of this planet for most of this century. Prediction occurs implicitly whenever we use familiar concepts, because they imply that their underlying assumptions will continue to be applicable. The vision put forward here is, in that same way, a prediction, but a prediction intended to demonstrate that predictions always have plausible alternatives.

The vision is personal to the extent that it represents my understanding of where nation-states came from and where they may be heading. It is not purely personal, however, in that I do not necessarily prefer it to other possibilities. In some ways I look forward to what lies ahead, and yet I know that there are dark sides which – were I to live long enough to experience them – I would no doubt denounce. I do not wish to offer personal evaluations at this point; they may become clear in later chapters. Instead my concern in this chapter is to define terms, set limits on this overly ambitious endeavour, open readers' minds to doubts and questions about current political situations, cast the arguments in ways which may help to differentiate between figure and ground (or between the forest and the trees), and to suggest that changes need not be either random or inevitable.

If the vision I set forth seems promising and beneficial, perhaps it can inspire action to bend history to its purpose. If the vision should seem deeply troubling, now would be a good time to begin working to subvert it, rather than waiting until the vision is so taken for granted that we cannot see that it is our own construction.

CONSTRUCTED WORLDS

There is a hard edge to parts of the reality humans inhabit. When we bump into the corner of a table, we bruise. When the brakes on a car fail, it crashes into something. But many aspects of our worlds are socially constructed. That is not the same as saying arbitrary, nor can solitary or defiant individuals construct another world. Over time, through micro-interactions, in countless ways they seldom notice, people who interact come to share concepts, terms, frames of reference, and assumptions which turn out to be constitutive of worlds that later seem as natural and real as tables, brakes, and car crashes. Short-run incremental micro-changes have the capacity to constitute large-scale macro-level changes in the longer run.

Socially constructed worlds, however, are not natural or 'given.' Of course, one may aver that tables are not 'given' either: having accepted the refined concepts of atom, molecule, and equivalence of energy and matter in quantum mechnics, we are lead to 'see' a different table than was 'given' in the eyes of our ancestors. That may reinforce the point that socially constructed concepts, even more than material bodies, should be viewed as malleable, as constitutive of our environment but ultimately derived from shared social experience. There are doubtless limits to the arbitrariness of constructions, but if concepts can be constructed, they can be deconstructed and reconstructed.

Most people feel no unease at the concept of 'creating' a nation by revolution (as happened in the United States in 1776 and France in 1789) or by writing a constitution, as Canadians did in the 1860s or Australians in the 1890s or so many Third World countries after the Second World War. But there are deeper levels of creation and construction: before you can write a constitution, you must have the idea that a constitution is a willed act of human agency and not just tradition or the revealed word of a diety; before you can argue for or create a nation, you must have the idea of a nation.

Words serve many helpful purposes, but they – like tables – often seem hard and definite when we need to see them as cages from which our thoughts should be freed. Is Canada one nation or two? Are aboriginal nations really nations, and if so, how many nations are there 'in' Canada? And how many angels can dance on the head of a pin? The answers to these questions – to the extent anyone can give an answer – are less significant than recognizing that the concept of nation (and angel) has changed a great deal over time, and 'nation' is undergoing, I argue, a fundamental transformation now.

Are gay or lesbian couples families? Are unmarried heterosexual couples families? If they have children? Does any family exist if there are only adults? The answers to these questions – to the extent anyone can give an answer – are less significant than recognizing that the concept of family has changed a great deal over the centuries, and it is evolving now. The new reproductive technologies will accelerate and complicate the changes in what 'family' means.

One reason it is difficult to think about nations sharing territory or coexisting within one place like Canada concerns the belief that nations are territorial.[8] In a similar vein, most people believe that families are about the sharing of sperm and egg in heterosexual relations. Both assumptions may be questioned, and one may then move on to a new understanding of 'nation' or 'family.' Of course, one may prefer to coin a new word in order to avoid confusion or to avoid arguments about what is 'really' a nation or a family. Whatever the word, one must confront questions about changing concepts, changing assumptions, and changing limits on what is feasible or plausible or decent or reasonable.

For present purposes, I intend to use 'nation' and 'nation-state' in several related ways because doing so will highlight the fact that an institution was created, evolved, feels familiar, but continues to evolve in ways that make me wonder if it is still the beast so many people feel comfortable with. Some readers will prefer new terms or adding explanatory adjectives ('couples' become 'partners' or heterosexual and homosexual couples), and I understand the urge. But I have chosen to stick with 'nation' for the reasons given. If 'nation' seems ambiguous, this may be inherent in current usage. Perhaps readers will feel more comfortable with the term in light of its universal recognition in the United Nations. Strictly speaking, *states* are allowed to become members, and only a few 'nations' have observer status. Mutual recognition by other 'nations' allows a new (or newly independent) nation-state to apply for membership in the United Nations.

SOVEREIGN TERRITORIAL STATES

No major group in Canada or any other country, so far as I know, has stated that a large portion of our current political problems stems from utilizing governments organized simply around a national territory. I propose to explore that possibility. By doing so, I do not necessarily assume that nation-states play no useful role, nor that they can be completely replaced by other political forms. Instead, I want to pose several distinct questions:

1. Why did the (Western) world come to assume that *one all-purpose political organization* was superior to several more narrowly focused organizations each with a more specific range of functions?

2. Why did Europeans come to assume, further, that a premier political organization must be territorially based; that is, it must occupy a piece of turf *exclusively* and its turf should be *continuous* and *contiguous*?

3. What are the implications of relaxing each of these assumptions about territoriality (as states have done at the local level for a very long time)?

4. What is likely to come after the nation-state, or at least to become more salient as part of the international or global political order?

Even a book cannot do justice to questions as broad or open-ended as these. One may speculate about implications of relaxing our assumptions about exclusivity, continuity, and contiguity of territory without fully understanding how everyone came to take them for granted. Nevertheless, some historical background is essential, as I argue in several chapters. Incomplete though my historical analysis may be, I hope that it is sufficient to undermine the assurance that readers now feel about the 'natural' or 'given' status of assumptions about territoriality.[9] Many of the subsequent chapters mix history and speculation about the future. Such speculations do not lead me to a single specific prediction about the organizational basis of the new world order which may lie beyond the nation-state, because I do not believe that any single mode of organization will achieve the hegemony in our minds that territorial nation-states have exercised for the past two or three centuries. Instead, I expect to find more differentiated political forms which suit or adapt to ecological niches, even if 'ecological' does not necessarily imply territoriality in all cases.

To question the assumptions about territoriality requires, as we shall see, that we also question the reliance on one all-purpose political organization. Since historically the all-purpose nation-state grew out of the increasingly territorial nature of the state, one can postpone the discussion of purposes until after examining assumptions about territory. Those assumptions must be situated in a very long historical context but in a very limited geographic context. They arose over many centuries solely in what we now call Western Europe and only later were they spread to every settled part of this planet by imperialism, exploration, conquest, settlement, and conversion.

Former prime minister Trudeau in his earlier incarnation as an academic described the origins of the territorial state in a succinct and pointed fashion:

It was not the population who decided by what states they would be governed; it was the states which, by wars (but not 'people's wars'), by alliances, by dynastic arrangements, by marriages, by inheritance, and by chance, determined the area of territory over which they would govern. And for that reason they could be called territorial states ... The important transition was from the *territorial state* to the *nation-state*.[10]

For more than a thousand years of the Christian era, some 'peoples' migrated across the face of what we now call Europe. They were inhibited in their movements only by force of arms and natural barriers and not at all by border inspections of passports or any other political boundaries. Over time, their movements became less common because they encountered more and more groups or 'peoples' who had already formed settled communities, because they chose to remain and cultivate certain areas, or because feudal obligations tied greater proportions of the population to particular parcels of land. By the eleventh or twelfth centuries, rudimentary states existed, whether called kingdoms, feudalities, or cities.[11] The process to which Trudeau refers encompasses the next few centuries (roughly 1200 to 1600), during which one might describe the process as the state coming to the sedentary people. The transition to the nation-state could be said to begin in the Thirty Years' War in the mid-seventeenth century and to reach its deification in the French Revolution.[12] All dates are arbitrary, as the process occurred earlier in some places and later in others. The point of 1648 and 1789 as significant events concerns how recent they are compared to the longer sweep of history. Despite what Trudeau implies, the nation-state was unremittingly a territorial state itself, but one sanctified or legitimized by popular consent. To continue the metaphor, the state and the nation ('the people') came together. Border disputes occurred, of course, but still one could assume that most people stayed in one place, 'their place,' and the rulers and the ruled agreed on the importance of that place to the nation.[13]

So strong was the assumption that people and state coincided in a compact territory that no one issued or asked for passports, except for diplomats.[14] Few people in Europe travelled and those who did were visitors, merchants, diplomats, or pilgrims rather than migrants: the exceptions were all outside Europe and are notable to us because they include Canada, the United States, Australia, and New Zealand. Not until the First World War were passports seen as a task for governments. The reason for the sudden change, I believe, concerned the fact that by then people acted as though they could come to the state, instead of the state coming to them or accepting the territorial expression of a state-people.[15] Formerly one could assume that people would, like E.T., go home eventually. When by 1920 it was evident that this presumption no longer held, nations took steps to control who entered their territory and for what purpose.

It is this type of tectonic change of assumption which I propose to explore. Unlike the historical examples just given, we have not yet witnessed the transition away from the assumptions that a nation-state must have territory and that the territory should be contiguous, continuous, and exclusive. I believe firmly that the transition is in progress and will be completed in a matter of decades.[16] Thus, it is timely to relax the components of territoriality and speculate about some directions in which political organization may proceed. To anticipate an important part of the argument, lessening our reliance on territory enhances our conception of citizenship.

Here and at several other places in the book, I emphasize the historical basis of concepts and assumptions. Perhaps it does not need statement explicitly, but let me explain why such history is essential to my argument about the future. For one thing, what led us to this point may help us understand what could lead us away from this point to something different. More important, however, is the way a grounded historical explanation forces us to see that events, institutions, or concepts are seldom as universal as we assume them to be. If they are acknowledged as local and contingent phenomena, it should be less traumatic to let go of them or to inquire how they may change or to keep an open mind about what one may find elsewhere or in the future. Social scientists hope to find 'universal laws' on the order of physical laws, but one of the few such laws (if it is) concerns the apparent need of social (or political or economic) forms to adapt to local conditions rather than take exactly the same form everywhere.

ANALOGIES

To soften our assumptions so that we can experience the hypothetical suspension of disbelief to imagine the future, let us consider an analogy with local government. Other analogies will be featured in subsequent chapters. Of course, analogies break down if pushed too far, so that we will not dwell on them but turn quickly to the territoriality of political forms.

Few people find incongruous the fact that local government involves organizations which share no common territory. It is true that some specific-purpose institutions – such as parks boards or school boards – may coincide with the territorial boundaries of a municipality. Many, however, are larger or smaller than a municipality: transit authorities, counties, water districts, gas pipelines, air traffic controls, community centres, harbour and bridge authorities, highway districts, and toll-free telephone areas are examples. It is not sufficient to respond that these are not all under the auspices of a municipal government or not even in the public sector at all in some areas. That is, in fact, the point: at the local level we do not assume that government must be based on exclusive territories operating under a single dominant authority. Why then should we take for granted such exclusivity at the national and provincial levels? The answer is that they are sovereign, but that is no answer at all. Why do we assume that the only kind of sovereignty must be territorial or that territorial continuity, contiguity, and exclusivity must be linked to sovereignty?

Again I emphasize that the answers to such questions, while interesting, are not sufficient. Instead we should focus on the fact that we seldom or never ask such questions and thus fail to note that the fundamental 'natural' unit of political analysis (nation-states) can be questioned, has not existed for very long in historical terms, and is very likely dissolving as we speak. Recent events in the USSR, Yugoslavia, and Czechoslovakia may offer intuitive evidence for this questioning of political units.

THE DECLINE OF NATIONS

What evidence can one offer – besides analogies – for the assertion that nations are no longer the hegemonic political units, that they have declined at least in relative terms compared to other political units, forces, norms, or ideas? This question can be fully answered only at the end of the book, but readers deserve some *prima facie* indicators at this point.[17]

The growth in number of nations in this century – from 60 members of the United Nations in 1950 to over 180 today – has been posited by many observers as a sign of the strength of nationalism in the postcolonial world.[18] That is probably correct if we emphasize the word 'nationalism' and thereby focus on heightened feelings of involvement in a nation; such feelings lead citizens to oppose its continued incorporation in a former empire (whether British, French, American, or Soviet). Strength of nationalist sentiment, however, may be distinguished from stability, durability, viability, or self-sufficiency of nations or nation-states as political building-blocks of the world system. There are many kinds of evidence to which one can point that suggest the nation as a political unit may be weaker than the sense of nationalism which may have called it into existence.[19] Many of these will feature in subsequent chapters; I will simply list them without elaboration at this juncture so that readers may begin to weigh the later points in this chapter against some of these issues.

Some signs of weakness relate directly to particular types of nations. The nations which were the centre of empires have been weakened by the end of empire, or perhaps their weakness hastened the end of empire. One thinks especially of Holland, Britain, and France in the post–Second World War era. Of course, the breakup of the Soviet Union itself – not to say its imperial decline as well – must count as evidence that specific nations cannot presume they will be permanent fixtures on the world stage.

Of the nations born of imperial decline after the Second World War or after the breakup of the Soviet Union and its empire, some have deep historical roots but most do not, and almost all contain substantial minorities who seek self-determination, autonomy, or devolution. Robert H. Jackson has characterized these African and some other Third World nations as 'quasi-states,' having 'external' sovereignty and lacking internal control, to emphasize their precarious existence as sovereign bodies.[20] The vitality and renewal of sub-national and transnational 'nations' such as the Palestinians, Kurds, Catalans, Scots, and Quebeckers should warn us that 'nations' which belong to the United Nations may be weakened by the claims of 'nations' yearning to be recognized. Tribes, religious groupings, and transnational corporations pose (as I argue below) quite different kinds of threats to 'nations,' but threats nonetheless.

Other signs of decline reflect the willingness to intervene in each other's affairs or to allow non-national bodies and groups to operate in a transnational fashion.[21] One may mention: the support for Kurdish 'safe zones' in Iraq; the boycotts of South Africa and of companies dealing with that country; imposition of conditions by the World Bank on developing countries; termination of aid to poor countries unable or unwilling to pay interest on debts; international regulation of shipping, air travel, and disease control; pressure for cross-border cooperation on environmental standards and clean-up; acceptance by many (though not all) countries of arms control verification inspections; and greater legitimacy for Amnesty International, PEN, Greenpeace, and a host of other private or voluntary organizations. Even more salient, in many eyes, as rivals to nations are transnational corporations, drug cartels, terrorists, and fundamentalist religious movements.

It is perhaps worth reiterating that nations or nation-states as we now understand them developed out of some very specific circumstances in Western Europe in the early modern period. The spread of the idea of the sovereign, all-purpose nation-state to the extent that it is the basic unit of politics in every part of Earth except in Antarctica has given the impression of moving from strength to strength. But one may equally argue that few areas that have embraced the idea also evince the conditions – social, political, economic, or technological – which allowed this form of organization to defeat contending norms (religious, civic, or feudal) in Europe in a long Darwinian struggle. The continuing urge to impose a territorial definition of nation may reveal the strength of *nationalism* as an ideology but its weakness as an organizational form. That nation-states have been relatively successful in some places and less so ('quasi-states') elsewhere suggests that technological, social, economic, and political variables interact in complex ways to create ecological niches for 'nations,' or to foster adaptation to the niches, which could explain why there are so many types of nation-states coexisting today. Thus, it may be the case that the increasing numbers of 'national' units demonstrate the dilution and weakening of the idea rather than its strength and inevitable hegemony.[22] This conclusion may be buttressed by looking at what is often called 'globalization.'

GLOBALIZATION: PROCESS AND PRODUCT

For most people, globalization means supra-national political units and/or more extensive economic interdependence. For them, the classic products of globalization include but go beyond the European Community, the Canada–United States Free Trade Agreement (and its potential extension to Latin America), and Japanese trade and investment in Europe and North America. These are surely worthy of consideration as products of the process of globalization. Note, however, that this way of thinking about globalization assumes, along with national units of analysis, that political and economic organizations will have territorial bases. Even if the process of globalization were to encompass a world government and worldwide free trade, it would be a less radical change in that respect than what I have suggested is under way – the demise of territory as the sole basis of political units and the consequent decline of sovereignty for all-purpose political units, especially nations.

I prefer to define globalization as a process, rather than equating it with these larger or more integrated political and economic units. Let us call these larger units 'globalism' to distinguish them from 'nationalism.' Of course, I do not deny that these events are happening or that new and larger communities are forming. What I propose, however, is to view these products as part of the evolution and adaptation of the Westphalian system to the economic and other interdependencies it has spawned. The reader can judge at the end whether it is a useful hypothesis to distinguish so sharply between globalism and globalization.

Globalization, by contrast, I conceive as the process by which ever larger proportions of the world's population become aware of differences in culture, style of life, affluence, and other matters. This increasing awareness has been under way forever, but it achieved an especially high pitch in the era of European exploration, imperialism, and settlement in the sixteenth and subsequent centuries. With the spread of independence of colonies from their empires, the process has become multilateral: instead of British opportunities to learn about India or Australia, and vice versa, almost all nations of the world may now learn about almost all other nations. This results from greater travel, more extensive trade (especially in consumer goods, which affect residents more directly than trade in machine tools or components), and massive diffusion of the media of telecommunications. The circumnavigation of the globe by Magellan marked the beginning of an era, and the circling of the globe by electronic means might be called the Second Magellanic Age.

Chapter 3 will return to this process in more detail, as will parts of other chapters. At this point, I want only to signal that awareness of difference may lead to emulation and thus reduction of differences, but globalization may also lead to amplification of differences. Greater differences could grow out of defensive intentions to foster and protect one's local culture or inadvertently because of increased affluence in some areas without sustained economic growth in others. Competition among species in nature does not seem to result in uniformity; indeed the opposite. Adaptation to complex ecological niches may be characteristic of political forms as well as living species. Might there be an analogous process among social and political units when freed from the constrictions of the territorial nation-state? No doubt some aspects of our lives as passengers on Spaceship Earth will converge while others will not. Although I discuss a number of these aspects in later chapters, I am not concerned with predicting precisely which elements will or will not converge. As I noted above, questioning assumptions is more difficult than, and precedes, making predictions. In this section I simply hope to plant seeds of doubt about the end products of the process of globalization so that readers will be more receptive to some new possibilities which I now address.

POLITICAL ECONOMY

Since the advent of nations, we have come to think of most economic activities in national territorial terms.[23] For example, we wonder whether Canadian car part manufacturers will compete successfully with their American or Mexican counterparts. We keep records of balance of payments on national bases, not on sectoral or other bases. We speak of Japanese banks, or Swiss or Canadian, because of the location of their headquarters, even though much of what banks do has no logical relationship to national territories: some are local, some are international, and telecommunication links mean that many banking activities operate on a twenty-four-hour basis in order to participate in the global economy.

These patterns reflect more than the effects of computer networks, important though they may be. They reflect even more the *relative* decline in significance of territory as a classification scheme and thus the more limited status of nations based on territory. Another statement of the same point has been more common in recent years: globalization has been conceptualized in economic terms more often than in political terms because certain economic relations can more easily be abstracted from territory, whereas few people have questioned the territorial basis of politics. One reason some political leaders press the case for deregulation, privatization, and government down-sizing concerns the difficulty in imagining non-territorial organizations of a political sort. Conversely, many economic organizations lack a territorial base: GATT, World Bank, IATA, and OPEC, to give some obvious examples.

But think about another view of the organizations just mentioned. Although economic in an overt sense, they are governments, or, more exactly, they involve governance and perform governmental functions. We rarely think of them as governmental institutions because they are neither sovereign nor occupy territory in an exclusive way. Yet they perform functions which are political or governmental, such as interest articulation and aggregation, rule-making, rule adjudication, and enforcement of sanctions in a few specific areas of jurisdiction. Furthermore, the organizations mentioned above are less directly economic than political; they do not 'add value' in a manufacturing, processing, or marketing sense; nor are they providing purely economic services in contrast to brokerage houses, supermarkets, or advertising agencies. Their essential purpose derives from the increasing need to regulate economic activities which coincide less and less closely with national or territorial boundaries. Which does not prove that nations or territorial units serve no useful purposes, but it demonstrates that they serve *fewer* purposes than they once did.

MULTIPLE IDENTITIES

As the idea of the nation-state achieved its hegemony as a territorial, all-purpose political organization, it affected aspects of citizens' identity. Out of the myriad ways in which each person can be characterized, one's territorial location in a nation has come to assume overwhelming importance. One is not just an Indian but an American Indian. One is not just a car manufacturer but a Japanese car manufacturer. One is no longer just a Catholic but an Irish Catholic or a Polish Catholic. Thus, slowly and incrementally, the idea of the territorial nation-state has changed the relative importance of identities, creating a hierarchy of identities which is arbitrary but has felt natural to 'Westerners' for generations. This hierarchy of identities coincides with nationalism, but its implications reach beyond nationalism.

I refer to this occlusion of identities as 'bundling.' The territorial nation has been the bundle or basket into which other facets of our lives are fit.[24] It is similar to the economic concept of a 'basket' of goods: you cannot easily get items individually but must take them collectively.[25] In a restaurant, one can order 'à la carte'; but as far as our identities are concerned, we must take what nations have bundled together, which amounts to 'table d'hôte.' Chapter 8 will develop a vision in which our choices will partially redress the balance between *à la carte* and *table d'hôte*. Government *à la carte* will seem natural to citizens in the twenty-first century. Those conclusions rest, however, on interconnected arguments, events, and processes outlined in intervening chapters.

These observations must be qualified. In the core areas where these processes of territorial bundling began, the hierarchy of identities seems most advanced.[26] In areas touched later by explorers from Europe and even later by imperialism and nationalism, some countries have been more 'resistant' to the virus of territoriality while others have had their own reasons for embracing these assumptions. To give two examples from Asia, one may hypothesize that India as a territorial agglomeration has probably not bundled its citizens' identities into as tight a hierarchy as has Japan. Caste, language, and religion contest quite successfully with nationalism for pride of place in the hierarchy of identities of many Indians. For most Japanese, however, homogeneity of a remarkable order in dimensions of language, race, and religion makes it difficult to say whether 'nation' as a set of islands is the pinnacle of Japanese identities or whether it may simply summarize (or thus bundle in another way) these other dimensions. Unbundling, as discussed below, seems in any event much less likely in Japan (or France or Germany) than in India (or Switzerland or Canada).

The United States, Australia, and a few other countries derived from European settlement provide another kind of evidence about bundling of identities. The United States showcases its tolerance, its welcome to immigrants from the rest of the world, even if its welcome sometimes includes discrimination. But the melting pot is aptly named, because there is a clear hierarchy of identities at least as a goal: one is an American first and foremost, to such an extent that the concept 'un-American' has had real resonance. Likewise, state and regional identities are strong, although often interlaced with some of a non-territorial sort: rock-ribbed New England Protestant Republicans, Southern Democrats, Texas (as contrasted to Oklahoma) cattle ranchers, and so on. The point is not that every American has the same hierarchy, but it is usually felt that in time every group will put 'American' ahead of race, class, religion, or place of origin. The 'bundle' or hierarchy of identities will never be exactly the same, but open borders, tolerance, and multicultural immigration are not usually seen as a threat to the United States and some other 'settler' countries because of the assumption that *place* and territoriality will win out over non-territorial identities and loyalties.

It takes an act of imagination to think back a few centuries and to realize that European imperialists made no such assumptions. One's identity was pre-eminently religious for many centuries, no matter where one lived or how often one moved. In feudal times, serfs and lords were tied to particular pieces of land, but their identities rested on the specific status and privileges of rank and mutual obligation and hardly at all on geographic place in the current sense of German or Italian or Dutch. The transformation of identities has thus been twofold: creation of powerful territorial loyalties, and the occlusion or bundling of many other identities and loyalties as subordinate to those of territorial nations. As we will see in later chapters, citizenship took on new meanings as the bundling of identities progressed, and it will mean something new in the twenty-first century when unbundling opens new 'spaces' in our minds and spirits.

A reverse process has been under way for some time, which can be called 'unbundling.'[27] When communists try to appeal to the working class across national boundaries, they represent a form of unbundling. When business leaders argue for free trade and deregulation, they unknowingly further the unbundling of national-territorial hegemony. When women make common cause between the First World and the Third World, their actions serve to make gender relatively more salient and nation or territory relatively less so. Unbundling probably always involves or follows from another form of bundling, another way to repackage identities; but from the point of view of the long-standing bundles called nations, unbundling is an undoing of what had been taken for granted. It may also be usefully conceived as a form of adaptation to evolving ecological niches.

Note that bundling or packaging never eliminated sub-national or non-territorial identities. What resulted was a hierarchy of identities. Unbundling may weaken the hierarchy and may change the *relative* significance of particular identities, but it need not eliminate any of them. More crucial is this: unbundling will create spaces in which the hierarchy of identities is replaced by multiple hierarchies. For some people, territorial identities like nation or province will still predominate, but for other people those identities will be closer to the bottom of their personal hierarchy.

Whether bundling will be eclipsed by unbundling everywhere, or only in some places, should receive due consideration. I will return to this issue in several chapters. In pondering such a question, we must not lose sight of an even more profound transformation of how one conceives of identities: change of identities need not involve *choosing* but can amount to *adding* new dimensions of our selves (or raising the salience of existing ones). Immigrants to Canada or the United States add a new dimension to their identity. Moving from one occupation to another need not entail changing one's religion or dress. And yet in earlier times and other places, one sort of change (to the extent it was allowed at all) entailed many related choices: moving to another territory may have required conversion to a different religion or denomination; entering a particular profession entitled one to wear distinctive clothing or live in a special type of housing; and the fealty and protection from one lord rather than another could affect whether or whom one married.

Those who partake of European culture have come by stages to believe that many identities are independent and open to choice, and thus to believe that choice may include the opportunity to add identities without discarding others. In short, historical instances of bundling and unbundling have eventually allowed many people to be comfortable with the concept and reality of *multiple identities*. Observers are learning, I believe, that this entails – for some people at least – the coexistence of *multiple loyalties*. Multiple loyalties may be a neutral label for what social scientists used to call 'cross-pressures.' Contrary to that earlier view, I envision multiple loyalties as one avenue to freedom by multiplying our choices.[28] This assertion will be pursued at length in the latter half of the book, so that it may be left undeveloped for now.

ENTITLEMENTS

Some people will interpret 'unbundling' as another description of national disintegration. And so it is in a very special sense: nations as territorial units yield pride of place among citizens' identities, and other identities come to equal or exceed them in salience, at least in some nations and probably for some people in all nations. In other words, 'national disintegration' used to mean the process of nations being carved into several territories, each of which would become a nation (the two Pakistans) or would be absorbed by adjacent nations (Poland). Unbundling in this book does not, however, refer to a particular nation but to the weakening of the *idea* of nation as a territorially based political organization. Unbundling is therefore less 'revolutionary' (because less visible) but perhaps more corrosive than the processes witnessed during these past three centuries of nationalism.

Nations will, I expect, continue to exist and play important roles indefinitely. But one may speculate about the durability of some of their roles or functions. Reasons have already been given for thinking that nations have much less of a role in economic matters. Social welfare safety nets and the health system may continue to be organized on a territorial basis, and perhaps primary and secondary education as well (although perhaps not post-secondary).[29] Likewise, passports would likely be issued by national (territorial) governments, since otherwise migration from poorer to affluent nations would almost certainly increase to catastrophic proportions, a point to which I will return repeatedly in various contexts.

Even border controls to limit immigration, however, might prove to be not necessarily territorial. First, as other identities – gender, religion, profession, sport, or whatever – become more salient, will those who share these features but happen to be born in other countries be viewed as essentially the same or essentially different? In other words, how will our 'selves' be defined in the concept of 'self-interest'? Second, the issue of entitlements can be resolved in non-territorial ways. Physical residence alone does not even today always lead to entitlement; for example, residence does not warrant voting, since nations also require citizenship. Where criteria for entitlement are 'invisible' (personal skills, payment of fees, membership in a group, etc.), passports might not be used simply to keep people out of a territory. Instead they might be used as markers within a territory. If so, national-territorial governments would not automatically have a monopoly over issuance of passports. Indeed, is it really necessary that there be a *monopoly*, or is that a corollary of assumptions about nations as exclusive territories?

Defined generally, passports are a form of proof of entitlement. But just as political organizations need not be 'all-purpose,' so we may ask whether specialized passports could be better suited to the unbundled world. In fact, specialized passports exist now, but we do not notice them as such because we do not call them that. Indeed, one's family name used to be a form of entitlement for people with titles and land. Think of some non-governmental 'passports' many people already carry: cards for telephone calling, airline lounges, medical insurance, library privileges, and private clubs, just to mention some in my wallet. These are distinct from credit cards, most of which are all-purpose. Instead I refer to 'passports' which allow one to gain *access* to a facility, benefit, or location and which are different from how one might *pay* for those things. Passports in this sense and credit (or payment) cards used to be much more closely linked or bundled than they are now. For example, each major gasoline company issued its own credit card, as did many department stores. These still exist, but they coexist with general purpose credit cards, which in turn coexist with specialized identification devices ('passports') for access to clubs, services, and places. Multiple identities are now visible as well as encoded in our sense of self.

Multiplication of 'passports' in this sense signals an unbundled conception of the self and thereby suggests new meanings of citizenship. If some people feel empowered by their first credit card, or having their credit limit raised, this also links them in some degree with other people who carry that card. Of course, this sense of community may be weak for widely held cards and stronger for those (American Express, Diners Club) with more stringent criteria for eligibility. As symbols of unbundling, all of the identity or access cards reveal the ways in which identity and entitlement may be linked.

As citizenship becomes an avenue to entitlement, it may become less

34 Beyond Sovereignty

constitutive of self-identity.[30] That is, as the total number of types of citizenship or membership or entitlement increases, the significance of each type shrinks. Loyalty to each realm of citizenship may then become dependent on the adequate provision of services. One may still not be able to switch countries as easily as banks or credit cards, but one may wish that were possible. Hence, national identitites or loyalties may be pushed down the ladder or hierarchy of identity, even though nothing fills the gap left by the declining resonance of 'my country, right or wrong.'

CORPORATIONS, RELIGIONS, AND OTHER BUNDLES

Unbundling is already quite advanced if we only know where to look. The tough question concerns whether unbundling will continue indefinitely or whether new bundles will replace old bundles like nations. Most of this book deals with implications of relaxing assumptions about territoriality; thus, unbundling is of greater concern than rebundling. Nevertheless, at this point – and again at a few other points – a few remarks about new bundles may be helpful. What comes after the territorial nation? Granting that nations will continue to operate, albeit with limited purposes, does not allow one to evade the question but makes it more precise: what other organizational forms might eventually constitute 'bundles' which push nations to a lower rung on the ladder or hierarchy of identities?

Religious revivals and movements have been accorded greater attention in recent years. Some are territorial (so far at least), in that they are limited to a particular country, as in the case of the religious right or Moral Majority in the United States. Some, however, are non-territorial, or at least supra-national, as in the case of Islamic movements of several kinds, or of Catholic liberation theology. The brevity of these remarks should not be interpreted as my judgment that such revivals or movements deserve no more attention. Instead, I am at this point merely opening a line of inquiry which cannot be completed in this book. More analysis is warranted, though I will be able to make only passing remarks in this direction in some of the subsequent chapters.

A more promising line of thought involves corporations. Many reports allege or assume that these organizations, especially multinational or transnational corporations, have grown too strong or are too undisciplined by governments. While that perspective may be valid, one might say that, from the perspective of this book, corporations are so prominent precisely because they are the characteristic organizational form of our era.[31] Note some of their features and how different they are from nations: voluntary, flexible, special-purpose (i.e., focused rather than 'all-purpose'), and non-territorial.[32] I will not know in my lifetime whether 'the age of nations' will be replaced by 'the age of corporations,' but I can speculate about the possibility. If corporations are becoming more prominent, this might be because they are well suited to certain ecological niches engendered by recent technological changes to which nations cannot easily adapt. I will return to aspects of corporate life repeatedly, but let me introduce a couple of salient features at this point.

If corporations are legal forms with 'personality,' then corporatism is a form of governance founded on the coexistence, cooperation, and connivance of a political order with 'corporate citizens' in its territory. Details of representation within business, labour, and government differ from one nation to another; and there is no value at this point in analysing the range of possibilities. Note, however, that in principle corporatism could involve more than these three fictive 'persons'; one could imagine collaborations involving other non-territorial interests (such as environmental groups or gender groups) depending on the salient political issues. Finally, note that the assumption that governmental elites will always play the leading or initiating role, even if true, might still involve such a degree of attenuation of sovereignty that it would be wise to search for a new label for the political system.

Let us move to the second feature by specifying a membership for these 'corporate citizens.' Suppose the corporate pillars were not just vague entities like 'business' and 'labour' organizations. Suppose that they consisted instead of representatives of specific organizations like the International Chamber of Commerce, the International Federation of Industrial Labour Unions, and the International Federation of National Farmers Unions. Now pose some questions that seem pertinent from today's 'national' perspective:

1. Each organization accepts the concept of nation (implicit in 'international',) but is that a serious concession or a token bow to a declining organizational mode?

2. Since these same organizations would no doubt meet with political representatives in several nations, does that make their representatives (CEO, Chair, whatever) a citizen of more than one nation? If not, what is the source of legitimacy of participation?

3. Since membership ('citizenship') in each of the corporate entities would be open to individuals or groups from many nations, in what sense do we understand citizenship in each nation?

4. If these questions were relevant to only some subset of nations (e.g., the G-7), would that make them any less significant? Must changes occur everywhere before we revise our concepts?

CITIZENSHIP OF WHAT?

I do not propose to try to provide detailed answers to these questions. Instead, the questions are rhetorical and provocative. What readers can gain from considering such questions is an altered notion of citizenship. That revision of citizenship is a central aim of this book. At base these sorts of queries compel us to ask *where* people may reside and still be *citizens of here*. Why should we assume that aboriginals who live in British Columbia cannot be part of the same province or nation as natives who live in Ontario or Quebec? Or that Mohawks in Quebec and New York are not citizens of one nation? It may be convenient that people who live nearby have the same government, but it is not necessary. Nor is it necessary that nations always and invariably have exclusive use of territory.

Not only do foreign nationals and other visitors often live amongst citizens without undue stress, but many aspects of citizens' lives are governed by institutions distant from their homes. These include professional associations, insurance companies, banks, churches, and some leisure facilities. Why do we now find it so odd that one might pass through a foreign country to get to another part of one's own country? Americans apparently do not have a problem with the fact that Alaska is not contiguous with the main part of the United States, or France with the fact that Tahiti and St Pierre et Miquelon are separate and very distant administrative units.

That contiguity is not universal should warn us that it may not be necessary. East and West Pakistan have been instanced as counter examples, but they were united as a country only briefly and then only because of Muslim League agitations at the time of Indian independence, and they did not share a language. One should note parenthetically that languages tend to be territorial. Of course, contiguity is useful and convenient for many purposes. The crucial point is to ask, as I do in chapters 4 and 5, for example, which purposes require contiguity and which do not. When we open that line of inquiry, we find that modern technology reduces the number of situations in which contiguity serves an *essential* purpose. Daycare facilities, hospital emergency services, and public transit may always require contiguity, until the advent of inexpensive transporters à la *Star Trek*, but many other purposes can be served in a territory in which people of different type or citizenship reside whether they receive different treatment or the same treatment.

SORTING PEOPLE

The central issue of services for citizens is our ability to sort people into the relevant categories. That can rarely be done by visual inspection. It can also be thwarted even when oral or written exchanges occur, since people may misrepresent themselves in order to receive certain valued services. Hence, we issue passports, medical insurance cards, and transit passes, and these often include a picture and signature. Electronic bands – such as on credit cards – will no doubt play a larger role in the future, as will microchips. Whatever the means utilized, they are justified if one must identify or sort the people entitled to a service from those not entitled to it.[33] If residence in a territory is not sufficient for entitlement, other markers will be used. Once one relies on those other markers, territoriality becomes largely irrelevant, with exceptions like those noted above.

But, many will ask, how can you have governance if different people are subject to different rules or laws? How can you tolerate that the same act may be treated differently – for example, be subject to criminal penalties – even if performed by people in the same territory but who hold different citizenship? Note that this question makes sense only because we assume that territory matters. More and more people ask a pertinent question with a different premise: how can we live in a world where members of the same group (such as women) are treated so differently just because they live elsewhere? Several avenues suggest themselves. First of all, criminal codes might be an exception; must they be territorially based?[34] Second, most countries now already have exemptions from many criminal and civil penalties for accredited diplomats and their families, and for young offenders. Is there a threshold of numbers of such exemptions above which the system breaks down? Is concern about this a product of assumptions about territoriality? Third, many instances can be cited of neighbours treated differently because they have characteristics the political authorities believe significant. Think, for example, of discounts for senior citizens, tax credits based on size of family, and affirmative action laws for businesses receiving government grants but not for other businesses. Obversely, governments often fail to treat differently people with radically different identities, needs, and situations. For example, in most Canadian provinces, people with no children and people who send their children to private schools pay school property taxes just as though they utilized public schools. In all of these examples, the point is that public authorities *choose* to find significance in certain distinctions but not in others. They could act differently, and other societies or other eras have done so.

By raising these possibilities, I do not claim that territoriality is never needed or helpful. Nor do I claim that enough cases have been considered so that we can dispense with territoriality as irrelevant to most cases. Nor am I certain that all the distinctions mentioned above should constitute different citizenships. Instead the point is to question something we take for granted. The reason I question these particular assumptions is because they are recent in origin: up until about three hundred years ago, Europeans never acted on these assumptions, and as recently as the early nineteenth-century Europeans did not take these assumptions as 'given.' Some parts of the world still resist such assumptions. Therefore, it is manifestly possible to conduct politics without them. Of course, we may not like the cost-benefit ratio in some alternative systems, but we will never know until we think through their implications.

There is another dimension to my argument. By questioning territoriality, I question whether *government* should perform certain functions, rather than other types of organizations. Surely that is historically justified as well. In the early nineteenth century in Europe, everyone assumed that governments need not concern themselves with the things to which they now devote most of their resources: universities, hospitals, controlling environmental hazards, regulating the advertising of food products, and licensing automobiles, to name only a few. If governments can evolve by assuming new roles, why can we not ask about a future in which they shed some of these roles.[35] Few national governments now own or operate airlines or railroads, although this was common until recently.

NON-TERRITORIAL CITIZENSHIPS

But, I hear someone say, what becomes of citizenship if the government gives these functions over to other types of organizations not based on territoriality? Exactly! The concept of citizenship will doubtless change.

Virtually all observers now *assume* that citizenship is tied to a territorial nation-state. Why must they assume that? Where is the harm in saying that I am a citizen of a professional organization? Or of a sports team? Or of a religious order? A second point may be independent of the first. Even now, citizenship as I understand it is not mutually exclusive: I am a citizen of two nations (Canada and the United States), so why not of other organizations as well?

If we wish to restrict the word *citizenship* to national entities, then consider other words. Instead of saying that I am a *citizen* of the Canadian Political Science Association, let me be a member or a participant or a holder of an entitlement to its services (perhaps 'titler' for short). The buzz-word in government circles recently has been 'stakeholders,' which includes clients, citizens, private organizations, businesses, and many other categories which might be equivalent to 'titlers.' If one distinguishes between citizens and titlers, then the concept of 'citizen' or 'citizenship' will have an ever more restricted significance as nation-states (and territoriality) serve fewer functions. The central issue for me has nothing to do with matters of nomenclature. More crucial than the terminology is whether we can relax or eliminate assumptions about exclusivity, continuity, and contiguity of territory in regard to political organizations. I believe we can; I believe these assumptions have already been undermined and attenuated; and I believe that we are passing into a new historical epoch in which non-territorial citizenship may seem as 'natural' or 'given' as citizenship in a territorial nation-state did for the past century or more. Whether or not I am right in these respects, this book offers a vision of the world I foresee. There is room for many visions, but if one grants that this particular vision *could* come true, then I have accomplished all that I really want to demonstrate: we have taken an awful lot for granted, and these tectonic assumptions may have blinded us to the world in which we already live.

2

Technology and Territory

In relaxing assumptions about the territorial basis of politics, we make implicit or explicit predictions about the future. Is there some way to discipline these predictions, or are all scenarios equally plausible? This chapter argues that technological changes in the past were important causes of the victory of territorial nation-states over alternative forms of political organization.[1] They were not sufficient causes, but they were among the necessary conditions which in Europe led to nations based on territorial exclusivity, continuity, and contiguity. Some of these technological developments contributed to European seapower and other aspects of military supremacy, thus ensuring the spread of ideas about territorial nations from Europe to all parts of the inhabited world, even though the technologies which favoured nations in Europe were not usually common in Asia, Africa, the Americas, or Oceania.[2]

If it can be shown that technological innovations in early modern and even medieval Europe contributed significantly to the 'bundling' of political functions along territorial lines, outlined in the previous chapter, then one should hypothesize that current technological changes may herald and partially explain the 'unbundling' now under way.[3] These aspects of technology may thus allow us to narrow the range of plausible scenarios predicted for the twenty-first century. Is there, in short, a lesson to be learned from the past about how technology 'tips the balance' between territorial and non-territorial forms of organization? 'Tips the balance' points us in one fruitful direction for this book, but there is a different dimension to be explored as well. Technology may interact with natural and social conditions to open up or to close off certain 'ecological niches.' In effect, I am arguing that technological changes in process now are opening up niches of a non-territorial sort, but of course some will remain or will become territorial. I believe that the net effect will be to favour more non-territorial niches than territorial ones, at least in the sense that people living very near each other may find themselves in quite different political or economic or social niches and linked to people far away who may come to live in similar niches.[4] If so, what can we foresee emerging from on-going technological changes?

To anticipate one objection, let me note that chapter 3 examines economic changes, and the evolution of economic ideas, which parallel and interact with these technological changes. They are not inherently separate processes, since economic organization is one way to utilize technology, but it is convenient to discuss them separately for analytic purposes.

One can also admit that 'technology' may not be the ideal term for what underlay some of the economic and political changes. Indeed, a broad spectrum of phenomena seem relevant.[5] These include technology in the usual sense but also the development of the idea of science in the seventeenth and eighteenth centuries, religious and other ideological changes (including economic ideas), and the spread of education, literacy, and secular knowledge generally.[6] Perhaps equally relevant but difficult to classify is 'globalization' as defined in the previous chapter; indeed, this might be another word for technology conceived broadly. Globalization means exposure to and awareness of other ways of life. Ways of life include cultures, languages, religions, and fashions, but they surely also include ideas and institutions like the plough, types of sails, types of weapons, banking, insurance, and limited liability corporations, that is, technologies.

Globalization did not begin with jet airplanes, satellite TV, or fax machines. It has always existed in one form or another. Migrations, nomadic wandering, caravan trade, exploration, diseases, and the Crusades may be mentioned as earlier examples without trying to be exhaustive.[7] Indeed, unintended consequences of the Crusades, for example, may have been decisive in setting in motion the process of state-building and territorial nationality which is our focus.

The Crusades were important in putting participants in touch with civilizations richer and more intellectual than Europe. Crusaders brought back various ideas and innovations which may have contributed to economic growth and to evolving styles of life, even though some of those ideas may have been Greek or Indian in origin rather than Islamic. But their significance went beyond specific innovations in at least two ways.[8] For one, the Crusades exposed people, as travel sometimes does today, to the fact that radically different ways of organizing and conducting one's life are not thereby necessarily 'heathen' or 'sinful.' The level of medical science in the Islamic world encountered by crusaders startled them, as did the opulence of courtly and city life. These 'revelations' have the effect of raising questions about the *necessity* of one's own assumptions. Perhaps, crusaders might have said, we can learn something after all from other peoples or cultures.[9]

The second effect, ironically, may have been to strengthen secular trends. Although the motive for the Crusades was primarily religious devotion, with touches of adventure and glory, they also revealed that the Christian God did not put all the benefits on one side. Furthermore, and even more significant, one could pick and *choose* among alternative lifestyles (clothing, food, horses, decorative art) as well as among economic and technological devices. This realization came slowly, and its duration should warn us that the dizzying array of technological changes confronting the world in the 1990s will not be assimilated quickly or easily nor with consequences we can imagine with assurance.

Both of these effects of the Crusades may have also been the effects of trade, commerce, travel, and exploration at other times. As Carlo M. Cipolla and others have argued, one of Europe's *cultural* advantages over China and some other places may have been less its inventiveness and more its tolerance and hence its ability to recognize value in other technologies, ideas, and products.[10] Few inventions originated in Europe, but many were adaptations and improvements on the artifacts and trinkets brought back to Europe.

THE SACRED AND THE PROFANE

If I may have conceived technology too broadly, I may have also presented it in a more favourable light than proper or judicious. At least we should consider the 'dark' side of technology before outlining some of its current and future effects. Perhaps the most famous exposition of pitfalls in the reliance on technology is Jacques Ellul's book *The Technological Society*.[11] Instead of focusing on that seminal work, however, it is more convenient to examine Jerry Mander's *In the Absence of the Sacred*.[12] My main reason for addressing the latter is Mander's explicit linking of concern about technology with aboriginal concepts of land and community, topics I explore in some detail, especially in chapter 5.

Several strengths of Mander's (and others') arguments should be accepted. He demonstrates, at least in regard to some 'high tech' innovations, that the benefits of technology are almost always better publicized than its costs or negative consequences. This follows from the fact that companies and industries – and increasingly governments – see advantages in the technology and have the resources to advertise or advocate or showcase them. Costs, by contrast, may be longer in coming or in becoming visible, and they may be diffuse (pollution, radiation, decline of literacy in the age of TV) and thus arouse no equivalent specific or focused interest group to respond on their behalf.[13] One can, I believe, accept that asymmetric information is the general case, although there may be some instances of technology with a different pattern of effects; and some people will argue, as I do in later chapters, that some costs or benefits may be miscalculated in early stages of diffusion, and so may the calculation of risk. Indeed, what is a cost in some observer's mind may be a benefit in the view of another; costs and benefits are partially defined by a culture and thus accountable most easily within it. Likewise, levels of acceptable risk may be culturally specific even if the calculations look scientific. These are also reasons why I raised questions in the Introduction about the value of labelling future scenarios as optimistic or pessimistic.

Mander makes another claim, however, which is more easily disputed. He avers that the benefits of technology are always less than its admirers allege and that the costs are always greater than they admit. Again, he may be right about some cases or even a majority of cases, but such sweeping generalizations are unlikely to be supportable. Also, as I argue below, there is one feature of current electronic technology which may make these generalizations less applicable, whatever their merits in prior cases.

Even more fantastic, Mander wishes to put in place a regime in which societies would vote on whether to develop and disseminate certain technologies. Whatever the abstract appeal of such an idea ('empowerment' is appealing to most of us), I will not discuss it because I believe it obvious that one could not stop a major technology like TV or fax or personal computers – which loom large in this book – even if a clear majority in every society in the world voted 'no.' If deplorable, expensive, and highly visible technology like military aircraft and nuclear weapons can proliferate, be traded, and be shipped around the globe, despite efforts to control them, I see no chance at all of halting research or production of small, inexpensive, and pleasurable devices like telecommunications equipment. Part of Mander's and Ellul's arguments rest on the belief that specific technologies have a 'logic,' and that logic is inimical of other values. I accept their observations about 'technologic' but put it to a different use: if they are correct, then that 'logic' constrains social, economic, and political evolution in the future, even if it is not fully deterministic. We may not like the constraints, but they may help us to envision the future, because they make some scenarios more plausible and others less so.

More efficacious than voting to ban certain technology, anticipation of 'best case' and 'worst case' scenarios or provision of incentives to channel technology in less harmful (e.g., less polluting) directions seem sensible and feasible. The plough has no doubt contributed mightily to erosion, but one can devise ploughs which do not cut so deep or one can educate every user to the value of contour ploughing. These do not solve all problems, but they do contain them while still feeding the world's population more adequately than a millennium ago.

One last point in Mander's book will serve to highlight some aspects of my argument about the likely effects of some of our new technology. He argues that new technologies have seldom been democratic in the sense of decentralizing power, control, or manipulation. He grants that a few have done so (e.g., solar heating of houses or solar-powered batteries), but more common have been strongly centralizing effects or more extensive central government regulation, as with nuclear energy, hydroelectric power, or the car as instigator of highway networks and sprawling cities. The flaw in Mander's argument, even if generally true up to now, concerns the role of territoriality. Most technologies which have survived the evolution of the last several centuries have favoured territorial consolidation or control and have thus facilitated large territorial nation-states. Such organizations have doubtless been 'centralizing' compared to feudal domains, medieval cities, or the silk trade, although perhaps not more so than the early Roman Empire or the Roman Catholic Church in the medieval period.

My argument – developed in different ways in each chapter – is that territorial forms of organization are not 'given' but invented, that they are quite recent inventions, and that some of the most prominent technological innovations of this century have been fundamentally non-territorial in their 'logic' or implications. To that degree, they need not fit Mander's definitions as inherently 'centralizing' or 'undemocratic.' Indeed, 'centralizing' and 'democratic' are not mutually exclusive concepts. More to the point, as I explain below, military technology has in some ways become non-territorial; and telecommunications advances may empower small groups and networks which will undermine nation-states and decentralize political, economic, and social life in ways imaginable but not fully specifiable yet.[14] Rather than continue this line of reasoning in terms of Mander or other thinkers like him, let me turn to some examples of technological changes in the past and in the present. This inventory will be illustrative rather than exhaustive; and it will consider only a few of the future effects because some other consequences will be the subject of later chapters.

CROSSROADS

In ancient times as well as more recently, 'crossroads' have been crucial in economic, social, and political life. Like many words, 'crossroads' means more than its literal interpretation: where roads cross. Of course, caravan routes intersect at oases, trade routes converge on key cities or isthmuses or river-crossings, and railroads interconnect. But 'crossroads' may also be used to refer to canals, rivers, ports, highways, airline hubs, and electronic networks. Especially crucial for economic development and urban growth have been instances where more than one means of communication or transportation intersected: for example, where a caravan route links up with a catchment area, or a canal ties a river system to a seaport, or a seaport like London or New York spawns a railroad network.

Crossroads, dense intersections, nodes, and centres of networks should help to explain why particular territorial organizations developed. They may also explain why territorial organization – especially contiguity – has declined in significance. Think of the relative costs and flexibilities of railroads, airplanes, and telecommunications. Rail lines are fixed in the fairly long run. If one puts a rail line between two points, but the traffic does not grow or generate additional tonnage, or later declines, one cannot easily dig up the tracks and move them elsewhere. Airports are also fixed, but not the routes connecting them, which can fluctuate in frequency of flights or size of craft on extremely short notice.[15] Likewise, airline 'hubs' are fixed in the short run but not in the medium or long run. Imagine how much easier it is to switch an airline hub from one city to another than to transfer the 'crossroads' of the rail network from Chicago to Denver.

Both examples, however, share certain features. Travel or shipment time is proportional to distance, and the energy costs are also roughly proportional to distance. Thus, they favour territorial organization in several ways: compact, contiguous territory is easier to supply than scattered, non-continuous, non-contiguous, or 'shared' territory. These features explain to some degree why certain places become organized as cities or as nations, although slightly different areas in the railroad era than in the age of airplanes, and they explain why nations were so eager to build railroads in the nineteenth century and to develop national airlines in recent decades.

As long as one wishes to move bulky material, like wheat or coal or heavy machinery, railroads would seem to have a continuing rationale. As long as people wish to travel extensively on holidays or to ship light, small, or perishable goods, airlines appear to have a future. But note that airlines now carry many of the goods and people that railroads previously did. Likewise, one can envision a transfer of function from airlines (and car and truck) to electronic networks, and hence to electronic 'crossroads' (like satellites). Indeed, the speed and capacity of electronic networks may reduce the occurrence of 'crossroads.' Think of the image of a switchboard such as telephone companies relied on not many years ago; all the telephones in a town went through the switchboard to another switchboard in another town, and thence to a house or business. This imagery no longer applies to telephone or most telecommunications networks. A switchboard implies centralization, whereas (contra Mander) electronic networks imply decentralization and more or less direct access. One may instance a phone call from Vancouver to Toronto which, because of busy circuits in Canada, is easily routed through various nodes in the United States. Obversely, busy rail traffic or congested airspace in central Canada cannot be compensated economically or without serious time delays by diversion to U.S. lines or hubs.

The 'unbundled' world introduced in the previous chapter will also depend on crossroads but in different ways than the inherently territorial technologies just analysed. For one thing, telecommunications are not in principle tied to territory. I will demonstrate this in a later section, but here I just note that the time difference as related to physical distance is trivial. The fraction of a second longer required for a telephone signal to reach between continents, as opposed to across town, is hardly detectable to telephone users. In addition, satellite retransmission with scrambled signals (rather than open broadcasting) means that contiguity has become almost completely irrelevant. At the other extreme, cable systems for TV or personal computers eliminate contiguity and continuity of territory in another way: neighbours may be linked to completely different communication networks, and thus for all practical purposes they might as well be quite distant physically, as they perhaps will be socially.

Chapter 6 explores some implications of these trends for our understanding of community.

Even more likely to decouple territory and communication is the movement of *information* rather than goods.[16] This will be obvious to anyone who relies on fax or who has used a credit card to access cash or traveller's cheques while on a trip far from home, but the next few decades will see more use of this principle in countless other ways. For example, mass-produced, virtually identical goods can be most efficiently manufactured in large factories and shipped to near or distant markets, although the shipping costs have already led to some decentralization (e.g., Japanese cars made or assembled in North America and Europe as well as in Japan and Australia). With customized products which have high value-added, some companies already find it cheaper and quicker to transmit specifications to many small, local manufacturing sites. There may still be a 'centre' in such cases, but if so, it is an 'information crossroads' and not a point of physical transshipment. Who knows? Perhaps a time will come, as foreseen in *Star Trek: The Next Generation*, when we use 'replicators' to make our meals, clothing, and office supplies as we need them. *Star Trek* is also famous for 'transporting' humans in the form of information, as in 'Beam me up, Scottie!' These possibilities are, I assume, far enough in the future that I can ignore them in this book, but I do not rule them out completely.

One can also move information rather than people. Of course, if one wants to scuba-dive on the Great Barrier Reef, travel will be necessary (at least until advanced forms of 'virtual reality' become locally accessible and relatively inexpensive). But business, government, and academic conferences have already declined in length and perhaps frequency as more adequate and less expensive teleconferencing has become available. Also significant here is the growing reluctance of busy professionals to spend needless hours or days in travel, only to come home with jet lag; of course, they do still travel, but mainly when a face-to-face relationship will be decisive.

Let me end this first set of illustrations of long-term technological changes with a caution. I have not tried to expound all the costs or benefits of changing from rail to air to electronic networks. Nor have I any certainty when manufacturers will transmit more goods by transmitting information than by physical movement. I repeat the warning issued several times already: the object is not to predict the future with precision but to tease out ways in which technology may have aided certain kinds of political or economic organization in the past and thus to identify the avenues to the future even if the destinations along the avenues are not yet visible. Scenarios may be demonstrative although not definitive.

MILITARY TECHNOLOGY, TERRITORY, AND NATIONS

The territorial state as we know it can be dated approximately from the Thirty Years' War in the seventeenth century. It was as a consequence of that savage era that rulers and ruled came to share languages and religious beliefs and otherwise exhibit the homogeneity we now find 'natural.' With the French Revolution, territoriality, homogeneous beliefs, and popular consent came together in the paradigm of the modern nation-state, even if the reality of France did not equal the ideal. The contrast with the formerly ubiquitous polyethnic empires was almost total.

The Peace of Westphalia in 1648 marked the end of the 'unbundled' political units of the medieval period and the beginning of the hegemony of the territorial state. Even today scholars still refer to 'the temple of Westphalia' to signify the lasting effects of consolidation in that era. The treaties themselves, of course, were not the significant cause of this territorialization of the nation-state. Instead the treaties represented the understanding at the time that previous forms of political organization, legitimation, and war-making were unsustainable. Part of the transformation can be attributed to changes in military technology.[17]

I have suggested that there are forces and trends leading to greater 'unbundling' of our territorial political units. We are not, however, simply reverting to a medieval world of jousting knights, jealous kings, guilds and syndicates in free cities, and a 'universal Church.' Nor are the affluent regions of the world likely to be headed for the poverty, disease, unhygienic conditions, or short life expectancies of that era.[18] Technology, I believe, has played critical roles in creating territorially based nations and in unbundling them, but not in the fashion of a pendulum. We may learn something important by examining how military technology helped to firm up territorial conceptions of politics, but the movement beyond territoriality involves new military technology and many other types of technological development. A few examples should be sufficient to make generally clear the processes at work then and now.

If military technology is one way to see the role that territory has played in our concept of nation, it is also a good way to see how technology can challenge our customary assumptions. Land armies have been and still are deterred by natural barriers, such as deserts, mountain ranges, rivers, and swamps. Compact, continuous, and contiguous territory has been more easily defended than territories which were elongated, which were divided into separate non-contiguous regions, or which had alien territory (enclaves) in their midst. Particularly where a country had a compact territory and had natural barriers at its borders, it benefited from short logistical support lines while its attackers suffered the obverse inconvenience. This explains Swiss independence among larger neighbours. Likewise, peripheral locations (such as Scandinavia) were less likely to be attacked; and if attacked, their attackers again had long supply lines.

Technology has decoupled territory and defence. Mountains and other natural barriers to a land army pose little deterrent to jet aircraft, rockets, missiles, and paratroops. Distance still buys time, but for missiles time is now measured in minutes rather than days or weeks. These technological changes do not prove that territory is irrelevant, but they suggest that its importance is circumscribed and its advantages not always permanent.[19]

A more specific set of examples involves towns and cities. The manors and walled castles of regional barons in the Dark Ages were a serious obstacle to territorial consolidation under aggressive monarchs. Likewise, free cities engaged in long-distance trade posed a threat to local territorial continuity. Both castles and towns could be defended more easily than captured, even in some cases after months or years of siege. As small cannon developed, the advantage to castles and cities increased, since they could devastate encircling troops or encampments, but small cannon were not powerful enough to demolish the walls of large castles or cities. Later, as metal-casting skills improved, larger and more accurate cannon tipped the advantage in the other direction: attackers could reduce to rubble in hours or days what had previously resisted destruction almost indefinitely. At that point, kings gained more secure hegemony over local barons, and cities began the process of incorporation in the territorial state of the absolutist monarchies.[20] The rise to supremacy of these European monarchies thus led to larger territorial political units, to a belief that territory should be exclusive, continuous, and contiguous, and to the reliance on one all-purpose sovereign centre.

Just to be fair, in the long run the cities may have lost the battle but won the war. As they were subordinated politically to state functions, they became even more economically essential to nations because of their 'crossroads' status, their value to hinterlands, and the vast reservoirs of voters (when voting became common) attached to them.[21] The usual narrative about the importance of over-representation of rural constituencies, while heartfelt by those areas, masks the greater truth that there are few rural constituencies anymore in most industrialized countries.

The trend to 'exurbia' and to small towns in scenic parts of North America should also be put in perspective. These are not direct analogues of local baronial castles or medieval free cities. They constitute a dispersion of population, but one more tightly connected electronically to city work-stations and centrally devised networks and crossroads than anything in previous centuries. Chapters 3 and 6 explore in detail some of these changes.

Military organization based on the technology developed after the Peace of Westphalia played another part in the narrative which links territory and nation. As Foucault has demonstrated, the nature of armies changed in a complex interaction of technology, ideology, education, policing, and patriotic feeling.[22] The cost of military technology rose in this period at rates greater than the ability of kings to finance it. Hence, efforts were made to raise conscript armies because they were cheaper than professional mercenaries. Although mercenaries and professional armies had, at least since Roman times, been highly disciplined, the new 'citizen' armies required new techniques. Even with seasoned officers, recruits needed much training and practice. Equally they had to be 'disciplined,' both in the sense of being punished and coordinated. They learned to drill, to march, to move in formation, and to coordinate strategy and tactics over greater distances; and some forms of punishment (e.g., drills, forced marches) were identical to the training. Foucault documents the long process of micro-changes in 'discipline' in related and reinforcing areas like schools, prisons, armies, and bureaucracies which culminated in efficient territorial administration and which reinforced the territorial foundations laid for the state by 1648.

As people came to equate territory and nation with populations which were mostly sedentary and homogeneous in many more ways (religion, vernacular languages, etc.), they came to realize that certain administrative problems were eased. If we can assume that people who are *here*, who speak *our* language, and who attend *our* church are part of *us*, then benefits, services, and entitlements can be rationed or delivered without much concern about mistaken identity.

Administration was particularly thought to be simpler and more effective where control rested exclusively with one sovereign centre. It was deemed to be complicated by non-continuous or non-contiguous territory. These ways of thinking about administration, though originally military, spread to many organizational domains that today we would lump together as business organization, private and public bureaucracy, or the public service generally. Of course, the belief in the efficacy of a single centre or sovereign was a belief and not necessarily a fact. For example, the Peace of Westphalia actually established the sovereign existence of only two states, the Netherlands and Switzerland, neither of which exemplified the idea of a single sovereign centre. Nevertheless, the Westphalian system came to be seen as demonstrating the efficacy and legitimacy of unified territorial states and as leaving behind the fragmentation and divided sovereignty of the feudal world. I will return to some of these changing beliefs in chapter 4, where I also examine administrative adaptations (such as networks and other 'flat' organizations) likely to follow from current technological changes. Much of the 'logic' of military and later administrative emphasis on territory relates to patterns of communication, which provide another distinct illustration of the fact that territoriality arose in a specific historical context and is not 'given.'

VERNACULAR LANGUAGES AND PRINTING

It has been generally accepted that the decline of Latin as a common language and the increasing use of vernacular languages occurred at the time we have been examining. That is, the greater concern with political territoriality went hand in hand (or mouth-to-mouth?) with linguistic territoriality. Indeed, Jean A. Laponce has argued convincingly that languages (especially oral versions) are inherently territorial: they need territorial exclusivity, continuity, and contiguity, and they help to define the limits of a territorial nation, although seldom coinciding perfectly even in relatively homogeneous countries like Japan.[23] At the same time, one must recognize that some languages – Chinese, Yiddish, and perhaps English recently – have non-spatial aspects because they have been languages of trade and commerce; nevertheless, they have 'core' areas where a concentration of native speakers can keep the language alive.

Languages did not always play exactly this role. Handwritten and illuminated manuscripts – however much devotion the monks evinced – could not satisfy demand in a world with more local vernaculars and growing popular literacy. Thus, printing (specifically movable type)

52 Beyond Sovereignty

came to play an unusually significant part in the story of territorial nations. Indeed, some scholars have gone so far as to argue that 'print capitalism' laid the conceptual, financial, and communication foundations for industrial and commercial capitalism, and the development of capitalism paralleled historically the consolidation of territorial nations.[24]

Whether print was the basis of capitalism need not divert us from the essentially undeniable point that inexpensive multiple copies of books, pamphlets, and newspapers were one of the key components in territorial political organizations. There may have been a mutual process of vernaculars offering a lucrative market, and rulers finding it expedient to utilize printed material in vernaculars to reduce labour costs of clerks and transcribers.[25] Other mutually reinforcing processes were caught up as well: commerce and literacy both encouraged and depended on easily accessible printed material; and education in vernacular languages (rather than in Latin) gained ground as the church was weakened by the Black Death and other pestilences which revealed its impotence; and the decline of the universal church opened avenues for monarchs to assimilate some ecclesiastial functions, such as training clerks, harnessing cities (including those of the bishops), and recording trade and taxes.[26]

Newspapers may have been the key element in some respects, since they fitted well with early modern social institutions such as coffee houses and commercial exchange centres. Equally significant – in this abbreviated historical overview – was the vast dissemination of the Bible in vernacular, which caused, reinforced, or resulted from various changes in religious beliefs and secular attitudes, and which culminated in the Reformation, which in turn helped to firm up territorial nation-states at the time of the Thirty Years' War and the Peace of Westphalia.

THE EVOLUTION OF MEDIA OF COMMUNICATION

The invention of the printing press, thus, had revolutionary effects and buttressed the assumptions about territoriality. Newspapers and magazines still have this effect, and radio and television broadcasting have until quite recently been biased toward territoriality. As I will show, the new generations of computers and telecommunications equipment have a non-territorial logic which will be mentioned below and developed at length in chapter 6.

Until recently newspapers had no value beyond a certain locality, except as historical record. Magazines eventually moved to a broader territorial concept, because they could be mailed and came out less frequently. Even airmail delivery has had very little effect on the linkage between newspapers and territory, except for the tiny proportion of audiences who read the *Sunday New York Times*.

In the past decade, however, remote and simultaneous printing via satellite has become feasible. Hence, the *Globe and Mail* can endeavour to be a nationwide Canadian newspaper, and the *Herald Tribune* a world newspaper. Regional advertising and regional variations in stories in magazines are now standard practice for the same reason. Nevertheless, because of the need so far to use printing presses as a crucial and unavoidable stage in news dissemination, print media have not moved beyond territoriality, just beyond narrow territories to wider ones. When we reach the stage at which individuals read their newspapers electronically, at home or office, then perhaps newspapers (without paper!) will no longer be territorial.

Consider radio and television by contrast and how the telecommunications revolution has affected and may change them. Even today we speak of the broadcast media, thereby building into our language assumptions no longer accurate. For decades, these two media were dependent on broadcasting, that is, on casting electromagnetic waves broadly or at large. That is still largely true of radio, especially for reception in cars or walkmans. Cable transmission and satellite signals, especially where 'scrambled,' have produced two changes which shatter the reliance on territory. These are multiplication of channels and fragmented or targeted audiences.

Broadcast media require public regulation. There is only a narrow band of usable broadcast frequencies, and the number must be kept small in any one area to avoid undue interference or impaired reception, even with new 'compression' technology.[27] Cable and satellite have the capacity for many more channels; indeed, fibre-optic cable has, in principle, infinite capacity. Practically speaking, however, the twenty to forty channels now available in most major localities in North America are sufficient to obviate the need for the earlier type of regulation and to break the monopoly of 'mass production' networks. It is manifestly pointless to use thirty channels to transmit two to four networks. Hence, one has witnessed in the past decade two changes: incipient additional networks (CNN, etc.); but, more significantly, the fragmentation of audiences because of channels with greater specialization. To call this a fragmentation of audiences is to use a negative word.[28] Instead we should think of it as engendering vastly greater choices for individuals, more accurately targeted advertising or other messages, and lower entry costs and thresholds for many topics long ignored by mass-oriented networks (such as multicultural programs, less popular or less well known sporting events, and religious preaching).

The changes already visible are far-reaching. Consider the meaning and value of audience ratings. If someone watches two or three programs with a remote 'flicker' – 'surfing' or 'grazing' as it has become known – what do ratings mean? Should surfers be counted as part of the audience for each program, fractionally for each, or not at all? If they are counted for each program, total audience for all programs may exceed 100 per cent of potential audience, if there are many 'surfers.' If fractionally or not at all, we may misunderstand the potential impact of any given program. Think also about advertising revenue. With many more channels, most of them reasonably specialized, should one charge less for advertising because any one channel has lower ratings, or more because the audience profile for each channel is more specific, more targeted on the type of person the advertisers wish to reach? Price schedules are now in flux because advertisers have not yet figured out which type of advertising is worth more.

Leaving aside such fascinating and genuinely important topics, let us return to territoriality. Oversimplifying, several conclusions may be asserted:

1. Satellites mean that broadcasting is not restricted to a specific territory, whether local, national, or continental.
2. Simultaneity of reception vanishes because of VCR taping capacities. Consequently, network 'prime time' has less and less meaning, and its share of revenue declines.
3. Individuals in a given area (even a common home) need not watch the same programs because of the multiplication of specialized channels.
4. Channels need not all rely on the same language; multicultural channels demonstrate that each channel may even use more than one language.
5. Pay television eliminates the need to go to theatres; in some areas there is already the capacity to schedule movies (and someday other programs) when each viewer wants them; and video rentals represent essentially infinite individual control over content and timing.

In short, innovations in telecommunications *to this point* have for all practical purposes eliminated the usefulness of the concept of a 'mass' audience. They have enabled so many specialized channels and such a level of individual control that it is quite unnecessary to have 'dense' transmissions based on territory, even though that condition remains necessary for newspapers and magazines. Further technological developments can only destroy more completely our assumption that communication and territory are linked. Some of these developments are now in progress, as is obvious when one thinks of fax machines in homes and cars and of personal computers and powerful work-stations at home. A few people have already begun 'cottage industry' careers based on these capabilities, visiting office buildings rarely or less often. I explore administrative and organizational implications of this form of decentralization and non-standard work patterns in chapter 4, and some personal and community implications in chapter 6.

Other developments available only to small, elite groups should soon become almost universally available in all industrialized countries. Professors at major universities have for about a decade been connected in a continent-wide and now almost worldwide network of computers. Besides the cost reductions from using couriers less often and making fewer long distance telephone calls, these networks facilitate collaborative research and expedite the dissemination of information, ideas, and data. Indeed, many scholarly journals are now published only in electronic form or simultaneously in electronic and hard copy. In addition to official publications, there are scores, perhaps hundreds, of 'bulletin boards.' Likewise, senior public servants, business managers, the administrative and medical staffs of hospitals, travel agents, and many other groups have equivalent networks.

The penetration of personal computers into private homes has not reached the level of telephones or TV or VCRs, but the dramatic reduction in cost and size of PCs suggest that a majority of homes will be so equipped in a few years or early in the next century. Even without personal computers or electronic notebooks, homes are almost ready to achieve worldwide two-way communication.

Within two or five years decisions will be made in most major countries (at least of the 'liberal democratic' type) to change the way TV and telephones are currently regulated.[29] In most countries, telephone companies have been regulated as public or private utilities for decades. Since it developed much later and involved broadcasting, TV has usually been regulated or licensed by a completely separate regime. Yet the technologies are identical and doubly parallel: TV cable systems duplicate telephone lines, and a growing amount of telephone traffic operates through satellite as does more and more TV. Thus, removing the artificial barrier between the regulatory regimes will allow the use of hardware in either system by the other. Whether telephone companies absorb TV companies, whether cable companies absorb telephone companies, whether a mixture occurs, or something wholly new, very soon every home or office with a telephone and a TV will have two-way visual and auditory communication facilities. Estimates of the number of residences and businesses with telephone and TV connections currently range up to 800 million worldwide. They will also be able soon after that linkage to transmit data in several forms. No wonder these developments are referred to as an information revolution.

To round out this set of illustrations, let us return to Mander's concern about the centralizing and anti-democratic logic of most technologies. I have argued that their logic derives in large part from their territoriality. It should be clear by now that telecommunications technology today and more so in the future has a different logic because it is non-territorial. There is no single centre, and as networks proliferate and intersect, there may be no centres at all. Computing capacity has been diffused beyond anyone's predictions of twenty to thirty years ago. Access to information and – more significantly, as I argue in chapter 6 – access to the precise individuals and groups who share one's interests can now and will increasingly occur in ways unmediated by central 'gatekeepers.'[30] Of course, some information may always be buffered and out of reach, but future users of electronic networks will face problems of information overload more often than lack of information. Indeed, the future 'gatekeepers' may be those who can interpret data. 'Information police' may arise, as suggested in a later section, but demand should outrun supply as the number of users grows exponentially. Whether Mander agrees that the trend to decentralization also presages democratization, I do not know, but that is how it looks to me.

COMMUNICATION AND NATIONS

If communication is largely decoupled from territory, is nation also decoupled from its turf? Karl Deutsch's analyses of nationalism and social communication would not be totally undermined, since face-to-face communication retains considerable value and appeal to most humans; but his other lines of analysis have been mostly negated.[31]

Neither the increase nor the diminution of territorially based feelings of nationalism or patriotism guarantee the survival or the demise of nation-states. Nationalism and the state are linked in very complex ways. Although nationalism may outlive the territorial state, it will not cause the decline of the state. In fact, I feel certain it will not have that effect in the near future; but the telecommunications changes outlined can have related effects. One would expect, specifically, that kindred feelings based on territorial boundaries (whether national, provincial, or local) should assume a *relatively* lower priority when other interests of a non-territorial sort satisfy basic needs and feelings of community. In light of the flexible telecommunications media, an equilibrium will be struck for certain periods in which the nation-state and non-territorial interests coexist.[32] These non-territorial interests may take many forms – political partisan, artistic, religious, occupational, educational, or sports and leisure – and are explored in chapter 6.

Over a period of years and decades, the competition between national (territorial) and non-territorial (personal or group) interests must have, I believe, a further effect. Why should feelings of nationality themselves be territorially bounded in the future? If the universal church (Christian or Islamic) was a meaningful concept for a millennium despite competing linguistic and political loyalties, why should there not be 'universal nations'? The question merits attention even though these new units may not be called nations because so many people in this century have been thoroughly imbued with the belief that nations are territorial. Some might say that such universal nations already exist, or have continued to exist, in the case of the Jews, Baha'i, and Islam, or perhaps all religions which have spread to large numbers of countries. There is no value in debating such an issue in a chapter on technology and territory, and in any event the point of these illustrations concerns the construction we have put on them and their deep 'taken-for-granted' quality. As Ellul argued, technology can warp or shape our 'mind-set' or ways of thinking. Territoriality and nation fell outside the ambit of his analysis but need not fall outside of our purview in this book.

RELIGION AND SEGREGATION

Religions were once thought of as 'universal,' and some still make those claims. Universal does not mean, in these cases, that every human accepts the tenets of the religion in question; nor that only one religion aspires to convert every person. Instead universal meant that one did

58 Beyond Sovereignty

not have to be born from a particular gene pool or in a particular place in order to enjoy the spiritual blessings of the church or community of believers. In terms of the assumptions about territoriality, religions could exist anywhere – space could be overcome so that if neighbours resisted the call, more distant (non-contiguous) peoples might prove more susceptible. As a result, continuity and exclusivity were also undermined in many places. These Hebrew, Christian, and later Islamic ideas (restricting this review to Europe and the Mediterranean world, as I have) contrast sharply with more ancient Greek and pagan religious ideas. The latter were unrelievedly territorial: a god or diety was unique to one place or city and was tied down, whereas Hebrew, Christian, and Islamic conceptions of their diety made no assumption of territoriality.[33] Nomadic peoples apparently prefer nomadic gods.[34]

In the early modern period, religion in Europe became territorial in a double sense. National religions were mandated and accepted, leading to some reshuffling of populations and even more conversions. Later as concepts of tolerance and separation of church and state (or private and public) became more common, churches served neighbourhoods or towns as focal points. In other words, 'the Church' had been transformed into 'churches.'

In recent years, territoriality has continued to be related to religious organization in both of these ways, but contrary trends may be noted. There are, for example, divisions within the Roman Catholic Church between national communities with distinct liturgies and 'liberal' or 'conservative' views of the mass, the priesthood, and celibacy, among other things. Alongside these groups are parallel groups of people who look still – or more so – to the pope as a counterweight to national or ideological divisions. Within Islam, one can find national 'centres of gravity' (Saudi, Iranian, Pakistani, etc.) and also pan-national or 'universal' strands (Sunni, Shia, Ishmaili).

Within the Protestant – and thus mainly 'national' – churches, one finds a non-territorial development which unites TV evangelism with fundamentalism and politics. European language differences inhibit transnational evangelism in ways less common in North America. In the latter case, telecommunications media create non-territorial audiences in the same ways they do for secular programs: they can target people anywhere without broadcasting to everyone in all places, and they can differentiate neighbour from neighbour. Of course, Protestant denominations have always exhibited a peculiar combination of territorial and non-territorial features of organization: in one nation but not in another, enclaves within a nation, and neighbourhoods, but the linkages were 'at the top' through pastors, bishops, and missionaries. Now individual believers can hear 'the word' directly from preachers far away and can 'witness' to each other over great distances. They can also participate in greater numbers in various ways: phone-ins, donation of money, travel to broadcast studios and theme parks, and attendance at schools or universities.

What emerges from examining a long time-frame is territorial intermingling of religions combined with the maintenance of social and ideological boundaries. Self-segregation occurs within national borders. Or has until now. Will telecommunications change this, as printing enhanced the relevance of territorial organization? The key to an answer may lie in the concept of sovereignty.

Most of the major world religions, especially those associated historically with Europe, have claimed a form of sovereignty. They asserted hegemony of belief and also usually wished to exercise detailed control over daily life. In some cases, religion was a matter of life or death, and certainly of life after death for Jews, Christians, and Muslims. Through the hold of these ideas on rulers of nations, and before nations of other political and social units, many people felt that religions should have their own territories. Indeed, a large part of the fury which lay behind the Thirty Years' War grew out of dispute over whether the churches should be universal or national. By deciding in favour of national – that is, territorial – church organizations under the protection of a monarch, Westphalia secured the territorial sovereignty of the monarch and the nation but eventually undermined the territoriality of religions.[35]

The compactness or 'boundedness' of religious believers gave way to intermingling of believers in the same area. Of many conclusions one might draw, the one I wish to emphasize concerns what type of organization can decide on segregation or intermingling. Religious organizations have been superseded by territorial nations as the sovereign or all-purpose units of analysis. Nations have been assumed to be impervious to intermingling: they should be exclusive, continuous, and contiguous in territorial use and control. It has been acceptable for some time to allow religions to violate these territorial assumptions, for believers to share national territory, local neighbourhoods, and even buildings. I have tried to show that technological changes mediated these profound transformations of our assumptions about territoriality, and I currently see evidence that technology may be challenging these assumptions which lie at the heart of many political cultures.

What is the new sovereign? What comes after national territories? What in the future will not allow any intermingling? What could enforce future versions of segregation? Can anything ever again prohibit intermingling? Have we passed beyond unitary, all-purpose, sovereign organizations?

No one knows the answers to these questions, although this book contains speculations relevant to them. As stated repeatedly, the contribution I most want to make is not predictions but the demonstration that there is value in asking such questions because they are too often assumed to have only one type of answer: nations, the state system, the temple of Westphalia.

Religious revivals and movements seem prevalent in many parts of the world, and the environmental movement may be a new religion for reasons Mander outlines. One must doubt, however, that religions could be the new sovereigns in such a secular era. The import of the questions about territoriality and sovereignty, if conceived in zero-sum terms, will be missed, since they suggest, I allege, that we must get past sovereignty as exclusively here or there. Instead the unbundled world features shared sovereignty, which may mean no sovereignty at all. Whether we will need to return to Hobbes for lessons about life being 'solitary, poor, nasty, brutish, and short' may be disputed, as I show in chapters 6 and 7. So long, however, as theorists cling to questions which imply that territory and sovereignty are inextricably linked, they cannot open their minds to another type of world, just as observers of warfare in the sixteenth and early seventeenth centuries did not envision what rulers were constructing. Can we, by analogy or with the benefit of hindsight or by understanding new technology, do a better job of prediction or at least of envisioning? This is, in a sense, the central focus of this book.

MASS SOCIETY AND TARGETED POPULATIONS

Until recently, communication has taken two forms: personal (or face-to-face); and mass, as in 'stump speeches,' church sermons, or modern mass media. Personal communication obviously depends on territorial proximity, and if any given person would have many personal interactions, it also depends on population density in towns or cities. Because of the intermingling discussed above, face-to-face communication occurs in an environment of 'noise'; that is, most of the information in the immediate environment of any given person is irrelevant or meaningless – if it is not in a foreign language, it might as well be.

Mass communication also succeeds best and is most efficient where territorial proximity and population density coexist. As with personal, so mass communication also involves 'noise' because the target audiences are heterogeneous. To the extent mass media aim to appeal to the 'lowest common denominator,' as they must, the messages vary greatly in appeal and relevance to different people. Any given program satisfies no one fully, or different programs satisfy different types of people in the network audience.[36]

One important way of identifying the salient features of the telecommunications advances outlined above concerns the ability to sort out types of people or groups and to target them accurately. There have been two dimensions or features of these new technologies which result in targeting. One concerns the profusion of channels (large but still increasing), which can thus be more specialized in content than 'network' or multi-purpose channels. The second involves the continental and worldwide reach of the media through cable systems and satellite hook-ups. A third dimension may be less significant; certainly scrambling and unscrambling devices are not necessary for targeting and extended reach, but they secure the channels so that only members, subscribers, or initiates can receive messages. To the extent that targeting accurately focuses messages on those most interested, it reduces 'noise' or 'noise-to-message ratio'; and descrambling devices restricted to members reduce 'noise' to near-zero levels.

The non-territorial media of communication do not require proximity or density of population. If numbers of a particular type of person or people who share a common interest are insufficient to warrant a dedicated local channel, this limitation loses its force when cable systems or satellites cover a continent or all continents. By the same token, personal communication (even if not 'face-to-face' literally) no longer requires physical proximity or local density. The computer – and eventually TV plus telephone – networks described above offer opportunities for individuals to interact with people living anywhere in the world who share their interests in art, science, sports, hobbies, religion, or politics. As Carlson and Goldman summarize it so pointedly, 'the small personal computer is the Protestant Revolution of technology."[37] Instead of a Protestant version of direct communion with one's god, these computer networks allow personal communion 'at a distance' with consequences for concepts of individuality and community which I expound in chapter 6.

In the next chapter I return to the opportunities for targeting particular types of consumers and how this may affect economic ideas and practice. Here let me just note that mass-produced goods for mass markets – like mass media in general – need not disappear in the future, but they may be supplemented on a larger and larger scale by higher priced, high value-added goods and services which target homogeneous groups of consumers, and perhaps not even types of consumers but individuals.[38] As this happens, we will find it easier to accept that telecommunications, economic production, and probably other domains of our lives will come to rest on our ability to sort and target particular people more accurately than has been feasible or imaginable in mass production or the mass media of communications.

Targeting and sorting require means of identification. How do we know who shares our interests, our concerns, our needs, or our beliefs? When territoriality was less 'given,' we also found different assumptions about appropriate markers of identification. Who could wear what type of hat? Who was allowed to wear certain colours of clothing? Who could carry a sword or dagger? These and other matters were legislated in sumptuary laws, and customs and traditions prevailed even in the absence of laws.

The descrambling devices on pay-TV systems are only one instance of modern forms of identification. Most businesses or governments no longer rely on outward signs – like accent, skin colour, clothing, or signet rings – to differentiate categories of people who deserve their attention or services. Other technical means include plasticized identity cards with photograph and signature, passports, and electronically encoded credit cards. In all of these cases, one can easily and reliably sort people into relevant categories of 'us' and 'them' or of those entitled to different services or treatment; these distinctions no longer need to bear any relationship to territory or to its corollary, local acquaintance. For example, contrast the role of bank managers in small towns two or three decades ago with their limited role in an era of automated teller machines, whereby few aspects of banking are face-to-face and many can be conducted from most areas on the earth, no matter how remote.

Politics too has been touched by technology and procedures which allow strategists to sort and target people or groups with the characteristics of interest to parties, candidates, and governments. Since overt features like age or gender or skin colour do not reveal all that political organizers wish to know about beliefs, attitudes, ideologies, voting intentions, or potential campaign donations, political marketers have devised other ways to penetrate personal privacy. Greatly enhanced accuracy of sampling, polling, and interviewing, combined with massive data profiles on neighbourhoods or even postal zip-code areas, now allow the identification of people most likely to be usefully approached by a candidate, solicited for a donation, mailed a brochure, or asked to work in a campaign. To be sure, sorting and targeting have not achieved perfection, but accuracy has increased by an order of magnitude.

If these technological and other changes related to proximity, density, and 'massness' contributed to the territorial basis of the nation-state, then the unbundling of the nation as the assumptions about territoriality are relaxed marks the end of mass society, that bugbear which so troubled decades of twentieth-century thinkers.[39] The reasoning to support this conclusion may be summarized briefly as it will resurface in various guises in later chapters. Territoriality became the progenitor and partner of the nation-state, and thus the nation-state was transformed from one of several coexisting political modes to an all-purpose, sovereign body which covered every inhabited part of the earth. Yet in this same time period, Europe invented the concept of the individual, or what Charles Taylor calls 'subjectivism.'[40] Nations reduced the salience and independence of other institutions and identities, as outlined in chapter 1, and thereby weakened or stripped away the networks, communities, and contexts which had defined people before they became 'unencumbered selves.'

The decline of territoriality and its handmaiden the all-purpose sovereign state is leading, I argued in the previous chapter, to fragmented organizational forms that allow, encourage, sustain, and feed on multiple identities and the revival or renewal of communities of interest. What was meant by 'mass society,' if not the exposure of the naked self to the weight of a nation-state with few or no mediating communities?[41] What can end the tyranny of mass society, if not the multiplication of social, economic, and political organizations independent of the nation-state and associated with the multiple ways in which each individual chooses to be identified, sorted, targeted, and appreciated?[42] Of course, only Candide could believe that every day in every way the world is getting better and better. However, to the extent 'mass society' was once a justifiable worry, perhaps we can now worry about something else. Many people will never honour or respect differences, but everyone will become more aware of them; and most should feel secure in their uniqueness as they come to realize that some others share their features and as technology allows them sustained contact with these significant alter egos.

POLICING AND THE NEW TECHNOLOGIES

The central image associated with the new technologies of the twentieth century has been 'Big Brother.' The political organization we have usually associated with the new technologies has been totalitarianism. The concept of 'the police state' grows out of these images. One would be foolish to dismiss these images, concerns, and fears as utterly groundless; but perhaps the collapse of the Second World has opened the door to another room in which technology plays a less sinister role. At the least we can perhaps distinguish totalitarian or police state images from some technologies and examine less global and more precise concerns. Many concerns will still prove worrisome, but some may be less so or even positive. Unbundling the implications of technology rather than lumping all technology together as good or bad may be just as hard as thinking about non-territorial political organizations, but both are worth the effort.

To begin relaxing assumptions about technology and policing, let me note first that 'police state' imagery rests on out-dated technology. Big Brother made sense in the 1950s, when the radio and TV networks were gaining almost total access to potential audiences. CBS, NBC, and ABC had, for several decades, more than 95 per cent of the audience with receivers in the United States. They now have about 60 per cent, and the figure will drop further, perhaps to zero. Network executives wonder if there will be only one network – or none – by the turn of the century. This change results from the multiplication and specialization of channels described above. It is not reversible, given current technology. Thus, one may reasonably ask how will Big Brother brainwash audiences so fragmented and exposed to so many different types of messages? Perhaps advertising executives will find a way, but perhaps not.

Totalitarian control without centralized technology seems implausible, if it were ever feasible even with big computers and media networks. After all, the only societies which have attempted totalitarianism (Nazi Germany and Soviet and Maoist Communism) have collapsed after more or less brief experiments. One cannot conclude that such experiments will never again be tried or that they must always fail, but the evidence favours those conclusions. Let us examine why that might be. This will involve attention to some technological changes already noted but also to alternative interpretations of why totalitarian experiments had some success, and thus why they may have less chance of success in the future.

Mass media, mass production, central planning, and police states share certain features. All involve in different ways assumptions about standardization within a territorial framework, and all are made possible by technologies which foster territoriality and standardization. Mass media, as we saw, presume audiences largely undifferentiated and almost identical as between a very small number of networks. Mass production presumes that some people have more and others less of pretty much the same things (cars, toasters, shirts, houses). Central planning presumes standardization and mass production because it is conceptually challenging to plan comprehensively if every type of place or person has different needs or tastes. A police state is one in which a single organization 'polices' all types of regulations, or at least all the domains deemed ideologically relevant.

All of these concepts have a territorial bias toward exclusivity, continuity, and contiguity. The media networks needed, until recently, physically dense populations of a regional or national scope. Mass production relies on shipments from one or a few central places, and non-continuous or non-contiguous territories are much more expensive to service. Planning also becomes more expensive and less efficient with diversity, distance, and intermingling of territories which are part of other plans. A non-territorial police state is an oxymoron, since its first condition must be the ability to seal off the borders, even if that means building an expensive cement wall through the middle of Berlin. Indeed, Berlin was the focal point of the Cold War in many ways, and one reason was that it violated the continuity and contiguity assumptions of First World and Second World nations.

We have already seen evidence that territoriality and standardization may be seriously challenged by the new technologies. Territorial exclusivity, continuity, and contiguity count for less in light of telecommunications advances; and standardization has been undermined by multiple channels, declining media networks, targeted messages, and personalized communications. Therefore, to the extent that Big Brother requires territoriality and standardization, Big Brother faces serious obstacles to a successful police state. Or at least the type of police state the twentieth century has felt to be most threatening.[43] I will return in several chapters to other potential threats which are less obvious from the recent past, but the totalitarianism which has been the focus of attention in this century seems to me to be a historical curiosity rather than a future threat.[44]

To drive home this conclusion, let me put the same novel interpretation on two events in recent years which have been interpreted in virtually opposite ways by most observers. I refer to the crushing of the demonstrations in Tiananmen Square in 1989 and the aborted *coup d'état* in the (then) USSR in 1991. Most people would, I believe, see the first example as the triumph of force and authoritarian power, whereas the latter example would be offered as proof of the failure of force and authoritarian power. My interpretation does not really disprove those views, but it casts them in a different light by noting a technological similarity between the two instances.

Both sets of events reveal in slightly different ways the limits on centralized power posed by the new technologies of telecommunications. In China in 1989, the student and other demonstrators remained in fairly close touch with the outside world because of the relatively wide distribution of fax machines and other communication devices.[45] Obversely, the whole world (outside China) knew what was happening because the authorities could not disrupt such decentralized communication capabilities.[46] Thus, the ordeal dragged on longer than one would have expected, given the overwhelming superiority of force on one side. Furthermore, the authorities apparently had some difficulties with troop units who did not wish to attack the students, at least partly because they knew more about the events than their superiors told them because of their own electronic connections and because of fraternization with the crowds.

It is easily overlooked that the Chinese leadership had a problem since the outcome went decisively to their advantage. Their problem may be viewed in hindsight as this: the monopoly of force can no longer sustain a monopoly of communication, either internally or with the rest of the world. The territorial borders do not define the information boundaries. Large-scale repression can and probably will continue, but it cannot be kept secret for more than a few hours or days. In the long run, that means that the repression itself becomes much more costly and difficult. Once Hong Kong is integrated into the main body of China, the information boundaries will be even more porous, and no one can put a finger in the dike.

This does not mean that China will suddenly become a democracy. It may remain authoritarian for as long as it chooses, as it has in the past. But totalitarian? Not again. And whatever happens, links to the outside cannot be severed without a total shutdown of the power grid and wholesale destruction of equipment. The same is true of Russia for slightly different reasons.

Why did the coup fail in 1991? Most observers at the time attributed the failure to two factors: Yeltsin had steadfast support from the populace, and the coup plotters were the gang who couldn't shoot straight. I leave aside the quality of leadership among the hardliners, because the way in which the first claim has an element of truth makes the latter claim irrelevant. I do not believe that Yeltsin had more than a tiny fraction of the population behind him, as subsequent events seem to confirm. However, TV portrayal of the street demonstrations in Moscow and Leningrad made it look as though there was wide support.

Note two distinct ways in which the new technology – this time in the form of mobile TV cameras – played key roles. First, as always, the coup leaders made sure to take command of the broadcasting facilities at the very beginning. But the TV coverage was not thereby hindered! There no longer exists, as there once did, a central 'crossroads' of broadcasting. The coup leaders did not know that, or could not figure out what to do about it. Second, the reason there was no 'crossroads,' no plug to unplug, or some other metaphor, concerns the transformation of telecommunications. Hand-held cameras in vans with satellite hook-ups cannot be unplugged without immense luck and enormous resources, and satellite reception dishes cannot be centrally controlled. Parenthetically one should note that the next generation of receiver dishes, now on the market, measure less than eighteen inches in diameter and are thus even more difficult to detect. What will come next? Dick Tracy wrist receivers?

As a result, cameras captured the surging crowds, and the world watched the action live. More important, Yeltsin watched and was heartened. Even more crucial, the hardliners watched and were disheartened. Yet what happened on the ground? This is speculation, but speculation informed by close observation of demonstrations in North America. For one thing, cameras draw crowds. Maybe there were large numbers of Russians in the streets of every town and city; but if so, you can be sure they went to the cameras and thus made it easy to portray the demonstrations as mass uprisings rather than 1 per cent of the population, which might be a generous estimate. One might ask also what conclusion to draw from the empty streets of most areas of Moscow and Leningrad. My conclusion fits with pre-camera Russia as well as today: nearly everyone keeps their heads down until they see who is winning. But there were not many pictures of the empty streets or of people hiding in their apartments. And so the hardliners – and the world – understood the pictures of demonstrators around the cameras as evidence that 'the people' opposed their actions and supported Yeltsin. Doubtful; but a picture is worth a thousand words.

UNBUNDLED POLICE

Think of a hierarchy of concepts with a reasonably clear continuum of degrees of authority or authoritarianism. The exact labels could be subjected to dispute, I suppose, but something like this seems plausible:

>control (most authoritarian)
>manage
>regulate
>coordinate
>police (surveillance) (least authoritarian)

The use of 'police' as the lowest level of authority or coercion is intentionally provocative in order to 'shake up' the usual knee-jerk assumptions about the efficacy of the police as brutes in hob-nailed boots. Of course, some are, but even in systems attempting to be totalitarian the police alone cannot control in the strong sense used above.

In most societies most of the time, however, this usage is appropriate because 'to police' means 'to keep an eye on' things. Think of phrases like 'we police that area regularly' or 'we patrol the 200-mile off-shore zone.' Policing functions generally involve intermittent observation and encompass a narrow range of activities. 'Surveillance' probably summarizes most police work. Indeed most police action results from response to non-police reports that something needs to be done, whether a citizen dialling '911' or an elected official suggesting the police should 'crack down' on drunk driving. 'Control,' at the other end of the continuum, involves continuous oversight and some enforcement mechanism. Think of how a chief executive officer of a corporation might control the organization (through a hierarchy of subordinates) or how a foreman controls a production line or how a commander controls an army or ship. One would find it odd, I think, to say merely that these people 'police' or keep under surveillance the activities for which they are responsible; they do that but much more as well.

This long introduction has a purpose. Note that – exact labels aside – this hypothesized continuum may be applied to the effects of technology. Different technologies fall at different points (or bands) on the continuum. As Mander argues, nuclear power or large hydroelectric dams would be at the high end, since they are territorial and centralizing. Once homes and businesses are hooked up, one controls their power. Solar power, by contrast, is less centralizing and might be at the 'regulate' or 'coordinate' level, since each user or local group has its own power source. Windmills and small water-wheels may be off the continuum altogether.[47]

Take computers or mass media. Mainframes and personal computers are at opposite ends of the continuum. TV networks and the plethora of channels on cable or satellites are at opposite ends of the continuum. Hence, what kind of political authority will each type of technology encourage, favour, reinforce, or 'prefer'? It is my argument that most if not all of the new technologies favour 'policing' rather than 'control,' that political and economic organizations of a non-territorial and decentralized sort are favoured, and the contrary forms are weakened even though not eliminated.[48] Where the balance or equilibrium will end up, I do not know; but the direction of evolution seems clear, and so this book examines the implications of this trend. In the remainder of the book, I will use 'police' and the other words on this continuum to refer to these degrees of authority or coerciveness.

But there is another step in the 'logic' of technology as it affects 'policing.' As nations 'unbundle' and technology favours decentralized non-territorial forms, so the police system itself comes unbundled. That does not mean it becomes less effective, however, only that policing (like nations) moves from multi-purpose to specific-purpose. Note that public police forces have become subdivided over this century into more and more specialized branches or separate services: local police, RCMP, Canadian Security and Intelligence Service (CSIS, which used to be a branch of the RCMP), Coast Guard, border patrol, Securities Commissions (federal and provincial), the customs branch of Revenue Canada, regulation of food quality (in Agriculture Canada), regulation and coordination of labelling and advertising by the Department of Consumer and Corporate Affairs, and probably many others. Some of these are territorial, some are not; some cover all of Canada, some very small areas or very specific topics. But they are highly specialized compared to nineteenth-century Mounties, Texas Rangers, or, until recently, sheriffs in the American West.

As governments 'privatize' some activities and generally 'downsize,' the private sector takes over more and more aspects of policing. One may mention airport security, office-building security forces in general, patrolling by neighbourhood and/or private groups (when residents are on holiday, or regularly), debugging and electronic scanning for surveillance devices, help in eliminating computer viruses, limousine driver-bodyguards, and 'walk-home' services for women students.

70 Beyond Sovereignty

Part of the appeal of 'the private sector' is precisely the fact that it has been unbundled for a very long time, basically ever since nations became all-purpose territorial organizations. Before that, one could say the opposite: knights and barons were all-purpose police who protected peasants and serfs in exchange for a proportion of the harvest, dispensed justice, and served the higher nobility and the king as soldiers and tax collectors. Only as capitalism and nation-states secured their hegemonic status in politics and economics did the 'invisible hand' replace the mailed fist in the private sector.[49] Indeed, as chapter 3 shows, capitalism and nation-states coexist by creating separate realms called 'economics' and 'politics' or, more generally, 'private' and 'public'; these realms intersect and their boundaries are blurred, but there is a faith that an unbundled private realm is essential to freedom and dignity. For good or ill, opinion still seems to be moving in that direction as territorial nations unbundle and something like capitalism regains its hegemony in the Second and Third Worlds as well as the First World.

SUPERCOMPUTERS AND DECENTRALIZATION

Mainframe computers were mentioned above as an example of centralizing technology, and supercomputers would thus appear as extreme versions of this generalization. To conclude these illustrations of unbundling and decentralizing technologies, I want to describe the next generation of supercomputers and show why they, contrary to intuitions, should be massively decentralizing in their implications.

Supercomputers are very large versions of mainframes. They are the Charles Atlas of computers. They are extremely inefficient because of the bottleneck inherent in all mainframes: they are 'single-minded' in the processing stage. They overpower problems by doing billions of operations per second on a single problem.

The current stage in super fast computing involves massively parallel processing, which sets up several types of activities simultaneously. Each processor may be slower or less powerful than any supercomputer, but together they are much more efficient and much less expensive. Supercomputers are priced at $100,000,000 and up; they are centralizing technology since few can afford them, and those few include military and intelligence agencies. Massively parallel computers priced at under $500,000 are now on the market and operate at about 70 to 80 per cent of the capacity of supercomputers. As they gain acceptance and production runs increase, unit costs will decrease, just as happened with personal computers. Predicting prices is uncertain, but the past thirty years offer guidelines. In the 1960s, a million-dollar computer had the memory and processing power of today's average personal computer priced in the $1,500 to $2,500 range. Thus, a conservative guess about massively parallel computers twenty to thirty years from now would price them well within the budget of millions of individuals and businesses.

What will one get for this investment? The experts agree on several features, and further advances may reveal others. For one thing, such computers will have memory capacity so vast that pocket-sized versions will be able to store the holdings of any major university research library. The second feature will involve voice interface in real time, which puts these computers in the realm of the ship's computer in *Star Trek*.[50] One will 'converse' with the computer rather than slowly typing in manuscripts or printing out information. Finally, massively parallel processing should allow translation between natural languages in real time. Thus, one could travel to various countries (or use voice transmission) and have one's own personal simultaneous translator.

It seems clear that massively parallel processing should engender extreme decentralization.[51] Small, inexpensive, powerful, flexible computers with awesome memories which can be accessed much more rapidly and efficiently than anything currently available may provide in our era what the printing press provided a few centuries ago, the transformation of individuals and small groups into autonomous repositories of knowledge. If personal computers, in a matter of a decade or so, can transform work places and decentralize many activities, imagine what could happen when many homes, offices, or organizations have access – in many languages – to much of the world's accumulated knowledge.[52]

There is little value in spinning out scenarios based on massively parallel computers for individuals. There is value, however, in taking note of the direction in which technology is headed and the potential it has for decentralization. Of course, challenging territoriality is an *incidental* feature of the technologies discussed in this chapter. Each form of technology has its own explicit primary purposes, and we should not lose sight of them. It is my belief that most users of technology can perceive these primary purposes once the technology penetrates society. Users will evaluate the purposes differently, as Mander demonstrates so well. My concern in this chapter has been to highlight *implicit* purposes, effects, consequences, and 'logic.' Doing so reminds us of the ways in which earlier technology helped quite incidentally to 'bundle' the world into territorial states – with consequences we now find 'given' or intractable – and in which the new technologies appear to aid (also incidentally) in 'unbundling' national political and economic units. Later chapters explore several ramifications of this unbundling. Those ramifications too will be evaluated differently by different readers.

THE FINAL FRONTIER?

As the voice-over on *Star Trek* reminds us, space is the final frontier. In the vocabulary of this book, it is the ultimate non-territorial jurisdiction. Work and play will be dispersed not only to homes rather than central locations, but to space stations and perhaps beyond. Think if you can about management issues in a team of three scientists or professionals or consultants – all three working at home – one in Detroit, one in Delhi, and one in deep space. Would that be more difficult than managing an assembly line spread across several city blocks? Why? Would it be more difficult than managing a research team in Vancouver, Montreal, and San Francisco? Why? All of these examples already happen, including an occasional hook-up to orbiting space craft. Thinking about the possibilities and imagining the potentialities are harder than actually doing these things.

There is another sense of space which I must mention. It is non-territorial to a further degree. I refer to 'cyberspace' and the world of virtual reality. Although crude, virtual reality gloves and suits exist; and cyberspace grows daily. But we cannot easily foresee what to do with them. Another book may attempt the task, but not this one. I wish only to note that virtual reality is a place, or feels like it, but one where exclusivity, contiguity, and continuity count for nothing. Each participant in a virtual reality program could be in the same place at the same time – or at different times but still together! Meet me on Holodeck Three and I will reveal more!

TYPES OF NATIONS?

Do my arguments about bundling and unbundling apply to all nations or only to certain types? What is an appropriate typology? Let us review briefly some reasons why unbundling might be more likely in certain cases or even not occur at all in some cases. Then we can assess more precisely the reasons why I believe it may be a general process.

One approach looks to history and finds that the earliest nations were based on a genealogical principle.[53] These groups, often called 'tribes,' would claim a common ancestor, whether fictive or historical. We now call such groups 'ethnic nations.' Later, territorial nations, based on principles or assumptions of territoriality, grew up in ways I have described. These are more often called 'nation-states' than simply nations, but both terms are commonly used. Territorial nations did not, however, replace ethnic nations; instead they have coexisted for centuries, and this is the cause of some tension since Palestinians, Kurds, Basques, Catalans, Scots, and Quebeckers claim that their status as ethnic nations entitles them to become territorial nations.

This analysis cuts both ways. It seems to provide grounds for a typology and thus support for the hypothesis that bundling and unbundling apply more to one type and less or not at all to the other. However, to my knowledge ethnic nations of any size above a handful of people want to be accorded the status of nation-states. If so, that suggests that this form of territorial bundling may still be going on in some cases. Thus, both types seem to be converging, so that unbundling might eventually apply to both types.

A cross-sectional typology may lead to a less equivocal conclusion. Imagine three types of nation-states which coexist at the same time. One might be called 'natural' nations (such as Japan or France) which have grown up incrementally over very long periods and in which ethnicity, language, and territory coincide quite closely, although never perfectly. A second type could be called 'quasi-states,' following Jackson, because they are almost completely artificial when viewed as territorially bounded groups but are sovereign nations for purposes of the international state system.[54] Examples include most African states below the Sahara. They represent borders imposed in the colonial period which bear no relationship to social, linguistic, ethnic, or genetic boundaries; they are arbitrary rather than natural. The third type (which could be further subdivided) consists of hybrids, or nation-states more diverse and less historically deep than the first type but much less arbitrary than the second. One thinks of India, Germany, Italy, the United States, and Canada.

We can agree that unbundling poses different degrees of threat to these types. The second or quasi-state type lacks 'internal' sovereignty and never 'bundled,' and thus is already in important ways 'unbundled.' The third or hybrid type appears much more vulnerable than the 'natural' nations. So a first glance suggests that my analysis should be focused on only the third type, and especially some of its members more than others; for example, Canada more than the United States because of the possibility of Quebec separation. I think there are several reasons why such a conclusion would be misleading, and their mention should help to clarify what this chapter has tried to accomplish.

The first counter-reason concerns what we mean by unbundling. If Quebec leaves Canada, becomes a sovereign nation, and joins the United Nations, that is confirmation of the continued vitality of the territoriality which has undergirded political forms for three centuries: likewise if the Scots, Catalans, and others achieve greater autonomy as Britain, Spain, and their partners integrate more fully in the European Community. Important and indeed momentous as these changes may be for the people who experience them, they concern larger or smaller territorial political units. By themselves, they do not challenge the *idea* of territorial political units.

A second response might focus therefore on technological changes which undermine territorial control, management, and policing, and which favour specialized non-territorial forms of organization. I have devoted this chapter to that end and do not want to repeat the arguments. Note that integration into larger units like the European Community or the North American Free Trade Area – with consequently greater scope for sub-national units to serve as focal points for identities or devolution of powers – could and probably will also make it easier for non-territorial organizations to thrive. As nation-states 'compete' with larger and with smaller territorial units, there is more scope for transnational corporations, religious revivals, and many other non-territorial modes of organization to find niches in which to exercise influence. And as these latter forms seem to work, to satisfy certain human needs, and to gain supporters, the territorial forms are weakened relatively if not absolutely. Note that these niches result from the way technology interacts with particular settings. Neither alone is a satisfactory explanation of the changes occuring now.

A third rejoinder concerns the 'natural' or first type of nation. There is no good reason to think they are exempt from the non-territorial forces we have been discussing. France and Japan are leaders in telecommunications technology, their transnational corporations participate actively in the global economy, and cross-border investments multiply. One may believe that separatist movements in such countries have dim prospects compared to Canada, but non-territorial modes of organization seem at home in these countries too. This book is not about whether the world will be organized territorially or non-territorially; it concerns the need to accept that both forms of organization have coexisted and will likely continue to do so indefinitely. The book endeavours to render more apparent or visible the non-territorial modes of organization which have been obscured by our assumption that territoriality underlies political authority.

LA LONGUE DURÉE

Casting the rejoinder in terms of larger and smaller territorial units competing with territorial nations usefully reminds us that competition among different types of political units has been under way for millennia. It is not a phenomenon brought on by the Cold War, the European Community, or satellite transmissions. One of the signs that we have taken for granted the assumptions of territoriality I outlined in the previous chapter is how hard it is for most people to recall the eras before territorial nation-states. A very brief recital of some history in *la longue durée* may be salutary.

Throughout large parts of the world, local governments and empires have coexisted, although not always and not everywhere. One thinks of Aztec and Incan empires in the pre-contact Americas, and the Iroquois Confederacy which combined large-scale and local-level organization. There were both village and regional political units in India and China as well as the empires which at various times overlay them from within or from without. Greek city-states existed alone sometimes, at other times in alliances, and occasionally as centres of empires. The Roman Empire, the Roman Catholic Church, Islamic empire and Islamic nations, the British Empire, and many other cases could be mentioned. But the point need not be pressed by endless examples.

The central point is that units smaller than what we call the nation-state and some vastly larger in area have coexisted since the dawn of recorded history.[55] As technologies evolved or spread to other areas, as personalities came and went, and as ideas about new forms of organization occurred to people, the balance between local and 'global' scales of politics and economics shifted back and forth. With the invention or consolidation of the territorial nation-state in Europe, a new rhythm entered the balance. The bundling of these new entities pushed down the autonomy of the local units and some non-territorial units. The new types of empires – especially the Spanish, Dutch, and British – reinforced European nationalism, which reached a peak in the nineteenth century. By the twentieth century, the nation-state had become the preferred form of political mode throughout the world, however awkwardly it overlaid the local and non-territorial loyalties in many places.

Now once again we see some movement to units larger than nations and units smaller than nations, but without the hierarchy implied in relations between empire and colony. Nations will, however, continue to coexist with these other political units. But recent decades have also witnessed the rise in importance of muscular new units and the non-territorial identities they engender. We move therefore out of an era – a brief era in historical perspective – in which one political unit called the nation-state won the Darwinian struggle with other units to become sovereign, that is, to become the only unit which could successfully claim authority over every function within its territorial reach. With the resurgence of local loyalties and the nurturing of broader loyalties by some nations, and with the revival of old non-territorial loyalties of religion and ethnicity, has come a new force which this book endeavours to explore: the ability of individuals and groups of various size to create communities for specific purposes and without concern for territorial integrity.

The five-hundred-channel 'deathstars' will eventually result in most areas of the earth receiving the same set of pictures, words, and cultural forces. Yet neighbours will live in different information universes because they will choose to watch some channels and not others. Therefore, it seems nearly certain that the variations in media exposure will occur at least as much *within* nation-states as *between* them.

There will obviously continue to be differences *between* and *within* nations in level of economic well-being. To the extent that some sectors, groups, or individuals in each nation are more likely than others to plug into the global economy, one would expect to see more rapid increase in variations *within* nations, especially in currently poor countries. For similar reasons, regional and ethnic differences in affluence may increase *within* nations. None of these events, should they occur, need mark the termination of national existence, but together with the tendencies summarized above they should weaken rather than strengthen most nation-states.

Technology made empires possible, and later technology tipped the balance in favour of nations. For reasons I have explained in this chapter, technology now seems likely to take us beyond nations. I doubt if technology and other forces will replace nations with another all-purpose political form with the hegemony territorial nations have exercised on our thinking. But it may be a useful prelude to subsequent chapters to ask what comes after nations.

AFTER THE NATION-STATE

Nation-states won the Darwinian struggle once, and so one should consider the chance that they might beat back these up-start challengers of a non-territorial sort. In chapter 1, I mentioned several reasons why the continued strength of nations and nationalism might be more apparent than real. Among them were incipient nations within their territories or overlapping that of several states, and the spread of ideas about human rights, environment, trade, and the values of market forces compared to planned economies. Here I wish to recall those reasons but not repeat them and to add some of a different sort.

In particular, consider that what comes after the nation-state may be a version of it, just as it came after ethnic nations founded on the genealogical principle. The common link is the word 'nation.' Consider, however, whether non-territorial (ethnic) nations, territorial nation-states, and non-territorial nations of the future have much more in common than that one word. And consider how the use of the same word for each may mask differences in concept.

Since 1648 the nation-state has undergone several significant changes. The most immediate involved the divine right of kings as justification for the absolutist state: 'L'état, c'est moi.' Sovereignty was seen as residing in the Crown, and in some countries it still is even though the monarch reigns but does not rule. Another momentous stage was enunciated first in the American Revolution and soon thereafter in the French Revolution, that the people were sovereign. There have been other important stages in the evolution of the nation-state since these. These are sufficient, however, to make the point that the twentieth-century understanding of what a nation is accords in only small degree with what contemporaries assumed at the Peace of Westphalia and even less with the genealogical principle of older nations.

Should we therefore conclude that the current challenges can be overcome because so many other 'revolutionary' concepts have entered our thinking about entities we still call nations? Or should we emphasize that this set of challenges involves a qualitative rather than a quantitative shift? We construct our world, we deconstruct it, and we reconstruct it, or at least to some degree. To that degree, we can use terms as we please so long as we admit what we are doing. I choose to emphasize the constructedness and historically bounded character of our territorial assumptions, and thus I find the current transformation more significant than others occurring since 1648. We bundled a lot of things together in

1648, or thereabouts, and now we unbundle them. As a consequence, I use the word 'nation' or 'nation-state' to refer to that all-purpose territorial political unit we have taken for granted for so long. A world in which nations continue to exist but in which they once again share power, sovereignty, and loyalty with non-territorial modes of organization constitutes to my way of thinking a radical departure from what contemporaries meant by territorial nation-states during the last three centuries.

Only time can prove whether I am right or wrong. If the new technologies have the 'logic' I attribute to them, territorial nation-states will be eclipsed even though they will likely continue to exist. Perhaps like monarchs, they will reign but not rule, be honoured but not obeyed. Perhaps they will be quite powerful but in fewer domains; multi-purpose rather than all-purpose organizations, as the next chapter argues.

Let us return one final time to technology. Recall that I have defined technology broadly. To oversimplify, technology consists of ideas made visible, usually in the form of machinery or energy sources, but also in the form of organization. Nations too are ideas, and they too are made visible by our awareness, our pride, our patriotism, our investing them with meaning. But if our awareness of other organizations, our pride, our loyalties, and our identities are shifted – in part or completely – from nations to non-territorial ideas, will nations still be visible? Or will they be like trophies on our shelf, or like monarchs whose pictures appear on our currency but who do not sustain the value of that coin?

Nations have another meaning. As organizations they exist in the form of patterns of activity – controlling, managing, regulating, and policing. If we have learned one thing about nations in our lifetime, it is that they are very poor at monopolizing ideas. Even where, as in the USSR for seventy-some years, national governments control the police, the media, the economy, and the borders, ideas penetrate, germinate, and follow their own course. In nations which actually encourage ideas and do not try to monopolize their transmission, nations-as-ideas must compete with more and more ideas not confined to territorial roots.

What then comes after or alongside nations? What lies beyond their sovereignty? That is the great and exciting question to which these chapters are devoted.

3

Economics and Territory

The extent of unbundling has been obscured by the lens of assumptions about territoriality. Since nations without a territorial base seem so unnatural to most people, a focus on the economic realm may make it easier to gauge the extent and the process of unbundling.[1] We should not, however, go to the opposite extreme and project the trend of unbundling forward to a world totally unbundled. Instead, as the previous chapter argued, technology and culture may shift the balance among political and economic forms, but *balance* deserves emphasis rather than one extreme or another.

One of the themes of this chapter concerns the simultaneous bundling of political units into territorial nations and unbundling (or decoupling) of economic functions from political organization. The unbundling has occurred in the 'real world' but equally important has been the unbundling of concepts once thought to be unitary. The chapter will examine changing concepts of property, ownership, and 'the economy'; and those changes will be shown to be part of a long-term process of separation between political and economic 'logics,' a separation which has now become accepted or 'natural.' The decoupling of political and economic realms, the chapter argues, rests on a cultural evolution in what counts as public and private domains and in what should be the appropriate balance between them. Much of the ideological debate in recent decades between 'liberals' and 'conservatives,' 'Keynesians' and 'free enterprisers,' would have been meaningless before these new assumptions were taken for granted. Prior to taking up such broad issues, we must examine a number of matters of economic history which most participants in political and economic debates today have conveniently forgotten.

MULTIPLE BUNDLINGS?

The bundling into territorial nations over several centuries coincided with the creation of the economic form we usually call capitalism. Freer markets, more extensive trade, and transnational corporations count among the forces which may be offered as evidence today for unbundling in the economic realm. Does this mean that capitalism has defeated the nation-state which called it forth? As with most grand questions, this one misses the mark. Economic factors undoubtedly played some role in the struggle which eventuated in the territorial state, or at least some types of states, and slightly different economic forces – as understood in a particular way by our culture – may be one important part of the explanation for unbundling or the shifting balance between territorial and non-territorial modes of political organization. It would, however, obscure more than it clarified to assert that capitalism was the child of the nation-state and may now come into its own by slaying its parent. It would be equally accurate (or equally misleading) to say that capitalism was the parent of the nation-state and may now be slaying its own progeny.

We can agree with Marx that economic systems have a base in technology, conceived broadly, without necessarily agreeing with his other propositions. Unlike Marx, I do not believe that 'the modes of production' uniquely determine economic organization or that the economy itself is a sufficient explanation of political superstructure. For one thing, there has been too much interdependence and interaction historically among social, religious, political, economic, and technological changes to single out one of them as *the* independent variable. Of course, many economic theories today treat these other factors as exogenous variables, with implications for causal explanations.[2] Eventually new economic theories should incorporate some of these variables. I feel certain that when exogenous variables become endogenous, they will not be related in simple or linear ways to each other or to other economic phenomena. Indeed, part of the argument of this chapter and of the book involves a belief that what constitute separate realms or separate types of variables are not constant over long time periods and are meaningful only within a particular cultural framework. There may, therefore, be room for several variants of economic theory, or even incommensurate theories.

A sharp division among social, religious, economic, political, and technological variables – however plausible to us now – would have seemed quite arbitrary to people living in the late medieval and early modern periods. This may be clarified by a brief review of some concurrent changes in these variables. The previous chapter recounted several links between technological, political, and religious changes. Now we can 'factor in' economic and social changes which occurred in the same historical eras. The point is to show that causal priority cannot be assigned to any one type of variable, and even more important one can only with great difficulty classify events and processes into such distinct categories.

As a starting point, consider the following schematic outline of linkages among demographic changes, monetization, and social organization. Population growth (for whatever reasons) from the tenth to the thirteenth century led to an increase in the number and size of towns and cities in Europe.[3] Commercial life in these urban areas increased as did the amount of specie and the frequency of cash transactions. Besides migration to cities, migration to open land on frontiers led to a weakening of strict feudal controls; and indeed the fact of both forms of migration indicated that attitudes about feudal obligations had perhaps already begun to change.[4] The accelerating cash economy favoured the commutation of feudal labour obligations for rent for some peasants, and the receipt of rent rather than service meant that lords of the manor had more cash to buy goods not locally available or of higher quality than those made locally. These purchases by lords and barons further increased commercial life in the cities and provided incentives to more extensive trade and urban growth.[5] With an economy ever more based on cash, kings could extract taxes more easily and rely less on goods or personal service. Kings thus gained an advantage in buying mercenaries and weapons (as shown in chapter 2) which helped to consolidate territorial political units at the expense of feudal lords and cities.

Cities were islands of commerce and incipient capitalism in a sea of feudalism. They were refuges for people escaping from bonds of fealty or serfdom. These were important functions, and they played a role in the evolution of political and economic life. Beyond these functions, however, one may speculate that the relative *balance* between feudal and civic institutions accounted in good part for why capitalism and territorial states took root earlier in some regions of Europe and much later in others. Charles Tilly has enunciated these views in detail, and an adequate summary would be a digression in what should only be a brief example.[6]

Another way of presenting the same information makes the process look more orderly, at least in our terms. The rise of the strong territorial state (as implied in consolidation of kingdoms) took advantage of economic changes which weakened the local lords and barons and thereby precipitated markets in land and labour which were essential to the rise of capitalism. But the rise of capitalism shaped the nature of the state because of the creation of classes (in the Marxist sense and in our modern sociological sense) which quickly (as these things go) saw the personal fealty which underlay feudalism (or was feudalism) replaced with a market in human labour.

During consolidation of territorial kingdoms of an absolutist bent, arguments of a mercantile sort were accepted as persuasive. That is, economic activity should be organized and utilized to enhance the wealth (especially in precious metals) of a territorial state, and this could be accomplished most effectively by 'freeing' markets from non-economic constraints such as the personal obligations and vassalage characteristic of feudalism, non-taxation of land, entail and other restrictions on sale of land, restrictions on personal mobility, and so on. All of this 'laissez-faire,' of course, was deemed an internal affair of a territorial state, not an injunction to break down barriers between states. It became more difficult, however, to deny across national borders what was advocated within those borders; and so eventually new theories (such as that by Adam Smith) gained acceptance because they persuaded many observers of the virtue of international trade and particularly of the virtue of a clear and sharp distinction between the political and economic realms.

Concomitant with the demographic and other changes just cited, European exploration and conquest got under way. Columbus, Magellan, and others opened new territory to Europeans and in the process brought ideas, plants, medicines, foods, and precious metals back to Europe.[7] This constituted a 'globalization' as extensive in its time as what we now witness in the age of telecommunications. How does one categorize these myriad events? Did exploration have a military or an economic motive? The sailors and conquistadors certainly sought glory and wealth through military means. But the gold and silver they funnelled into Europe served to expand the money supply, in our terminology, and thus hasten the process of monetization and commercial development associated with the dominance of monarchs and the territorial state. Thus, the consequences were undeniably economic but also political and social. Scientific interest in new flora and fauna, of course, may often have been inseparable from issues of profit and prestige. The demand for written reports of 'new worlds' helped stimulate profitable printing companies and enlivened the discussions which took place in coffee-houses. Coffee-houses were a new social and economic phenomenon, since they were not feasible until coffee and tobacco were brought from the 'new worlds' to Europe in large quantities. They were precursors of insurance and stock markets.

In short, the many processes at work can only be classified with the aid of hindsight as economic, political, social, or whatever. Two very grand, interconnected, and parallel 'revolutions' were apparently under way. One we call political because eventually it led to the victory of absolutist monarchs ruling territorial states. The other we call economic because it led to capitalism. In one sense these new ways of acting in the world and their attendant assumptions were of a piece, were threads in the same tapestry, were one 'bundle.' It would be difficult to envision them separately at that time because so much of what happened in one realm seems inexplicable without knowledge of what was occurring in the other realm.

From our vantage point, however, we must conceptualize them as two quite distinct processes or chains of events. Today we create or construct our world as conceptually subdivided into categories of political and economic, as well as others like social, religious, and scientific. The point is not whether we 'moderns' are right and the benighted 'medievals' wrong, but rather that we cannot understand our world in the terms they used a few centuries ago. We 'see' sharply delineated subdivisions and organize, justify, and understand events in these terms. The deep structure of this way of seeing our world constitutes a form of unbundling because it denies the equation of political with economic activities, institutions, or values, a matter to which I will return repeatedly.[8] That there may be some 'real world' validity to seeing capitalism and the nation-state as separate historical processes gains credibility from the facts that some states were never capitalist and that capitalism is now transnational in significant sectors.

If territorial states and capitalism may be seen as two different ways of 'bundling' the many strands of politics or economics, they must thereby have developed by following somewhat different 'logics.' The belief that the economy is a separate realm beyond or above or underlying the political realm has been sanctified by capitalist economists as more than a fact, indeed as a dogma which should be placed beyond question. Hence, no matter how politics has been bundled territorially, so that nation-states have come to be seen as all-purpose organizations, the economy has been unbundled from it for almost as long.

SPECIALIZED INSTITUTIONS AND UNBUNDLING

The merchants, bishops, kings, and artisans of the late medieval world did not have a plan. They could not foresee the nature of bundling that was occurring or its consequences. They did not sit around asking themselves what they could do to encourage or discourage nation-states or capitalism. Nevertheless, the complex and connected 'micro-changes' outlined above resulted in new perceptions, and these perceptions were eventually rationalized in theories and concepts about politics and economics. We must now guard against letting words like 'nation' or 'capitalism' enslave our thoughts.[9] These words were coined to capture significant elements of a very complex historical reality. As this reality has changed slowly, analysts and the public have continued to use the same words. At some point, and now may be such a point, we should question whether the concepts have changed enough to warrant using different words. For example, economic historians have conceptualized some economic changes by referring to commercial capitalism giving way to industrial capitalism; and we may ask if global capitalism is a new phenomenon.

One reason the buzzing complexity of events, personalities, and activities could be conceptualized and theorized concerns the stabilization of specialized institutions. By describing in abbreviated form the development of institutions in several specialized domains, we will see that conceptual clarity and unbundling were related phenomena. This may also serve to remind us of the point with which this chapter began, that we should seek to understand the balance among forces leading to bundling and to unbundling. For three centuries bundling in territorial political units called nations has clouded our vision in ways which made it difficult to see that unbundling in non-territorial realms proceeded on a parallel track.[10]

This discussion of institutionalization will not endeavour to be exhaustive. Some examples drawn from what we see as quite different domains should serve to make the point that bundling in small, specialized non-territorial packages is also a form of unbundling compared to some earlier ways of thinking about human activities. Several examples also reinforce the point that matters we classify as 'economic' or 'political' or 'scientific' were not always so clearly distinct.

Let us begin with science. We now think of science as an institution separate from art, technique, religion, magic, and the economy. Of course, that is not to say that we fail to see how science might influence religion (creation vs evolution), the productivity of the economy, the decline of belief in magic or miracles, and so on. But we conceptualize a world in which certain types of people (scientists mainly, but also teachers, intellectuals, and others) have a specialized role to play in perpetuating knowledge and in expanding knowledge. By so doing, we institutionalize knowledge, and eventually we have come to speak of the knowledge industry.

Yet in origins, science as 'objective' knowledge was not really distinct from many other realms. Artisans who made shoes or textiles or bricks learned, modified, and passed on techniques because they were good ways of earning a living, not primarily for the pursuit of knowledge or in the hope of a scientific breakthrough. Likewise, 'art' as purely expressive activity was not until recent centuries seen as distinct from the activities of artisans and thus of science and technology; it served economic and decorative purposes and not just 'cultural' ones. We still have linguistic holdovers, such as 'the art of medicine' or 'the medical arts,' which remind us that art and science were not antithetical, and these phrases certainly would not be misunderstood even today as concerning paintings or sculpture with a medical theme.

Science also had close affinities with the church in medieval and early modern times, as well as famous clashes, for example, Galileo's trial for heresy. In past centuries, activities we might call scientific had religious motives and connotations. For example, practical, economic, and artful activities might be undertaken to demonstrate the orderliness of God's creation; and one of the most powerful arguments for the existence of God has been the metaphor of the universe as a clocklike mechanism and God as the clock-maker.

Turning to another example, bureaucracy has existed in various forms (such as empires) throughout history, but in the early modern period we have been discussing it became more like what we recognize today. In the previous chapter, I used Foucault's analysis of 'discipline,' and it is relevant here as well. Regular and repetitive techniques of organization or drill, routinized activities, and standardized conduct became the norm in tax collection, armies, prisons, schools, and business. Thus, bureaucracy as a concept and a goal or norm became distinct from political or religious life; and equally crucial, multiple bureaucracies with specialized functions proliferated.

Bureaucracy (by whatever name) enables the development of other institutions. Without the standardization and routinization made possible by bureaucracies, it is difficult to conceive of absolutist monarchs establishing effective control over the large territories and populations of European states.[11] As these bureaucracies – and related institutions like legislatures and judicial courts – were differentiated conceptually and functionally from the monarchs, kingship itself was transformed into an institution. Instead of the personality of the king being the most salient feature, orderly successions and bureaucratic continuity enabled and encouraged concepts of 'law' and 'justice' which were not purely arbitrary edicts of the monarch but generalized rules, whether written or unwritten in form. Some of this process may be conveyed by the phrase 'rule of law.'

As bureaucracy, technology, absolutist monarchy, and territory grew more intimate and interdependent, sovereignty took on the meaning we have understood for three centuries. Sovereignty justified the consolidation of national territories under kings who commanded a state which claimed to have authority over every person and activity within the borders of the political unit. Thus, territorially based politics had the interesting consequence that Europe would have a pluralism of nations rather than a single overarching authority.[12] In other words, the pluralism of the modern state system itself became institutionalized, as sovereign entities were too strong to be subdued by a single great power. After 1648 it was also embodied in legal doctrines we still utilize, even if they appear increasingly anachronistic[13]

Specialization is a two-edged sword: it divides functions, and it creates interdependence. These two consequences may be seen at the individual level, at the institutional level, and at the national level. To use medieval knights as an example, those individuals were simultaneously soldiers, managers of property, judges, and tax collectors, and they lived in largely self-sufficient manors. They were replaced by people with special expertise in these several activities, thereby creating interdependencies among people whose enhanced power in one domain (economic or political or military) was counterbalanced by the need to rely on experts who were powerful in the other domains. Globalization today involves, by analogy, greater interdependencies and thus a changing balance of power among political, economic, and social domains.

As I have implied above, specialization among institutions also had the same result. It made each institution more effective, whether in science, as a bureaucracy, or in politics, but none was self-sufficient. The interdependence of the institutions within the borders of the territorial nation strengthened the state as an actor in the state system. New concepts of economics showed why a division of labour and specialized skills, whether within the economy or more broadly, should generate wealth and strength, which in turn enhanced the nation's sovereignty. As trade between nations increased and as Adam Smith, Ricardo, and others gave proofs that a division of labour was beneficial between nations ('comparative advantage'), so interdependence among the European states threatened (or was believed to threaten) the sovereignty of each nation.[14] Hence, resort was made for a period to mercantile defensive postures and later to overseas empires and colonies. Eventually, however, trade was accepted as a necessity, and later still efforts were undertaken to regularize it with alliances, common markets, and other concepts.

Let us return to the themes introduced at the beginning of this section. Territorial and non-territorial institutions or modes of organization compete, contest, or vie with each other and for a time achieve a balance. But only for a time, and then the balance shifts. In the previous chapter and in this one, we have seen that a great many processes and activities 'conspired' (albeit unconsciously) to become bundled in territorial fashion. More and more activities we count as distinct – economic, political, social, religious, linguistic – became interdependent and reinforcing parts of territorially based nation-states. That balance could not last forever, partly because some things were not fully territorialized, partly because other parts of the world had other ideas about appropriate organization, and partly because the 'bundle' of all these elements contained internal tensions and contradictions. We now turn to some of these ideas, tensions, and non-territorial 'logics' to see some more of the relevant background or context for the apparently greater unbundling most areas of the world are now experiencing.

PROPERTY AND OWNERSHIP

What constitutes property has evolved in the centuries under review in this book, and the meanings of property rights and of ownership have also changed.[15] Property and ownership seem likely to be among the concepts which will change further as the balance shifts from territorial to non-territorial assumptions, since a particular notion of property rights has coexisted uneasily with the nation-state for three centuries. In addition, ownership and management have become increasingly separate functions because of joint-stock companies, pension funds, and mutual funds.

Ownership in European culture has, at least for a few hundred years, rested on a zero-sum orientation. What belongs to A cannot also belong to B. Of course, there are joint-stock companies and partnerships, but even in such instances one would say that the stockholders or partners own the company to the exclusion of everyone else. Likewise, I may invite guests to my home, but this usage of the house does not in any way imply that I do not own it exclusively. Ownership in this narrow sense involves the power to dispose of or use the object without reference to the wishes of non-owners, and to exclude them from its use.[16] Historically, this concept of ownership may be related, in its emphasis on exclusivity, to the notion of territory as the exclusive base of nations. It is also the analogue of the concept of sovereignty in the state system. It is also, historically, closely related to the rise of the modern concept of the individual as the bearer of rights, a topic to which I will turn shortly. Concepts of property, ownership, and individualism bear also on the relative decline of certain conceptions of community and citizenship which are addressed in chapter 6.

For personal items like a home or clothing or one's law practice, exclusive ownership has a natural appeal. For many objects, however, there is another, older, subdominant conception. Shared usage or complementary usage does not entail ownership. Instead, 'the commons' has been a meaningful concept for centuries. In an earlier period, for example, certain people had the right to collect firewood from land they did not own, and others might have had a right to graze cattle on that land, and the local 'lord' might have had the exclusive right to fish for salmon. Who owned the land? All of them? None of them? The question seems relevant to us because we assume that usage somehow entails ownership. Other cultures do not make that assumption, and thus we can learn something about the arbitrariness of cultural understandings. After all the arguments, perhaps we would prefer the way we now assume to be correct or natural, but perhaps not. Until we take seriously other possibilities, we cannot be sure that our way makes sense.

We are belatedly coming to realize that many of our environmental concerns derive in part from narrow cultural conceptions. 'Who owns the land?' is a question less relevant to sustainable development than one about usage by humans and other species. The aboriginal concept of the land owning us, or conceptions of seasonal usage, might serve us better. Whatever the definitions of ownership in different nations, the arbitrary nature of geographic boundaries ensures that nations are less and less relevant to environmental concerns. They may also be irrelevant to many economic concerns, to which I now turn.

If a concept of ownership was related to the assumptions about territoriality which underlay the nation-state, the connection probably stems from what people meant by property. Since our understanding of property has expanded greatly in the past century or so, the concept of ownership may now be separable from territory. Property has meant, for most of human history, 'things,' physical things, tangible things; and most importantly in the last thousand years in Europe it has meant land. One's relationship to land in Europe has not always involved ownership, but it did in the early modern period; and so we find again a convergence of capitalism and the territorial state which yields a new set of rights and privileges and which may now be yielding to new forces and concepts.

Medieval knights and lords were attached to particular places and had control over the activities on their land. The peasants were tied to the land and obliged to devote a significant portion of their labour to clearing and cultivating the lord's property. Although lord and peasant were both connected to the land, they did not own it in our sense, but it brought them certain rights and privileges. For the peasant, the rights and privileges were not very generous, but they ensured a home and food for the family and its descendants. For the lord, the opportunities were greater and life more rewarding; but sale of the land was not an option, so that ownership had a more limited meaning than for us. However, that was perhaps compensated by the prestige and power it brought, the ties of fealty with the higher lords or kings, and the possibility that valour might cause the king to enlarge the estate and thus the power and prestige of the lord and his family and heirs. 'Glory' and honour were the peak virtues for ambitious men, and only much later were they displaced by motives of 'profit.'[17]

The processes of monetization, commercial development, and population movement described above changed the nature of landed property. To oversimplify, with a market for labour and eventually for land, it became important to own property for a different reason. Whereas land had previously created and symbolized the feudal bonds of vassalage and fealty, the new concepts meant that land was a basis for independence. There arose, in another of those unwitting micro-processes, an understanding that only property – and preferably property in land and estates – could protect one from the overweening power of the newly dominant territorial state. John Locke was the great voice of this interest, although no one person authored the idea. This is why only men of property were deemed worthy of the vote, and as the new bourgeois industrialists expanded the concept of property (and bought land), they were eventually granted the right to vote. The upper houses of nineteenth-century legislatures were seen as bulwarks against democracy because the landed and wealthy lords or senators (whether in Britain, Canada, or the United States) could not be 'bought' by the state, whereas labourers were all too easily bought, or so it was assumed. Since women generally could not own property, and thereby achieve independence, this logic required that they be denied the vote.[18]

Two lessons may be drawn from this brief review which relate directly to the relations between economics and territory. First, property ownership and enjoyment of its benefits rested on the authority of the state. Only the all-purpose state and its judiciary could enforce concepts of ownership which concentrated property so exclusively and in so few hands. And yet, ironically, property was seen as the only thing that could give a man (and it was at that time men only) the independence of mind and action that warranted full citizenship, including the vote and the opportunity to enter politics.

Second, the individual enjoyment of property rights had a collective corollary. The economic growth which kings and their states needed in order to consolidate power and gain sovereignty rested on property rights. Only with the right kinds of property rights would there be sufficient incentives to invest, to innovate, to organize efficiently, to make a profit, and then to reinvest the profits and increase employment and production.[19] The state which was in process of creation in the late medieval and early modern periods depended heavily, therefore, on economic concepts of ownership and property; but the individuals who stood to gain the most could not benefit fully without the state's enforcement of property rights against free riders. In this way, and others suggested above, the territorial states and capitalism achieved a balance among their interests with extraordinary results, as the subsequent affluence shows. But the 'logic' of the political state and its economic Siamese twin were different for several reasons to be addressed throughout much of the remainder of this chapter. Today and in the near future, capitalism, property, and the state are being redefined in order to achieve a new balance between their 'logics.'

Several scholars have noted that the mutual dependence of capitalists and the state creates a new political dynamic. Marx is probably the best-known exponent of this view, but Lindblom has also come to a similar conclusion from quite different premises.[20] An extended quote from a legal scholar will add a helpful perspective, to which I will return in a later section:

There can be no doubt that our property laws do confer sovereign power on our captains of industry and even more on our captains of finance. Now it would be unworthy of a philosopher to shy at government by captains of industry and finance. Humanity has been ruled by priests, soldiers, hereditary landlords, and even antiquarian scholars. The results are not such as to make us view with alarm a new type of ruler. But if we are entering a new era involving a new set of rulers, it is well to recognize it and reflect on what is involved.[21]

Although this point of view may serve us well as we enter the twenty-first century, it is humbling to note that Morris Cohen published these remarks in 1927.

THE SERVICE ECONOMY

The first step in exhibiting the tensions between state and economy involves a quick look at changing concepts of property. Each successive stage in our understanding of property (other than items for personal use) has involved the inclusion of more and more intangible things which have less 'need' for a territorial state and which favour or encourage non-territorial enforcement mechanisms. We have already seen that property was conceptually broadened to include commercial and industrial versions. These activities are less fixed in space or territory than land, but once factories are built, transportation networks set up, and favourable laws passed, the mobility of capital looks fairly limited in the short run.

This change of 'property' is closely related to the shifting centre of gravity of economic activity from the primary sector (especially agriculture) to secondary (especially manufacturing). Without trying to be comprehensive, let us turn immediately to how property and ownership change as the focal point of the economy shifts to the tertiary or service sector. Of course, all three sectors have always coexisted, but here I want to draw attention to the expansion of the concept of property as more and more economic activity revolves around services.

'Services' covers a very wide range of activities and concepts, as must be true when they encompass 70 per cent or more of the value in modern economies like those of G-7.[22] Many people also have the idea that these are boring and low-wage jobs compared to those in manufacturing, and this attitude has been captured by the stereotype of 'McJobs.' Of course, many jobs in the service sector fit the stereotype, but more and more jobs do not. Doctors and other health-care professionals, lawyers, management consultants, motivation-seminar leaders, fashion designers, advertising directors, movie and television workers, computer software programmers, school, college, and university teachers, genetic engineers, and a host of other educated, skilled, and well-paid individuals work in careers which have grown in number alongside short-order cooks, hairstylists, secretaries, and taxi drivers.[23]

What tangible products can one own in this sector? Traditional service workers – such as cooks or barbers – 'produce' meals and short hair. Neither product would be described as 'owned' by clients, but they are, in the sense of 'used exclusively.' The workers themselves have certain skills which are in greater or lesser demand, more for cooks and less for barbers, and they command prices accordingly. The same is true of professionals like lawyers, doctors, and writers. But the intangibles count for more and more as product and as a source of value. One can sell 'good will'; that is part of the value created in certain kinds of businesses involving sales, legal practices, and the like. Similarly, 'intellectual property' has expanded by increasing the categories exemplifying it (synthetic drugs, engineered genes, computer software) and by increasing volume within categories (more novels, more legal documents, more software). One no longer patents only 'tangible' inventions like light bulbs; one also patents genes. One no longer copyrights only 'tangible' objects like books; one also copyrights electronic images, data, and computer software. And more countries have come to realize the importance of respecting patents and copyrights, even former 'outlaws' or 'pirates' like Taiwan.

We should not make too much out of concepts like tangible and intangible, but they signal an important shift in economic activity. Virtually all of the skills and activities in the new sectors of the service economy, and many in the more traditional sectors, are 'intangible' in at least two senses. For one, they involve knowledge and skills and are not visible in the way a factory or a car is. We can drive the car and see if we like it. How does one 'test drive' a genetic engineer? One goes by her experience, training, 'dynamic energy,' and 'track record.'

The second feature most of these 'service' activities share is their mobility.[24] This implies they are easily transferred to a new jurisdiction or territory compared to moving a factory, but it means much more than that. If a company moves its factory, it leaves behind a building and perhaps equipment. When a person moves, the skills, knowledge, and experience go too. In different terms, we can say that *assets* have been broadened and transformed. Buy a manufacturing firm and you get the assets in the form of a production line and a set of known suppliers of material. Buy a software company and the 'assets' may leave to work for another company. So what do you own, what is your 'property,' when you buy a company 'making' software or special genes? How do you keep in place the employees who are your most valuable assets when they can move to a new employer (or start their own company) in another town or country or next door to you?

The purpose of these questions is not to seek answers, but to indicate that such questions imply very different understandings of economic ideas like property, assets, and ownership. And we are not talking small changes here. In dollar terms, software companies in North America generate more revenue and 'value-added' than does the manufacture of the computers on which the software runs, and software or computers alone have surpassed car and truck manufacturing in value.[25]

Most service industries which are growing today depend on information. They 'produce' or analyse information, they store it and transmit it, or they utilize a particular configuration of it to generate added value in production. That is why these areas of activity are often called 'information industries,' and their rapid rise to prominence has been labelled an 'information revolution.' When these tertiary activities are described in these ways, we naturally ask such questions as the following, which at first glance make sense: who owns information? what is transferred when it is sold? and how do you get exclusive control of it, when the seller retains it no matter how many times it is sold? The peculiarity of such questions reminds us that concepts of property, property rights, and ownership may be changing in degrees which require us to ask different questions. Sharing ideas may sound less profitable than selling them, but ideas are shared even when bought or sold; land once sold is not shared.[26] It is my argument that many of the new questions imply that territorial states are less and less compatible with or necessary as the locus of many important economic activities. Politics and economics exhibit, more and more, different 'logics.'

Recall the points made above about the mutual dependence of the territorial state and capitalism. The state needs economic activity, and capitalism needs enforcement of property rights, contracts, and the like. Mobility of largely intangible skills and products in a global (or at least multinational) market means that nations can be less sure of retaining companies and employment opportunities, and the state is less and less effective as enforcer except when all the relevant states cooperate, which they feel compelled to do more and more often in order to keep skills at

EXTERNALITIES

home. It may not be fair to say, as Cohen did in the quotation above, that the captains of industry are sovereign, but nation-states certainly feel less sovereign in the global economy, and for good reasons.

EXTERNALITIES

Externalities have always been difficult for any group to handle. They have also been a problem for accurate measures of economic activity and value. They are, by definition, external to the specific activity under examination, and they include positive and negative externalities. How they are measured and whether they show up in the national accounts depends on cultural features of the organization of family and of work, on what we see or ignore, and on the scope of the externality.

Positive externalities, being favourable to someone, pose fewer problems politically, even though they are conceptually identical to negative externalities. Thus, let us examine a couple of examples of negative externalities and some of their economic and political implications. The most commonly noted externalities in recent years have been environmental. Pollution of the air or of streams and rivers has costs in health care, unpleasant tastes and odours, and reduced visibility, among others. These costs are virtually never included in the prices of products sold as a result of the economic activity which caused the pollution. Of course, governments sometimes try to capture some of the costs in fines or in mandating new equipment to reduce future pollution. These rules and regulations have real dollar costs, and they show up as part of GDP. Many costs of pollution, however, are not monetized and so do not get measured as economic activity. For example, an employee who would be an economic benefit to a company or town leaves or does not accept a job there because of the pollution of air or water in the area, and thus economic activity is less than it could have been.[27]

A different kind of example involves day care. Many employees must make private arrangements for day care. These show up as part of economic activity in GDP only where money changes hands and is reported as income. But consider the many ways in which GDP does not get augmented by day care: 'underground economy' transactions with cash and no receipt; quid pro quo in which people care for other people's children at one time in return for reciprocal care at another time; and most commonly a spouse (nearly always the wife) who stays at home and thereby forgoes income in the money economy. Many points – practical, moral, or economic – might be worth exploring, but only one is directly relevant here: the costs and opportunities foregone do not show up on balance sheets and thus do not enter into decisions about pricing of products. The costs are borne privately by individuals or families, or they are borne publicly as expenditures from tax revenues for unemployment insurance and social welfare, as lower tax revenues, and probably many other ways.

There is no need to proliferate examples, as these can serve to point up several conclusions. First, what counts as economic activity has changed over the centuries and is still evolving. We still do not measure 'housework' when performed by family members or in the underground economy. Many activities which used to be 'internal' to households are now rarely performed there, but has the level of activities really increased by counting in GDP the dollars spent on baking bread, canning jam, cooking restaurant meals, and so on? Of course, there are a few things which have been removed from the money economy as a result of changing values; for example, certain government offices were bought and sold on the market in earlier centuries in Europe, but not now.[28]

Second, efforts to include these activities in GDP – for example, housework by non-market participants such as wives – have foundered on the impossibility of measuring their market value. Although cleaning carpets and babysitting exist in markets, one cannot assume that the non-market versions of these activities need have an inputted value equal to the current market prices. For example, if one were forced to pay a family member at going market rates, one might choose to eliminate the activity, to buy less of it, or to plead inability to pay the price. Hence, the markets would not clear, and prices would change.

Third, many non-market costs or externalities are really negative benefits, as are many things in the market economy. If one forced companies to clean up all the pollution they created, that would certainly show up as extra economic activity. But prices of products might be higher, and profit margins no doubt lower, so that fewer companies might remain in operation.[29] Whether the economy would appear to be larger or not, there would clearly be no more goods or services on the market, even if we felt better about a cleaner environment. If one exports most of the product in question, then a higher price would be a benefit to the exporting country. But there is no guarantee that the product will command a higher price, especially as many foreign countries have low environmental quality standards, or like Canada have high standards which they rarely enforce, thus ensuring lower prices for their products, which may compete with the ones we are trying to export.

Fourth, one way to 'internalize' externalities, especially for some industries, involves government expenditures.[30] The costs of education, social welfare, pollution clean-ups, public security, national defence, and a host of other activities can be seen in public revenues and expenditures. Businesses usually complain about these as costs, burdens, and wasteful interference – and sometimes they are – but they are not directly attributable to a given company because they are often better conceptualized as infrastructure and other public goods. The nature of public goods consists in being available to everyone, but no one has an incentive to provide them because there would be 'free riders.' Why should I build a road if you can use it for free? Even if I can charge a toll, traffic may be too low to recover the costs. Hence, we expect governments to provide public goods and use their coercive powers to raise taxes from users or potential users. Because of the absence of a competitive market, public goods often end up being produced in inefficient quantities, either too much or too little.

The fifth and final point about externalities concerns territoriality. Many externalities – like pollution – reach beyond the borders of any given country. Likewise, public goods may result in subsidizing of one country by another, and this is more and more true of economic activities in the service and information sectors. For example, it may be cheaper to send students abroad for advanced education, since public universities in many advanced countries recover only a small fraction of their real costs through tuition and other fees. This amounts, it appears, to North subsidizing South, or developed subsidizing underdeveloped countries. However, what about the very common case in which the student does not return home after earning the PhD? In that case, South has subsidized North with a skilled human resource it can ill afford to lose. In a world where factors of production are mobile, and skills and knowledge are the most mobile factors, national borders have less and less relevance. One can refuse to allow students to come from abroad or one can insist that they leave, but both policies have costs and neither is easily enforced. A later section will focus specifically on migration across national boundaries, so that no more need be said here.

In summary, more and more externalities cross national borders. These include pollution, migration, and what appear to be subsidies arising from the difficulties of adjusting prices to take account of provision of public goods. In addition, whether an activity is counted as economic depends on such things as cultural modes of family organization and work and which activities can continue to operate underground.

Countries which export pollution are subsidized by other countries which do not do so. Countries which – directly or indirectly – subsidize export industries thereby also subsidize consumers in the importing countries. As trade increases, so do externalities. Regulation of externalities and provision of public goods which cannot be territorially contained require supra-national governments or international agreements, to which I will return in a later section. Before that, it is necessary to explore a broader implication of some of the topics raised so far which relate to the different 'logic' of the economy in its non-territorial aspects compared to that of the territorial state.

PUBLIC AND PRIVATE REALMS

At the beginning of this chapter, a question was raised about the relationship between capitalism and the territorial state. The first answer suggested that a division into distinct political and economic developments might be nothing more than our current perceptions imposed on an earlier age. In exploring the institutionalization of different realms such as bureaucracy, the military, science, and business, it seemed more reasonable to suggest that our categories were not just perceptual but might indicate that specialization and interdependence were actually increasing in the real world. Consideration of changing concepts of property, ownership, assets, externalities, and indeed what activities we include in 'the economy' has now lead to the conclusion that there has been a growing separation of political and economic logics – one based mostly on territoriality and sovereignty and the other less and less on territorial organization. The disjuncture or decoupling or unbundling of these large domains, it will now be argued, rests on a cultural change in what we count as public and private realms. This is a very broad topic, and the surface can barely be scratched in this chapter. Other chapters consider some related aspects in greater depth.

In relating the disjuncture between political and economic realms to a tectonic change of cultural assumptions about public and private arenas, I leave completely open the issue of which is cause and which is effect or whether they are just part of a syndrome. Let us not be distracted by such issues but focus instead on how changing concepts of 'public' and 'private' may help us to see linkages among many apparently separate aspects of economic or political life in the last few hundred years and, by extension, in the future.

Public and private have come to be understood as antithetical or at least as mutually exclusive. This has not always been so. In classical political theory, a person could achieve his (yes, his not her) full potential and purpose only by participating in the public life of his city or *polis*. Of course, there was a sense of private life, including one's relationship to family and household; but it was very constricted in comparison to our modern conceptions.[31] For one thing, religion in pre-Christian Europe was a public activity and not a private sanctuary. Indeed, that continued in some degree until the Protestant Reformation, literacy, and vernacular scriptures established the personal, private, individualized relationship between a believer and the Christian God. One need hardly mention that we are discussing Europe in this book, but a reminder may be helpful because many religions are not private or personal spiritual realms. That is part of what Weber realized in arguing that 'the Protestant ethic' was a cause of capitalism in Europe.

The process of personalizing religion in the era of the Reformation was an important part of a broader development, and economic changes leading to capitalism should also be seen as strands in the new cloth. The overall perspective may be characterized in our modern terms as the creation of the individual.[32] Obviously, people have noticed for a long time that human individuals exist as physical entities bounded by skin. What needs to be brought to consciousness is that the concept of the morally autonomous individual was invented at just about the same time as nations were bundled into territorial states. Over several centuries these historical processes led people to believe that the basic building blocks of society were human individuals, that each individual has value and dignity, that each bears certain fundamental rights, and that governments or groups which fail to recognize individual sanctity behave immorally and improperly.

This is not the place to recount in detail the creation of the individual, or what Charles Taylor calls 'subjectivism.'[33] But a few remarks may make it easier to step outside our current assumptions about individuality and thus to see it as a historical creation. In discussing concepts of community in chapter 6, I will return to individuality and try to show how in the future our notion of free and equal individuals may be enriched and reconciled with new types of community. That will also reveal that 'individual' is a concept evolving now in a 'postmodern' direction. At this point, however, I want simply to mention a number of historical changes which we take for granted but which are related to the development of the concept of the individual as part of the differentiation of public and private realms. One might begin by pointing out that 'private' must have a fairly narrow compass if one does not have a conception of autonomous individuals.

The division of labour and specialized institutions were unintentionally part of the process. As noted above, the creation of separate domains of science, economy, and religion laid a foundation in which some things could be public without everything being so. Obversely, some matters could be private – that is, not regulated by any public figure or public institution – without entailing a complete negation of public order. Just as religion could be personal, so other choices or activities could be personal. For example, medieval lords of the manor could arrange or forbid marriages for their serfs, and the king might 'give' in marriage men or women in vassalage to him. As feudal ties weakened, marriage became a more personal decision, even though our ideas about suitable partners still depend to large extent on socialization within a particular group and culture.

Clothing, furniture, and style of house have become personal for us, restricted by climate and income but not by public edict. Yet for centuries, sumptuary laws prescribed who could wear certain colours or styles of clothing, who could have a tile roof, and who could exhibit certain types of art or decoration. That is, individuals did not have rights or privileges, only groups or statuses had these rights or privileges. Those restrictions seemed natural to people who believed that individual preferences were signs of wilfulness or sin, that society must be ordered in all its aspects to reflect God's ordained order and hierarchy, and that this life mattered little compared to the everlasting life revealed in Scriptures. Besides, with no exposure to or awareness of alternative ways of leading a life, how could one imagine entirely different arrangements, let alone effectuate them? Globalization – whether through caravan trade, the Crusades, exploration, settlement, or telecommunications – can have that liberating effect on our minds, but it is most effective in conjunction with all of these other changes in society, religion, and the economy.

The idea that economic activities should be somehow outside of government or other public control developed slowly. Of course, there are many people who do not accept that view even today. City life in the centuries after the fall of the Roman Empire was relatively autonomous of political controls by nobility or landed knights. City dwellers were much more oriented toward economic gain than to the 'glory' and 'honour' which motivated the lords and kings. But even in city life, individualism in our sense was stifled or not even contemplated. Cities were, after all, social contracts among groups of people organized communally in the form of religious orders, guilds, syndicates, and corporations. The economic competition and free flow of ideas we take for granted were intentionally restricted by these organizations to try to maintain 'trade secrets,' whether in artisan works or religious mysteries or financial accounting.

The truly revolutionary aspects of Adam Smith's theory about the wealth of nations were twofold. As mentioned before, he focused on nations as territorial units, and most economic theories since then have also done so. The 'global economy' has forced some reconsideration, but not much when one thinks that Michael Porter's book is entitled *The Competitive Advantage of Nations* (even though he actually argues that the unit of analysis should be industries, not nations).[34] The second – and still most controversial – feature concerned 'the invisible hand.' This was the idea that each person or firm could make the decision which best served their personal interest or advantage and the market would guarantee that this was also the optimal result for the society and nation as a whole. As noted above, this idea fit well with the broad 'agenda' of modernity involving rationalism and positivism.

Economic man (or woman) has ever since then been an individual or an individualist.[35] The theory of the market has been a powerful motive and rationalization for our reliance on individual preferences unfettered by government or social or public intervention. Of course, these economic theories would have been unthinkable without some of the concomitant changes we have observed in technology, religion, and politics. For example, bureaucracy assumes routines, standard behaviour, and elimination of arbitrary privileges. Likewise, changing concepts of ownership were related to the idea of property rights beyond the reach of absolute monarchs and their whims, which led to the belief that property was the basis of personal freedom, as recounted above.

Literacy and mass printing in vernaculars had the effects noted in the previous chapter, including the diffusion of ideas and the Protestant Reformation. They were also part of other ways in which thinking was altered and a private sphere was enlarged. Literacy and printing led, for example, to reading as a sometimes private activity rather than continuing to be entirely a public activity. When few copies exist, reading to a group is efficient. When each person has access to a copy of a book (owned or borrowed), the ability to read silently to oneself must be learned, but once learned it enhances the concept of an interior space of privacy and autonomy.[36] Literacy in vernaculars has another effect; one can understand that universal truths may find local expression in different ways. Diversity comes to be more tolerable, and when encountered it need not be as threatening. The growth of a scientific approach, attitude, or ideology would be impossible without the liberation from revealed truth, without the concept of personal rationality, and without the exposure to alternative ways of thinking and acting. Natural laws come to displace divine laws, or to exist alongside them in an autonomous domain.

One more aspect of individuality should be mentioned. The concept of rights as inherent in the individual – rather than just in a city or a guild or a class of landowners – was a momentous step, and we have not yet seen where all it will lead.[37] Rights and the concept of the individual were parts of the same interdependent process of creating a sharper line between public and private realms. Again causal priority need not be an issue in this context. Personal rights to property, speech, belief, association, and the vote clearly involve the carving out of a private realm of autonomy which we believe should limit what public authorities may do to us in our private capacities.[38] By a different but related route, we have arrived at the idea of separation of spiritual matters from political control (even if one church is 'established'); and we have witnessed the almost universal spread of the idea that science should be beyond either spiritual or political control. Not everyone agrees, but these forms of autonomy have become the dominant view in most parts of the world and unquestionably in the 'European' world-view.

The creation of the individual and the assumption that a private realm deserves sanctuary from public authority occurred concurrently with the building of authority on territorial lines, as outlined in the previous chapter. Tension was inevitable as a state was created which claimed sovereignty and purported to be an all-purpose organization in regard to the people and activities within its borders.[39] The greater the ability of the state to make good on such claims, the greater the felt need to protect a private realm. At one point, the resistance came primarily from the religious or spiritual realm; at another from science; and after the late eighteenth century from the private realm of individual rights. The more recent the era we study, the greater prominence given to economic freedom or autonomy in this effort to achieve some degree of arm's length from the territorial state. The apogee of nationalism occurred in the nineteenth century, and it is no accident that the dominant economic ideology of that period in Europe and its offshoots around the world was 'laissez-faire' liberalism.

If one questions the equation of the 'political' with a territorial state, one may more easily question the need to see 'public' and 'private' as mutually exclusive or competing realms. There are some indications that re-conceptualization is under way. For example, the feminist injunction that 'the personal is political' encounters opposition, in part, because it appears to challenge the public-private dichotomy, as well as because it challenges patriarchy. Of course, 'private' as it has been used in the previous few pages means 'not government' in the civic republican tradition now taken for granted in the 'European' cultures. 'Personal' in the feminist sense would refer to a subset, at most, of the 'private' realm of civil society, since 'the personal is political' points to the power relations within families or other gendered relationships and to the way these are 'sheltered' from government to the detriment of women and children. Another example mentioned above was Drucker's concept of the 'third force,' those public activities which are non-governmental but also not-for-profit (and thus not 'private' enterprise). Whatever examples one considers, one may hypothesize that some parts of the global culture are redefining the boundaries between the public and private spheres.

GOVERNMENT INTERVENTION AND SOCIAL EQUALITY

For most of this century, political debate about public and private realms has focused on the acceptable or appropriate type or degree of intervention in the economy. Obviously no such debate could occur until it was generally accepted that politics and economics constitute distinct domains. The ways in which that separation gained acceptance has been the principal theme running through this chapter. My point has been to remind readers that a balance was being struck between territorial and non-territorial forms of organization. For the period after 1648, the balance seemed to favour territorial organizations in almost all aspects of life – religious denominations, social intercourse, economic transactions, harnessing cities to national economies, and in general the consolidation of political authority in territorial nation-states. The ubiquity of the assumptions in favour of territoriality explains why 'sovereignty' remains a central concern of governments.

Concurrent with that territorialization was an underground resistance which has gained respectability in several areas. Such resistance was especially notable, from this chapter's perspective, in the economic realm. The eventual success of industrial capital in its quest for relative autonomy from the territorial state set in motion a reaction based on notions of social equality which were in turn an outgrowth of the creation of the individual. If individuals were rights-bearing producers and consumers, how could one justify the grotesque degrees and types of inequality in economic and political terms? If one believed in *human* rights or *individual* rights, rather than in class rights or ownership rights, why would one allow businesses to hire children whose health was at risk or tolerate business use of violence to suppress union organization? Eventually people more often came to believe that governments had responsibilities to intervene in the economy to correct the market or to counter some of its worst consequences.

Since the publication of Keynes's theory in 1936, Keynesian ideas have justified many more forms of intervention. These include, most prominently, government intervention in fiscal and monetary policy, which in turn made feasible the funding of the welfare state. Resistance to these public intrusions into the private realm of economics has been couched most often in the language of privacy, efficiency, and national economic health. These arguments are still used, and they will undoubtedly continue to be the dominant vocabulary at the political and mass media level. In business circles, and to some extent in academic circles, the language is somewhat different. Without retreating from concepts of property rights, individual initiative and dignity, or the private sector as the engine of economic health, more and more emphasis is being placed on the inherent lack of fit between territorial forms of political authority and the increasingly global and non-territorial logic of markets and the economy, as will be shown in later sections in more detail.

Privatization, rationalization of government services, and globalization of the economy have come to be code words in some circles for a return to the ruthlessness of nineteenth-century capitalism. The collapse of the USSR, the almost total retreat from communism, and the transformation of many socialists and social democrats into advocates of 'economic restructuring' or more lean and efficient governments have convinced many observers that they must redouble efforts to achieve social equality through political means. These concerns are serious and sincerely felt; and I want to explore them and some possible responses to them. Before pursuing those topics, I should try to pull together the broad lessons which can easily be overlooked in current controversies.

Bundling and unbundling occur at the same time. One or the other may predominate – and I believe that unbundling will hold the upper hand in the next century – but a balance is struck only for a time. Technology, culture, and other matters evolve and disrupt the balance, or the different 'logics' built into the forms of bundling may create tensions which lead to a shift of balance, as we have just seen. Furthermore, bundling and unbundling occur in our minds – as concepts, assumptions, or theories – and they occur in the 'real world' out there. The first step in understanding the forms of bundling and unbundling 'out there' involves questioning our own ways of constructing concepts and theories and questioning critically the assumptions so taken for granted that they appear to be part of the natural order. Assumptions about territoriality provide the door or window through which I have tried to enter the realm of reconstruction of our forms of political authority. Opening the door a crack and finding another room with very different assumptions about territoriality may help us bring to consciousness other matters we now take for granted.

SERVICE DELIVERY AND SOCIAL JUSTICE

For some people, privatization, rationalization, and globalization have become code words for cutting off or reducing the aid and support for individuals and families who seem unable to care for themselves. Various countries, including Canada, have seen attacks on unemployment insurance, public pensions, universality of health care, and even public schools. Both the proponents of greater public services and the proponents of market solutions should be taken seriously. Many on each side are sincerely motivated in seeking ways to foster the greatest good for the greatest number, while many on each side also have vested interests, whether bureaucratic feather-bedding or a desire to transfer wealth regressively. It is not necessary to state a personal opinion about motives or even about which side has more 'economical' solutions to the problems everyone may identify.

This book tries to avoid blame and vituperation. Some will interpret that stance as actually favouring one side over another. Perhaps so, but I hope readers will wait until the end of the book before deciding which side I favour, if either. Part of my justification for this position of 'neutrality' (for the time-being) concerns shared assumptions underlying the different ideologies in conflict. In particular, I believe that an examination of the subtle ways in which assumptions about territoriality have distorted our ideologies and forms of political organization may put these controversies in a different light. For example, welfare-state advocates seem to assume that the state administering the welfare must be territorial. Similarly, advocates of 'less government intervention' often oppose government actions on the grounds (implicit in nearly all cases) that governments which are inherently territorial in operation cannot deal efficiently with an economy which is more and more global and non-territorial. Can government be more effective but less ambitious by refusing to be shackled to territory, and thus meet at least some objections from both camps? Most of the remaining chapters return to this question, in various guises, but the basic argument should be previewed in this context.

Calling into question the premises of these opponents may reveal that one side has more realistic premises, and thus the other side may be weakened. But if both sides have untenable premises, then new possibilities are opened beyond the limited options presumed by the original debate. Consider the way the issue has usually been framed, as in the following quotation:

Certain things have to be done in a community and the question whether they should be left to private enterprise dominated by the profit motive, or to the government dominated by political considerations, is not a question of man versus the state, but simply a question of which organization and motive can best do the job.[40]

While I agree that an important question is which type of organization can do which job better, I will argue a different position than either of those above. I will not allege that one side or both sides are completely wrong in what they take for granted. Instead I argue in the next chapter that some political and economic functions are inherently territorial (and of varying scope or scale) while others need (or even should) not be organized territorially. Thus, one can ask whether we are organizing particular functions in the most effective way. Ideologies answer such questions in general and categorical terms, whereas I have been arguing that the answers must take account of technological and cultural factors, and thus that the balance between territorial and non-territorial means of achieving collective actions will vary significantly over time. I noted in the previous chapter that new technologies may open up new ecological niches for particular social formations. I believe it is reasonable to consider that economic goals and ideologies thrive better in some niches than in others, and thus that one should be on the lookout for changes in technology which interact with political, economic, social, and cultural institutions. Hence, we must periodically query the adequacy of our means as well as our goals. How do we go about fitting the solution to the problem?

Assumptions about territoriality have kept citizens of most countries from seeing certain problems in the proper perspective and have thereby limited their vision of appropriate solutions. Just as I do not want to make specific predictions about the exact shape of political organizations or what may replace nations, if anything will, I also do not want to take particular positions on how to resolve issues such as more or less social welfare expenditures or more or less expenditures on private schools. Instead, I want to open up the discussion of those issues by showing how the current controversies are limited by shared assumptions about territoriality. How one delivers social services may turn out to be as important as whether the amount of money spent on them should be increased or decreased.

These are complex and highly contested issues which have generated more than a little emotion and bad feeling. The re-analysis of foundations which I can offer will be equally complex, drawing on a number of aspects of politics, economics, social change, and technological innovation. Several economic factors will be addressed in ensuing sections of this chapter which may be ways of mitigating concern that an unbundled world will necessarily be more cruel, lean, or heartless than today's bundled territorial states. These sections open up important issues, but they will need to be addressed again in chapter 8 after some related, and largely non-economic, matters have been spelled out. For example, chapter 4 will ask what political and administrative functions are inherently territorial (given current technology) and which might be better organized in non-territorial fashions. Chapter 5 will build on that analysis by asking whether, even if inherently territorial (given current technology), some political or administrative functions might be better or more efficient if assigned to larger or smaller political territories than nations.

Chapters 6 and 7 move the analysis into social dimensions, although social and political may be more convenient categories than rigidly separate realities. For example, chapter 6 looks at changing conceptions of community, particularly those 'lost' by the invention of the concept of the individual. That chapter speculates about how technology may enable new communities to support social life more effectively where we feel that social 'safety nets' are most threatened by free market solutions. Chapter 7 addresses what we mean by 'a people' (or nation in an older sense) and whether majoritarian forms of government can be adapted to a non-territorial base so that minorities in one place may be majorities in a new conceptual space.

Each chapter omits many details or concerns in the interest of a coherent analysis of territoriality. Each chapter could be a book, but I am writing only one volume and so must leave out much that others will think crucial. If that is so, then I hope the reader will wait until the end to reach that conclusion. Even more strongly, I hope that this interconnected set of speculations will have challenged readers' assumptions sufficiently to stimulate them to write the books which I have been unable to include within this one volume.

MARKETING IN THE BORDERLESS WORLD

Most proponents of free markets and private enterprise usually advocate that governments should do as little as possible for those individuals who do not succeed in economic competition or who lack the resources for competition on a level playing field. That particular combination of ideas has come to be called the conservative or neo-conservative ideology, although in the era of its ascendance in the nineteenth century it was called liberalism because of its association with the emerging idea of the individual as the social building block. Liberalism is still used in that sense in the names of some European political parties and in the Liberal Party of Australia. Whatever one calls it today, the ideology persists and may even be gaining strength relative to ideologies which advocate a more comprehensive welfare state or more government regulation of the market-place.[41]

A very different perspective has been gaining adherents in certain circles. This view envisions an economic world largely decoupled from territorial nations – 'the borderless world' of the interlinked economies of Japan, Europe, and North America.[42] That much fits with 'liberal' analysis, but the new perspective asserts that national governments should invest more rather than less in human resources and other infrastructure, and so it directly contradicts the usual liberal analysis.[43] It will be helpful to outline very briefly some components of this perspective, since they serve several purposes in my analysis. They remind us of some technological developments related to economic 'policing,' targeting, and sorting of people which were discussed in the previous chapter. They demonstrate that some serious business leaders and analysts reject the simplistic dichotomy between political and economic realms which has been premised on assumptions about territoriality. And finally they suggest ways in which some social welfare functions may be justified more easily in the unbundled world about which concern was expressed above.

The nature of markets should be mentioned first. For a period, it was assumed that larger markets were always better than smaller markets because they could achieve and encourage economies of scale.[44] Many theorists therefore assumed that larger countries had an advantage since the larger home markets would be more amenable to products manufactured at home. Then, on the basis of profitable home markets with minimal shipping costs because of proximity, firms could launch successful foreign trading ventures. Even if larger markets are better than smaller ones, that does not ensure that large countries represent large markets or that small countries are not part of large markets. Several aspects of markets and cost structures, it is alleged, have dramatically altered earlier conditions enough to call forth new strategies.

Larger local markets represent the ideal when a product with few or no variations is in demand and when economies of scale obtain. That is to say, mass produced goods for mass consumption favour larger local markets. If consumers in different regions or with different styles of life demand different models or variations, the logic of large markets carries less weight. Variations in quality or luxury may be just as important as optional features such as colours or extra functions (CD player plus radio in a car, for example). To the extent a product can be customized, or must be customized, to appeal to a specialized type of consumer, economies of scale arising from mass production are pretty much irrelevant, particularly since for many products profit margins are higher the greater the degree of customizing.

Some specialized types of consumers may be geographically concentrated. For example, people in warm areas buy more air conditioners for cars or homes. Many types of consumers, however, are not linked strongly to territorial clusters, except perhaps high or low income ghettos, but these are spread across the world or country. Thus, to maximize any particular market – let us suppose for alligator handbags or chronometers – one must target a market which is spread over wide geographical areas but is composed of specific groups that may be quite rare in any one location. Large countries may still have an advantage, if they are affluent, because the targeted consumer group may be fairly large even if rare. Obviously, the inclusion of foreign markets will be more and more necessary, the smaller the proportion of individuals who fall into target groups in any one area.

Once one begins to think in terms of customized products for specialized tastes or needs, the concept of 'home market' makes less sense, since most of the people in the 'home' market fall outside the target group. If a consumer needs a more effective artificial leg or wants a sound system with exquisite tweeters, country of origin takes second place to quality and price. In such cases, large countries with large 'home' markets have an advantage only if one assumes they automatically have quality products or cost advantages. The examples of Switzerland, Singapore, Hong Kong, South Korea, and other countries belie that assumption.[45] Of course, trade restrictions affect these generalizations, but the consensus seems to favour fewer restrictions among the major economic powers. The Introduction considered trade wars, and I will not repeat that discussion.

Furthermore, it seems clear by now that import-replacement or import-substitution strategies work better with products for local mass markets.[46] By definition, such products are less difficult to manufacture than esoteric ones and are assured of lower shipping costs if produced locally. Thus, India can manufacture many mass products but will import products which require greater technology or offer no mass markets.

These and other related reasons explain why territorial (national or regional) markets have been more and more bypassed by firms seeking to enhance profit margins by focusing on customized products for specialized consumer groups. They do not constitute complete explanations since they were not feasible strategies until technologies enabled them. Targeted advertising, flexible production made possible by microchips, cheaper air freight, and many other advances have contributed to the creation of new markets and to their greater accessibility. Even more important, I believe, globalization has made more people aware of options about which they were formerly ignorant, and thus new demands in very particular groups have been stimulated by awareness of options. Again we see how technologies may serve to link human (in this case 'economic)' activities with specialized ecological niches.

Note a structural feature of these changing market conditions. One could not at any time during the past couple of centuries speak of a single market-place, but it is particularly true recently that each type of product has a different market. Of course, gold, commodity futures, and shoes have almost always been handled by specialized traders or in different exchange settings; but now that many markets are less territorial, overlapping and non-congruent market targets have proliferated. Which countries receive more or less attention, and what types of consumers may be targeted in each, have become more specific to each product and probably less stable over time as well.

110 Beyond Sovereignty

Finally, consider how firms have responded to these and other aspects of globalization. For one thing, more of them operate across national borders, and not only in areas with free trade or common markets such as the European Community. In doing so, however, they have changed the nature of their organization, and the way we refer to them reflects this evolution. Multinational corporations were the norm. They were essentially national corporations which had foreign branches for marketing and distribution. A car was manufactured, for example, in country A and then sold in country B or C. Watches were carefully crafted in Switzerland and sold in Europe and North America. Such companies still operate, but they have been joined by a growing number of what we may call, by contrast, transnational corporations.

Transnational corporations have no national 'home' since in several ways they operate as though borders did not exist. Headquarters may be located in more than one place, since research and development may not be in the same country as accounting, banks from many countries are utilized, and members of management teams may carry a wide range of passports. Ownership too will often be widely spread among several countries. Furthermore, if the firm produces physical output rather than a service, manufacturing may be located in several countries, but not in the sense of branch-plants. For example, different components may be produced in different countries, and assembly may occur in another country or indeed in any country where there is a large market. Decisions about what stage of a product to make in which country depends on access to materials, cost of labour, special skills of the population, types of environmental or other regulations, and so on. Cost and reliability of transportation (especially air cargo) have decentralized the production process and made international import and export *within* the corporation more common than after the final product has been completed.

INFRASTRUCTURE IN THE BORDERLESS WORLD

If national borders have become less relevant in manufacturing by transnational corporations, other consequences also follow logically.[47] These corporations are more mobile than any previous types. They seek out cost or other advantages piecemeal, and thus they less often have to make choices between things like low wage labour versus proximity to materials. Their needs are conceptualized in different ways from earlier forms of business firms. Instead of needing a pleasant setting for management near banks and cheap land for plants, all of these activities may be decoupled or unbundled into entirely separate operations linked just as effectively by jet airplanes and telecommunications facilities.

National governments can do little to regulate such corporations, and they must attract their operations by offering appropriate infrastructure. Hence, analysts have realized what some governments saw earlier: that the task of governments should be more focused on providing infrastructure including human resources.[48] Besides providing world-class airports, harbours, and electronic crossroads, governments come to realize that stable regimes, healthy workers, and skilled populations are worthy investments if they attract the right types of companies.

Contrast this situation with the heyday of laissez-faire capitalism in the late nineteenth century. Governments in Europe and North America did not see it as their responsibility to provide extensive infrastructure. They provided loan guarantees for railroads, of course, and sponsored trade fairs, but they did not (with minor exceptions) support health care facilities such as hospitals or insurance, universal public schooling, university or industrial research, and many other endeavours we now take for granted.

Put in broader terms, the range of public goods which governments feel they should provide has greatly expanded during the past century or so. At the present we may be witnessing a change in the priorities among these public goods, even an absolute reduction when activities have been privatized. Whether some activities may be reduced and focused or just allowed to atrophy, enhancement of human resources through education, skill development, medical and health plans, employment information, and other activities or services has taken on a new urgency. Whereas formerly such issues were the preserve of 'the left' as a way to repair damage done to individuals by the market, such issues have come more and more to engage the active interest of business leaders and politicians who otherwise deserve the label 'right' or conservative. Of course, not every owner or manager of a business feels this way, nor will they; interest runs highest among multinational and transnational corporations. But their greater prominence in the future and the example they set should, I believe, lead to more support for government spending and activities in these areas, while fiscal restraints will curtail other activities such as regulation or attempted regulation of business operations.

Returning to the concern that the unbundled world will have fewer or less effective 'safety nets' for individuals, this evolving view of infrastructure suggests a more precise conclusion: there may be *fewer but more effective safety nets*. We may have to devise different types of safety nets, or we may have to reconceptualize them in order to justify their continuation, but there seems no reason to predict their complete termination.

REGULATION OF THE BORDERLESS WORLD

Will governments retreat from major areas of control or regulation over the economy? If so, will economic activities by large corporations or financial institutions take on more of the character of heartless engines which exploit or victimize employees in order to provide ever more wonderful products to affluent customers? No one can claim with certainty that ethical practices or humane compassion will come to dominate business decisions, or even to provide moderation of their worst effects. However, besides the reasons already given for thinking that some welfare state functions will continue or even improve, there is another aspect of the globalizing economy which may continue to gain in significance.[49]

To set in context this new aspect of the economy, let me first point out that there are hidden assumptions behind the questions in the previous paragraph. To ask about governments and what they do would be understood by most people to mean territorial governments, usually national but also state and local governments. When we specify that national or other territorial governments may be unable or unwilling to regulate certain economic activities, the question then remains whether there are now non-territorial governments to perform these tasks or whether such governments could be developed. Several kinds of non-territorial governments do exist and may be gaining in number and importance, but we easily overlook them because they are non-territorial and usually very specialized rather than claiming all-purpose sovereignty.

In chapter 1, I referred to a number of examples of such organizations which look economic but perform political or governmental functions. They include, but are not restricted to, GATT, the World Bank and IMF, IATA, OPEC, G-7, the European Community, the Canada-U.S. Free Trade Agreement, and several agencies of the United Nations such as the World Health Organization and the International Commission on Refugees. A few of these – especially the European Community – look like territorial governments. The European Community has institutions which may someday become all-purpose governments, leaving the twelve national governments in positions analogous to provinces, states, or cities.[50] Be that as it may, this is not territorial government in quite the form we have taken for granted for three centuries: new territory may be added without conquest as nations (or parts of nations) ask to join;[51] the current pieces are not continuous and contiguous; the degree of integration is forecast to be quite strong in some domains (such as currency and exchange rates) and extremely weak in many other domains; and one can envision secession without civil war in certain cases.

To state the perspective in other ways, larger territorial political units may be called forth or encouraged in order to match the scale of the new economic units and activities in the borderless world. More common now and likely even more common in the future than these larger territorial units will be non-territorial organizations which fulfil political or governmental functions relevant to the economy.[52] The examples mentioned above (leaving aside perhaps the European Community) share at least three pertinent features. Each of these features augers well for the realistic performance of functions which may mitigate some of the possible negative consequences of the lack of fit between political-territorial nations and economic-non-territorial organizations. These three characteristics are as follows:

1. They are specific purpose organizations rather than all-purpose; as such they are created, evaluated, and modified step-by-step as needed.
2. They have not been set up as enemies of nations (although they reduce national sovereignty) but by the governments of key nations.
3. They have blurred the lines between economy and polity; or, more exactly, they constitute new ways of performing political functions without violating our tacit notions of the economy as a private sphere beyond government intervention.

No doubt some nations may refuse to participate in any such organizations. Perhaps some participating nations will from time to time refuse to abide by their decisions.[53] Such eventualities have occurred among nations as sovereign entities in the past whether such transnational or multinational organizations existed or not, so that we should hardly be surprised at some instances of maverick behaviour. What we should not lose sight of, however, are at least two related points. For one, many nations have felt it necessary and desirable to set up these organizations because they felt unable to respond effectively to certain kinds of non-territorial or global challenges, usually of an economic sort but also concerning other matters such as disease and refugees. For another, these organizations work, they accomplish some goals, and they have gained some legitimacy, which allows them a degree of independence of any one nation, although not of all their member states if acting in concert. One explanation of their legitimacy concerns the fact they have been conceived and organized 'from the bottom up' rather than being imposed by a few countries on the rest 'top down.'

It is perhaps worth noting that some of these bodies have formal constitutions and statements of rights. The most visible has been the Universal Declaration on Human Rights, but others exist as well. Any government of a nation may ignore such rights, and most have at some point or other, but over time the moral force of such documents gains momentum. That does not ensure that their legitimacy will grow, but I will argue in later chapters that there are technological and social developments which favour enhanced concern for rights in one country by citizens of other countries.

We are in effect talking about transfer of sovereignty. If nations give up – tentatively, to be sure – some aspects of sovereignty over specific matters, the organizations exercising the formerly national prerogatives grow in relative importance. No single organization (again perhaps excepting the European Community) is likely to rival territorial nations as such, because these are generally single-purpose bodies, but jointly they pose challenges which nations will find hard to counter. If these supra-national agencies prove to be quite independent of their national progenitors, they will be able to do their job better but will threaten to a degree the sovereignty of their creators. If they fail to become independent actors, they will fail to serve the purposes for which they were established. After all, these entities were set up by the nations involved because they serve useful purposes in the nations' interests. Add to usefulness and self-interest the growing consciousness of rights and the supremacy of nations seems weakened well beyond the economic sphere. The greatest strength of these challenges, however, may come in the growth or reinforcement of a private sphere partly beyond political control.

MIGRATION OF PEOPLE AND IDEAS

Throughout recorded history, people who have become dissatisfied with their situation in a particular place sometimes found it possible or expedient to move to another place. People have 'voted with their feet.' That is indeed how most of the 'Europeans' got where they are. Some migrated from the steppes of Asia, some from the Middle East, and some from one part of Europe to another (such as the Norman French who now reside in England and who were mostly Vikings at an earlier date). Likewise, millions of people left Europe to settle in colonies in North and South America, South Africa, Australia, and elsewhere.

The 'safety valve' effect of migration, while important, may not be its most important feature. Many scholars have observed that the diffusion of ideas has most often been the result of migration of skilled people, particularly persecuted minorities and groups out of favour with the government of the day. North America has benefited greatly in this century by the persecution of talented people elsewhere. Of course, ideas and skills are not the only baggage migrants bring to new territories. Diseases travel well, too, and when first arriving in a place may be even more damaging than the weapons used by settlers.[54] There are few, if any, areas of the world where large groups have never been exposed to the major diseases (except perhaps AIDS), so that this result of migration may have declined in significance. The skills, knowledge, culture, beliefs, technology, and ideas which migrants bring with them continue to be significant.

Within nations, migration has often been allowed or encouraged as a means to stimulate economic growth. For example, the vast movement of population to the western regions of Canada and the United States in this century has created new productivity in the west as well as creating new markets for products from the east. Migration may also be encouraged because a region in decline can regain some of its productivity if its manufacturing, service, or extractive capacities are handled by fewer workers. In short, nations generally encourage workers to go where the jobs are, and there are excellent theoretical justifications for migration. Furthermore, most observers believe that migration between regions in a nation helps the individuals who move, the regions which receive them, and often the regions they left. Migration often appears to be a 'no-lose' situation.

By contrast, we discourage migration on a global scale. Indeed, one of the most central functions of territorial states has been to keep their populations at home (or at least within settler colonies) and to keep out other people 'belonging' to other nations. The exceptions have been small in numbers and few in type. They include exile of dissidents or overthrown rulers, and the recruitment of a small number of people with special skills in short supply. Recently many nations, although not all, have seen fit to take in refugees on a modest scale.

How can citizens justify on a global scale the opposite of the policy they believe so beneficial within a national context? This question will become more compelling as economies evolve in the directions outlined above, and I will return to it in chapter 8. That people are the ultimate resource, especially when educated, trained, and healthy, would seem to lead to the conclusion that we want more of them in our place rather than in a place where our competition may use them. (One should note that 'place' presumes that territory matters. It does to emigrants, but as far as the economy is concerned, one might say that we want these sorts of people helping us wherever they are.) Regardless of whether they want more immigrants, the developed and affluent countries may have little choice. Birth rates in most of the richest countries will not lead to expanded populations, and may even result in declining populations with more elderly and retired groups. By contrast, populations in the less developed areas of the world have very high growth rates.[55] Even if, as in Somalia and other such places, war and famine take their toll, the net growth of world population seems inevitable and largely confined to the poorer countries with the least productive economies.

Given the imbalance in affluence between areas of the world and given the greater awareness of economic disparities by poor and rich, there seem to be three choices: massive migration from poor overpopulated areas to rich areas with lower densities, massive 'migration' of jobs and affluence to poor areas, and new ways of sharing economic success in widely separated areas without migration. Let us consider these in turn, and let us begin by assuming (as seems plausible) that most people in the rich, developed nations prefer to keep immigration at current levels, or a bit higher or lower, but certainly not at the levels suggested by scenarios which would solve overpopulation and unemployment in Africa or Asia. Thus, for the moment, we assume away the first solution.

The second solution has been happening for a long time and especially in the past couple of decades. Many firms and industries have built branch-plants in other countries, especially in low-wage countries, rather than export from North America, Europe, or Japan. Transnational corporations, as explained above, have decentralized their operations even further and created jobs in developing countries like Thailand, Singapore, and Mexico. The negotiation of the North American Free Trade Agreement should see this process occur at a faster rate, especially if other countries in Latin America join NAFTA in the future.[56] Then one can expect some transfer of plants from Canada and the United States to Mexico and parts of Central or South America. Indeed, most labour unions in Canada and the United States strongly oppose NAFTA for this reason. If high-skill and high-wage jobs replace those lost to poorer areas, however, everyone is better off all round. Even if they do not, one might still find the economic costs acceptable as a way of avoiding massive immigration of relatively low-skill workers who will agree to work at wages below what affluent workers in affluent societies deem reasonable.

Thus, the third alternative would appear to have benefits if for no other reason than it cannot be worse than the first two scenarios, at least in some people's perspectives. It will be more convenient to evaluate this possibility after some matters have been discussed in more detail in the next few chapters. A few points may be noted, however, by way of preview of the argument even though supporting evidence will await later chapters.

Do computer networks, telecommunications facilities, and enhanced transportation modes mean that we can have it both ways? Can one increase jobs and prosperity in at least some areas rich in people but poor in material wealth without beggaring the countries rich in material goods but with stagnant or declining populations?

It is easy to outline some plausible scenarios. The one above seems plausible: export low-wage jobs or industries while creating or expanding high-wage jobs or industries here. One other possibility concerns 'cottage industries,' in which employees work at home on their computers. This has proved feasible for workers in suburban or ex-urban centres employed by firms in city centres, and some examples suggest that greater distances can be bridged so that some of this work might be done in other nations. Furthermore, the organization of transnational corporations already suggests a growing propensity to locate more low-skill jobs in the poorest countries, more medium-skill jobs in newly developing countries, and more of the high-skill jobs (research, legal services, computer programming) in areas with the most educated populations. The process has already begun, and it seems likely to become more and more common.

Technology makes these options plausible, although it may not 'force' particular options. As has so often been the case, technology enables certain possibilities, or 'liberties of action,' without determining that they will be pursued.[57] Another factor which can enable or hinder them is government, especially at the national level. Rather than allowing the export of certain types of jobs and encouraging creation of better jobs, all of which take time, governments facing elections often prefer to 'save' jobs by propping up existing plants or industries and by trade restrictions of various kinds. Thus, the electoral calculus may forestall this device of 'sharing' jobs in rich and poor countries, at least for years to come. Eventually, the markets will prevail, barring another all-out world war or a trade war leading to a depression on the scale of the 1930s. As more people come to realize the value of long-range solutions, governments may find their calculus also leads them to support sharing rather than protection or migration.[58]

As noted above, there are only three main options; and two of them would probably be viewed as less desirable than sharing of networks of jobs. Thus, eventually it seems likely that the least of three evils may be chosen. The crucial question may not be which option is chosen but when it is chosen – in time to forestall the other 'evils' (if they are that) or too late to preserve our way of life. The evaluation of these alternatives will be the subject of comment in later chapters, as will the ability of national governments to help and hinder their occurrence. Nevertheless, if implemented, this third option – of substituting one type of job for another – might go some way to allaying the fears summarized above about the safety nets to be expected or needed in the unbundled world. In chapter 1, I raised the question of where one can reside and be a citizen of here; now I propose the question of where one may be employed without being a citizen of here.[59] Both questions will arise repeatedly.

GLOBALIZATION AGAIN

The more global or universal the standard, the more it makes visible the local, the unique, the different, and the distinct. The global economy in tandem with global telecommunications have made visible the successes and failures in economic development. This is true within nations – and it is one reason for the rise of the welfare state – but it is now true between nations and regions and sectors on a global scale. Just as awareness of regional economies or cultures within a nation has not usually led to all regions becoming the same, so there is no clear reason to predict that the global economy will make all nations equally rich or poor or lead to all nations sharing the same language or religion or culture.

Early analyses of economic or political development assumed, more or less explicitly, that there was only one model (usually the United States) or one path to development. Over time many analysts have come more and more to realize that there may be different models or goals or end-states – or no end – to development, and even if the goals of affluence and industrialization be shared, the means to those goals may differ in Japan, the European Community, and India. The collapse of the Second World, and especially the Soviet Union, may have led some people to believe that only one avenue to one goal remains, that is, free markets leading to a world of capitalism. Even if that turns out to be true, there may be several paths to capitalism. Equally if not more critical, there may be several capitalisms.[60] Perhaps the least developed countries will have to pass through agrarian capitalism to commercial capitalism and then industrial capitalism before they join the new order of global capitalism.[61] If that road looks familiar, it will still mean that during any given period, the regions of the world will experience quite different forms of economic organization. If capitalist development fails to occur, as seems likely in some places, world heterogeneity seems destined to be even greater.

Penetration of markets and monetization has already occurred in all major and most minor national economies. Globalization as measured by penetration of transnational corporations need not lead to homogeneity. As Ohmae and others illustrate with numerous examples, flexible production and improved feedback and marketing will often lead to products tailored for culturally distinct populations of consumers, whether in luxury goods or in 'mass' products such as cars and refrigerators. No good practical or theoretical reasons have yet been offered to explain why sensitivity to cultural tastes should decrease as technology enables such customizing with greater ease.

When one examines what are usually called global trends, many of these seem certain to sustain cultural distinctiveness on a large scale for many decades to come, if not indefinitely. Several of these trends are totally unrelated to national boundaries – for example, penetration of market systems into the Second World, environmental degradation, and refugees – but some are in part sustained by national policies or by national rivalries – for example, Islamic fundamentalism, Arab solidarity, and debt or liquidity crises. Such varied forces, at work in different degree in different places, seem poor candidates for homogenization of world cultures, societies, or economies, regardless of whether territorial nation-states decline and become unbundled (as I predict) or not.

Marshall McLuhan caught the world's attention with his arresting image of the global village. By this he meant, and nearly everyone took him to mean, that communication will lead to a world as homogeneous as a village. Leaving aside the fact that most villages I know are riven by social cleavages, economic rivalries, and often religious differences, the arguments above suggest that the world will not be a homogeneous place. We will probably never know whether watching the same TV programs must eventually lead to cultural convergence among the nations of this planet, since not everyone will watch the same programs. Even if cultural convergence may have been a danger in the era of mass audiences, the specialized and fragmented channels and audiences of the present and even more so of the future bode ill for predictions of homogeneity.

One alternative has seldom been analysed, but it seems to me a likely possibility. As all major nations reach the capability of receiving scores or hundreds of TV and radio signals, the range of messages may be less varied *between* nations than it is now, since many if not all signals would be available everywhere. Instead, the range and relative distribution of messages may increase dramatically *within* nations. Then, the crucial comparison will be the relative size of audience for the common signals compared to the size of local or less common signals. For me, the relative decline of the territorial nation-state in the unbundled world seems to demonstrate that several types of heterogeneity should count for more than whether nations (or what is left of them) come to seem more similar in some specific ways.

I argued above that globalization should not be defined as homogenization. That should be an empirical question based on a process of globalization which involves information exchange. My definition of globalization, therefore, rests on an understanding of the enhanced degree of exposure of units (a country, a firm, a scholar, a sports fan, or whatever) to regular information from virtually every area of the globe, and exposed quickly and indeed often 'live,' by means of TV channels, fax, telephone, computer networks, and reports from friends recently returned. The result of global information could be homogeneity, à la McLuhan, but that would be most likely to occur in technical areas. For example, scientific or business competition may result in rapid emulation of some new ideas or techniques or standards, but these may also consist frequently of copying the *means* to ends which are defined locally.

In most cases, how an individual, firm, or country responds to global information should be a function in large degree of existing information, knowledge, beliefs, and culture. Ideology, religion, historical memories, type of political system, and cultural understandings enter into the processing and use of information. Hence, full convergence seems as unlikely as a world in which everyone becomes Catholic or Islamic or

Buddhist. Indeed, the central point of this book may exemplify the problem: global citizens find it extremely difficult today to see or comprehend the information bombarding them daily about the declining importance of territoriality because those assumptions are the lens through which they see the world and find it natural. To extend the point by means of a personal example, an explanation of why I may have been able to see past these assumptions about territorial nations concerns my having been a citizen of two nations (first the United States and then Canada) and my having lived so long in Canada, a country consisting of at least two and probably three types of nations and which has never had a strong sense of its security as a nation-state. The 'threats' of the United States giant next door and the national rivalries between French and English (and now aboriginals) have made assumptions of a long-lasting Canadian nation laughable (or pitiable) to most citizens.

Despite the likelihood that universal convergence on common cultural standards or ways of life cannot be the outcome of the global economy or of other globalization processes, some common patterns may be predicted. Global information should, as noted above, result in envy and resentment among the four-fifths of the world now living in poverty or at least well outside the level of affluence North Americans take as their rightful reward for having the wit to be born in such a developed place. As residents of North America, Europe, and Japan become more and more aware of their favoured status, so do the less favoured peoples on this planet.

Such awareness leads more people, I hope, to reflect on the alternatives outlined above. Do affluent countries wish to welcome hundreds of millions of migrants to their shores? Do they instead propose to help the poor nations or peoples to prosper, if that is possible, because it will protect them from migration? Or might we try to enable people to partake of *here* while residing *there*? How one might be able to utilize technology and wealth to achieve one or another of these ends cannot be spelled out in complete detail here. But subsequent chapters contain my vision of one way to actualize the third option before others are forced upon the most affluent countries. In the end, if the third option heads off truly massive migrations, it will have done so because many countries moved beyond the nation-state and, more importantly, beyond sovereignty, although that may not have been their aim at all. Chapter 8 will return to such inadvertent possibilities.

4

Functions and Administration

One may distinguish between functions and administration. The former refers to topics, heads of power, jurisdictions, or kinds of services delivered (or rules imposed). The latter refers to how the delivery occurs, how policies or rules or incentives are managed. Most analysts assume that public administration is usually quite similar to private administration, though differing in scale and in sovereignty.[1] In particular, both usually involve bureaucracy or a hierarchical form with impersonal (non-arbitrary) application of rules.

When one keeps separate the issues of *what* is delivered and *how* it is delivered, there is more scope for a refined analysis of both dimensions. For example, there may be some functions or jurisdictions which must be administered territorially, while others could just as well be administered without reference to territory because they are targeted on specific types of persons wherever they live. Obversely, when one imagines territorial and non-territorial forms of administration, there may be significant differences in the way these administrative structures operate.

Currently, most public administration (although not all) assumes that nations, provinces, and most political units should be based on territoriality, as defined in this book as exclusive, continuous, and contiguous territory. When one examines what governments do, it is immediately clear that only a few functions are inherently territorial. As technology has evolved, fewer jurisdictions have remained inherently territorial; and it may be that eventually very few will be. Observers of businesses, especially in the service sector, have noted that management has become flatter, that networks have partially replaced hierarchy, and that customized service sometimes replaces standardized service. Public administration, I will argue, can also move in those directions, particularly where it is decoupled from territory.

This chapter thus has two broad purposes. For one, it will explore functions to see which are inherently territorial and which are not. This will lay the groundwork for the second purpose, which involves a rethinking of public administration.[2] If one relaxes assumptions about territoriality, one can envision types and forms of administration which are more precisely fitted to particular heads of power or jurisdictions. Both of these purposes in turn provide the foundations for chapter 5, which looks at whether it would be feasible and preferable to construct some non-territorial provinces (or other sub-national units, whatever the label). Chapter 5 also addresses the question of whether, even if some functions are inherently territorial, administration might be more efficient or effective if larger or smaller in area.

Running through this chapter and the next, but less explicitly than the two purposes just mentioned, are several questions closely related to territoriality of jurisdictions and administration. They include the following: What jurisdictions or functions should be performed by governments rather than privately? What mix of public and private administration would be optimal, and how does the mix vary across jurisdictions? Can governments in the future be more effective by doing less but doing it better? The central organizing concept in all cases, given the focus of this book, is territory. The deeper question, therefore, which lies behind these specific questions may be put very starkly: if governments are best at territorial functions, and other organizations can perform just as effectively the non-territorial delivery of many services, will we eventually end up with governments which do almost nothing since technology has had the habit of transforming more and more jurisdictions from territorial to non-territorial? This question cannot be answered definitely, but it will come up again in chapter 8 in speculation about the future. One reason no definitive answer seems likely concerns qualifications to be considered in this and several other chapters.

PUBLIC GOODS AND COMMON RESOURCES

Economists have long made use of the concept of public goods. Pure public goods consist of goods which people desire but which must be shared with other people even if they did not contribute to the cost. They entail the non-excludability of such people, who are thus called 'free-riders.' For example, it is not possible to provide military defence for a nation while restricting that good only to certain types of people resident there. Likewise, if air pollution has been reduced, everyone in that area enjoys the benefit. In cases such as these, where free-riders are possible, there is little incentive for any given person or organization to expend money or other resources to provide the good. Even when some people can be excluded but some cannot – that is, partial public goods rather than pure ones – the problem of free-riders still affects the incentive structure in the same way.

The concept of public goods has been used to attempt to answer the question of what jurisdictions or functions governments should have. Specifically, if public goods can only be provided through coercion (such as compulsory taxes or fees), then governments can do so more effectively than private organizations. Although the usual problem with public goods concerns quantity – that is, not enough provided – rather than complete absence, the issue of an appropriate level of the good is usually assumed to require government action. For example, some roads might be built by private citizens, but highway systems are presumed to be the prerogative and obligation of governments. Thus, in reviewing jurisdictions, we will be interested in whether they involve public goods or whether they involve other types of activities which might be effectively provided by private organizations.

The key factor in public goods for our purposes is excludability. One of the crucial issues therefore concerns identifying who is entitled to a service and how they might be included while others are excluded. One of the consequences of technological change is that one may more easily exclude people in some cases, although perhaps not in all cases. In other words, what is a public good depends in part at least on the state of technology at a point in time. For example, radio and TV broadcasting was – and in many areas still is – a public good to the degree that anyone nearby can pick up the signals. Cable systems or scrambling of signals from satellites can with almost complete certainty exclude non-subscribers. As we examine functions and administration, we should be mindful of such technological changes and their implications for *who* should perform *what* services and *how* they may most effectively be delivered.

Some things do not need to be produced; they are just there. Water in rivers or streams, scenery in some places, forests, and wildlife are just a few examples. Other things are there naturally but not in useful form, and thus investment is needed to make them available. Examples include water in irrigation systems, underground minerals and ores, and forests in remote or inaccessible areas. Both of these types of things may be called common resources, or 'the commons,' in distinction from public goods. The distinctions are subtle but crucial. Public goods generally involve joint supply and joint use. Common resources, however, mostly involve joint supply but personal use. That is, 'using' a public good like clean air or military defence does not 'use up' the resource and thus keep others from using it. Using a common resource, however, does remove some amount from use by others, as when upstream farmers divert water from downstream farmers. There are grey areas where public good and common resource might be equally applicable labels; for example, a highway is a public good but may become so crowded and congested that use by some limits use by others, in which case it might fall into the category of a common resource.

If one can make a persuasive case that governments should provide public goods, it is nevertheless not obvious who can best control the use of common resources. Since we have become accustomed to governments doing more in this century, some people conclude that they must manage common resources. And in some cases they must, but experience has shown that in other cases, governments may be very inappropriate managers of common resources or that a mix of public and private bodies serves the function better.[3] Our knowledge at this point does not provide complete understanding of appropriate spheres for public and private management of common resources. Instead, I believe we have enough evidence to warrant the conclusion that some particular activities we now assign to governments may need re-evaluation in regard to other modes. This, I shall argue, seems especially urgent where jurisdictions are non-territorial in nature.

One would not want to conclude that governments must perform all the territorial functions or that only governments can perform those functions. These are first approximations, however, which may be useful as hypotheses in raising queries about who should do what and how. A second set of hypotheses or approximations would involve public goods. If they are likely candidates for government jurisdiction, they may be even more obviously so when the public good is inherently territorial. Whatever general conclusions one may draw about who should do what, there is always some degree of choice – as a community, whether nation, province, or municipality, we can decide to use government or private organizations or both for some functions. Choices should not generally be viewed in all-or-nothing terms. By the same token, the choice is never final; we can re-evaluate the way things have been done, and technological changes may make it especially desirable that we do so intermittently. This chapter is one such occasion.

INHERENTLY TERRITORIAL FUNCTIONS

If territoriality involves exclusive control or use of territory which is continuous and contiguous, there are relatively few jurisdictions or functions which are inherently and unequivocally territorial. Even if we relax these conditions slightly, to mean that proximity is the ultimate criterion, that is, a combination of contiguity and continuity, there are still a great many non-territorial jurisdictions. In chapter 1, several functions were mentioned as territorial, including primary health care (such as in emergency wards), mass transit, and day care centres for children. In passing, defence and military matters were noted above. These are quite different types of jurisdictions, and they share only a few features.

One thing each of these functions shares is that distance has negative consequences. If one is too far from primary health care, accidents or illnesses are more likely to be fatal. Mass transit works most effectively where everyone in an area shares the system, rather than having separate systems for different groups, as South Africa had for many years with separate bus and train systems restricted to whites or non-whites. Day care centres would serve little useful purpose for parents who had to drive hours to drop off and pick up their children. In military affairs, distance from the enemy may be beneficial, but non-continuous areas are much more difficult to defend.

The fact that they are territorial functions, however, does not entail that they must be provided by governments. Of course, each has been provided by governments in some times and places. Probably most people today believe that only military defence must be governmental, but even that is debatable, as Alvin and Heidi Toffler argue.[4] Public and private hospitals and day care centres exist in different nations or side-by-side in a particular nation. Mass transit systems are usually publicly owned but not always. For example, in Japan, public and private railways coexist and compete. Furthermore, the only 'public good' in this list is military defence. It is easy to avoid 'free-riders' in mass transit, day care, and (in most circumstances) primary health care. Thus, we can conclude that territoriality, governmental provision, and being a public good can be relatively independent dimensions.

Another example of a territorial function will serve to make another kind of point. The provision of postal services could be set up in a non-territorial manner, but that would be enormously more expensive. For example, one could have separate systems for men and women, or one for businesses and another for residences. But both systems would have to cover the same territory and would thus duplicate basic overhead costs. Hence, it seems reasonable to state that postal services are inherently territorial. If we redefine postal service to mean messenger service, then it will not be inherently territorial because electronic messages can be non-territorial. For example, academics have a different electronic mail system than do some hospitals, and most people in an area do not participate in such systems yet. With the penetration of telephones, fax, E-mail, and the like, postal services in the traditional sense (carrying hard copy) have had less and less to do with messages.[5] The important conclusion is simple: technology can and does affect what counts as inherently territorial. As postal systems come to have less and less to do with messaging, their remaining functions are almost totally territorial.

Currency and coinage provide an intriguing example of territoriality, because in some respects they are inherently territorial and in other respects they are not or are becoming less so. By currency, I mean the unit of currency – Canadian dollar, Japanese yen, German mark, and so on. Obviously, if one means 'money' in the broad sense, then most of what is measured under that label is non-territorial. For example, promissory notes, negotiable securities, lines of credit, and credit cards can be handled case-by-case, so that some individuals or firms in a territory have access to them while others do not, and equally crucial one may use them almost anywhere in the world even if one's own country's currency would not be accepted in a commercial establishment. They are thus non-territorial and perhaps even anti-territorial, since one would never expect everyone in any given territory and only in that territory to have access to each of these instruments.

Sticking to currency as a unit of monetary value, it appears that currency can probably only be handled territorially. This may be true in two distinct senses. First of all, it is difficult to imagine how a territory can have two or more legitimate currencies. Of course, we should not be too hasty, since counter-examples occur. For example, quite a few U.S. towns near the Canadian border have at times accepted at face value Canadian dollars from Canadians and American dollars from Americans. Similar situations may be found in some areas of Florida. Nevertheless, the novelty of these instances argues for the view that currency is primarily a territorial function.

The second sense in which currency may be inherently territorial concerns exchange rates. It really is quite difficult to imagine how one might maintain two different exchange rates for one currency, if there is an open market for currencies. Of course, with blocked currencies, black markets result in widely different exchange rates, but in the global economy at the centre of attention in this book, one and only one exchange rate will be sustainable.

One way to look at why only one currency is allowed in a territory and only one exchange rate at a time is to think of currency as a common resource. Like a common resource, supply is joint (each person cannot print their own money), but use is not joint; once on the market, anyone with resources can 'hoard' the currency or buy or sell it. By the same token, it is 'your' money in that it is your property just as though it were clothing or furniture or jewelry. To avoid there being too much currency, one must restrict the source – and we usually assume that the government (or central bank) will handle that job. Avoiding counterfeit currency, although a job for government, may be a non-territorial function, since it does not matter where in the world the fake notes are printed or distributed.

There may be in progress some changes in currency which could result in different conclusions about its territoriality. First, transnational corporations and large national corporations with foreign suppliers have largely moved beyond territorial currencies. They may rely on a single currency for all transactions worldwide (the U.S. dollar usually), or they may engage in hedging currencies to avoid nasty surprises in exchange rates between order and delivery of products. Second, the European Community may move (although it has not yet) to a common currency, as opposed to the notional currency (ECU) which is not actually carried in wallets or offered in stores. Being a multinational currency, it would thus be non-territorial in the strict sense. Third, the large-scale trade in Eurodollars and petrodollars may lead to collapse of the U.S. dollar, or it may lead to what is, in effect, a specialized type of currency of a non-territorial sort. None of these speculations go to the heart of this section. The crucial point is that up to now and in many foreseeable circumstances, currency and especially exchange rates are inherently territorial.

There is little value, I believe, in trying to identify all of the current functions which are inherently territorial. There are some; it is difficult to see how there could come a time when there are none; and those which are territorial will probably shrink in number over time or become more circumscribed. Thus, we turn to a series of examples of functions which are currently administered by territorial governments but which could just as well be handled by non-territorial organizations. Many of these could not have been conceived in non-territorial terms a century ago. So again we see how technology *enables* administrative or political changes, although it rarely forecloses all options or determines how a function will be administered.

TAXATION

Some taxes seem to be territorial and others non-territorial, even though at the present time all taxes are administered by territorial governments. Retail sales taxes, GST (goods and services tax) and VAT (value-added tax) are currently territorial, although there are exceptions which may grow in extent as technology changes. Income taxes, by contrast, need not be territorial, or at least not to the same degree as retail taxes.

Retail sales taxes appear to be inherently territorial; that is, everyone in a particular area will be charged the same tax.[6] Fairness as well as practicality may require that each customer in a store be charged the same tax, rather than a tax rate determined by their country or province of residence. But perhaps not, since in some jurisdictions today certain types of people are exempted; for example, clothing for children under a certain age or equipment for the handicapped may be exempt from sales tax. Even now, when purchases are made by mail, certain kinds of taxes are not collected for some foreigners or residents of some provinces. Thus, as electronic shopping (for example, by use of TV catalogues) becomes more common, it may happen that VAT, GST, and retail sales taxes will be assessed according to place of residence rather than place of purchase. Such taxes would then be non-territorial in application even though territorial governments would still set the rates. Of course, even when sales or other taxes prove to be territorial or when we choose to administer them territorially, the size of the territorial unit could be varied, as we will see in the next chapter.

Income taxes have not been territorial for a long time, even though they too are administered by territorial governments. Although the basic rates are thought to apply to everyone who is resident in a territory, there are a great many non-territorial features. For one thing, official residence in a province or country does not entail physical presence; one may live away from home for extended periods and still maintain the home as official residence. Second, tax codes everywhere make distinctions of a non-territorial sort about tax rates, tax deductions, tax credits, exemptions, and surtaxes. For example, capital gains may be taxed at a different rate from salaries, wages, or dividends. Likewise, individuals incorporated as a business may be treated differently from salaried individuals. In some areas, income below a certain level attracts negative income tax. Almost everywhere, family structure affects tax rates by determining who counts as a spouse or a child eligible for deductions for dependents. In short, people pay income taxes only in small part because of territorial residence; they are treated as *types* of individuals more than as a territorial group.

Rather than proliferate examples, let us consider some implications of these observations. The first is this: if many taxes (or even all taxes in some degree) are non-territorial, then they need not be administered by a territorially based organization, although they can be. Second, even if all taxes must fall under the jurisdiction of governments, and thus cannot be private, those governments are not forced to be territorially based because of the nature of taxation, although other factors may induce some governments to be territorial. This conclusion will be especially important in the next chapter, where I consider non-territorial provinces. Third, one feature to be kept in mind in designing governments – and even more in designing administrative structures – concerns the particular mix of taxes envisioned, so that there are sensible matches between the territoriality (or lack of it) of each.

WEIGHTS AND MEASURES

Weights and measures are public goods. If fair and accurate weights and measures can be assured, it is hard to see how any person or group can be denied the benefits. Thus, they must be a function of governments, and so we naturally assume that they will be administered in a territorial fashion. Strictly speaking, however, this is not accurate, although for most practical purposes, it is accurate. In Canada there are two legally sanctioned systems of weights and measures (Imperial and metric), so that exclusivity is not enforced. Likewise, metric is essentially a universal system, although overlaying local systems as in the Canadian example, and thus it is non-territorial in a trivial sense.

For daily business purposes, weights and measures almost everywhere are territorial. The Imperial and metric systems in Canada – and probably most mixed systems elsewhere – are equivalent, can be translated easily into each other, and do not result in unfair trading or deceptive pricing. Thus, in the way in which we experience them, weights and

Functions and Administration 131

measures are territorial in the sense that customers or clients are not treated differently (for example, charged higher prices) because of requesting one system rather than another in the same territory. As a result, we can conclude that weights and measures are not only a job for government but probably also must be administered in a territorial manner. It is worth adding, however, that standards are most useful when they have global scope.

EDUCATION

Nearly everyone thinks of education as a quintessentially territorial jurisdiction. After all, one wishes to send children to schools near home, so that they do not have long commutes; and taxes on residential and business property in the community are the largest source of revenues for schools in most parts of North America and several other countries as well. Yet there are many significant ways in which education is not handled territorially, and these may be increasing in frequency and importance.

One must recall that parallel systems exist in most areas, thus violating the assumption of exclusivity. Parallel systems take several forms. In Canadian provinces, there are public systems and private systems of schooling. In some provinces, there are two public systems: one with instruction in English and another in French 'where numbers warrant.' In some provinces, more than one private system may exist; for example, Catholic schools and secular private schools. Therefore, several forms of non-exclusive use of territory may occur, even where all schools ultimately fall under the jurisdiction of a territorial government, since licensing and accreditation, safety standards, and other matters require enabling legislation or constitutional sanction.

The higher the level of schooling, the less likely the education will have a clear territorial basis. Elementary schools are almost uniformly neighbourhood based, and thus proximity and contiguity (if not exclusivity) are emphasized. Secondary schools not only serve a wider area in most cases but are also, more often than the elementary schools, private and/or residential. At the post-secondary level of colleges and universities, students often choose to attend nearby institutions. But they need not do so; many foreign students attend such institutions; and programs are often not available in each institution, so that local students must go to live elsewhere for them. Some colleges and universities house high proportions of their students in residences, while others consist almost entirely of commuter students living at home. At the highest levels – especially doctoral programs in major research universities – students are recruited from all over the world, and students rarely limit their choice to nearby schools, except for reasons of family obligations. Since advanced degrees are more and more necessary in the global economy, one should expect ever larger numbers of students to migrate over great distances – and across language boundaries – to secure the optimal education.

Distance education exists at all levels, although it is most common at the post-secondary level. It is worth remembering that many school children in rural or remote areas have been taught by correspondence for decades. Australian children in the Outback have had instruction by radio for most of this century. Some universities specialize in distance education and in fact have relatively large numbers of students who seldom or never visit the campus, and some offer only distance education. Besides the Open University in Britain and the University of South Africa, which focus almost entirely on distance education, some universities have aimed for a balance between on-campus and off-campus enrolments, including Faculté Saint-Jean (University of Alberta), the University of New England (Australia), and the new University of Northern British Columbia.

Any form of distance education violates assumptions about contiguity and continuity, and often that of exclusivity. When education 'goes to the people' rather than asking them to attend a central location, territoriality has little meaning, even if most of the potential students reside within the national borders. As telecommunications grow in sophistication and flexibility and decline in cost, one should anticipate that distance education will become more common, encompass larger numbers of students, and perhaps involve a higher proportion of students. Even if neighbourhood schools continue to dominate basic education, distance education at that level could gain in importance, and it will almost certainly become a serious alternative for higher levels or more specialized types of education and training.

As with taxes, education need not be exclusively non-territorial before we recognize the implications for how we deliver this service. As with taxes, a mix of territorial and non-territorial administrative structures appears to offer benefits compared to rigid or traditional adherence to a territorial model. In the extreme, one may point to voucher systems as the ultimate non-territorial administrative structure. Many fellowships and scholarships, such as from the Canadian granting councils or the

Commonwealth, constitute vouchers since they may be used at almost any university in the world, whereas others (such as Rhodes) are tied to a particular place (Oxford). This is not the place to decide whether voucher systems are a panacea, a curse, or one of several useful options. But it is worth considering the extent to which at least some resistance to voucher systems – in education or in other domains – may be a result of our habit of assuming that territorial systems of governance or administration have all the advantages. We will return to this possibility in several later chapters.

SOCIALIZATION OF RISK

'Socialization of risk' encompasses what we normally mean by insurance, but it is a better term because it has broader connotations. Most people think of insurance in a narrow sense of paying premiums to an organization in anticipation of future risks of a financial sort, involving car repairs or hospitalization costs, among others. The idea behind insurance in this sense is that some occurrences are essentially lotteries – random, arbitrary accidents – beyond anyone's ability to foresee or forestall. In other words, they could happen to anyone, but in fact they only happen to a few. Some people can absorb the cost of such events, but most cannot do so. Thus, it makes sense to share the risk and minimize the maximum cost to each individual. Another description for that strategy is 'socialization of risk.' This strategy makes sense primarily when people have little control over events. When they do have control, others sharing the risk subsidize these voluntary acts. For example, one may purchase insurance against earthquake but not against going bankrupt, losing an election, or losing money in currency speculation.

The larger and more diverse the group among whom risk is socialized, the lower the premiums on insurance. This follows from the fact that diversification almost always leads to greater stability and less risk. When one extends the concept to some government jurisdictions and to aspects of one's life which most people do not bother to insure, the term 'socialization of risk' signals that the concept of insurance has been expanded. Let us examine some of these types of insurance and their relationship to assumptions of territoriality.

Military and defence functions may be thought of as forms of insurance. Some types of police or fire protection may also involve socialization of risk. In all of these matters, one can reasonably ask how much it would cost to provide equivalent or sufficient protection (from invasion or theft or whatever) and thus how much of a 'bargain' one's taxes are. I think everyone in advanced economies and liberal democracies accepts that taxes to support armies and police forces are cheaper and more effective than private security forces would be. One cannot thereby extrapolate to all situations, because we in 'Western' countries (now including some countries not originally Western) take for granted several critical assumptions. For example, we assume that armies obey civilian and elected rulers, that they intend to protect civilians rather than victimize them, and that minimum force is likely to be used. Likewise, we assume that police forces are law enforcement agencies rather than law-makers or law-breakers. Leaving aside occasional lapses or some corruption, most of these assumptions are valid most of the time.

One reason citizens accept these assumptions stems from the provision of these services by governments as public goods. That is, they are available to everyone (joint use) and are supported by taxpayers (joint supply). When they become essentially private services – 'protection' rackets or enforcers of laws only against certain types of residents – armies and police generally do not serve to socialize risk even-handedly or at all. This is part of what political theorists have meant by noting that the state has a monopoly on the legitimate exercise of force or coercion in its domain.

Sometimes particular people feel that they need more protection or a special type of protection, and so they set up or hire their own security services. For example, business leaders may pay a bodyguard-driver to prevent kidnappings, office buildings have private security guards at least at certain times of the day, and Neighbourhood Watch abets police functions. These examples demonstrate that governments provide standardized services and thus tolerate some non-competing services. They also generally license or regulate private security services.

From a practical point of view, some of these services could be provided or administered in a non-territorial manner. For example, some areas have privatized fire-fighting and allow competing services. Another example concerns very specialized forms of police protection: Interpol; international task forces on terrorism or drug trafficking; and securities commissions. Some services either must be territorial (most military defence) or must be territorial so long as they are provided by territorial governments. Local police patrols are probably inherently territorial under all forms of government. Like postal services, police services would be more expensive and less effective if they were devoted solely to one type of person in an area – for example, youth patrols, elderly assistance patrols, and assault patrols.

The logical categories among such services grow out of conceptions of entitlement. Can one exclude 'free-riders'? Under what circumstances would one want to exclude free-riders? Why would one want to socialize the risk over a smaller rather than a larger group, with consequently higher cost? As with other functions discussed above, some combination of territoriality and public-good-ness seems to determine the usefulness of particular ways of socializing risk. Let us examine a few more examples before trying to draw general conclusions.

Take unemployment insurance. Governments which provide this service usually organize it in a territorial fashion. In Canada, for example, this is a federal jurisdiction which is administered in a regional mode. To the extent that premiums are regionally risk-adjusted, they determine the extent of regional subsidy. Thus, regions (a whole province or a sub-provincial region) are classified in terms of rates of unemployment, so that individuals in areas of highest unemployment are required to work (and thus contribute) for shorter periods in order to qualify for benefits. In principle, however, this is not necessary, as this program could be administered in a non-territorial mode in at least two different ways. First, one could categorize industries rather than regions in order to identify individuals who should be asked to work longer or shorter periods to qualify for benefits. Seasonal or declining industries, wherever they happen to be located, might be targeted. Second, whether administered by region or by industry, one could encourage job-seeking by paying benefits anywhere in the country rather than in the region where one lost one's job. Thus, one could provide incentives to seek similar work elsewhere or different types of work at home or elsewhere.

Victim assistance programs serve as another example. Even if one grants that some people seem to be more vulnerable or live in homes more likely to invite burglary, few people are mugged, robbed, or burgled. Likewise, rape and other forms of assault are no longer assumed by most observers to derive from 'inviting' behaviour. Thus, a form of insurance has been devised in regard to some of these crimes, in that governments may pay compensation to victims when this cannot be recovered from the perpetrator. Enforcement of alimony payments and child support seems to fulfil the same purposes, that is, to socialize risk and to recognize that incidence is largely unpredictable.

Such victim assistance programs have territorial and non-territorial aspects. They are territorial to the degree that one wishes to socialize risk over an entire nation or continent (for example, all of the European Community because of ease of travel, or Canada and the United States). They are non-territorial in the very specific identification of entitlements, since few people are victims in any particular area or of any specific type of prohibited behaviour. Thus, administration should probably reflect some mix of territorial and non-territorial modes, which means it should not be exclusively territorial. Which government should have jurisdiction, however, will vary depending on the behaviour and incentives to flee. Thus, avoidance of child support or alimony should be a national (or international) jurisdiction, whereas some other types of victim assistance such as compensation for burglary might be local or subnational.

Some governments have entered the insurance business in the narrow sense of, for example, automobile or health and hospitalization insurance. They have, however, done so in quite different ways. So far as I know, 'no fault' insurance provided by governments has always been territorially based. That means that everyone resident in the government's jurisdiction (provinces in the Canadian case) must purchase the service through the government agency. Health and hospitalization insurance, by contrast, is administered territorially in Canada but non-territorially in the United States. Health is a provincial jurisdiction in Canada, and the provincial schemes are coordinated under a federal umbrella which ensures universal access and portability across provincial borders. The specific way in which individuals enter the program differs according to employment status and so on, but everyone in a province is part of that plan. In the United States, however, most coverage is through private health plans (non-territorial), and the Medicare-Medicaid plans of the federal government are targeted on specific types of individuals (such as the elderly, welfare recipients, etc.) and are hence also non-territorial. Of course, since states administer most of the Medicare-Medicaid plans, there may be exceptions (such as Oregon), but the broad national differences still exist.

Perhaps these examples offer sufficient variety to warrant some hypotheses or conclusions. The most obvious point concerns the frequency of territorial administration. Virtually every program mentioned has a territorial base, although there are exceptions like Medicare-Medicaid. The second and more important point derives from observations about the non-territorial possibilities in almost all jurisdictions. Although territorial administration is common, it need not be as common as it is. Third, and equally crucial, many of these activities could be

Functions and Administration   137

handled by governmental agencies or by private organizations, except for military and some police functions. Since most private organizations are focused on particular types of individuals wherever they may be and not on all individuals in one place, they are almost never inherently territorial.

The implicit motive behind socialization of risk can be conceptualized in terms of cost or of fairness. In terms of cost, one wishes to limit the maximum damage to particular individuals when the occasions are largely beyond individual (or perhaps even collective) control. In terms of fairness, random costs should not fall unfairly on individuals who did nothing to cause the misfortune. Either way of conceptualizing costs reminds us that we are part of communities, that these are not all the same in scope or inclusiveness, that we can benefit from sharing risk if the sharing is mutual rather than exploitative, and that one way to specify preferred communities concerns whose risks we are willing to share. Chapter 6 will develop more fully these aspects of community and fairness.

For present purposes, we can leave these reflections on risks and return to the issue of functions and administration. I have tried to approach questions of governmental and non-governmental jurisdictions, territorial and non-territorial functions, and types of services (public goods, common resources, types of risk). All of these avenues should help us to answer two questions: the next section will ask about some administrative implications of the existence of non-territorial functions or jurisdictions; and the next chapter will ask about some of their implications for federalism and politics generally.

ENVISIONING ADMINISTRATIVE FUTURES

If it is now clear that many functions are not inherently territorial, then their administration need not be organized territorially. If fewer jurisdictions remain territorial as technology changes, then more instances of administrative organization will likely be non-territorial. Thus I will assume that a trend away from purely territorial administration is under way, and that over time there will be more non-territorial administrative structures, either on their own or as part of a mix of territorial and non-territorial delivery of services.

Since I have repeatedly stressed that precise prediction is not my goal, let me reiterate that point. I cannot foresee exactly which jurisdictions will be administered non-territorially, since governments have a choice and are not fully constrained by the nature of the function. Likewise, I cannot be certain whether at some point most administrative structures will be set up in a non-territorial mode, or whether they will remain a minority orientation. Regardless of such uncertainties, I feel sure that some forms of administration will be non-territorial, since some already are and since they may prove cheaper or more effective. The first part of this chapter has demonstrated conclusively that a great many functions are not inherently territorial. Thus, we can move beyond that debate and the question of exactly how much non-territorial administration will eventually occur. The remainder of this chapter will focus instead on *administrative* implications and challenges posed by taking seriously the increasing number of non-territorial jurisdictions. The next chapter will look closely at several *political* implications of non-territorial organizations.

Recall a number of points set out in previous chapters. We are exploring some consequences of relaxing assumptions about territorial exclusivity, contiguity, and continuity. Together these assumptions have generally ensured that political boundaries are congruent, that is, the jurisdictions occupy the same territory. When there is only one centre of power or sovereign for these jurisdictions, congruent territories amount to *all-purpose* organizations, which is what nations aspire to be. Non-territorial organizations, we have noted, can be and usually are more specialized in function; thus they can be more flexibly adapted to the issues relevant to service delivery.

If many services or administrative structures are divorced from a territorial base, then they will inevitably overlap and intersect each other in cross-cutting fashion. Even if some must retain a bounded territorial base, we may see more and more organizations whose boundaries are not congruent. By definition, non-territorial administrative structures will almost always be non-congruent also. When boundaries are not congruent or when administration consists of non-congruent networks unrelated to territory, there can be little doubt that *exclusivity* diminishes as a valid assumption. Those groups and individuals who advocate voucher systems for public services like education or waste disposal have implicitly moved out of the realm of territorially based services to non-territorial forms of administration. Although there are some valid concerns about voucher systems – not least, that they impose information costs which may exceed the capacities of some groups of people – they also offer certain advantages of flexibility, portability, and simplicity of administration.[7]

As we have seen, at the municipal or local level we do not assume that organizations must be territorially exclusive or congruent and operate under a single government. Why then should we so often take for granted that exclusivity or congruence is essential at the provincial or federal level.[8] One answer is that these higher governments are sovereign, but that is no answer at all.[9] Why should we assume that sovereignty must be territorial or that territorial exclusivity must be linked to sovereignty? The choice may come down to choosing between *all-purpose* organizations which are territorially based and *specialized* organizations which may or may not be based on territory.[10] Put in this way, it appears that the burden of proof should be on those who prefer general or non-specialized organizations.

Exclusive and congruent territories constitute bundles. Non-exclusive or non-congruent territories are a form of unbundling. Vouchers constitute an extreme form of unbundling. Non-territorial organization offers even more flexibility than any type of territorial organization. If one must move to another province or country to receive (or to avoid) certain services, one may have to give up valued services as well as incur transition costs. If one can subscribe to or join unbundled services or networks or organizations without moving, choice is greater and costs are lower.

Canada and most countries are currently moving away from bundled and territorial organizations and toward unbundled organizations. There has been much more discussion of unbundling in the economic realm than in the political or administrative arenas, under the general heading of 'globalization.'[11] Nevertheless, it is a general process which will not be confined to purely economic matters. These new organizations may be mostly non-territorial, although in many cases they may involve non-congruent territories. If these assertions are correct – and let's assume for purposes of argument that they are – then we can turn away from proof and examine some implications of unbundling for public (and perhaps private) administration. For convenience, they are grouped into four broad categories: structure of organizations, output of organizations, careers, and accountability.

STRUCTURAL IMPLICATIONS

It should be clear by now that unbundled organizational structures will contrast, in many if not all cases, with traditional organizations. Because they do not flow from all-purpose central authorities or from congruent territories, one would expect them to be less hierarchical, or to involve multiple hierarchies.[12] to be described more often as webs or networks; to involve face-to-face interactions less often, whether among staff or with clients, because they are not always territorially based; and, if territorial, to be non-congruent with territories of other organizations with the consequence that 'centres' or 'headquarters' of organizations may not be concentrated in proximity to each other. Indeed, what counts as 'core' and 'periphery' may be relatively obscure in a network; and multiple, specialized, non-congruent networks may make this distinction meaningless.[13] Less certain but very probable is that employees may be moved among jobs, departments, or networks as tasks are tailored to specific issues or problems. In other words, these structures may be less 'bureaucratic' than existing agencies or departments. These changes may be interesting in their own right, but they should be evaluated most carefully in light of their manifestations in outputs, career structure, and accountability.

OUTPUTS AND OUTCOMES

Many organizations, especially in the public sector, measure output, productivity, and the like in standard categories, indeed often categories of inputs, which persist for long periods of time.[14] For example, the Food Safety Branch might try to demonstrate improved levels of performance by the increased number of inspections or by infractions identified per inspector. Customs officers would no doubt report success in terms of contraband seized. Treasury Board might express pride in the reduction of person-years in the system as a whole. In these and many other examples, two assumptions recur which may never have been valid or which may be less valid or useful as unbundling proceeds. First, output equals activity; or, worse yet, output equals input, rather than goal attainment in a broader sense. Is the food safe? or just inspected more often? Is the contraband seized an increasing or decreasing proportion of all dangerous contraband? Has Treasury Board crippled some branches or has it increased their productivity by removing person-years? Second, output is standardized, so that it can be quantified for answers during parliamentary question periods and for other publicity purposes. For some services and some purposes, that method suffices, but qualitative judgments may lead to different evaluations.

If we posit another terminology, we could contrast output (as standardized activity) with outcomes. What are the goals of this organization, and how effectively are we achieving them? The answer will rarely be found wholly in standardized activity measures, although some standard measures may be relevant some of the time. Each organization and each policy will need evaluation in specialized terms. As each organization becomes more specialized and more targeted on particular clients or situations, output alone becomes less and less relevant. Non-standard services tailored to special circumstances should be more common, and thus outcomes (goal attainment) more varied and specific.

Presumably, goals change, unless stated extremely broadly. For example, 'reduce poverty' could be a goal that never changes; but an attainable or measurable goal might be 'provide incentives to high school drop-outs to gain skills in order to reduce reliance on welfare.' Of course, the more specific the goals, the more different goals one will find within a broad problem area. Also the more specific the goals, the easier it may be to demonstrate success *or failure* in attaining the goals, with implications for career progress and accountability. Thus, one can expect resistance in some quarters to unbundling and to functional outcome (rather than only output) assessment.

If goals are precisely specified and if services are targeted or tailored to particular client groups, then one may discover that fine-grained policy must change quickly even while the basic policy remains constant. For example, as one moves in or out of recession, broad policy on welfare, literacy, or food safety may not change, but quick response to localized or specialized client groups may be desirable. That almost certainly means that activities (outputs) should change in order to expedite goal attainment (outcomes). If accountability or career advancement depend on standard output, how would one expect most employees to react under these changed conditions? How would one expect their unions to react?

CAREER PATTERNS

Recall what we have posited: organizations which are less hierarchical, have ever-changing specific goals, require rapid redeployment of at least some individuals in ways that are hard to foresee, and may involve individuals in fewer personal interactions and in more 'electronic network' interactions. Surely these new features raise questions about the types of people one should recruit, the kinds and frequency of training for them, methods of supervision, and the ways one assesses performance. By extension, these aspects of institutional adaptation raise questions about accountability (below), about individual compared to team performance, and about concepts of career progress and promotion.[15] Most concretely, the challenges will involve how to write job descriptions for such people and to coordinate them in a linear career.[16]

Career progress for most people has usually meant 'moving up the ladder,' whether in terms of salary or wages, span of authority, or impressiveness of title. One may presume that salary or wages will continue to increase with experience and training in these new organizational circumstances. Span of authority, however, loses some of its allure where hierarchy has been replaced by networks of teams; and titles might be 'professional' designations more often than reflections of status. Leaving aside some tasks which may not change their character although they may be less common (secretarial, routine clerical, janitorial services, security guards, etc.), most employees, we have speculated, would have relatively vague job descriptions (or else scores of them), would be working on their own (whether at home or away from 'the centre' if there is one), and may be judged as much by how well the team approximates its goals as by the activities the individual performs. One will, in these circumstances, need highly motivated, self-reliant employees who relate easily to new people and adjust quickly to new situations. In other words, a higher proportion of public servants will come to resemble those in professional and entrepreneurial categories as we currently understand them.[17]

Even where we can evaluate individuals in terms similar to current output measures, we may see substantial changes in the categories. Coordination and brokering or 'policing' may be more common and more important than managing or regulating or controlling.[18] Promotion may need to be based on a concept of 'entrusted with a wider and wider range of activities' instead of moving to a 'higher level' in the hierarchy or supervising more subordinates.

Public service unions will be challenged by these developments as much as senior managers. Just to mention a few possibilities should be sufficient to suggest how difficult it could be for unions to adapt. How will grievances be framed if job descriptions are less specific and if skill usage changes rapidly with experience and in-service training? To which union will employees report or belong if – without any physical removal – employees are 'transferred' to a new or different web or network because their skills are appropriate for the new target of that team?

Under such circumstances, unions would probably be well advised to 'get on with the job' and not try to negotiate each transfer, each new job description, or each retraining. Instead, one can imagine that the difficult tasks will be union-management collaboration on modes of evaluating performance or outcomes. Furthermore, performance and outcomes will be team efforts, but only individuals belong to the union; and a team may involve members of more than one union. 'Company unions' may be an exception. Current bargaining over pay and benefits will, in retrospect, look straightforward by comparison. Indeed, pay, promotion, and advancement may depend more on access to training than on security of tenure in a current position.

ACCOUNTABILITY

The structural, personnel, and career changes outlined above, if even halfway accurate, should affect substantially our ways of assessing accountability. To whom is one accountable in a network or web? When many teams are linked in complex and less hierarchical ways, an employee may have, in effect, several 'bosses,' each responsible for different tasks related to sub-goals attained at different rates.[19] Where teams are critical elements, whose job it was and how did they perform it become conundrums which may defy clear lines of authority or accountability.[20]

We have speculated that goals may evolve fairly rapidly and that goals may be somewhat different for specific target client groups. If so, how do we know when the task is finished? If the termination date is unclear, how do we measure progress?

We have reason to believe that in the future departments or agencies may not exist in the compact and distinct sense they do now. That is, who is 'in' which unit may become blurred. For one thing, 'mobile' teams which can provide specific, time-constrained services may migrate among units or may be shared on an on-going basis. These eventualities would affect accountability and responsibility for ministers as well as for employees within any given unit. Needless to say, such arrangements also make difficult the assignment of person-years to particular units; this might lead to a greater reliance on contracting for specific services within the public service or outside it.

Contracting out would be only one of several developments which blur the line between public and private administration. Non-congruent and non-territorial administrative arrangements imply, as we saw at the local government level, a multiplication of specific-purpose organizations. Each unit would have a different 'reach,' a different territory, or a different blend of public-private collaboration. Without going into details, one can speculate that more structures will come to look like 'half-way houses' bridging the public sector and the private sector. The more blurred that line, the greater chance of apparent conflicts of interest. Again, accountability arises in a double aspect: who is responsible for what, and who should answer to whom?

A NEW ORGANIZATIONAL CULTURE?

From questioning the need for our assumptions about the territorial basis of nations or provinces, we have been led to think about radically different types of administrative structures, careers, and other concepts. But are they really that new or radical? Certainly they seem to diverge widely from some of the textbook wisdom about public administration and perhaps business administration as well. Nevertheless, I propose to draw together some strands of these ruminations by arguing that the model for the future – or the metaphor for understanding the new organizational culture – is that found in universities.[21] This may have two beneficial effects, since it could reassure some sceptics about whether any organization can function under these conditions and it may relieve some pressure on universities to become more 'businesslike.' Most universities are publicly funded, but they are nevertheless insulated by 'arm's length' fiduciary arrangements.

Universities are relatively 'flat' organizations in that there are not many layers in the hierarchy. More important, 'hierarchy' is a misleading word because there are actually several relatively independent hierarchies: faculty ranks, support staff and supervisors, administrative committees at department, faculty, and senate levels, and so on.

Several characteristics identified above as related to non-territorial or non-congruent administrative structures find a prominent place in university governance and goal attainment. These include: autonomous work units, self-governance, non-territorial networks of scholars, overlapping networks, a premium on knowledge and continual updating of knowledge, professional titles and careers, and no clear 'bottom line.' Appropriate metaphors to describe authority focus neither on command nor on consensus but on integrity, innovation, and personalized service. Universities have been caricatured – and sometimes praised – as places

Functions and Administration 145

of 'constrained anarchy.' If so, they may have inadvertently pioneered the path along which public administration will evolve as we confront the challenges of globalization and therefore rely on fewer territorial forms of organization.

Drucker has chronicled a related and broader concept as evidence of new forms of administration. Called 'the third force,' because it is non-profit but also non-governmental, it includes universities, certain kinds of hospitals, orchestras and many arts groups, and most charitable organizations.[22] Drucker claims it already constitutes a very large proportion of American organizational life and employment and thus explains why overall taxes (relative to GDP) are lower in the United States than in almost all European countries. Canada apparently falls between American and European poles on this dimension.

The third force represents non-territorial and non-congruent organizational structures. Like my example of universities, many of these organizations evidence the features or incipient aspects of the features of administration outlined above.

Drucker argues that the third force challenges our conceptions of management. Instead of a focus on hierarchy, control, planning, or strict accountability, Drucker defines management in the third force, and more broadly in the future, as that which makes it possible for people to pursue joint endeavours. Whether Drucker is correct in predicting the direction of change, his analysis challenges us to question our usual assumptions about types of organizations, types of management, and standards of evaluation. Whether I am correct that universities may prove a fruitful model for public administration, analysis of non-territorial and non-congruent territorial organizations should challenge us to question some hidden or unconscious assumptions built into our administrative arrangements.

Many people will see in these processes of non-territorial administration, or unbundling, dangers of fragmentation and weakening of government. They will fear that people will suffer because the governments 'taking care' of them will decline in importance. Although those fears may be justified in particular instances, and thus we should watch carefully for them if we implement these changes, there is another perspective on unbundling or non-territorial administration. One can equally see these adjustments as institutional flexibility, functional adaptation, customized service, and fitting the solution to the problem. The intricate and ingenious efforts at governing the commons which Elinor Ostrom has described emphasize the value of devising better institutions and of finding an optimal balance of public and private institutions. In other words, let us keep separate the questions of jurisdiction, governance, and administration. Efficiency and responsiveness then become functional rather than structural issues.

5

Non-Territorial Federalism

For at least 150 years, Canada has wrestled with the political implications of an uneven social distribution of population across its territory.[1] Upper Canada was almost totally Protestant and English, but Lower Canada was a mixture of English and French, Protestant and Catholic. After Lord Durham's famous report to the British government, Upper and Lower Canada were joined in 1841 and became the United Province of Canada.[2] By bringing together the English of both areas, it was felt that the assimilation of the French was only a matter of time because of the rapidly expanding English population of Upper Canada. In fact, by 1851 the majority of the population of the Canadas was for the first time English instead of French.[3]

Assimilation did not occur. For awhile, 'dual ministries' in the legislature kept the process of governance working by ensuring that departments were run jointly by two ministers, one French (Catholic) and one English (Protestant).[4] Concurrent majorities among French and English were the norm. This system could only work when leaders on both sides were committed to it, and not all were. Hence, throughout the 1850s, Canada proposed various federal schemes – on its own or with the other colonies of British North America – as a solution to its own inner dilemma.

The achievement of the 'wider union' in 1867 was heralded as satisfying several goals – military defence, debt management, and railroad construction, but perhaps most of all the alleviation of territorial fights between English and French. The Fathers of Confederation believed that tensions could be managed or eliminated by allowing provincial legislatures and governments to administer matters of local concern.[5] That is, ethnic, religious, and linguistic conflict could be quelled by territorial division of protagonists.

148 Beyond Sovereignty

People move, however, and political boundaries have failed to separate English and French. Yet history has shown that assimilation of one by the other could not be accomplished either. And so began the peculiar puzzle that has been central to Canadian history for a century and a half. This feature was accurately described as a fundamental characteristic of Canada in section 2(1)(a) of the Meech Lake Accord of 1987:

> ... the existence of French-speaking Canadians, centered in Quebec but also present elsewhere in Canada, and English-speaking Canadians, concentrated outside Quebec but also present in Quebec, constitutes a fundamental characteristic of Canada.

THE CANADIAN CONUNDRUM

The puzzle or dilemma consists in this: Canadians have been tantalized by geographic or territorial boundaries as a means to solve a conflict between social groups. At no point has it been possible to draw provincial boundaries so that Protestant and Catholic, English and French, had exclusive control of their own territory. Yet the 'fit' between social and political boundaries was always close enough to tempt Canadians to try to deal with one set of boundaries as a surrogate for the other. By enshrining provinces as territorial units with powers appropriate to the protection of local social customs and ways of life, federalism ensured that a non-territorial problem (ethnic conflict, as we would say today) has been assigned to territorial governments.[6] A further complication, of course, concerns the non-coincidence of the non-territorial cleavages; religion and language have diverged ever more widely as Irish Catholics settled in Ontario and other groups such as Italians came to reside in various parts of the country.

One previous effort to separate French and English by forced removal involved the expulsion of the Acadians in the eighteenth century. As we now know, this was unsuccessful; and today New Brunswick is an officially bilingual province with a population that is one-third Acadian. Such a forceful relocation of thousands – or today millions – of Canadian citizens would be unthinkable in light of liberal traditions and democratic rights. Besides, the Charter of Rights and Freedoms gives (in section 6) every Canadian resident the right to enter or leave any province or territory in Canada. Of course, voluntary movement sometimes clarifies the social distribution. For example, many English-speaking Canadians after the Parti Québécois took power in 1976 have chosen to leave Quebec as a result of the province's redefined role as champion of

French-speaking Quebeckers rather than, as previously, guardian of all francophones wherever they lived in Canada.

At the present, Canadians face again the need to think creatively about their institutions and about protection of rights and ways of life. Since the creative use of territory has not provided a permanent solution to social problems, perhaps the next step in political evolution should be to question the need for territorial governments and institutions. The need for creative political thinking is not restricted to Canada, but much can be learned from detailed examination of particular cases, and I will thus focus on Canada for present purposes.

Rather than looking further at the historical record, we can make the analysis more concrete and provocative by envisioning two non-territorial provinces. The first would consist of francophones living outside of Quebec, and the second would comprise aboriginals across the country and in particular south of 60°. Thus, there would be two predominantly French provinces, Quebec and the one I propose here, one territorial and the other non-territorial. Likewise, if the new Territory of Nunavut becomes a province, as most observers expect, it would be in most respects a territorial one not unlike the existing provinces.[7] That is why I focus on aboriginals other than Inuit, and on territory within the borders of existing provinces.

For certain purposes, both types of non-territorial provinces are quite similar since both types violate one or more of the assumptions about territoriality mentioned at several points. It is worth discussing them separately, however, because they violate different assumptions, pose different kinds of challenges to our thinking about federalism, and may require different forms of administration.

LA FRANCOPHONIE

The francophone province which I hypothesize might be called 'La Francophonie' to distinguish it from Quebec.[8] It would consist of all francophones in Canada living outside of Quebec. At some point, it might become necessary to determine who is or is not a francophone, but I hope that can be left to personal choice. Since I propose that individuals or families be able to decide if they wish to reside officially with La Francophonie or not, one will not end up with a totally francophone province nor will all francophones outside of Quebec choose this option. If we relied, however, on criteria involving mother tongue, language of work, or language spoken at home, this might affect in some small degree the number of residents of the province. Any consistent application of criteria of this sort will yield the same geographic distribution: almost all francophones will turn out to live within what is now Ontario and New Brunswick, with scattered pockets elsewhere.

La Francophonie would need very special powers, not exactly like those of a territorially based province. Hence, one value of speculating about this province derives from the need to shift our focus from an exclusive concern with federal and provincial jurisdictions. Instead – or in addition – we must consider which powers can only be administered by territorial governments or agencies and which services could be delivered by institutions without a territorial base.

In the previous chapter we have seen that quite a few jurisdictions do not require a territorially based administration. Thus, there is no danger that this hypothesized francophone province would have no functions or jurisdictions. We have concluded that education, most health services, and individual welfare or unemployment insurance payments can be handled either territorially or non-territorially. Since French-language education and some health services in French would rank at the top of most francophones' priorities, these could easily be met. There are already French-language radio and TV services throughout Canada, and there are several French-language newspapers and magazines. As argued in chapter 4, income tax is inherently non-territorial, and so La Francophonie would have a tax base similar to that of existing provinces, although sales taxes might pose certain administrative problems.

The difficulties posed by retail sales taxes – and perhaps certain localized health services – provide an opportunity to begin discussion of one of the features these non-territorial provinces have in common. Both provinces will need to share certain services with existing, territorially based provinces. I will discuss the example of sales tax revenue at this point and return to other examples when discussing the province for aboriginals.

I concluded in chapter 4 that retail sales taxes – or equivalents like GST – require a territorial base, at least outside of mail-order or electronic shopping. One cannot easily distinguish at the cash register between people who live in different jurisdictions. Would this pose a problem in financing La Francophonie? In particular, would it be deprived of the revenue from such taxes? If so, this could be crippling, judging by the degree of dependence of nine of the ten existing provinces on sales taxes (Alberta having none so far).

There are at least three major choices for dealing with this issue. The first involves self-identification by customers in the retail outlet. One would charge a particular tax on each purchaser and remit it to La Francophonie if the customer is a francophone self-proclaimed to be a resident of that province, and all other tax collected from customers would go directly to the territorial province within which the retail outlet was located. This would be possible but expensive for retailers to administer. It might also be time-consuming at the point of check-out. So let us consider two other procedures.

As a second option, one might designate each retail outlet as francophone or not, depending on the official place of residence of the owner (if a local business) or manager (if a branch of a regional or national company). Francophone stores would remit tax to La Francophonie, while all others would do so to the territorial province surrounding the store. This method has the merit of simplicity and low cost of administration. If it were felt, however, that one or the other of the provinces got an unfair share because of patterns of ownership or management, then one could consider choice number three.

As a third option, one could monitor the usage of retail outlets by francophones and non-francophones, and then allocate tax revenues proportionally. In other words, one need not record every transaction (as in the first procedure above) but simply have spot-checks. These would be analogous to labour-force surveys on unemployment, which are now done once a month on samples of people rather than on everyone. A combination of the second and third methods might be most reasonable: one would divide the tax revenues according to the residence of the owner (or manager) unless a survey indicated deviation from the norm beyond a certain margin.

The purpose of this extended example is twofold. I want to show, for one thing, that a non-territorial province could be funded by a reasonable mix of tax sources. These would obviously be supplemented as necessary by transfer payments collected and disbursed by the federal government, as occurs now among all provinces. But those transfers would be distorted if La Francophonie (or any other province) made no effort to collect its own taxes. Taxes are, after all, public goods in the sense indicated in chapter 4; they require an enforcement mechanism to deter free-riders, whether individuals or provinces.

My second purpose in dwelling on sales taxes – and another example in a later section – concerns the need for interprovincial cooperation. Instead of each province collecting and keeping its own sales tax revenues, these would be handled in a cooperative manner to ensure that neither territorial nor non-territorial provinces suffered. One might also perceive the issue from the residents' vantage point, since they would like to be assured that their taxes were destined for their province's treasury. There is already considerable cooperation of this type currently, and one should encourage rather than discourage it. For example, residents of a province travelling or residing temporarily in other provinces continue to pay income taxes and health insurance premiums to their province of residence, but all provinces reimburse each other for certain costs such as hospitalization, automobile accidents involving residents of more than one province, and the like.

Before turning to the second type of province, let me just mention several implications of La Francophonie besides jurisdictional issues. If education can be delivered by a non-territorial province, as I believe it can, then the concern at present with services 'where numbers warrant' becomes superfluous. Instead the question is what kind of education should be provided for which kinds of people wherever they reside. When provided from one or more central offices, the numbers will always 'warrant' the provision of services. Furthermore, there may be economies of scale because one does not need to replicate certain facilities or administrative structures in small local enclaves. Of course, there may be some disadvantages or personal costs, such as children taught by distance education not having the same types of social life centred on a neighbourhood school. In such cases, francophone parents will need to weigh the trade-off between French education and other benefits in an English-language school. This dilemma is, in principle, no different than asking whether one cares enough about French-language schooling for one's children to move to another neighbourhood, city, or province. Instead of only one way to deal with a dilemma, parents would have two radically different means of coping: moving to Quebec or to a neighbourhood with a French school, or 'moving' to La Francophonie.

One can expect that La Francophonie will find itself behaving in some ways more like a national government than a provincial one. Such a province will face the same degree of regional diversity that the federal government in Ottawa currently confronts. Regional disparities and regional perspectives become critical for such a province even though it is not regional (territorial) itself. One of those details – hours of operation of polling stations in an election – might result in pressures on the federal government to consider uniform hours in its elections.

Notice that the need to address regional diversity seems to us natural, and thus we contrast La Francophonie with Quebec. But that assumes that one kind of diversity or homogeneity takes precedence over others. Why should it be better that a province be homogeneous in language but divided regionally, rather than the reverse case, which now obtains in Quebec? Forcing ourselves to reason out these unexamined assumptions is the principal benefit, in my view, of questioning territoriality.

ABORIGINAL PEOPLES PROVINCE

The second type of non-territorial province could be called Aboriginal Peoples Province.[9] Its basis would probably not be individual, as with La Francophonie, but more likely it would be land-based without the assumptions of contiguity and continuity. Whether the basis was existing reserves or the outcome of current comprehensive land claims, the results would be similar in type, although different in area. The reserves south of 60° are now exclusively for aboriginals (status Indians, actually), and the land claims settlements might or might not involve exclusive use of territory.[10] Neither basis assumes a single contiguous territory; in fact there would very likely be several hundred territories. (There are currently more than 2,000 reserves among over 600 bands, comprising about forty to fifty 'nations.') Nor would Aboriginal Peoples Province necessarily be continuous since there might well be enclaves of non-native settlement within at least some of the larger parts of this province. And certainly reserves today form 'islands' within each province.

It should be noted that there are several additional obstacles to the establishment of Aboriginal Peoples Province, beyond the general resistance to non-territorial political formations. For one, the Métis (mixed aboriginal and non-aboriginal) have no reserves, and except in Alberta they have no land base at all in a collective sense. Thus, federal or provincial Crown lands may have to be set aside for their use. A second concern relates to Indians who live off-reserve but who wish to maintain their identity and status as aboriginals. This actually consists of at least two distinct issues – citizenship and delivery of services. By citizenship I mean the privileges and duties of membership, how one acquires them or loses them, and the ways in which that status is compatible with citizenship in Canada. I have explored 'aboriginal citizenship' elsewhere, and I will address some aspects of it in chapters 6 and 7, so that in this chapter I will leave it aside.[11] Delivery of services receives some attention below.

Like Canada and to some degree like La Francophonie, Aboriginal Peoples Province would be very diverse in language, cultures, economic situations, and affluence. It would therefore have a government which felt the pressures of national diversity currently felt by Ottawa. That could prove beneficial to the extent such provinces achieved a broader perspective than the narrow regional perspectives common in the existing territorial provinces. Such diversity should, however, be mentioned as a third obstacle to the creation of Aboriginal Peoples Province. If we ignore the diversity among reserves and bands, as largely creations of the Indian Act and imposed by the federal government, there is still the diversity represented by the forty to fifty 'nations' which historically used the land we now call Canada before and at the time of European contact and settlement. Would such groupings agree to subsume their historic differences and to coexist within a single province?[12]

The resistance to amalgamation in a province may be seen in several respects, not least of which is the demand for a 'third order of government' within Canada. By definition, a third order would have a somewhat different status from the other two orders – federal and provincial. Hence, it may seem a bit of a comedown to be designated a province. There are, I believe, several strong counter-arguments. We know what provinces are, whereas no one knows anything concrete about a third order of government; and so one might avoid years or decades of negotiations and litigation by using the label of province as one's point of analytic departure. As I point out in some detail in a later section, there are substantial differences among existing provinces in effective powers and jurisdictions. Thus, it cannot be ruled out *a priori* that Aboriginal Peoples Province might have unique combinations of functions or jurisdictions.

For Aboriginal Peoples Province, as perhaps for La Francophonie, an objection might stem from the distances which separate the constituents. I find this concern relatively minor and less of a problem as time passes. For one thing, telecommunications satellites and the like would allow for an immediacy of mutual experience at least as great as Canadians derive from the CBC or Radio Canada. In addition, flying time is the relevant measure these days, and large reserves or major settlements could have airfields. From the perspective of someone who lives in Vancouver, there is little reason to differentiate between the distances to Montreal or to Kamloops – each is five hours away, one by jet and the other by car. Cost may be a consideration, but time as a function of distance can be overcome.

Distance has another consequence. The 'nations' mentioned above are generally clustered in that most members of any one nation reside on reserves near each other, or else live in nearby towns or cities. Exceptions occur, such as people from the east or west who live in Ottawa because they work in the Department of Indian Affairs, but these are proportionately small groups. Thus, the desire for personal interaction might not be thwarted by great distances, anymore than it is for the vast majority of Canadians who live in a province where most of their colleagues and friends live. For all people, travel may be pleasant or unpleasant, but aboriginals should be no more 'alienated' by distance within a third order or a province than Canadians are now.

If one considers simultaneously the question of distance and of 'nations,' perhaps a solution can be found in the idea that Aboriginal Peoples Province could be a federation or confederation of 'nations,' just as Canada is a federation of provinces.[13] Of course, the units within Aboriginal Peoples Province would not be exactly like provinces in Canada; otherwise, one might as well have forty to fifty provinces and dispense with the concept of an overarching political unit called Aboriginal Peoples Province. However, I put forward the concept of a federation within a province to show that diversity may be accommodated in many ways. This is not the place to develop this hypothesis in detail, although some aspects are pursued implicitly in later sections and in chapter 7. Instead I want to return to the main line of argument – implications of non-territorial federalism – after this excursion into why some aboriginals might object to Aboriginal Peoples Province.

Unlike La Francophonie, jurisdictions in Aboriginal Peoples Province might be defined differently because of the peculiar combination of territorial and non-territorial assumptions or aspects. For example, as far as taxes were concerned, property taxes as a base for education on reserves would be feasible, and income taxes could be highly varied, as they are in Canada, because of varied personal circumstances. Education would almost certainly be territorially based, because it would reflect language needs which happen to be bounded territorially, except for urban aboriginals. Haida could be the language of instruction in the Queen Charlotte Islands, Cree in other places, and Micmac elsewhere. How education was delivered could thus be extremely different from the agencies in La Francophonie. That flexibility seems to me one of the most attractive features of having different kinds of provinces. I will return to some implications of this flexibility in a later section.

THE VALUE OF SHARED JURISDICTIONS

A great deal of effort has been expended – by theorists and judges as well as politicians – in trying to clarify the division of powers in federal systems. After all, the reasoning goes, federalism was created in order to keep distinct national issues and matters of local concern. Therefore, each order of government should have jurisdictions which are clearly delimited and defined. I propose to challenge this doctrine from two points of view.[14] In this section, I examine the joint delivery of services by provinces, and in the next section, I extend that logic of cooperation to encompass concurrent jurisdictions between federal and provincial orders of government, and, if it should come to pass, a third order of government as well.

The first specific example which this section will analyse is the delivery of health and hospital services in the non-territorial province of Aboriginal Peoples Province. I have already stated several times that emergency wards and other primary health care seem to be inherently territorial in the sense that proximity must prevail or else more fatalities and greater suffering will occur because of the link between distance and time lapse. For all other types of health and hospital care, contiguity may be convenient, but it is not essential. Elective surgery, expensive diagnostic procedures, rarely used treatment facilities, and experimental programs should not be located in or near every neighbourhood or community, since the expense of doing so would take resources away from other governmental programs or from private disposable income. For ease of reference, I will refer to these latter types of services as 'secondary' or specialized, to distinguish them from 'primary' or all-purpose emergency services.

In the existing territorial provinces, allocation of secondary facilities and services among communities has been accepted from the beginning of the Canadian universal care system in the 1950s and 1960s. Where a community cannot fully utilize a specialized facility, ambulance or air ambulance transportation becomes an extra service so that artificial or arbitrary barriers to use are minimized. In some cases, provincial health plans even pay (including travel costs) for the procedure to be performed in other provinces, the United States, or elsewhere. Since there is a central clearing-house for payments, use anywhere in the system has the same effect; and thus where use should occur can be determined on the basis of efficiency, costs, and fairness rather than proximity.

As hypothesized, Aboriginal Peoples Province would consist of about 2,000 pockets of reserve land, which vary in population from a handful to several thousand. In addition, about half of all aboriginals live off-reserve, permanently or temporarily, and their numbers and demographic composition change frequently. Thus, one cannot realistically expect to set up the full range of secondary services in all locations, whether on reserves or off-reserve. Some reserves will be too small, even if several are located near each other; and urban or other off-reserve sites would often duplicate existing specialized facilities run by territorial provinces.

As a result of these considerations, I propose that Aboriginal Peoples Province share its jurisdiction over health with the other territorial provinces, at least where reserves or groups of reserves may not allow sufficient population base for elaborate facilities. Sharing will include several related aspects: sharing the use of facilities, sharing the cost of operating them, sharing capital costs, and sharing responsibility for quality and accountability. Some of these aspects are already shared among existing provinces, since federal coordination ensures that members of any provincial health plan can utilize facilities in the other provinces and have the usage paid for by the 'home' province. Capital and other costs are shared between federal and provincial governments, which follows logically from equalization grants and other transfer payments between 'have' and 'have not' provinces. These would presumably continue but not be limited to transfers among territorial units alone.

Since aboriginals have expressed a desire to maintain their traditional medicine, I propose that it be included in the cost-sharing arrangements too. Indeed, I would assume that Canadian society will – if not now, then more and more as time passes – want to share the knowledge and expertise that traditional medical practitioners and elders possess. Sharing, in my usage, should be a two-way process wherever possible.

The sharing I have in mind would, on a practical level, be quite simple. Imagine a band or reserve which is too small to justify a full-service hospital but is relatively near a town or city with such a facility. The members of the band or reserve will have identity cards which entitle them to service, just as all Canadians have now. When they make use of a service in a territorial province next to their homes, billing will occur – electronically if possible, by mail if not – so that the relevant province pays for the service. At regular intervals, the two provinces can determine proportions of use by residents of the two provinces – such as during a yearly audit – and thereby apportion the operating and capital costs for the next fiscal year accordingly. If all billing were handled electronically, as it surely will be in the future, such cost-sharing could be done weekly, monthly, quarterly, or whatever. By the same token, accountability and responsibility would be transparent; and ministers of health in each province would be able to answer questions about usage, cost, efficiencies, and planning in the time-frame defined by the audits or monitoring.

Note that exactly the same sharing and accounting would also be feasible for off-reserve citizens of Aboriginal Peoples Province. Instead of a short car or bus ride from reserve to town, these people would travel from one part of a city to a nearby hospital of their choice (or their doctor's choice). Billing would be automatic. Since income tax is, as we have seen, non-territorial, those citizens of Aboriginal Peoples Province who reside for extended periods off-reserve would (or at least could) declare their wish to be official residents, in which case their income taxes would revert to that province. The territorial province would then reclaim a portion of revenue from the non-territorial province to pay for the shared operating and capital costs. These procedures would require some legislative changes to take account of long-term physical residence without a change of official residence. There is, presumably, no reason why such changes could not apply among territorial provinces as well if that seemed to be preferred. Part of the value, I believe, in exploring these alternatives to territoriality concerns the potential benefits even when territorial provinces are retained. This could result in greater choice and flexibility for citizens.

The scale of sharing in the envisioned system would obviously greatly exceed what now occurs as a result of tourism, business travel, and temporary residence in another province. As just suggested, however, the example of joint or shared jurisdiction and administration between Aboriginal Peoples Province and territorial provinces might have a demonstration effect. Then the territorial provinces might find it advantageous – either for cost reasons or to satisfy citizens with unusual living arrangements such as 'commuting couples' who live or work in different provinces – to share some or all of their health systems.

These suggestions may not seem very radical since they constitute incremental changes beyond current practice. By themselves they may not involve fundamentally different arrangements. But they represent a new and beneficial mind-set based on a habit of cooperation rather than conflict, sharing for mutual benefit of citizens rather than the zero-sum attitudes of 'what you get, I lose.' This orientation should become more visible and marked, the more jurisdictions or functions which are shared. Besides health, provinces might share with Aboriginal Peoples Province many other jurisdictions, including highway construction and maintenance, fire fighting, secondary and post-secondary education, tax collection and auditing staffs, environmental regulation, licensing of some private businesses, and many others. Some jurisdictions might never be shared, since most aboriginal communities seem to place great emphasis on their own police and administration of justice.[15] Leaving aside such jurisdictions, one can ask next whether the territorial provinces might benefit from joint jurisdiction in some of these areas. This already occurs in the Maritime region to a limited extent, but more of it might be helpful. This topic deserves much greater treatment, but it would be a digression in this context.

In earlier chapters, I observed that one value of all-purpose territorial political units has been simplicity of administration. People who are *here* are part of *us*, and thus they share in *our* entitlements. As the technology of identification has evolved, so has the value of territory as a device for sorting and targeting people. When we all some day carry 'smart cards' or use electronic sensing of fingerprints or retinal scans, physical location will have less and less relevance for entitlement, billing for services, or sharing costs. Indeed, technology affects some of the other jurisdictions mentioned above. For example, very large-scale, efficient road-building equipment or forest-fire-fighting bombers may be more than some provinces need, whereas earlier, cheaper, and less efficient versions may have been suited to smaller localities.

Let us be clear, however, about what is being suggested or recommended. I am not arguing that sharing jurisdictions will solve all problems or that all political units should be non-territorial. Instead I am asserting that we should get past our longheld assumptions about territoriality and exclusive jurisdictions so that we can address questions about the most fair, beneficial, or efficient mix of political units. By focusing on some non-territorial provinces, one may try to achieve greater equity or justice for groups which have been marginalized, as many francophones and aboriginals have, for decades or centuries. What this chapter and the previous one have tried to show is that there are no obstacles to doing so which are inherent in either federalism or administration. Whether we should undertake shared jurisdictions or create non-territorial provinces are political questions now that technology has enabled their execution. The next section will explore a further implication of the underlying logic of greater cooperation by examining concurrent federal and provincial jurisdictions.

ASYMMETRIC FEDERALISM

The faith in exclusive jurisdictions for federal and provincial governments has proved groundless.[16] Except for a few cases, such as currency and military defence, none of the jurisdictions has remained exclusive in practice. In some cases, deceptive terminology disguises overlap; for example, exclusive provincial jurisdiction over 'education' but federal jurisdiction over 'training.' In other cases, courts have delineated 'aspects' of the same jurisdictions; for example, different aspects of banking or insurance or trade. In three cases, concurrent jurisdictions have been entrenched in the Constitution Act: immigration and agriculture with federal paramountcy; and old age pensions with provincial paramountcy.

It is time, I believe, to recognize that both orders of government have legitimate interests in many, if not most, jurisdictions now considered exclusive to one or the other. These jurisdictions should become concurrent with paramountcy by one or the other order of government. Usually paramountcy can be decided on the basis of which domain currently has exclusive jurisdiction in s. 91 (federal) and s. 92 (provincial) of the Constitution Act, 1867. At the least, that could be the 'default' option; changes would have to be negotiated item by item. As a result, one would deal with several issues now causing difficulties. One could reduce the amount of litigation over which order of government has jurisdiction, thereby saving money on court costs and, even more importantly, reducing delays in implementing programs. One might also foster an attitude of cooperation and responsibility, as argued in the previous section. This would be a welcome change, from citizens' points of view at least, in avoiding the now common efforts to protect one's turf and avoid responsibility for contentious or costly issues.

Even more beneficial would be the sense of empowerment in some provinces – notably Quebec, but also British Columbia and Alberta – which have long argued that their needs and local circumstances, being different, should result in extra powers to meet those needs or to reflect locally specific political demands. This would not constitute, as many so-called Canadian 'nationalists' have alleged, an evisceration of federal powers or 'caving in' to the provinces, since the federal government would gain access to some provincial jurisdictions without the bullying or subterfuge now so common.

The largest single benefit of shared jurisdictions, in my estimation, would be the entrenchment of a flexible form of asymmetric federalism. This type of federalism has usually been resisted for three reasons. The first has been an assumption that it runs counter to the equality of the provinces. The concept of equality has several meanings – equal legal standing, fair treatment, uniformity, homogeneity, reciprocity, and equal opportunity, among others. One should note that the provinces have equal standing in most respects – in constitutional revisions, in the right to attend first ministers' conferences, in reference cases, and a host of other matters. They also vary enormously in treatment: number of senators (some are parts of regions, others constitute a whole region), equalization grants, transfer payments, deviations from proportional representation in the House of Commons (small provinces are over-represented, large ones are under-represented), provisions regarding terms of entry into Confederation, provisions regarding the status of Catholic or dissentient schools and of the two official languages, and many others. There is no homogeneity or uniformity; and thus legal equality rather than these types of equality should be our focus. If all were to share jurisdictions legally, equality would be preserved. Equality is not the same as uniformity.

The second objection revolves around the role of members of Parliament. If a province has jurisdiction over some matters that other provinces have left to the federal government, then MPs from the former province, it is alleged, should not vote on those matters since that federal legislation would not affect their province.[17] Concurrent jurisdictions clearly do not raise this issue, or otherwise one would have heard concerns about the three concurrent jurisdictions now shared or about problems in countries using mainly concurrent jurisdictions. They also fail to raise the issue because exercise of a head of power is totally voluntary and can be taken up or put aside as needs be, whether under the present examples of concurrent jurisdiction or any future instances. Thus, no MPs would have to abstain on any issues before Parliament, and one would not need elaborate procedures for determining who was allowed to vote on which bills or amendments. Differential treatment of provinces in a particular piece of legislation has never up to now disqualified some MPs from voting on any bill, whether concerning unemployment insurance, fisheries, regional economic stimulus, the Quebec Pension Plan, or transfer payments – all of which differ enormously in intent and in impact on different provinces or regions within provinces. Urban MPs vote on farm subsidies, and rural MPs on urban airports, ports, hospitals, and the like.

The final objection concerns 'special status,' and especially its entrenchment in the constitution. When entrenched, it cannot change in response to evolving circumstances. The most common example hypothesizes that Quebec might someday be notably less French, and thus not deserve special powers to protect its Frenchness. Leaving aside the fact that no projection of current trends has envisioned French becoming a minority language in Quebec within the next century or more, one should note that, once concurrent jurisdictions were established, the current proposal requires no constitutional change to reflect changing circumstances. If Quebec decided that French could not or need not be protected, it could simply cease to exercise the powers available to it, or to exercise them less vigorously. Likewise, as Ontario's francophone population grows, that province could use such powers more than at present, or leave the problem to La Francophonie.

Let us put aside these objections and focus on how concurrent jurisdictions would work in practice. Then we can assess their value in asymmetric federalism. The simplest description of what would occur in the immediate future might be that Quebec and British Columbia would occupy most heads of jurisdiction, Alberta and Ontario almost as many, and the less affluent provinces fewer of them. Furthermore, what each province chose to do in any given concurrent jurisdiction would be, to a greater or lesser degree, different from activities in that jurisdiction undertaken by the other provinces. In other words, provincial experimentation would occur, and sometimes other provinces or the federal government would emulate the program. Sometimes, unique local needs would engender programs in one or more provinces which were of no interest to the rest of the provinces. Federal programs in areas of concurrent jurisdiction might also be quite different in each province or region, as they often are now in areas of exclusive jurisdiction. All of this variety should be judged by its value in reaching the stated objectives; it should not be sought soley for its own sake or condemned simply because it occurs. Variety does not in itself weaken Canada, despite what some advocates of federal power claim.

Consider one further likely consequence of concurrent jurisdictions. At present most governments feel obliged to 'occupy' their jurisdictions in order to 'head off' potential encroachments by the other order of government. 'Use it or lose it' seems to cover many situations. If the constitution made plain that each order could move in or out of a domain without risking a battle, retaliation, or loss of standing, concerns might be lessened and tempers might subside. If these speculations proved correct, then each order of government could rationally consider as a course of action the option of doing less but doing it better. One might see, thereby, a variety of mixes of public and private administration in different places or different orders of government.[18] Some mixtures might prove less costly or more effective or more popular, and thus other governments might learn from them. As noted in chapter 1, this occurs at the municipal level.

But some critics will assert that this recommendation is purely academic. No political leaders would wish to share jurisdictions. Of course, one may point to other federal systems such as those of Australia and the United States, where shared jurisdictions are much more common, indeed the norm. Even in Canada, there has been considerable enthusiasm for concurrent jurisdictions, and that is why I have proposed them here. The fact that the most recent advocacy of these ideas came from Quebec – and, in particular, from the Allaire Report in 1991[19] – has meant that most observers reacted negatively, fearing that they would be labelled separatists or be seen as weakening the federal government or as 'giving in' to Quebec. Regardless of the source and regardless of the motives of the Allaire Committee, these innovative ideas deserve evaluation in their own right.

So few have been the solutions offered for Canada's political difficulties, that one cannot afford to overlook any that seem to have support from influential groups. When analysis from the perspective of non-territorial solutions to aboriginal and francophone problems converges with suggestions designed to keep Quebec within the constitutional framework, one should be especially careful to weigh their advantages and disadvantages reasonably and not be put off by facile assumptions. Numbers alone would require us to consider these ideas seriously, since the combined populations of Quebec, La Francophonie, and Aboriginal Peoples Province add up to about nine million citizens, or almost one-third of the population of Canada.

There have always been many ways in which the provinces have been different or unique. Size, affluence, mix of economic activities, ethnic origins of population, proportion of aboriginals, types of natural resources, and climate constitute only a few of these dimensions. If one were to allow each province to choose the jurisdictions it deemed most important to its well-being – even if some chose to let the federal government exercise them on its behalf, as currently happens in many cases – the asymmetry would be one more way in which federalism tried to balance local and national interests. Another way of stating the point would note that asymmetry amounts to respecting regional differences. If one went one step further, one could imagine a different pattern of public and private means of service delivery in each province. Finally, the ultimate asymmetry would involve creating some non-territorial provinces when those could more adequately answer the needs of groups long neglected in the politics of territorial provinces.

SCOPE AND SCALE OF GOVERNMENTS

Existing provinces vary widely in area and population. The hypothesized non-territorial provinces would, of course, vary in area – essentially none for La Francophonie and modest for Aboriginal Peoples Province. In population, they would both be medium in size, in the range of just under to just over a million, putting them in the same range as, or slightly larger than, Manitoba or Saskatchewan. As suggested, neither province would exercise exclusive jurisdiction over the full panoply of services taken as normal for territorial provinces. However, Aboriginal Peoples Province might undertake functions less common in some existing provinces, such as some aspects of punishment for criminal offences ('community policing'). In short, these two provinces might provide the occasion to think about the appropriate scope and scale of government. That follows partly from the asymmetries noted in the previous section, but it also grows out of a broader debate. Are there economies of scale in governments? Would jurisdictions of differing scope or scale be cheaper, more efficient, more effective, or more fair?

Robert Dahl raised some of these concerns over a quarter of a century ago in his article 'The City in the Future of Democracy.'[20] His central point was put starkly: the really important issues fall within the jurisdiction of political units (nation-states or sometimes states or provinces) which are much too large for meaningful citizen participation, and the political units where such participation can most meaningfully occur (cities and towns) lack jurisdiction over the big issues. Dahl recognized, of course, that there are exceptions, but he believed that these observations or generalizations were sufficiently accurate that they posed an extremely frustrating dilemma for modern politics.

It seems certain that some issues can only be dealt with on a large scale. Global warming, arms control, international trade, and the like cannot be left to private citizens or local governments. Many other topics which we currently assign to large national or sub-national units, however, do not have to be handled that way. Some can be administered centrally but non-territorially; some in very decentralized ways, whether territorially or not; and some might be just as well left in private hands. The *scale* of an activity does have many of the negative qualities which Dahl identified, but he neglected other dimensions. If one relaxes assumptions about territoriality – as I have tried to show in this chapter and the previous one – two aspects open up. First, *scope* of government (that is, public vs private provision of services) can be more easily addressed because it is generally true that private organizations are non-territorial. Secondly, one may entertain the possibility that different elements of government may have different scale; that is, congruent boundaries are not necessary even in territorial jurisdictions but less so in non-territorial. Finally, one may speculate that the federal deficit may motivate a devolution of fiscal responsibility to provincial and municipal levels, which thereby puts matters closer to the people affected.

Chapter 1 noted that much of local government consisted of non-congruent territorial units, and thus of units that violate some assumptions about territoriality (especially exclusivity). By considering non-territorial aspects of administration in chapter 4 and non-territorial federalism in this chapter, the debate Dahl canvassed may be seen in very different perspectives. Why must one choose between large and remote jurisdictions versus small but insignificant ones? Why not experiment with mixes of territorial and non-territorial forms and with different mixes of public and private delivery of services? Why not, in short, try to fit the solution to the scope and scale of the problem? That is, I believe, the fundamental idea behind the vivid slogan of the environmental movement: think globally, act locally.

The hypothesized provinces discussed here will not solve all the serious problems. They were not meant to be all-purpose solutions. They were intended to offer ways of dealing with specific problems of long neglected groups. Beyond that, of course, they should serve to stimulate thought about ways in which we limit our thinking by accepting as given some long-standing assumptions about territoriality and the many consequences which flow from them. Just as 'think globally, act locally' also means 'do not think or act dichotomously; question your assumptions when faced with a dilemma,' so one may use concepts like non-territorial federalism to unblock apparent dilemmas such as Dahl posed. This book constitutes an attempt to unblock our thinking on a wide range of issues.

Unconventionalizing or deconventionalizing our thinking also involves questioning the labels we apply to institutions. Once one considers non-territorial forms of federalism seriously, one can address more flexibly matters like the scope and scale of government because one may decouple the usual means to common ends. When federalism has this more adaptable meaning, one can perhaps see that non-territorial federalism has been discussed under other labels for decades. For example, 'consociationalism' generally means two (or more) parallel social formations (such as Calvinist and Catholic in the Netherlands) which share the same territory but are bounded and distinct in political and social organization. So are Aboriginal Peoples Province and La Francophonie. Another example is 'corporatism,' which involves trilateral decision-making about economic matters by joint bodies of business, labour, and government organization: a mixture of territorial and non-territorial forms as well as public and private. So are Aboriginal Peoples Province and La Francophonie.

To a person with only a hammer, the saying goes, all problems look like a nail. We can have more tools if we question territoriality, and so let us fit the solution more sensitively to the problem. This chapter has tried to do so for some political problems, and the next will examine some social implications of this perspective.

# 6

A Community of Communities

Assumptions about territoriality lead directly and indirectly to particular concepts of community. Because these assumptions narrow the focus of attention to certain kinds of communities, relaxing the assumptions permits a consideration of other types or forms of community. Just as territorial exclusivity and sovereignty imply that some all-purpose political organization is necessary, so these ideas together lead one to believe that there should be some overarching community: for most people today that community is the nation or nation-state, although historically it has taken other forms such as a universal religion or a city-state or a small town. To question the need for an all-purpose political organization also calls into question the notion of an overarching community, except in the sense of a community which serves as a framework for a multiplicity of non-competing communities – in short, a community of communities.[1]

The modern concept of individual citizenship grew up in tandem with the idea of the nation-state, especially after the French Revolution. Dwellers in nation-states now take for granted that the state defines and reflects their citizenship.[2] As we question the basis and durability of nation-states, we implicitly question the nature and basis of citizenship. Thus, as this chapter explores new or heightened forms of community, it will return repeatedly to implications for understanding citizenship.

What specific kinds of communities, therefore, would flourish or be more visible in the unbundled world envisioned here? One can also inquire about the potential for greater democracy or authoritarianism under these new conditions. These queries have special urgency because most people react to the idea of an unbundled world in two ways: either they fear that the centre cannot hold and 'things fall apart' or that the apparent looseness and informality of political structures will tempt would-be dictators to impose a new order. Since both fears are not unreasonable, we should weigh these possibilities carefully. Although they may be addressed at several points, I will try to pull the threads together in the later section entitled 'Tyranny à la carte.'

At the outset it should be stated that 'community' will be used in this chapter in a fairly strict sense. The concept of *Gemeinschaft* was an ideal type, and it is doubtful that many communities instantiated its features.[3] At the other end of the continuum is another ideal type which Tönnies called *Gesellschaft*. The latter might be translated as group or aggregate and rested on an instrumental or contractual basis in contrast to the 'natural' or 'organic' community defined by *Gemeinschaft*. For present purposes, I will focus on communities united on the basis of strong ties of various kinds. Thus these hypothesized communities will be closer to the *Gemeinschaft* than to the *Gesellschaft* pole of the continuum, although they will differ in degree of approximation and in the mixture of characteristics. Territory has been one of the strong ties underlying many communities – whether tribe, nation, or neighbourhood. But there are other strong ties, as we shall see, and they may suggest by contrast what a territorial community actually means.

The reason I emphasize that the entities discussed below are communities rather than mere categories of individuals concerns responsibility. A community consists of people who care about or feel responsible for each other's well-being. Relationships involve caring and responsibility and may be thought of as a form of community at a fairly intimate level. We will see below that they can be an important bridge between the individual and collective levels of analysis, even in something as legal and public as basic human rights. The extent of responsibility may be limited in different ways depending on the basis or type of community, but to use 'community' meaningfully there should be mutual obligations. One expects that the members of a community may share a fellow-feeling for each other, a warmth, pride in belonging, or something equivalent. Those feelings would seem natural for most members of most kinds of communities, but the defining core feature of a community is a sense of obligation, of mutual responsibility. As we shall see, territoriality is not a necessary condition for mutual responsibility. This is obvious where ethnic groups, families, or private clubs are concerned, but many other types of community may be distinguished as well.

One frequently encounters assertions that there has been a loss of community in the modern world. While this could signify different concerns for different people, I will focus on the loss of territorial community. The use of the singular form – loss of community rather than loss of communities – suggests to me that a focus on the all-purpose territorial community can be defended. In doing so, I should not be understood as denigrating concerns about other types of community, such as families or marriages. Instead, the focus in this book on territoriality finds its parallel in territorial communities and in a concern with their apparent decline in absolute or relative importance.

A final caveat should be mentioned. The fact that I will focus on communities which are in process of forming will suggest to some people that they are not 'natural' communities and thus can hardly stand in the place of natural communities like nations, races, or families. The reader will recall the discussion in chapter 1 about the 'constructedness' of nations and should therefore be prepared to accept that 'natural' is a label one can apply only after forgetting how the community – or the idea of the community – was constructed. I have also mentioned various alternative types and forms of nations, families, and other constructs; and that variety should also remind us that evolution of communities and concepts has a historical basis and is not 'given' or preordained in the manner implied by words like 'natural.' The feeling of loss of some communities derives in part from the multiple uses of communities and in part from ignorance of how those communities came to be what they are because they have existed a long time.

So the first task in this chapter is to unpack some of the assumptions which seem to underlie 'old fashioned' territorial communities. Then I will examine in turn four other concepts of community which seem likely to play a more and more important role in the future, or at least to take on added significance when territory is less often the basis of community. In some cases, I will raise questions about consent and community, and in others about obligations not based on consent. In all cases, discussion of types of community cannot be separated from the nature of 'the individual' or 'individuality.' For a considerable period of time, roughly since the Enlightenment in the eighteenth century, it has been assumed that individuals needed protection from at least some kinds of communities or collectivities; this dichotomy should be questioned, since different kinds of community pose different threats or offer different benefits. Finally, I will reconsider the territorial community in light of the discussion of the other four; this review should highlight any contrasts among them. Non-territorial communities are unlikely to replace territorial communities, but they will supplement the territorial communities and will gain in number and significance. Each type of community appears to have its own benefits and costs, and one hopes that by deploying them in better balance, the benefits can be exploited more often and the costs minimized.

GREATER AND LESSER NEIGHBOURHOODS

Territorial communities have taken many forms over the centuries. Among them, one should note especially parishes, villages, towns and cities, city-states, nation-states, and in recent periods neighbourhoods. Of course, all might be called neighbourhoods, except that the word has come to mean something like 'small residential areas without political autonomy.' They are, therefore, sub-units of some wider geographic or territorial organization such as a town or city. They might equally be viewed, however, as templates of what a territorial community has to offer: intimacy, connectedness, fellow-feeling, rootedness, and a host of other presumptions. All of these 'neighbourly' characteristics have been deemed important in many times and places; they are in a sense the sinews of a society. Such features are said to be less common or less strong in the anonymity of the city and in an era of rapid mobility.

Indeed, it is easy to imagine that the unbundled world would lack many of these appealing attributes. Yet people would presumably still live in a neighbourhood, and I shall argue that one may even live in many more such neighbourhoods. Before coming to that conclusion, however, we should examine carefully these territorial communities, and we should be particularly careful to keep separate myth and reality.

Robert Bellah and his colleagues, in *Habits of the Heart*, have written a poignant book. The subtitle reveals the concerns which motivated the research: 'Individualism and Commitment in American Life.'[4] They argue that individualism is a modern phenomenon, unknown in older, traditional societies; it represents 'the new man' which several nineteenth-century observers found in America. 'We are concerned that this individualism may have grown cancerous – that it may be destroying those social integuments that Tocqueville saw as moderating its more destructive potentialities ...' (p. vii). Elsewhere they refer to 'ontological individualism, the idea that the individual is the only firm reality' (p. 276).

Many of the people they interviewed expressed concerns about how individualism had become too much of a good thing. The retreat into nuclear family, career, leisure activities, and the like had weakened or made impossible the older kind of community, which seemed to be conceived by them along the lines of a New England town with its town meeting and a 'commons.' And, of course, with industrialization, social and geographic mobility, and urban sprawl, such towns or communities have become less solidary than heretofore.

The issue in this context, however, is not the survival of such communities but their nature. Was territory an essential part of their strength or their appeal? If we relax the assumptions of territoriality, what kinds of communities – with what strengths and appeals – might fill the gap? We will also find that the concept of the individual personality takes on new meanings which some have called 'postmodern.'

The first thing to note about territorial communities is that they were not based entirely or even primarily on shared interests or values. This is, I believe, a fair assessment of them, whether we think of a village, a city, or a nation. Instead, there were some shared values and interests, some complementary ones (a division of labour, in effect), and some conflicting or competing interests and values. Although there may be instances of communities which all shared the same religion, these have been exceptional in the last few centuries in the West. And even those were internally divided along economic and class lines, leadership in the community, type of family, gender roles, race, and the like. Of course, the larger the community, the more obvious the lines of cleavage (compared to shared values) would appear. Indeed, at the level of cities, provinces, and nations, what was shared were often grievances as much as values: one thinks of the Prairie farmers or Maritime fishermen and their common appreciation of the exploiters in central Canada. Sharing in broad communities often came down to civic pride, nationalism, regional assertiveness, or (in Canada especially) loyalty to a local hockey team.

It is crucial to emphasize the relative rarity of shared values and interests. It is all too easy to wax nostalgic about the warm and cosy organic communities of yesteryear, and thus to overlook differences of gender, religion, class, affluence, status, ancestry, and education. Of course, each village shared its 'commons' and associated facilities like wells or bridges, but common values were not always obvious.

Territory played a role that was invisible so long as we concentrate on values, interests, and feelings of solidarity. In all of human history until very recently, living in a place threw you together with others whether you wanted their company or not. Propinquity was the underlying, taken-for-granted variable which explains several features of these communities. Of course, there have always been mavericks, rebels, and strong-willed risk-takers who found ways to move on, especially in nineteenth-century North America and other 'frontier societies.' In settled times and places – that is, most of the world, most of the time – face-to-face, cheek-by-jowl, and living together through thick-and-thin have been the norm. Even when avenues of mobility became institutionalized, as in the case, for instance, of priests, traders, and warriors, most had a 'home base,' a community that they came back to, although it might not be where they started. That *place* – natal or found – determined many if not all of one's intimate relations and eventually one's identities.

For many people, territorial propinquity was a blessing to be cherished. Closeness to family, rooted identity, familiar traditions, a shared way of life, and spiritual closeness combined to provide a meaning and richness that a great many people today feel are missing or weak. For others, propinquity was a curse represented by many clichés: conformity, snobbishness, intolerance, clannishness, inwardness, and isolation. One person's rootedness in an organic community became another's claustrophobia in a suffocating prison without walls. The balance or proportion of such feelings must have varied in different places and over time.

This chapter returns to these images of community based on territory. But they can be appreciated more fully, I believe, by comparing them to unbundled communities of several kinds. They are all communities of responsibility; they differ in terms of to whom one is responsible, for what one is responsible, and for whom one is responsible. This is also true of one's roles in territorial communities, but there 'to whom,' 'for what,' and 'for whom' are heavily dependent on propinquity; when unbundled, our responsibilities will be more focused and specific while wider in territorial extent.

TECHNOLOGY AND COMMUNITY

Before examining my hypothesized communities, let us review very briefly our earlier conclusions about the role of technology. One should most of all recall that technology enables (or disables) rather than determines situations. It opens or makes more visible previously blocked or unnoticed options; but having more or newer options does not guarantee which option someone will choose. Thus, the four types or aspects of unbundled communities discussed here represent hypotheses; they encompass envisioning of options rather than predictions about specific behaviour or institutions.

A Community of Communities 173

It is worth reminding ourselves that, as Mander argued, many technologies have evinced a 'logic' favouring centralization. The technologies of the near future, by contrast, should have a different thrust. Decentralizing would be an adequate description, I suppose, for technologies like cable or satellite television since they induce fragmented or specialized audiences and undermine the networks. Others, however, are neither centralizing nor decentralizing since they involve no centre and no satellite centres. Networks or webs are not generally centralizing, but what I envision is the multiplication of so many independent webs or networks that decentralization fails to capture the dimension at issue or the degree of autonomy. Thus, I have relied throughout this book on 'unbundled' as a more appropriate image.

To capture the sense of what it might be like in unbundled communities, imagine yourself in a telecommunications network in your home – TV, fax, personal computer, electronic-mail, and whatever new gizmos may soon appear. If you wish to hook up with all the people in the world who share an interest with you, the limits consist only of language barriers and the time and money you are willing to devote to the task. The interests might be lofty – spiritual, religious, artistic, or humanitarian – or quite mundane – model airplanes, scuba diving, or *Star Trek* trivia. The technology enables you to further those interests or values which matter to you.

Cost should be borne in mind. Most of the relevant technology on which the hypothesized communities will be based seems likely to be very inexpensive. Already we have seen telephones, radios, TV, and personal computers steadily reduced in price – both absolutely and relative to other technologies such as cars, refrigerators, or golf clubs. Newer and related technologies – such as fax, cellular phones, and fibre optic networks – are certain to be improved while becoming cheaper. Ironically, these ever cheaper technologies may also prove to be extremely profitable as enterprises (e.g., cable companies or cellular phone producers). Even technology which is expensive has seen unit costs decline. For example, airplanes go up in price but carry more passengers and are deployed more efficiently, so that the real cost in constant dollars per passenger mile has gone down dramatically. Likewise, long distance telephone rates are now a fraction of what they were in our parents' generation or even a decade ago. Thus, even if there are entry fees for 'electronic highways,' it should be the case that participation in the hypothesized communities will be open to the majority of the populations of affluent countries and significant proportions of every country. In short, we are not speculating only about socially elite communities.

Finally, let me remind the reader about the size of personal communications technology. Not only do lap-top computers and pocket cellular phones occupy less space, they are thus less visible and more easily concealed, moved, and disguised. If one is concerned about Big Brother, these and other devices should continue to be more and more difficult to keep track of as they proliferate, shrink, and become cheaper. This is perhaps another dimension of decentralization and another aspect of 'enabling.'

With these features of new and future technology in mind, let us turn to four types of community of a non-territorial nature. Some implications will be mentioned as we proceed, but later sections will build on the basic descriptions in an effort to show how revolutionary are the changes discussed here. In particular, the chapter leads most fundamentally to new or enhanced understandings of citizenship.

COMPLEMENTARY VALUES

For over a century, sociologists have contrasted the organic local community (*Gemeinschaft*) with its modern replacement. This newer community, and it is a community, derives its cohesion from a division of labour which is primarily economic and occupational, but which perhaps exists in other ways as well. A central feature of the division of labour is complementarity. People stay together because they are different; they can do things for each other in a non-competitive (or not entirely competitive) way without losing their individuality in sameness, conformity, or shared values and interests.

What has been true of territorial communities organized around a division of labour will also be true of non-territorial communities organized around a division of labour. It is pointless and probably futile to try to categorize all such communities, depending on the particular type of division of labour. This is especially true when the new types are only now coming into focus and changing rapidly. Instead consider two types of unbundled communities which have existed long enough to provide a basis of generalization – 'multinational' corporations and universities as centres of research.

Chapter 3 reviewed many features of 'multinational' corporations. One conclusion, of course, was that 'multinational' may be a misnomer because that label implies that nations are involved. Instead we saw that these large corporations have become increasingly de-coupled from any particular nations. This is one reason the label 'transnational' is used frequently and 'multinational' less often. Fellow-feeling among employees would today probably derive more from complementarity of activity in the shared community of the corporation. Even that overstates the simplicity of the contrast, since there would almost certainly be several communities – teams, networks, multiple hierarchies – and, of course, 'the corporation' might be a conglomerate of several vertically or horizontally linked companies, each with a sense of community. Interdependence would take several forms, including stages of production, joint supplies, and friendships, among others. Perhaps one could speak of such corporations as forms of non-territorial federalism.

One must recall that this sort of community is not territorial. Of course, all employees live somewhere, and many may live in the same somewhere, especially if they are involved in a particular stage of goods manufacturing. They live near people who are not part of this particular community (the corporation) but have their own equivalent. Corporate communities, however, are knitted together by their complementarity, just as nations are by theirs. The inclusiveness may be different, the kinds of fellow-feeling may be different, and the territorial base contrasts with the non-territorial, but they are communities deriving a major part of their strength from complementary interests and values. In terms of the metaphor of communities of responsibility, members of corporations and other organizations of this sort find cohesion in the question: on whom do I depend and who depends on me, reciprocally?

The academic research community (and perhaps related researchers in business, government, etc.) also exemplifies a division of labour, and thus complementary values and interests, without necessarily having a territorial base. Teaching, by contrast, may often have a territorial base (in each university) because of the interconnectedness of curricula and programs, although 'distance education' does not. Within the research community, there is obviously a broad division of labour: physics, chemistry, history, political science, etc. For many academics, that complementarity may well define a community (especially when government funding or threats to academic freedom are concerned). A more specific community derives from a more detailed division of labour. Within one 'discipline' (physics, history, etc.), scholars depend on each other in quite literal senses. They are peers (of greater or lesser renown, but peers) who rely on the work of others because specialization is unavoidable. No one can master all of one discipline, and very often the degree of specialization is extremely narrow. One comes to trust and depend on one's peers, and they on you, because of the need to know more than one can learn alone. Although some communities involve more than this sense of trust, division of labour can create durable and significant communities.

Specialization and communal endeavour must be put in perspective. There are also shared values and interests (such as integrity, non-plagiarism, openness of sources, and academic freedom). And, of course, there are rivalries and conflicts and a degree of ignorance. At bottom, however, the recognition of complementarity is surely as crucial as the shared values and interests, since the latter are usually shared across disciplines but do not lead to as much interaction or fellow-feeling as do the specializations within a discipline. Lest we glorify these specialties, one should recall that they are occasionally barriers to fruitful collaboration (e.g., between political scientists and economists, or between people working on the politics of different countries or periods). Whatever those 'costs' or deficiencies, the point here is that a strong, vibrant, enduring community can find a base in complementary interests with no territorial base or limits.

Both of these examples, corporate and academic, reveal the same underlying 'ethic' which provides the sinews or integuments (as Bellah et al. call them). Knowing that others depend on you, as you on them, not only means that one is linked by an interest in a joint endeavour. It can also mean a sense of obligation and responsibility for each other even if you have never met face-to-face, and even if you have never 'consented' to these mutual obligations in any explicit form. If you do not do your job well, someone else will suffer; and vice versa. This can be highly motivating if presented reasonably and organized non-hierarchically. Coordination may be more obvious in a corporation, if for no other reason than the need for scheduling the arrival of parts or components, but it is also the hallmark of academic conferences, publications, and electronic 'colleges' or networks. Responsibility for each other, a sense of common endeavour, and motivation to cooperate in pursuit of excellence or productivity: these are hardly descriptions of superficial communities compared to 'organic' traditional communities. To the extent one expects that such complementary communities without a territorial base will become more common (or more visible) in the unbundled world, one need not fear that they herald the end of community.

SHARED VALUES AND INTERESTS

To share values or interests requires a focus, since each person embodies many values and interests. In most cases, communities come to realize or actualize only a few that are deemed socially acceptable, useful, or in some other manner especially significant in the local culture. For example, handedness has, to my knowledge, never been considered a significant basis of shared values or interest, especially by right-handers. Other features wax and wane in significance: in 'Western' societies, religion used to be more important than it has been recently; and birth or ancestry has declined in proportion to increased emphasis on education, occupation, and other achieved statuses. Gender and sexual preference loom larger as bases of shared values or interests than in most eras or societies, at least for women or minority sexual orientations; males and heterosexuals have (usually unconsciously) shared the dominant values and interests because they have been the 'norms' for the dominant values.[5]

Sharing a value or interest is often a relatively weak basis of community since each person generally has many values and many interests, and they do not always reinforce or coincide. In particular, one is frequently 'cross-pressured' by sharing one value with someone but sharing another value with someone else. Class, religion, and recreation often pull one into different orbits. Of course, at some points in history, and even today in some countries, religion has proven a powerful community and not just within a nation. The Christian church in Europe until the Reformation, and Islam today, are examples of strongly coherent communities of shared values. That they have been replaced in most countries by other value systems, or at least must share their influence with other sources of value systems, can hardly be denied. But powerful 'world-view' systems are not the only basis of a shared community. Many forms of sharing rest on what by comparison to religions seem slender reeds like sports, a job, a type of automobile, whether children attend the same school, and living in a neighbourhood threatened in some way (the NIMBY phenomenon).

It was noted in the previous section that communities of complementary values often also involve shared values. But the former communities often are stronger or more intense or provide firmer motives for common action. This should not be surprising when we think back to earlier chapters on technology or economic relationships. Many of the newly prominent or more visible communities are best described by words like team, network, coordination, and function. Thus, one asks, who is like me in this respect? with whom do I share an interest in this or that? with whom am I 'in the same boat'? Because they involve specific relations in a non-territorial framework, there is no overarching value, interest, or community, again leaving aside religious communities where they still carry significant weight.

One suspects that these features go some way in explaining why many people lament the 'loss of community.'[6] If overarching, all-purpose, multifaceted communities are replaced by multiple communities, each of which brings out or highlights or rests on one specific characteristic, value, or interest, many people would feel that a richness has been lost. One might – indeed, almost certainly would – have a greater diversity of relationships in the unbundled world described here, but the specific communities might not overlap, or only slightly. Of course, some people – like myself – find that liberating, lending a degree of diversity and complexity to one's life which no single community can sustain.

Therefore, even if one finds these special-purpose communities of shared values more and more common, one can easily overlook the fact that they are 'community.' The use of singular or plural is perhaps the key: belonging to 'a community' is not the same as belonging to many communities (which do not coincide or fully overlap). Thus, judgments and evaluations of the unbundled world will surely differ. Nevertheless, bases of community have changed before in history, and people do not feel the loss of those now long forgotten. In time, most individuals come to know and appreciate the communities which matter in their own situations. In the transition period, it is easy to focus on what is lost rather than what is gained.

SOME IMPLICATIONS

Communities of shared values and those of complementary values have always existed. What seems to me novel about such communities – and perhaps the other types below – derives from the unbundling process described throughout this book. Instead of overlapping, congruent, and multi-purpose or multifaceted communities, 'packaged' as nation-bundles, I detect an increasing disjunction among communities. They are of different size, scope, and type; their boundaries do not coincide much or at all; memberships do not overlap in easily predictable ways; and knowing that an individual belongs to a particular group offers little purchase on predictions about that person's other communities of involvement. Many observers have summarized some of these new features of individual identity and community organization as 'postmodern.' I prefer to use 'unbundled,' but this is a very similar orientation.[7]

Although we may come to recognize many surprising implications of these new communities as they become more prominent, I want to speculate about three likely consequences for our ways of thinking about individuals and their communities. By noting them here, the reader may more readily evaluate them in this and subsequent chapters. They will be sketched briefly even though their potential significance might warrant more extensive exploration.

The first implication concerns the mutual compatibility of the communities. As noted above, each person has countless characteristics, interests, and values; and so each may use these features to become part of a great many communities. Involvement in a community represents an affirmation of that feature of an individual's identity. It may also be a means of developing an identity or aspect of one's identity, a way to 'find oneself.' One may be limited to active involvement in only a few of the possible communities by energy, time constraints, or one's chosen balance between focus and diversity. One need not generally be limited, however, by incommensurable communities. That is, most unbundled communities may be *added* to an individual's repertoire and identity rather than substituted one for another. In this, they are similar to what social scientists used to call 'reference groups.' This has always been true of some communities, but the emphasis in certain periods on religion, nation, race, gender, or other mutually exclusive communities or categories may have obscured this feature or made it less remarkable.

Consider, for example, that chess fanatics linked by a computer network or other means may belong to many other communities too. These might include other hobbies, professional or occupational associations, charities, neighbourhood support groups, and a host of others. Adding new memberships does not entail choosing between them and one's prior involvement in other communities. They enlarge the person because they do not pose an 'either-or' choice, nor are they limited to territorially close neighbours. Of course, some communities may try to be 'exclusive' and thus to forbid some kinds of other memberships, as many religions have done. But most communities today can involve additions to one's identity rather than force one to make painful choices among these expressions of one's identity.

The second implication may be another way of stating what has just been described, but it is sufficiently important to warrant its own designation. This point involves what has usually been called 'cross-pressures' and concerns a positive evaluation in contrast to most previous analyses of them as debilitating, frustrating, or conflictual.[8] Of course, when communities pose contradictory injunctions or try to impose conformity to beliefs or codes of conduct in opposition to each other, individuals may have to choose among them; and this form of cross-pressure may have the consequences of delay or avoidance of decision-making commonly noted in the psychological literature. But when communities 'go their own way' and thus do not force choices among them, what look like cross-pressures from one point of view may look like extra options from another. In short, at least for many of the communities in the unbundled world, cross-pressures should turn out to enhance freedom of choice rather than to restrict it. They represent a multiplication of identities and hence an expansion of options and choices.

Finally, let us ask what an individual is and whether individuals and communities represent contradictory modes of organization. In the modern European world-view – that is, since the Enlightenment at least – political and social theories have argued, assumed, or concluded that individualism requires a lesser role for communities, and that communities can pose a threat to autonomous individuals. This debate goes to the heart of so many issues over the past few centuries that it would be fatuous of me to say it no longer should concern us. But there is, I believe, some reason to hope that the unbundled world can now move beyond that debate, not because of a consensual resolution of the intellectual challenge it poses but as a result of new types of communities which are less – or not at all – threatening to individualism, and as a result of post-modernist conceptualizations of what it means to be an individual.

In particular, one might say that an individual in the unbundled world consists of the intersection of multiple communities. One thing that makes a person uniquely different from others is the matrix of communities (some freely chosen and others inherited) as arenas of involvement and as expressions of the various facets of personality. Even if it were to happen that two individuals had identical community involvements, this would likely be seen as a bond between them rather than reason for concern about the viability of their individuality. Individual rights as defences or 'trumps' against oppressive political or social regimes still have value, but they need not be seen as antithetical to the rights of communities based on choice and responsibility to maintain themselves in order to strengthen individual's identities and to keep open their options. After all, the usual concern about 'mass society' has been that there were not enough competing or autonomous communities; hence, the right to maintain many communities can be viewed as both an individual and a collective right.[9]

The ability to add identities rather than being forced to substitute one for another; multiple identities and 'cross-pressures' enhancing rather than inhibiting one's options; and the anchoring of one's uniqueness in the complex constellation of communities to which one chooses to make commitments: these three implications of communities in the unbundled world appear to be mutually reinforcing elements of a broad syndrome which fits with our current self-image as autonomous individuals and stands in marked contrast to older notions of rank, status, and duty within an overarching community which claims all our loyalties. It also constitutes a postmodernist step beyond the dichotomy of individual and community. If each individual is, in effect, a community of the communities individually accepted or chosen, their threat to individuality dissolves in the choices freely made. The more extensive the globalization – and by definition the wider the awareness of diverse communities available – the greater support an individual's communities of choice offer to that uniqueness. The more global the standard, the more visible the uniqueness of local choice.

INSURANCE, THE SOCIALIZATION OF RISK,
AND DIVERSIFICATION

There are many risks in life, and only some are suitable as the basis of community. But insurance or socialization of risk can, I believe, be a powerful basis of community; and one which has territorial and non-territorial aspects. The question is: as territorial communities give way to non-territorial ones, how does the socialization of risk change? Most precisely, should one share the risks and attendant costs among categories of citizens or among residents of a place? This is a moral or 'fairness' question, but it is also a practical or administrative question about enforcement, efficiency, and types of risks.

One must make plain what insurance consists of; otherwise, the significance of the socialization of risk may be overlooked. Insurance obviously covers things like home fire and theft, various types of life insurance, and liability and collision for automobiles. Those are subject to the questions just posed, but so are a host of other matters that we often call by other names. These include military defence, health standards for food and drugs, workers' compensation, unemployment insurance, licensing of doctors and other professionals, and police functions like traffic control and personal security. In short, socialization of risk often involves functions of government and the provision of 'public goods.' Village life often involves this sense of insurance, as in cooperation against flood or fire or in gathering the harvest.

For present purposes, insurance as a form of community derives from inquiring about a sequence of questions relating to shared responsibility for certain kinds of risk. If something terrible happens to an individual, under what circumstances should responsibility rest on the person or family as opposed to sharing the costs more widely? Different eras and different societies have answered that question very differently. One has only to think of public hospital and medical insurance in Canada contrasted with private insurance in the 'free enterprise' climate of the United States. American doctors rant against 'socialized medicine' with an implicit definition of socialism as that which restricts their ability to set fees in a free market. But 'socialized' is the correct word in another sense, because the costs to individuals are spread across society. Of course, medical insurance in the United States also 'spreads the risks,' but only among the individuals who have voluntarily chosen to pay premiums to a particular company. In Canada, by contrast, the costs are amortized across the entire population of a province, and participation is almost entirely compulsory.

Ideological dispute over health and medical insurance may be contrasted with lack of dispute about other forms of insurance like military defence or most police functions. I doubt if anyone in Canada seriously believes that there should be private armies rather than the Canadian Forces. But these concepts of risk and insurance involve a continuum: public army; public police (RCMP, municipal, etc.), but also private police (department store detectives, home security patrols, and 'neighbourhood watch'); private 'policing' of many professional groups (doctors, accountants, etc.), but with recourse to the courts when one believes a breach has been ignored; governmental guarantee of bank solvency, but only up to a fixed amount and no guarantees about losses on the stock market (except where fraud can be proven); and so on with environmental externalities, noise regulations, and health codes for restaurants.

In all such examples, each nation, society, or group makes a judgment that certain kinds of risks should be shared, or shared up to some point or beyond some point. Other risks are personal, private affairs. The line is drawn differently in different periods as well, partly to reflect changing conceptions of justice or fairness and partly to reflect technological change. The rationales offered usually rest on various understandings of 'random' or 'unforeseen' events, disasters, catastrophes, and the like.

That is, problems arising from risks easily foreseen (stock market, futures trading) or from things 'brought on yourself' (leaving jewelry in the washroom at the airport) are virtually never deemed to be other than a personal responsibility. Others we believe should be shared because they could 'happen to anyone' (and you were just unlucky) or because people involved have characteristics which make them especially likely to be affected (workers in dangerous occupations which are socially useful) or because the subjects lack control of their life chances (children, mentally retarded or disturbed, destitute).

There are several key points relevant to community:

1. Cultural definitions of appropriate types or degrees of risk define, in effect, the community, as those who share the assumptions.

2. Social conventions about the balance between 'taking responsibility' and 'sharing the burden' imply boundaries around a community sharing the conventions but may also involve ideological debates not shared by other communities. (Is smoking still a private activity?)

3. As technology changes, what is 'random' shrinks or expands, and thus we adopt new community standards of acceptable risk and degree of risk-sharing.

4. If risks are to be shared, that sharing creates a moral community, even though one may never meet most members of the community, because it amounts to an answer to questions like the following: From whom do I have the right to expect help? To whom do I owe an obligation to help? Under what circumstances?

5. 'Public' insurance has nearly always been territorially based (provincial health insurance, workers' compensation boards, federal food inspection), whereas 'private' insurance (home, car, life, etc.) has almost never been territorial because it has spread the risk among people who choose to join rather than among every resident of a place.

What is public and what is private has been changing, and the unbundled world reflects these (and other) changes. In part one may recognize these trends by more frequent reference to government 'overload,' the desire to 'privatize' government functions, or the need to encourage government to 'shoulder its responsibilities' (for the poor, for the environment, for visible minorities, etc.). It is not entirely a one-way street: government probably ought to do less of some things but more of others. Doing less usually involves, as we saw in chapter 3, opening up the markets for 'free enterprise,' while doing more generally entails socializing risks which did not receive as much emphasis in the past (right to employment equity, lifestyles such as smoking or promiscuity, and environmental damage).

As assumptions about territoriality change, are relaxed, or disappear completely, the unbundled world should conceptualize insurance in new ways. In particular, public as well as private insurance will see a shift in focus from sharing risks among residents of a place (neighbourhood, province, nation) to sharing risks among categories of citizens (who are often not all in one place like a nation). One dimension has already come to prominence: international responsibility for environmental degradation is leading to a more common belief that nations should not be entirely sovereign because of the costs to their neighbours. Another dimension may gain prominence: what are seen by the majority as 'needless risks' (smoking, sky-diving, bearing unwanted children) may be excluded from the socialization of risk because the activities are deemed 'anti-social' and are judged to have costly repercussions for more 'responsible' citizens.[10] Put in these stark terms – 'why should I pay for your mistakes?' – the degree to which a community may be based on socialization of risk (or threatened by it) is made visible.

Without wishing to debate the particular issues, I do want to emphasize the intimate connection among these issues and the nature of communities in the unbundled world. The connection, as suggested above, takes several forms:

1. The debate, the lines of cleavage, the 'sides,' are forced to deal with each other and therefore constitute a community, however divided, whereas other people do not share that debate.

2. The debate takes place because the risks are agreed upon by most categories of citizens; that is, a new understanding of what risks are acceptable or not, which are personal or not, has developed; and agreeing upon those matters creates a sense of community.

3. As the previous two chapters argued, administration of a policy (including socializing a risk) will sometimes be better carried out in a non-territorial fashion. This is especially clear when 'socialization of risk' involves global or very large-scale externalities, but also when socialization occurs across generations. We have already seen the beginnings of a debate about what types and amounts of budgetary deficits are unfair to future generations, as well as the implications of environmental use for future residents of Earth. Up to now, 'future generations'

have been assumed to be those in 'our territory,' but this should be less true in the unbundled world.

These trends should not mark the end of territorial risk-sharing. Instead I assume there will emerge a new balance among territorial and non-territorial communities of risk. Whether wholly non-territorial or only partly so, communities founded on or built around risk-sharing count as real communities. After all, they address more directly than most types of communities the question of who shares my burdens and who has the right to expect my help, however indirectly. It may not be neighbours who share as often or as exclusively as heretofore, but communities of sharing will exist.

Risk has another meaning in economics. It means that one can calculate the odds and thereby decide if one finds them acceptable. Risk in economic theory and practice stands in contrast to uncertainty, which consists of an inability to calculate the odds at all. Uncertainty in this sense probably corresponds to what most people understand by risk as I have used it above. Let us turn briefly to the economist's sense of risk and ask if we might wish to 'socialize' it.

Whether we realize it or not, each society does socialize risk in businesses to some degree. Forms of insurance vary in terminology and extent, but they include food and building inspections, auditing requirements, depletion allowances for non-renewable resources, and a host of others. Part of the rationale for these types of risk-sharing concerns the protection of businesses from liability by imposing requirements on all businesses in a certain category; another part derives from using incentives to induce behaviour rather than using threats or punishment; and part involves a recognition that society benefits from the particular business activity and thus should share the risk (or really uncertainty).

Economists have argued that the new global economy will depend more and more on research and development (R & D). One feature of R & D involves uncertainty because one cannot know which avenues of R & D will pay off; and another involves risk because of long delays in approval of a product for use or sale. To the extent governments wish to encourage R & D, socialization of both risk and uncertainty may be warranted. This may take the form of tax deductions or credits, government subsidies, or government-business joint ventures. It can also be more direct; for example, by government-funded research facilities or increased funding of granting agencies for university research.

The interesting question about communities in the unbundled world concerns the potential disjuncture between who pays and who benefits. If taxpayers in only one locality or nation share the uncertainty or risk, the enhanced or new product may nevertheless be sold throughout the world. If all localities or nations follow this practice, then new or improved products should proliferate everywhere; and there should be relatively little unfairness or sense of subsidizing someone else, even though perceptions of uneven benefits may persist. The vision of a global economy usually presumes such widely dispersed costs and benefits. This is only partly a matter of 'free-riders' on public goods, since a company may find it profitable to proceed whether or not a subsidy or other socialization of risk has been offered. To the extent governments delay the process of R & D by requiring lengthy and costly tests (as for all new drugs), they reduce the potential profit and thus the world may never realize certain benefits.

This example could easily be developed into a chapter of its own, and I do not want to engage in such an extensive digression. For present purposes, the point concerns concepts of community and how socialization of risk requires that people consider with whom they are prepared to share uncertainty or risk and why. At the beginning of this section, I defined risk (really, uncertainty) as growing out of random, unforeseeable, arbitrary events or calamity. The example of the riskiness of R & D, however, suggests that economic risks of a certain kind (but not others like currency speculations) may be candidates for socialization of risk, particularly when the public wishes government to impose strict health or safety regulations which serve to delay marketing and thereby increase risk or uncertainty.[11] Whether involving risk or uncertainty, sharing can help to mark or create communities which have strong integuments.

MORAL COMMUNITY

Each type of community discussed so far has a moral dimension, because each involves different ways of handling obligations and responsibilities. By a moral community, however, I have a more specific focus in mind – namely, to whom do we owe an explanation or a justification for our actions? The answer to this question sometimes involves a territorial community, but more often it does not. This may be inferred in several ways, but the one I will pursue here involves demonstrating this moral dimension in each type of community just reviewed.

Each of the types of communities involves obligations to specific people about specific matters. Failure to meet those obligations requires an explanation or justification to those specific people and only rarely to others. For example, in the case of a division of labour or a community of complementary values, failure of obligation would mean that other people cannot do their job (or do it as well) because you have let them down in some way. In a corporation, it could involve absenteeism, inaccurate designs, carelessness on the shop floor, misuse of funds, or many other production or service deficiencies. In the academic realm, it might take the form of plagiarism, falsifying data, not sharing data, refusal to publish results (but sharing them privately), or falsely questioning a colleague's integrity. The people with whom you had been involved and who counted on you have a right to ask for an explanation. If public money is at stake (business subsidy, research grant, etc.), public agencies may also feel it necessary to investigate.

In communities of shared value, a slightly different account may be demanded. If one brings discredit on oneself, a cloud could be cast over the members of the community, since by definition they are just like oneself in at least that one salient respect. An athlete, for example, who is caught in a random drug test may bring disrepute to the team or to all athletes at that level or in that event. Likewise, a stockbroker convicted of insider trading becomes a symbol which may lead many investors to think less highly of all other brokers or to demand proof of innocence.

The socialization of risk entails costs for every member of the community. Since the costs arise out of 'random' catastrophes, we usually feel sympathy instead of the need to demand an explanation, but not always. Sometimes we ask whether the victim might have been culpable, as in the case of health costs escalating among smokers, or of benefits provided by 'no fault' insurance to drunk drivers. Even if there is no suspicion of self-inflicted injuries, we still feel entitled to ask what happened. Of course, one would rarely raise questions as a single individual inquiring about a particular event. Instead we have 'police' who monitor and regulate the various types of insurance to reassure us that fraud is minimized. Thus, we rely on securities and exchange commissions, bank inspectors, government food inspectors, the provincial law societies or bars, and police commissions. In all of these examples, members of the community of risk have the right to know if the costs passed on to them are reasonable, whether the answers are to be sought directly or through intermediaries of one sort or another. People who do not share the potential costs are unlikely to ask these questions and generally lack standing even if they seek answers.

Even territorial communities involve this form of accountability. The difference between various kinds of non-territorial communities, on the one hand, and nations, provinces, towns, and neighbourhoods, on the other, is that the people of whom explanations may be asked are limited in the latter cases by territorial jurisdictions. 'That is out of my jurisdiction' (because in another city or country) is a very frustrating answer to someone who has been injured or affected prejudiciously *here*. Of course, in non-territorial organizations, one can get the run-around ('you should take that up with the Workers' Compensation Board'). In these latter cases, however, one usually only has to walk across the street; one rarely finds that the matter is completely beyond one's reach.

Whatever the type of community, this moral dimension counts as a strong bond, even if it is not the only bond, nor an overarching one for all communities. It rests on noting that the limits of the particular community often coincide with the answer to such questions as: To whom do you feel responsible? and Who has the right to call you to account?

It is worth observing that nations have proven permeable in this respect. Sovereignty in the macho nineteenth-century form – in which each nation (or at least each colonial power) went its own way and thumbed its nose at the others – has been steadily eroded by these moral communities, and not just by the economic globalization reviewed in chapter 3. For example, besides some United Nations agencies and their sanctions, there are private organizations like Amnesty International, the Red Cross, World Watch, PEN, and the World Council of Churches which feel it appropriate to call attention to alleged abuses of rights or persons regardless of national borders. Indeed, even national governments have been moving in the direction of intervening – by word and deed – in the affairs of other nations. One has only to think of Commonwealth sanctions on South Africa, relief aid to insurgents in some Third World countries, the boycott of the 1980 Olympics by several countries to protest the Soviet invasion of Afghanistan, intrusive verification procedures in arms control agreements, and most visibly the armed removal of Iraq from Kuwait. Whether one applauds any or all of these activities, the more fundamental points are that they occur more frequently than they used to, they are often effective, and they are part of the unbundling on which I have commented repeatedly, since they challenge or weaken state sovereignty. They are perhaps a continuation of an earlier era's reaction against colonialism and empire.

The effectiveness of moral communities – or, if you will, the moral dimension of newly assertive communities – underlines the importance of forms of organization not based on territorial assumptions. More and more, assumptions about territoriality are questioned; and the more they are questioned, the less their force. Important as territoriality was in creating the world of hegemonic nation-states, territorial communities now share centre stage with other forms of community which may have always been there but in the background.

ALL-PURPOSE AND CONGRUENT COMMUNITIES

We can now return to our 'old-fashioned' community based on territory and highlight some of its features which are quite distinct from those of the non-territorial communities just examined. There are two features above all which should be emphasized: territorial communities are generally multi-purpose or all-purpose; and they are 'congruent' – that is, the boundaries or borders of their many purposes coincide. Of course, there are exceptions, but these features are so rare among non-territorial communities and so common among territorial ones that they are worth comment. These features – or their absence – turn out to have some non-obvious consequences which should become more visible over time.

The previous chapter explored some administrative implications of non-congruent territories or organizations. Now I intend to examine the obverse – some implications of congruence among communities, especially territorial communities.

Where several jurisdictions coincide, we can refer to a multi-purpose organization of territory. The state as conceived in the last couple of centuries has become, in effect, an all-purpose organization. By serving many purposes and by congruence among the implicit communities defined by those purposes, the state gains a broad allegiance. This is a good part of its strength, that it rests not on a single reed but on a bundle of them. But according to an older concept, this constitutes a form of tyranny since power is concentrated rather than dispersed. Hence, the centuries-long debate over taming, civilizing, and democratizing the state.

Likewise with social and local communities. The old-fashioned township or village, whose demise is now mourned, was a place of congruence, an all-purpose (or multi-purpose) community. There are two ways of approaching this feature of territorial communities – congruence of networks of status and overlap of membership. Both pose, in attenuated but direct fashion, the issue of 'tyranny' also found at the state level and its 'democratization' in the unbundled world.

In the local territorial communities – and even in some wider ones –

an individual usually held many statuses which were linked or at least visible to other residents of that community. As a homeowner, worker or operator of a business, church-goer, coach of Little League, or 'pillar of the community,' a person belonged to several (sub-)communities or networks whose boundaries by and large coincided with each other and with that of the local community. Not only were they congruent but one had little or no choice within a type of (sub-)community; for example, you could not be a Little League coach elsewhere. Another way of seeing these linkages and congruences is to note that many of these statuses or memberships connected you to a wider network *mediately*; for example, the local Rotary Club was part of a national and international network with which one had very little or no direct contact, and similarly with the Presbyterian Church or Boy Scouts. In the unbundled world, by contrast, one may belong to many communities beyond the residential locale directly without the mediation of local or intermediate levels. *Immediate* rather than mediated associations are generally non-congruent with other such linkages locally or elsewhere. More communities, more choice, but without congruence of communities; therefore, less 'real community'? As noted in chapter 1, neighbours may be linked into quite different networks, while distant connections are becoming more common, durable, and even intimate.

Besides congruence, territorial organizations, especially local ones, involve correlated memberships. That is, an individual will find that the same people reappear in many networks, groups, and sub-communities as fellow members, and often that they know each other. In the unbundled world, however, many communities will be non-congruent in boundaries, and the members of one network will be unlikely to know those of another, let alone to be members. For example, the chances are slim that the members of your aerobics class know each other through common membership in other groups (like a church or children at the same school), and yet it is exactly that degree of correlated membership which makes local territorial communities special.

Some people will argue that correlated, coincident, and overlapping sources of community make territorial communities strong and satisfying. If the sources of community exist independently of each other, the argument goes, there will be an absence of 'roots' and not a very deep sense of community. This may be true for some people, but the unbundled world provides another perspective which is also valid for many individuals.

Special, close, strong, and appealing to many people – but tyrannical to many eyes. In a large enough local community, one may find sufficient options for one's interests and for facets of one's personality, but in 'old-fashioned' communities, remembered nostalgically, options were limited. Thus, to highlight – and perhaps exaggerate – the nature of territorial communities, I want to point to some positive features of 'anonymous' large communities and non-congruent communities.

Anonymity is another word for privacy. Privacy lays a foundation for autonomy. Autonomy must involve, to some significant degree, choosing one's associates on the basis of shared interests, functional specificity, or sheer challenge of something new or different. Thus, getting out of a system of congruent communities with correlated memberships can be liberating and enhancing at the same time that it can involve risk.

Cross-pressures can also enhance freedom of action, challenge one's mind and personality, and enliven one's life. Of course, we often conceptualize cross-pressures or conflicting reference groups in terms of indecision, confusion, delayed implementation, and paralysis. For example, early voting studies emphasized these features as they related to when or how easily a voter decided how to vote. But true as that analysis may be, the obverse can also be painted negatively: being rushed and bullied to a decision by all the constellations of one's environment ganging up on you.

Notice a final feature of non-congruent communities and uncorrelated memberships. If each activity in which one engages (work, play, love, church, etc.) brings one into contact with different people who may not themselves be connected, *one can be different people*, if one wishes, or be 'de-centred' in postmodernist terminology. The alternative is always to present the same facade to everyone one encounters. Not everyone will want to be an actor playing several roles, but for those who do, the unbundled world may hold many attractions.

For some, congruence, correlated statuses and memberships, coherence, and homogeneity prove to be appealing and their absence threatening. For others, such communities can be tolerated only if one can move away; for them, openness, variety, cross-pressures, new experiences, and trying out different personas have a great appeal. Thus, different kinds of community will be evaluated in opposite ways by these types of people. But more than evaluation, one can say that the types of community may help to shape the kinds of people who live in them, and as the balance among communities changes, we may create a different distribution of types of people. Again, the transition is what we find difficult, because we can see and feel what has disappeared or weakened, but it is much more difficult to appreciate the new communities.

Bellah et al. write of 'the invisible complexity' of society.[12] They note that what seems simple may be so only through familiarity. Equally, what appears complex and daunting may be so only because we do not yet know it well or understand how to use it. Much of what I have suggested about communities in the unbundled world will strike many people as a buzzing confusion. And it does have that aspect, of course, in comparison to medieval cities or to small towns in nineteenth-century North America. But it also has many compensating virtues, and only time will tell if they are worth the 'loss of community' in another sense.

Recall some of the features we might expect in the near future, based on these concepts of communities:

1. functional interdependence through specialized activities
2. integration through expertise and shared values
3. multiplication of communities and thereby of loyalties and identities, rather than substitution of one for another community or identity
4. communities of choice because one can choose from the whole world and not just from one's local place of residence
5. moral and ethical concerns highlighted by feelings of obligation and accountability to people and groups beyond one's local horizons

COMMUNITY AND CITIZENSHIP

Citizenship involves community because it entails inclusion and exclusion. One person alone cannot create citizenship. Robinson Crusoe could not be a citizen of his desert island, at least not before Friday appeared in his life. (Like so many 'Europeans' in the Americas, Crusoe could forget that he was the immigrant, and it was Friday's island.) Likewise, citizenship implies that there must be a group or category of non-citizens: a group which is 'other' and thereby makes vivid what citizens share.

Citizenship has come to signify rights and privileges, duties and responsibilities in a political community. It encompasses how one may gain or lose the status of citizen, what opportunities or liabilities follow from the status, and whether other loyalties or identities can coexist as equals or will be subsumed by it. A good part of our concept of citizenship derives from the same set of historical circumstances which engendered the modern nation-state and the concept of individualism. As territorial units bundled the varied and competing political forms into an all-purpose, sovereign entity, they blurred the distinctions of estates, cities, statuses, roles, and fealty.[13] Rights and duties, and thus citizenship, were divorced from offices or roles and attached to the personality of the incumbent. As bearers of rights, individuals gained in significance and became equal in crucial respects. Hence, they became invested with citizenship rather than being simply subjects or vassals or lords.

Traditionally we reserve the word 'citizenship' for our inclusive territorial communities.[14] At earlier points in time, of course, citizenship was not extended to every resident but was restricted on the basis of class, gender, race, and the like. In this century, most such restrictions carry less weight in many countries. For other types of associations, we use other words, like 'membership,' 'user,' 'stakeholder,' 'partner,' or 'beneficiary.' So long as we all understand the conventions, these usages will do. But thinking of how territorial communities may be giving ground to other communities, I prefer to argue for a broader use of 'citizenship.' Perhaps it should not apply to every membership; do I really want to be a 'citizen' of the Canadian Automobile Association? But many increasingly important non-territorial communities deserve the concept of 'citizenship.'[15] As with several other concepts in previous chapters, I do not want to be diverted by nomenclature. If readers feel uncomfortable with stretching the word 'citizenship' as I do here, they may substitute some of the terms above. I will use 'citizenship' in the wider sense, however, because I wish to be provocative. After all, even in regard to many of these private groups or communities, we find members urging each other to 'be a good citizen.'

'Citizenship' is the right word, I argue also, because of the moral force it conveys. In its national meaning, it has connotations also appropriate to the communities of responsibility discussed here. It goes beyond membership because it involves a sense of commitment, of being engaged by actions related to a given community. It presumes characteristics of maturity, concern, and self-awareness, and it is a concept that takes us beyond individualism, self-interest, and self-centredness. In these ways, it is inherently related to concepts of community.[16] It asks what one can contribute and what one owes to others, as well as implying a mutuality of obligations. As I urged above, these new communities – like the older forms – remind us that there are others who have a right to call us to account, and in politics all citizens and only citizens have that right. This has not always been the case; in earlier ages, people were called to account by the pope or his bishops, and later by kings who were the state in which people were subjects rather than citizens.

Whatever else one may learn by relaxing assumptions about territoriality and exploring new concepts of community, it should be obvious that these entail a broader understanding of citizenship. Where can I live and still be a citizen of here? Of what community can I be a citizen without giving up too much of here? What do I have to give up in order to be accorded the status of citizen?

In Roman times and throughout most of the medieval period in Europe, laws were 'personal' rather than territorial. That meant that a political group's laws did not apply to members of other groups, even if they lived among the group.[17] The criminal law became local and territorial fairly early, as it was felt that individual personal law should not interfere with public law, of which the criminal law was a supreme example. Eventually almost all laws became local and territorial in this sense. This process was cause and consequence of the creation of territorial nation-states. The relaxation of assumptions about territoriality and the development of various non-territorial forms of political organization and citizenship may be indirectly recreating conditions of the first millennium of the Christian era, and perhaps also of 'tribal' law in other parts of the world.[18] Of course, conditions are quite different today because of travel, commerce, and communication on a global scale, but it is salutary to recall that non-territorial political and legal systems have existed and functioned for hundreds if not thousands of years. The territorial model and its related concept of citizenship are the late-comers and probably a passing phase, however dominant they may seem.

Citizenship in our modern sense of national rootedness and civic rights and duties has never been unchallenged. There have always been some people who felt that duties as 'citizens of the world' could compete with, be balanced by, or override duties as citizens of a nation. Obversely, the growth over the past two centuries of the concept of individual human rights has limited citizen subservience to the nation and its state. The concept of war crimes underlines that circumstances may dictate responsibilities which run contrary to national citizenship. More recently still, as Canadians are learning, sharing a Charter of Rights and Freedoms can serve as a potent basis for a sense of common citizenship.[19] Sharing a medical insurance scheme may also be part of this conception of rights of citizenship.

Yet the growth of supra-national loyalties and the legitimation of individual or human rights have obscured a once powerful strand of community and citizenship. Formerly, corporate or collective rights of several types coexisted. Cities had rights and autonomy, and their citizens partook of those rights and autonomy, not by their merit as individuals, but by residing for a year and a day in the city.[20] Likewise, for centuries, the church, convents, monasteries, and holy orders were communities which did not answer to an overarching political authority, as they came to do when the state gained its pre-eminence. In short, there existed many types of citizenship based on several types of community. Perhaps we find ourselves coming full circle to multiple citizenships, albeit integral to quite different kinds of communities.

However different city-states, religious orders, or medieval guilds may seem to our modern sensibility, they constituted self-chosen, self-governing, and self-enhancing communities. They did not grow out of an aggrandizement of other forms of authority, nor did they endeavour – as modern nation-states have done – to be all-purpose, sovereign, and unchallenged. Of course, the Roman Catholic Church at one time aspired to omnipotence, but not for long and never with quite the universal success of nations. Thus, in startling ways, the new unbundled communities hypothesized in this book offer parallels to earlier communities which also guarded as best they could their rights as autonomous entities. Pre-modern communities, modern nations, and the future unbundled communities share the goal of harbouring, protecting, and fostering a way of life. However individualistic modern people have become, they still seek and welcome communities to sustain them, as did their ancestors. But just as nations supplanted or submerged some earlier communities, so unbundled communities represent a stage beyond nations.

In a 'postmodern' development in which multiple identities are sustained and created by multiple communities, 'the self is redefined as no longer an essence in itself, but relational.[21] And so our concept of citizenship will evolve too. Jennifer Nedelsky has reached a similar conclusion by re-conceptualizing 'rights' as involving relationships.[22] I do not want to repeat her arguments, interesting as they are, but she presents a bridge between individual and collective levels of analysis. If rights are viewed as goals and relationships as means of sustaining individual pursuit of those goals, there is less chance of a zero-sum confrontation between an individual and a collectivity. She contrasts her analysis with the liberal individualism which has permeated assumptions about political authority in territorial states: '... what is wrong with this [liberal] individualism is that it fails to account for the ways in which our essential humanity is neither possible nor comprehensible without the network of relationships of which it is a part ... The anti-individualism theorists claim that we are literally constituted by the relationships of which we are a part' (p. 12).

By largely forgetting earlier forms of community and understandings of citizenship, we have also lost the sense that neither community nor citizenship need be zero-sum. Indeed, we are so thoroughly imbued with territoriality and national citizenship, we have mostly lost touch with the historical nature of institutions. As earlier chapters showed, nations – and the idea of nations – were constructed over an extended period, eventually becoming hegemonic as European assumptions about territoriality became hegemonic throughout the whole world.[23] Also noted were the origins of passports less than a century ago, and yet most citizens now equate their passport with their citizenship.

How easy to forget older ideas. Think, for example, of the views of many French Canadians at the time of Confederation, which (being the mid-nineteenth century) coincided with the apex of modern nationalism. They accused English-speaking supporters and opponents of Confederation of having loyalty to two nations – Britain and Canada – and thus fully to neither. They argued that French-speaking Canadians, on the contrary, had only one country, and that was Canada. In our time, ironically, English-Canadian nationalists trumpet their singular nationality while denouncing the dual loyalty of Quebeckers as only equivocally Canadian. Furthermore, large sectors of English Canada (speaking for what it believes to be all of Canada) propose measures to insulate Canadian culture from American influence, to preserve whatever tenuous national sentiments they perceive, while condemning Quebec for using its state powers to preserve and promote its 'distinct society.' Obversely, Quebec's treatment of its English community may be more generous than Canada's treatment of Quebec.

The coexistence in Canada of Canadian nationalism, Quebec nationalism, and an incipient aboriginal nationalism underlines the arbitrary nature of notions of exclusive communities and all-encompassing citizenship. Former prime minister Trudeau used to taunt advocates of provincial autonomy by asking if they were British Columbians first or Canadians first, Quebeckers first or Canadians first. This was then, as it is now, a false dilemma. One does not have to choose one identity and discard the other, and one does not have to embrace one community to the exclusion of another more encompassing community. How much more true when one considers the unbundled communities discussed here.

Just as fifteenth-century Europeans would have been puzzled or fearful if told that each individual must choose only one community – sovereign above all others – to which loyalty would be owed, so perhaps we now find it hard to give up that singularity. It is hard for us to conceive that we now can and soon must think of citizenship as residing in several independent communities. Our puzzlement is the mirror-image of theirs. Our fear of multiple citizenships as threatening to national order and stability is the obverse of their fear of a sovereign territorial state as imbalanced and as threatening to the order and stability so familiar to them.

With individualism and an ever widening concept of rights have come new and muscular identities. Some are ancient but have been eclipsed or in the shadows; others have been constructed in our time as nations were constructed in an earlier time. Examples of enhanced identities which draw their new or renewed strength from the language of rights include aboriginals, women, gays and lesbians, the disabled or 'challenged,' and ethnicity. The question posed by Trudeau about whether provincial or national identity came first can no longer seem so simple, if it ever was, when one factors in these emergent identities and the communities they represent.

The psychological space of citizens in many – although not all – countries has become conditional as it has expanded and contracted. It has expanded by witnessing the legitimation of many identities which were once very private – family, sexual identity or preference, and physical disability. These are now 'public' identities fostered by the rhetoric of rights and freedoms. The psychological space has contracted, however, to the degree that many people view these once-private identities as more central to their well-being; they are unwilling to stay in the closet. The privatization of identities parallels their more public display. As identities and loyalties become more varied and distinct, the concept of citizenship unbundles. A person's identity is conditioned more and more by circumstances and by what aspect of identity is activated or threatened by public events – and not just events 'at home' in one's country or locale: 'Those who live alone need not be pitied, however, for from the present view, we are never alone, even if isolated from others' physical presence. So long as our actions are intelligible, they are intelligible within a system of meaning. And meaning, as we have seen, is not the product of individual minds but of relationships. To act before witnesses does not render such actions more social.'[24]

UNIVERSAL INDIVIDUALISM

Individuals were created or constructed at the same time as nations.[25] In both processes, strenuous efforts were required to play down the significance of certain aspects of individuals. Especially troublesome were labels or categories which corresponded to status, role, or rank in the old order. In endeavouring to obliterate the signs of inequality, hierarchy, privilege, and rank from feudal times, emphasis was placed more and more on the legal equality of individuals. This process continues in our own day – for example, in the debate over what descriptors should be mentioned in news reports, whether to forbid reference to race or age or disability, among others. By trying to be fair, we have concluded that we should be 'blind' to personal markers. Although this can lead to injustices, if remedial action based on knowledge of particular circumstances would be ruled out by this forced anonymity, it has been generally accepted that the advantages outweigh the disadvantages. 'Blind' refereeing of scholarly manuscripts may be seen as a specific instance of this broad phenomenon.

The communities discussed in this chapter may turn out to further this anonymity, and they could thereby support the multifaceted complexity of each individual. Think for a moment about E-mail, fax, electronic bulletin boards, and generally about the entrance of a particular individual into a 'virtual community' or network of people focused on a topic of mutual concern, whether politics, hobby, sport, or religion.[26] They do not need to see each other or hear each other's voice or know all the myriad details that make up the others' personalities, although over time they may come to know all this about a few of their colleagues. How will they manage to discriminate? How will each be able to differentiate responses along the lines we frequently worry about when we try to keep 'blind' certain features? Unless full names are used, will they be able to identify individuals as men or women? How does one ascertain age, race, ethnicity, occupation, status, income, or disability unless mentioned by the message sender? In short, it is extremely likely that we can learn to have extended interactions with featureless individuals. But not really featureless because we will know the crucial features, namely, those which we share with them and which they want to share with us by way of interests and concerns.

Yet the paucity of features visible to the network is its strength for the individual: to be judged on that feature of self which you want to put forward as the one relevant to the network or community at hand, rather than risk being judged on the basis of 'extraneous' features. The multiplicity of networks or communities provides thereby support for as many sides of one's personality as the number of communities one cares

A Community of Communities 199

to join. Each network 'sees' what you want its members to focus on, and you thus can be many distinct people if you wish. But there can be a 'whole' or integral you, in the sense of your 'will' or choice in joining a particular set of relationships and communities; and that integrity of personality equals individuality. And so once again we see how an individual may be defined as a community of communities, a community of relationships, or a relationship among communities.

There are other implications of the new citizenship which deserve brief mention. Beyond sovereignty in the unbundled world, these specialized, focused, anonymous but personal communities may be seen as the opposite of mass society. If secondary and voluntary groups as conventionally understood can serve as mediators between the naked self and the government of mass society, how much more effective these new communities should be. They will be public – open to all who share their interest – but as private as one wishes. They can be activated at any hour on any day by an electronic command. They will encompass the world far and near. Their 'citizens' will be a mixture of strong and weak, assertive and passive, nurturing and distant, and may include scores of people or millions. What government or society could compete effectively with such battalions? Of course, over time, perhaps more sinister governments, gangs, or rulers will find ways to harness these communities, as William Gibson's dark vision of cyberspace suggests.[27] But until then, these communities should bolster each individual's unique combination of multiple identities by multiplying their communal links.

Another implication already noted should be highlighted. These new communities should enhance the trend toward greater concern by citizens of one country about rights and well-being of people in other countries, and thus greater respect for diversity. Such 'fellow-feeling' occurs now but has been limited by opportunity. For example, immigrants or their descendants may maintain active concern about people in the former homeland, but common as this may be in settler societies (Canada, United States, Australia, and a few others) it is almost unknown to most people in most countries. Electronic networks of individuals sharing a passionate interest may create similar levels of concern, or even greater because one can interact directly with those in one's network.

Finally, note another way in which the unbundled world may bring us full circle. In the medieval and ancient world, manuscripts were read aloud because few copies could exist. Learning, knowledge, and growth were communal, but not communal in the sense of 'clannish'; instead, one chose to join and enhance a community, and one result was a shared experience of its knowledge. Likewise aboriginal communities – traditionally in all non-literate societies and even in some today – maintained a similar awareness of shared or communal knowledge because of oral traditions passed from each generation to the next. With vernacular printing, as noted in chapter 2, learning became a more 'personal' or solitary endeavour. By reading to oneself, one carried on an interior monologue, although one might feel part of a tradition of scholarship. And today's trends are returning again to shared and communal knowledge. 'Invisible colleges' have for some time circulated pre-publication scholarly papers. Electronic publishing and networks will lead participants to share 'books' and yet to possess them privately as well. Since this chapter should not be the occasion to speculate what analogy to the Protestant Reformation may befall electronic publishing, I will resist writing more.

All of these implications and the analysis of unbundled communities from which they flow centre around the question of what comes after citizenship in nations. As I have pointed out in other chapters, this question does not presume that something will *replace* nations. What comes after, what is now germinating, what can be built on these new concepts of community? This book offers several answers to these queries, but one that seems especially pertinent to this chapter is that real communities constructed on the basis of universal individualism may grow 'from the bottom up.' That will be their strength, and it should make them forceful competitors of nations even though posing no threat to the survival of nations.

TYRANNY À LA CARTE?

The picture of vibrant communities supporting or defining autonomous individuals linked by relationships of mutual caring will seem too benign by far for many readers. And, of course, they will be correct. There are dangerous possibilities to which I should address a few remarks, even though my main concern has been to show that 'loss of community' may have been exaggerated and new communities may have the positive and beneficial consequences just outlined.

Since Althusius and especially since Montesquieu, divided authority has been prescribed as an antidote to tyranny. Federalism and other devices such as checks and balances have been justified in this way. A thorough and comprehensive analysis of such 'compound republics' by Ostrom reveals how deep the roots are of this perspective.[28] For at least two centuries, however, most observers have applied these concepts to territorial political authorities and communities. I have suggested an alternative view in which non-territorial communities and forms of governance may gain in visibility and influence. If pluralism among territorial authorities may serve as a check on tyranny, can we expect the same from non-territorial pluralism? I will give a preliminary answer of 'yes' at this point, but the next chapter raises the question in another form.

Unbundled, single-purpose, or highly focused political or social units without a territorial base should have the benefits outlined in this chapter and elsewhere. But might any one of them turn out to be tyrannical? The 'virtual communities' in electronic space will probably provide no protection against 'majority rule' within each network. Their value lies in providing a multiplicity of niches for individuals with well-defined interests or values. Protection of members from each other seems unnecessary, however, since membership would be voluntary, exit would be easy, and start-up costs of a new community should be minimal. If there are two primary motives or principles in politics – loyalty and revenge – then we may ask whether the multiple loyalties embedded in these focused and non-congruent communities may make it less clear on whom vengeance should be wreaked.

The key constitutional issue, therefore, involves an assurance that *limited (or single-) purpose* communities do not appropriate or aggrandize purposes otherwise controlled by other limited purpose communities. I cannot see how this could happen for the 'virtual communities,' for the reasons just given. For transnational corporations or other hierarchical or 'command' structures, there may be some potential in this regard since employees may not feel free to 'exit' because of limited alternative employment options. One might, however, expect the focus on 'bottom lines' in a globally competitive environment to discipline or restrict such tendencies to appropriate functions. If so, the primary threat may continue to come from territorial political units, especially if they try to 'claw back' functions or purposes leaking away to non-territorial organizations or communities. If physical location in a strong multi-purpose unit is coupled with a bloody-minded majority, what can be done to protect the minority? The next chapter takes up this issue, because it involves quite different considerations than the social or economic communities we have analysed in this chapter.

7

Majority Rules

Politics involves differences: some can be reconciled with each other through persuasion, compromise, redefinition, or log-rolling, but others seem to be incompatible. Authoritative decisions about which values shall prevail, or in what degree, go to the heart of politics. Democratic polities have developed rules about such imposed outcomes. Majority rule is the best known and most frequent example. As Robert Dahl has noted, majority rule is generally acceptable among people who are actively concerned with the issue at hand and likely to be affected (although perhaps in different ways) by the outcome.[1] Even though majority rule must entail some possibility that one will be on the losing side, one accepts that possibility on the assumption that one will not always be on the losing side on all issues and that one has a reasonable chance of trying to convince a majority that this outcome is better than that one. As former prime minister Trudeau has argued, '... a true democracy must permit the periodic transformation of political minorities into majorities.[2]

Consider, however, that winning and losing under majority rule can take two radically different forms:

1. Each time (or most times) an issue arises, there is a different 'coalition' forming the majority, and hence the minority shifts from issue to issue.

2. On many (although not necessarily all) issues, a certain group ends up in the minority position; they may not be the only group in the minority, others moving in and out, depending on the issue.

The second situation is especially likely to arise when there are cultural, ethnic, or religious cleavages which are still salient. (Not all such cleavages retain their salience, in which case the following observations would be less apt.) These particular cleavages might have the effect of engendering 'permanent minorities' because the groups which define the cleavage have a way of life whose coherence among many facets or aspects of life ensures that positions on many issues are not independent of each other. For them, 'way of life' means that many issues are decided in a particular and interdependent way. For other groups, the issues may be united but in a way that puts them on the 'winning' side, or the issues may be largely unrelated and thus allow members to end up on the winning side often enough to accept majority rule without feeling perennially threatened. Those in a minority culture, however, are virtually guaranteed to react cohesively and end up in the minority or 'losing' side more often than for most other members of society. Furthermore, many members of this minority culture will have intense feelings about these issues, since they touch beliefs or activities which define their culture or way of life. That is why we say the cleavages are salient.

There are several very important assumptions lurking behind these two ways of losing under majority rule. The situation faced by apparently permanent minorities reveals that 'majority' or 'minority' may consist of groups, collectivities, or societies rather than disembodied individuals who are largely interchangeable except for their views on the issue at vote. Obversely, Trudeau and Dahl take for granted that the units of analysis are generally individuals – or very small groups like families – and thus not cohesive collectivities. Dahl is quite clear that majorities are simply coalitions of minorities and individuals who find it convenient to work together for particular goals. One way to highlight the contrast is to ask whether the voters are seen as 'people' (individuals) or as 'a people' (a society, an ethnic community). The singular form has a different meaning in many contexts from its plural cousin. For example, people have certain rights and freedoms (speech, presumed innocence, etc.), whereas 'a people' has the right to self-determination under the United Nations' International Covenant on Economic, Social and Cultural Rights, its International Covenant on Civil and Political Rights, and other agreements.[3]

Note another instance in which the singular and the plural of words have quite distinct connotations if not denotations. Take 'majority' and 'minority' and contrast them to 'majorities' and 'minorities.' Although there are exceptions, the plural form of each word carries an implication of shifting boundaries and composition, as when we say that there is only a partial overlap among the majorities favouring the Canadian public health system, the policy of bilingualism, the Free Trade Agreement between Canada and the United States, and the deregulation of the airline industry. In validating such assertions, we have recourse to public opinion polls and the like, which presume that individuals are the appropriate units of analysis. Unfortunately, polls often fail to measure the degree of overlap among issues or address the implications of lack of overlap.[4]

The singular forms carry quite different implications. For example, we say that the majority speaks English, and that French is the minority language in Canada, except in Quebec, where English is the minority language. We would generally not say that 'the majority position' favours bilingualism or the other issues listed above, because that would invest those positions with a sense of permanence. The linguistic or ethnic or religious majorities and minorities in Canada do change but exceedingly slowly by comparison to opinions on current public policies.

Thus, one might say that the most common defences of majority rule – such as those by Dahl or Trudeau – rest on a set of assumptions similar to those underlying 'mass society' as outlined in chapter 2. That is, interchangeable individuals capable of shifting opinions or subject to shifting moods and peer pressures may not have tightly integrated ideological positions; and to that extent they bounce back and forth between majority and minority positions depending on the issue being debated at the moment. This set of assumptions contrasts starkly with the view of 'a majority' and one or more cohesive ethnic communities, each constituting a minority with correlated and interdependent views. In the latter cases, more or less permanent minority status does not derive from individual monads making separate decisions about a host of political or social issues. Being a minority, in short, may not be a momentary accident but a long-standing disability.

There have been many suggestions about how to deal with this danger in majority rule. Several common alternatives include the following:

1. requiring special majorities on key issues; that is, requiring more than 50 per cent plus one, such as a two-thirds majority or even higher;
2. giving certain groups a veto over certain issues;
3. letting groups opt-in to certain provisions only if they choose;
4. letting groups opt-out of certain provisions under specified circumstances;
5. entrenching defined rights and freedoms so that the minority (or

each individual) has an area of sanctuary which no majority can violate.

Notice a deep assumption behind these procedures or safeguards. All presume that the majority and the minority share the same political system. In particular, they take for granted a territorial system with a heterogeneous population, and they try to identify groups (or individuals in the case of many rights and freedoms) which have non-territorial boundaries. In chapter 5, I explored how one might use social boundaries to define provincial political memberships instead of relying solely on territorial borders.

This chapter takes seriously that suggestion and endeavours to expound several non-obvious implications of non-territorial majorities. It will contain a fair amount of detailed examination of some Canadian situations and some abstract considerations with scant empirical detail. The focus on Canada is opportunistic; one could equally examine several other countries such as South Africa, Switzerland, Belgium, or India, and some references to these cases will appear. Since my knowledge of Canadian situations greatly exceeds my knowledge of those other cases, the empirical analysis will be limited mostly to Canada; but the practical problem of dealing with majority rule comes up in almost all polities at one time or another.

COMPLEXITY AND THE PROTECTION OF MINORITIES

European concern for two hundred years has been to protect dissident individuals and groups from government actions. This concern grew out of the earlier success of the territorial nation-state and its coalescence around the absolute monarch. During that earlier process, the central theoretical issue was how to subdue the local, particularistic, centrifugal forces represented by feudal and civic institutions. At a later stage, however, reactions to arbitrary rule by monarchs and their courts – captured perhaps by the expression 'l'état, c'est moi' – led to greater emphasis on how to protect the majority of the national population from a tyrannical minority. The minority has at various times been identified as a monarch, the nobility, an established clergy, or a social class controlling the means of production. In all such instances, the theoretical challenge has concerned the issues on which everyone should count equally so that social decisions reflect the full range of views.

Who needs protection has thus been remarkably different in different eras. Our own era has focused the question of protection in two contradictory ways, both of which lead to more visible complexity within nation-states and thereby greatly complicate the issue of protection for whom. These two strands in the twentieth-century represent the culmination of the nineteenth-century hegemony of the nation-state in its liberal individualist and colonial manifestations. So today we live with the consequences of the end of colonialism and the universal use of the rhetoric of rights and freedoms.

The first element of complexity is the end of colonialism in the period since the Second World War. As noted in chapter 1, the dramatic increase in the number of nations eligible for or holding membership in the United Nations has encouraged many groups to assert their claims to self-determination and state sovereignty. Some, of course, have succeeded, including most recently the former republics of the Soviet Union. The more successes we witness, the more noteworthy are the remaining groups who have not succeeded. The contrast between success and (so far) failure corresponds almost exactly to the difference between groups who were a majority in a territorially defined political unit (a former colony or a Soviet republic) and groups who are inextricably intermingled with a larger majority group in a territorial nation. The latter include Kurds in several nations, the Basques in France and Spain, Tamils in Sri Lanka, the Maya in Central America, and the French in Canada, to name only a few.

The second element making for greater complexity seems to be virtually universal. The rhetoric of rights and freedoms – as noted in chapter 6 – has fostered an awareness of groupness for some and has heightened that awareness for others. The most clear-cut examples of groups activated, mobilized, or made visible by gaining rights and thus some degree of acceptability involve totally non-territorial categories of people. These include women, gays and lesbians, the disabled or 'challenged,' and immigrant ethnic groups, again to mention only a few. Aboriginals stand as a partial exception, since some (Inuit in Canada or aboriginal groups in the Australian Northern Territory) have a degree of territoriality. For most aboriginals, however, reserves are non-contiguous, and many live and work off-reserve among 'whites.' Aboriginals are a partial exception for another reason: although not exempt from the rhetoric of rights, they have in some parts of the world justified their claims in other ways, most notably by the assertion of aboriginal title and unbroken possession of land and culture.

These abstract considerations about majority rule have serious practical manifestations in Canada and in many societies. Three current instances should be mentioned. For one, French-speaking Quebeckers have been keenly aware that majority rule threatens their way of life because they have been a permanent minority since the 1850s and were a conquered people before that (although a numerical majority). Furthermore, aboriginal groups claim the status of coequals with Canada and its white, European society, and thus they reject individual equality of the one-person-one-vote variety, at least on certain issues. Finally, advocates of a triple-E Senate insist that the enormous differences in population between large and small provinces make a mockery of majority rule, since the West or the Atlantic provinces will always lose in a conflict with Central Canada (that is, Ontario and Quebec), which contains two-thirds of the total population.

The first of these examples explains in large part why Canada became a federal state. As noted in other chapters, the Fathers of Confederation tried to solve a religious or social problem by territorial separation of antagonists. By giving provinces powers over language, education, property and civil rights, local business and commerce, and 'local affairs,' Canada created provinces in which the locally dominant group could exercise majority rule and protect its way of life without infringing on the majority rule of groups in other provinces or regions. Note that this stands in sharp contrast to the motives behind the adoption of federalism in the United States. There the concern was how to divide an otherwise potential majority into locally focused groups; federalism was seen as of a piece with the division of powers, checks and balances, and an unelected Senate: all were antidotes to the concentration of opinion which would allow 'the masses' to impose their will on government.[5] Of course, Canadian politicians in the 1860s also feared 'mob rule' and opted for an unelected Senate. But their concern was how to achieve majority rule in each province more than how to thwart it.[6]

This perspective on federalism found expression in many forms, and it has continued to exert influence on thinking in Quebec, although less so in some other parts of Canada. For example, the Tremblay Report in the 1950s, in expressing concern for the long-term viability of French culture in Quebec, put the point succinctly:

... the initiative of creating their own political and economic system according to their own concepts of order, liberty and progress was never entirely in their own hands ... That, let it be remembered, is essentially the drama of the conquest ... Only one thing could quiet their [French Catholic] fears but could not, however, fully reassure them, and that was the prospect of a provincial state whose government it would control by its votes and to which could be entrusted the guardianship of its ethnic, religious and cultural interests.[7]

Aboriginal groups refer to themselves as nations. They wish to deal with Canada on the basis of government-to-government. The renewed emphasis in recent years on treaty rights and obligations constitutes another version of this orientation. The agreement-in-principle in 1992 on the creation of a 'third order of government' to parallel the federal and provincial orders, although rejected in a referendum in October of that year, was thought feasible because it reflected the aspirations of self-determination and sovereignty, even if limited to 'within Canada.' Likewise, creation of the Territory of Nunavut – by splitting the Northwest Territories – has been viewed by most participants and observers as a step along the path to a province which would be overwhelmingly Inuit in composition, so that majority rule would help rather than hinder that group.

Demands by several provinces that the Canadian Senate be elected, effective, and equal (i.e., each province have an equal numbers of seats) may be evaluated from the perspective enunciated for Quebec and aboriginals. That is, the fear of a majority whose interests can be imposed on a more or less permanent minority (the West, the Maritimes) leads logically – in some minds – to an institution within the federal government in which Ontario and Quebec would be minorities. Thus, their dominance of the House of Commons (roughly 60 per cent of the seats) could be thwarted by a different majority in the Senate.

All of these examples involve, to one degree or another, a conflict or tension over the fundamental units of society. Should one conceive of society as composed of individuals whose preferences are to be counted equally, added up, and the majority rules? Or should one seek means to temper majority rule in light of the fundamental importance of groups or communities, whether religious, ethnic, racial, or regional? Much ink has been spilled over these questions, and yet more needs to be said. Instead of addressing them directly in the terms just stated, this chapter will come at these matters from another perspective to see if that sheds new light on them. In particular, we can ask whether our assumptions about the importance of territory may obscure reasoning about majority rule vs minority rights. Does it matter that some minorities are territorially based while others are not? Does having one's own territory protect a minority by providing a place where it can be the majority on certain issues? Are there ways of achieving the same goal in a non-territorial jurisdiction?

It turns out that answering this family of questions may help us to understand other matters not obviously, or at first sight, related to them. Hence, we will find that this exploration also offers insights into criteria for allocating jurisdictions between federal, provincial, and local governments. It also puts corporatism in a new perspective, and by extension raises questions about whether democracy needs a territorial base. Finally, self-determination, secession, and status as 'a people' turn out to be illuminated to some extent by these ruminations on majority rule. No doubt these large areas cannot be covered adequately in one chapter – or even in several – but as with most parts of this book, my concern is to open up topics for debate rather than to find answers which terminate a debate – to challenge our assumptions so that they may either be changed or be more firmly grounded because protected from this new challenge.

Non-territorial solutions to the sorts of problems just discussed should be considered seriously for at least three reasons. For one, there are only so many 'levels' of territorial government which can coexist, or at least so it seems. Even if one imagines a third order of government for aboriginals, that must be non-territorial in some fundamental aspects, as outlined in regard to Aboriginal Peoples Province in chapter 5. Second, the proliferation of cleavages in this century dwarfs the intellectual and political challenges posed by the religious cleavage of the nineteenth-century. It is essential to recall that the issue in the minds of Canadian politicians (and their British Colonial Office overseers) involved a single cleavage: Protestant vs Catholic. French and English language rights were an aspect of religion, not the separate issue that language has become. French-Catholic-rural culture constituted a package or bundle, as did Protestant–English language–British culture–parliamentary institutions. With immigration and with the rhetoric of rights, these dimensions have come unbundled for most Canadians, although arguably not for French-speaking Catholic native-born Quebeckers.

To the extent the bundles exist (at least in people's minds or perceptions), a very restricted number of levels of government are needed. At the time of Confederation, two levels or domains seemed sufficient. Had aboriginals figured more prominently in the deliberations, perhaps three orders of government would have been established, or perhaps different kinds and numbers of provinces. Today, one must think in terms of many more groups – as the agenda for constitutional change in 1992 and the debate over its ratification in the October referendum revealed.

The number of groups which feel they need political protection has mushroomed. That many groups have been legitimated by mention in the Charter of Rights and Freedoms has raised expectations by groups not mentioned that they too may aspire to greater freedom and liberty and to more effective protection from whatever majority they fear.[8] Thus, one may question whether territoriality ever served as full protection of minorities, and even more one may question whether it offers any promise to the plethora of groups occupying political stages in many countries.

LIBERTY AGAINST GOVERNMENT AND LIBERTY THROUGH GOVERNMENT

The third reason why non-territorial solutions to majority rule should be considered returns us in quite a different way to the historical evolution mentioned at the beginning of the last section. There we noted major differences over time in the emphasis placed on strengthening government or on shielding people from government. As with many choices, one should be wary of zero-sum thinking. If a strong government is helpful at times, and if strong rights are helpful at other times, might one more fruitfully ask whether they may both be beneficial under certain circumstances, rather than which to accept and which to reject?

Avoiding false dichotomies may be especially pertinent when one recalls the observation above that most successful 'separatist' movements (of colonies or of former Soviet republics) have been able to take control of existing governments. Obversely, many (although not all) unsuccessful ones have had no government they could commandeer. Thus, one may hypothesize that territorial integrity could be less important and governmental control more so than previously imagined. One approach to this question concerns non-territorial governments, but before returning to that theme, let us explore further the question of balance between government and rights.

Observe that some groups can be protected sufficiently – or even solely – by the Charter of Rights and Freedoms or by federal and provincial human rights codes. One thinks here of individual religious freedom, as well as rights against discrimination for groups like the disabled, women, gays and lesbians, and the elderly. One can always debate whether particular provisions are adequate or whether all relevant groups or types of individuals have been covered, but the broader point is that these types of people may be satisfied with non-discrimination and affirmative action guarantees.

Other minorities – especially those encompassing a 'way of life' – may require active government assistance or, indeed, even control of their own government in order to establish and maintain a range of institutions to meet their social and cultural needs. Quebeckers certainly believe this, although they disagree over whether it is enough to control a province or whether they must become a sovereign nation. As noted above, the origins of Confederation rest in part on the belief that provincial legislatures would reflect local majorities, whereas matters of common concern to all groups would be dealt with by the government in Ottawa. Aboriginals have long since come to the conclusion that their needs can be met only by some form of self-government. Of course, these many types of cohesive minorities do not eschew rights and freedoms, but they argue that those protections are not sufficient even if necessary. The reason in virtually all cases concerns the assumption that communities or collectivities need protection, and that individual rights do not generally serve that end.

This faith in government has a long and honourable history in Canada. Herschel Hardin characterizes it as the 'public enterprise' culture.[9] Frank Scott expounded a related perspective. He showed how 'liberty against government' had been, historically, the great battleground of the American and French Revolutions. He believed, however, that such liberty was not enough and that Canadians in particular had come to see that 'liberty through government' had some positive attractions.[10]

Although Scott's distinction between the two types of liberty is important, both types signify a lack of trust. In one case, individuals or minorities do not trust government to embody their needs or wishes and strive to entrench protections against government actions in appropriate topics of concern. In the other case, minorities trust the government they control and wish to strengthen its hand against another government which represents a larger majority within which they are a minority. In both cases, one feels more secure with entrenched constitutional provisions than with ordinary legislation or custom. The kinds of entrenched provisions differ, of course, between the two types of liberty, and they are easily confused with a debate about whether individual rights are more fundamental than collective rights. As Christian Dufour has framed the issue, 'in North America, where law has replaced war, constitutional rules represent the ultimate power.[11] Much of the debate over Canadian constitutional reform in the past two or three decades has reflected these concerns about using government to protect one's way of life.[12]

I have demonstrated elsewhere that the Canadian Charter of Rights and Freedoms contains several aspects of 'liberty through government.'[13] These include, most conspicuously, the 'notwithstanding clause' (section 33), which allows government to exempt a piece of legislation from some provisions of the Charter of Rights and Freedoms for up to five years; and the provision in section 1 that various rights and freedoms may be balanced or limited when benefits can be shown to be 'demonstrably justified in a free and democratic society.' These provisions – like the two types of liberty themselves – can and do come in conflict with other rights, and they have caused much debate. They should also make plain that even rights and freedoms in the category of liberty against government are to some degree at the mercy of liberty through government. Thus, it seems all the more necessary that a minority which feels threatened by broader majorities have access to governments sympathetic to its interests and point of view. In positing the two non-territorial provinces of Aboriginal Peoples Province and La Francophonie, in chapter 5, I have tried to show how their control of provincial governments with special powers suited to their needs would serve the cause of justice. This remains true of both territorial and non-territorial governments.

One can take the argument one step further by combining the concern about complexity with the present point about liberty through government. One may ask whether the increasing complexity of groups demanding rights or governments of their own has a logical conclusion. Part of the answer depends on perceptions which change as the culture changes (or vice versa), but a considerable portion also depends on new understandings of public and private, as outlined in earlier chapters.

At some points in history, political life took note of only a few 'interests.' At times these were 'estates'; at other times they were closer to occupations or classes – such as peasant, military, and commercial interests. During such historical periods, one could have a relatively clear-cut, even simple, organization of government. For example, the House of Lords represented estates, such as the nobility, clergy, and the like, while the House of Commons represented 'newer' interests, such as the gentry and later the commercial or industrial classes. These interests and estates were largely non-territorial. As greater emphasis was placed on territorial bases of political authority, people developed and used devices like federalism in conjunction with earlier ones like a bicameral legislature.

One should not conclude that these institutions could be relatively simple because society was more simple. Instead certain groups and interests were ignored, were deemed worthy of no notice, or were literally invisible. It is tempting to criticize such 'blind' ancestors and their benighted views. But charity to their incomplete vision may help to lessen the sting of criticism which will be heaped upon our era for 'blindly' ignoring so many groups and interests patently obvious to future generations. I do not know which these will be, but I am quite certain that we have ignored or undervalued some groups or individuals. As a left-hander, I like to think this feature will in the future attract more sympathy. Other possibilities include single parents and children or partners who have been abused; these groups may demand Charter rights so that they can seek compensation for our failure to protect them even though we know they suffer. We would perhaps defend ourselves by noting that these matters are 'private.' But feminist theorists have long since demonstrated many ways in which 'the personal is political.' As in other chapters, prediction is not my game. I wish only to make the point that our ability to see what earlier societies missed is no guarantee that we will be more insightful about ourselves than they were about their own blind spots.

Even if society is not more complex 'in reality,' there have been changes which make it appear more complex and thus pose new challenges. As democratic presumptions have become more engrained in our culture, we find it increasingly difficult to counter the claims of newly assertive groups. After all, if so many are worthy of inclusion in our politics, why would we want to exclude this new candidate? Thus, as social interests become more dense, complex, and competitive, they undergo what Coleman and Skogstad refer to as 'organizational development.'[14] This involves increasingly differentiated structures, more stable organizational bases, and greater professionalism. Whereas once an invisible hand served to coordinate individuals or firms, or small cohesive groups like estates seemed 'natural,' we are entering a stage when everyone must be consciously organized, and the question becomes whether they will organize themselves or be organized by others.

Organizational development has a compelling logic. As more and more interests, values, functions, and facets come into play – as, for instance, with the new communities outlined in chapter 6, or with the 'Charter groups' in Canada (those, as noted above, in s. 15) – it is not obvious who shares what interests with whom. Or, more precisely, only the members know; or maybe each member knows only about a few other people in the network. This follows from the unbundling I have repeatedly stressed. From particular roles or statuses, one used to be able to predict what other features a person would have. With unbundling, each person may play up certain features by joining electronic (or local) communities. But, as we saw in chapter 6, this can mean that one may 'be a different person' in each distinct community. Who 'belongs' may well be known within the community, but there are few overt 'markers' which are visible to outsiders.

Organizations or communities which just want to be left alone – as many do – can usually be so because they are, in effect, part of 'the majority.' That is, they fit or 'pass' within the accepted range of variants deemed 'normal.' Most of the communities hypothesized in chapter 6 would be invisible and accepted as 'mainstream,' and in part this reflects the fact that they do not represent a 'way of life' but a very specific focus for individual identities.

When a group wants to use government, the government will usually want proof that the organization does in fact speak for the community it claims to represent. In response, some private organizations take on characteristics of public, governmental bodies with their own bureaucracies, internal elections, formal dues or fees, accountability for money spent, and so forth. Some such organizations have been set up and/or funded by governments, raising serious questions about who is representing whose interests to whom. Even 'independent' organizations often receive tax credits or subsidies from governments, and that too is part of 'liberty through government.' But all of these valuable services, when taken in the aggregate, result in a blurring of the line between 'public' and 'private.' That is not necessarily bad, but it has been done inadvertently. I have repeatedly noted how assumptions sink below the threshold of awareness, and thus we lose conscious control of some aspects of our public or private lives. By calling attention to this blurring of a formerly clear line between public and private, I hope to focus attention without prejudging the value society will place on the outcome.

To conclude this section, let us recall its larger purpose: in considering reasons for seeking non-territorial solutions to problems of majority rule, we distinguished between liberty against government and liberty through government. In chapter 5, I explained why at least two communities in Canada need their own government and thus their own province or order of government. In chapter 6, I outlined some new communities likely to become prominent or common in the unbundled world. The latter part of this section has speculated that the line will blur between encompassing communities which constitute 'a people' and seek public endorsement for their 'way of life' and those new communities of choice ('virtual communities') in the unbundled world. Once again I prefer to think of these speculations as scenarios rather than predictions. Some of the ways in which we try to solve problems of majority rule may lead us to blur the lines – or perhaps just to evolve a new balance – between the public and private realms which were a product of the historical forces producing territorial nations, individualism, and rights.

CONDITIONS FOR MAJORITY RULE

Because I intend this chapter to focus on situations in which we surmise that majority rule may be an unjust imposition on a minority, it might be helpful to point out many situations in which majority rule does not appear to cause concern. Although one cannot easily quantify these conditions, my guess is that they greatly outnumber the occasions which concern us. That does not remove the need to deal with the problem when it arises, but it puts the severity of the problem in perspective.

Majority rule is not a problem when everyone agrees. Some societies are very consensual, and most societies have areas or topics of consensus even when deep divisions exist on other topics. This observation – banal though it appears – has significant import because it suggests that majority rule is a tool to be used only under certain conditions. The choice should not be all or nothing, always majority rule or never majority rule.

Majority rule may be more easily justified when the issue arouses weak preferences rather than intense ones or when the decision concerns allowing something rather than forbidding something. For example, Sunday shopping probably falls into both of these conditions: few people put it near the top of the agenda, and no one is forced to shop or work on Sunday anyway, at least in the provinces where it has been implemented.

Majority rule may not pose a problem when the 'permanent minority' can be given a territory of its own where it will be a majority. That was the justification for adopting a federal system in Canada: Protestant and Catholic, English and French, would each have majority status somewhere. Of course, any given minority may not be concentrated so that it can have its own territory. I will elaborate this point in the next section, and it remains the principal justification for seeking non-territorial solutions to majority rule.

Majority rule is not a problem when membership is voluntary. If you do not approve of what the majority chooses in your club, you can 'exit.' This is rarely an option for cultural minorities in a nation-state. Even when it is an option – as many 'separatists' in Quebec claim – it is difficult to accomplish and has severe transition costs. Nevertheless, I will return to this option at other points in the chapter, since non-territorial accommodations for minorities may put secession in a slightly different light. Perhaps there is greater voluntarism in nations than our assumptions about territory have allowed us to see.

If consensus, voluntary membership, and federalism allow for fair use of majority rule, then their obverses should specify the conditions under which we would express concern about imposing majority rule. Majority rule is a *prima facie* problem when diversity occurs within a territory with a relatively fixed or immobile population and when issues must be resolved authoritatively, that is, must apply to everyone in the territory. Even then, we may alleviate the problem by privacy provisions, charters of rights, appeal courts, and the like. Nevertheless, it is worth exploring other avenues in order to see whether assumptions about territoriality are part of the problem.

NON-TERRITORIAL MINORITIES

All minorities are non-territorial. It is a matter of degree. The exceptions (such as some Hutterite communities in the Prairies) are so few or small that they fail to qualify this generalization to any serious degree.[15] By non-territorial, I mean that the minority cannot be given its own exclusive territory without movement of people on a scale we would regard as dictatorial and insensitive. Non-territoriality comes in two forms in the case of cultural minorities (and many other types of minorities, too): some members of the minority do not reside in the territory and so do not benefit from being part of the majority there; and some non-members of the cultural group reside in the territory and are thus 'permanent' minorities there. The former problem questions the assumption of contiguity, while the latter problem challenges the assumption of continuity.

It is perhaps helpful to recall the discussion in chapter 5 of La Francophonie and of Aboriginal Peoples Province. Each was a hypothetical solution to minority status, each being quite different because the territorial situations of the minorities were different. The difference between Quebec and La Francophonie as protectors of French-language rights highlights the essentially non-territorial nature of francophones outside Quebec as a minority: their community occupies territory which is neither continuous nor contiguous. Aboriginal Peoples Province would also violate the assumption of contiguity, but one cannot foresee the degree to which continuity might be violated. Nevertheless, to some degree aboriginal peoples – considered for the moment as a single minority – are a non-territorial minority and one which is non-territorial in a somewhat different way than are francophones.

No one, I am certain, will challenge the conclusion that most minorities are non-territorial. For example, it is not plausible to define 'their own territory' for the working class, gays and lesbians, women, the disabled, youth, the elderly, left-handers, or large immigrant groups. No one has given serious consideration to the possibility, and thus for those minorities Canadians have deemed worth protecting (in one way or another, all of the above except left-handers), we have relied on non-territorial solutions such as rights, privacy provisions, and non-discrimination codes. These devices are subject to criticism and could be improved, but they are generally viewed as significant advances over informal protections in earlier eras.

Yet most people persist in suggesting that territorial solutions would be appropriate for certain groups, especially aboriginals and francophones, which is why I return to those examples repeatedly. As I have argued, territorial solutions for these groups have serious flaws. Thus, I offer the conclusion that non-territorial solutions to the problem of 'permanent' minorities under majority rule are generally preferable to territorial solutions. Since this may not have been true in all historical periods, it is not a 'law' of human society; but our technological situation makes some non-territorial solutions more and more attractive.

TARGETING AND SORTING PEOPLE

Territorially based majority rule without opting-out founders on the problem of cultural minorities intermingled with majority groups. A non-territorial 'solution' to the use of majority rule, therefore, requires that we be able to identify, sort, and target individuals according to group membership. That can be done visually for some 'visible minorities,' although affirmative action programs usually find that some (or even most) members of the visible group refuse to be classified in that way. Regardless of that, most minorities must be identified in non-visible fashion; and we need to keep track of them so that they can be targeted whenever a decision involving them needs to be made.

We saw in chapter 1 that technology now exists for these purposes, though many people fear that these very purposes could be subverted, and authoritarian rather than minority-protective regimes could be put in place. That is a legitimate concern. Here let us note only that the intent is benign, that only certain groups and issues raise the concern, and that the threat may be reduced or eliminated by reliance on more specialized organizations rather than on 'all-purpose' territorial political forms. Whatever the dangers in practice, let us at least explore the possibilities on paper.

The serious conceptual problem – as opposed to the authoritarian threat we have set aside – concerns specifying criteria for membership in a general way. Once we have criteria in place, the technology can do the sorting and targeting.

Let me pose the question in a different way. We have adduced examples of cultural minorities which might be 'permanent' minorities under majority rule, but they are relatively obvious and membership is easy to specify. Whatever ambiguities may arise at the margins about who is a francophone or an aboriginal, we have no difficulty in seeing why their ways of life might result in their being in the minority on 'too many' issues. But how do we decide on the particular groups or ways of life which should be protected or insulated to some degree from majority rule? This involves in part a question of how individuals identify with groups, but also how groups relate to each other. If we are not careful, we could find every group entitled to special protection. Of course, historically we have often made the judgment on the basis of who had the political clout to get themselves mentioned in the Charter of Rights, human rights codes, and similar instruments. That may work politically, but this sort of analytic exploration of territoriality requires a more systematic set of criteria. The next section will open the debate by exploring a few candidates as 'permanent minorities' in need of protection and the implicit criteria which thereby bar other groups from this status and protection.

WHAT IS 'A PEOPLE'?

In the abstract one might argue convincingly that 'a people' – having, as they do, the right to self-determination – should have special protection from a dominant majority society. Otherwise, such a people might, depending on territorial configuraitons, try to separate and form its own country. That option may be attractive, and I will explore below the sense in which we might encourage separatism in some cases. Presumably our concern about majority rule, however, rests on the hope or assumption that separatism is too costly or otherwise not a realistic option. Thus, the question of who deserves a majority status in some non-territorial political unit may be specified as whether a particular group constitutes 'a people.'

The first conceptual clarification here involves acknowledging that *categories or groups* may be constituted by the sum of individual choices. They do not constitute 'a people.' Two sub-types may be mentioned for Canada. There are a host of groups or categories which have a specific common interest but are otherwise indistinguishable from the rest of society. I include here almost all the so-called 'Charter Canadians': women, elderly, disabled, gays and lesbians, and others listed in s. 15 of the Charter. One might also include left-handers, smokers, non-smokers, red-heads, tall or short people, obese individuals, and a host of others. Such categories consist of individuals who may form support groups or lobbying organizations but who cannot be imagined in isolation from whatever society or country one is discussing. By themselves, no single category like any of these could ever be 'a people.'

The second type at the individual level of analysis comprises – for Canada – all immigrants and their descendants who came to Canada since the late eighteenth-century, that is, since the founding of the British colonies which eventually came to constitute what we now call Canada. The exceptions will be mentioned in the next paragraph, but they are an extremely small proportion of immigrants. Here I have in mind all of the usual census categories of immigrants and their descendants, including Irish, Germans, Italians, Japanese, Indians (often called East Indians), Vietnamese, and so on. These people chose Canada as a home or refuge *as individuals or families*. They consciously chose to leave another society or were forcibly removed from somewhere and chose to settle in Canada. In other words, they did not come to Canada as a collectivity, even though they may now self-identify as a distinct group within the Canadian mosaic.

The importance of this distinction may be noted by contrasting these types of people with groups who chose to come to Canada as collectivities. Examples include several groups of Hutterites and Old-Order Mennonites who made community-wide decisions about leaving their homes in Europe and moving to Canada. They negotiated with the

Canadian government *as a group* for concessions to their uniquely collective way of life, including joint ownership of land, exemption from military service, and other matters. They explored options in other countries but chose Canada because of a combination of concessions and economic opportunities.[16]

In quite a different sense, one could say that some provinces chose to join Canada as collectivities also. The initial provinces made such a choice, and so Ontario, Quebec, Nova Scotia, and New Brunswick 'founded' Canada. Then other British colonies made a collective choice to join later, including British Columbia, Prince Edward Island, Manitoba, and most recently, in 1949, Newfoundland. Only Alberta and Saskatchewan did not enter as colonies; instead, the federal government created them on its own initiative (and also greatly enlarged a few other provinces) by incorporating what had formerly been Rupert's Land and parts of the Northwest Territories.

The significance of collective choices by some of these groups lies in what they gained. Hutterites and Mennonites gained enough concessions to make them exempt in very important ways from majority rule. They are to be left alone and allowed to opt out of certain 'mainstream' duties, obligations, or rules. They pay income tax collectively rather than individually, for example, and have different rules about property and inheritance. The provinces – even those not joining Canada as pre-existing units – have their own governments with important jurisdictions. Thus, they constitute 'the majority' somewhere and do not need the nonterritorial solutions proposed in this book. Of course, as noted above, some of the provinces do feel threatened by federal government actions and have proposed a triple-E Senate, redrawing of jurisdictions, or other reforms. They are not, nevertheless, permanent or temporary minorities without governments to act on their behalf.

There are two categories of groups not considered so far. The first consists of groups who chose Canada but failed to get concessions or their own government. In Canada, this is a null category, but it could be quite significant in some other countries. I do not wish to discuss it in the abstract, because any such groups could be handled in the same way as the last group to be mentioned.

The final category consists of the two communities for whom I have proposed non-territorial provinces. Stated in general terms, they deserve to become non-territorial majorities to whom a government should be accountable. There is a simple reason for this: they did not choose to come to Canada, either individually or collectively. Instead Canada was

Majority Rules 221

imposed on them by force, by settlement, by treaties honoured or not honoured, incrementally in the case of aboriginals and all at once by the conquest of New France during 1759–60.[17]

The situations of these two groups may be contrasted sharply with the others mentioned. Aboriginals and francophones did not come to Canada; they were here first. At the time of Confederation, aboriginals got no concessions except to be wards of the federal government through the device of the Indian Act. That act embodied a policy of assimilation, not of protection, although, as it happens, an unsuccessful policy of assimilation. At Confederation, Quebec was granted bilingual status, although that was to protect the English minority more than the French majority. Quebec did get certain important concessions, besides all the jurisdictions of a province; the most notable being the Civil Code rather than the Common Law, which applies in the rest of Canada. Francophones outside of Quebec, however, were given no protections, or those protections (the Manitoba Schools Act among them) were ignored or overridden.

The other groups came to Canada collectively with concessions to their way of life, or they came as individuals. As individuals, they did not expect or demand concessions to their way of life beyond whatever all residents or citizens enjoyed. It has only been in our lifetimes that Germans, Italians, and others have argued that their communities deserve special protections. These pressures, in consort with those from non-ethnic groups like women, the disabled, gays and lesbians, and labour unions, account for most of the major advances in rights codes, affirmative actions, and similar measures. Collective institutions have not led to a view of these communities as potential non-territorial majorities.

EXIT, VOICE, LOYALTY

It is not necessary at this point to codify precisely what 'a people' need be in order to ground a presumptive right to be a non-territorial majority rather than a permanent minority. Just as I have no urge to make specific predictions in this book, I also do not want to 'legislate' hard and fast rules for identifying what 'a people' must be in the unbundled world. I do believe that it was necessary to demonstrate that plausible criteria can be enunciated, so that one does not have to accept the claim of every group that they too need a province or other non-territorial government or political unit. I think the criteria specified above have that plausibility.

In this section, I want to recapitulate the argument in terms of Albert O. Hirschman's concepts of exit, voice, and loyalty.[18]

The immigrant groups, whether arriving individually or collectively, have already exercised the 'exit' option. That is how they got to Canada, and in principle it is an option for leaving Canada in the future. Indeed, some Doukhobors split off from the main group in Canada and moved as a group to Latin America. Aboriginals and francophones did not arrive in Canada by exercising the option to 'exit' from elsewhere, although as individuals they can move elsewhere. Since Canada came to them, rather than the reverse, it would be unreasonable to ask them to 'exit.'

Aboriginals and francophones have exercised the 'loyalty' option in different ways. Treaties embody this option for many aboriginal groups, although not for all. In constitutional discussions in recent years, most aboriginal leaders – with notable exceptions like Joe Norton of the Mohawks – have stated that self-determination or a third order of government will occur 'within Canada.' Francophones outside Quebec have actively supported the policy of bilingualism, minority language rights, French schools and school boards, and other measures and thereby have repeatedly affirmed 'loyalty' to the existing Canadian political system, albeit reformed in various ways.

The non-territorial provinces I have proposed represent, to my way of thinking, an innovative way of letting these groups have a new or enhanced 'voice' in Canada. Such 'voice' has never been offered to aboriginals until this past decade, when local self-government, Nunavut, and a third order of government have been mooted. There has been, however, a history of 'voice' for francophones outside Quebec. A brief review of some of that history reveals why the option outlined here needs consideration, since the previous 'voice' has been weakened in various ways.

French-speaking Quebeckers were, at the time of Confederation, very Quebec-centred. They were largely ignorant of, or unconcerned with, other French groups in Acadia, the West, or Ontario. Confederation, for them, represented a way of gaining a homeland, an exclusive territory where they could be the majority. In the late nineteenth century, however, French Quebeckers came to identify with and to offer assistance to some of the French minorities, especially Métis groups and other French speakers in the Prairies and Franco-Americans in New England. One may conceptualize these ties as a form of 'extra-territoriality.'[19] A.I. Silver attributes a good part of these attitudes to an understanding of British imperialism, which was, of course, at its apex at the time of Confederation. Imperialism, many French Canadians believed, validated the idea that 'home base' could intervene in far-away (i.e., noncontiguous) places in order to correct wrongs and set things right.

Once French Quebeckers 'reached out' to other francophones, they could begin to conceptualize Confederation as a bicultural deal in a way that was difficult previously. Up until then, federalism was just a way of gaining a province of their own. When redefined as a bilingual or bicultural deal, Confederation could be seen as an agreement between 'two nations.' By the early part of this century, André Siegfried focused on the 'racial' (or, as we would say, ethnic or national) basis of Canada,[20] harking back in a way to Lord Durham's striking phrase in 1839 of 'two nations warring in the bosom of a single country.' By the 1950s and 1960s, Pierre Trudeau revived these concepts indirectly when he championed Henri Bourassa's notion of a country-wide bilingualism.

So long as Quebec saw itself as the protector of French in all regions of Canada, francophone minorities in other provinces had 'voice.' At the time of the Quiet Revolution in the 1960s and even more during the government formed by the Parti Québécois (1976–84), Quebec turned 'inward' – 'Maîtres chez nous' (Masters of our home) became the motto – and gave up on the viability of the pockets of francophones outside its borders. The French language in Quebec has 'voice' and need have few fears about disappearing. The French communities outside of Quebec (and perhaps outside Acadia in New Brunswick) have lost 'voice' and are indeed fearful and threatened. Thus, I propose a non-territorial province tentatively named La Francophonie.

MORE ALTERNATIVES

Even if a group does not constitute 'a people' entitled to its own territorial or non-territorial government, we should consider mechanisms which could benefit it. Some are territorial while others are non-territorial. Some have been tried in Canada; others have not. Some can be utilized in conjunction with other solutions; some cannot.

The first alternative has been used in Canada in several ways. It involves sharing or rotation of majority and minority in key positions. In each double-member constituency in provincial elections in Prince Edward Island, it has been the practice of all major parties to nominate one Catholic and one Protestant. Obviously, voters determine whether the proportions elected turn out to reflect precisely that balance. The relevant point here takes note of the decision to share positions as equitably as possible. Another example involves the rotation of Speakers of the House of Commons between English and French. Likewise, the Liberal Party has tried throughout this century to ensure an alternation of English and French leaders, although the balance is not equal in terms of years of service and the formal rules do not require this alternation. Indeed, the very concept of government and official opposition in a parliamentary system rests on the belief that it is beneficial that parties alternate in office, even if not at specific or regular intervals, because parties represent different mixtures of interests.

Experiments with double majorities – or, in Calhoun's phrase, 'concurrent majorities' – have proven cumbersome but often effective in protecting localized or diffuse minorities. The American Congress might serve as one example, since the House of Representatives closely reflects population in single-member districts, whereas each of the fifty states has equal representation (two) in the Senate. Both chambers must agree on every piece of legislation. A Canadian example occurred in the United Provinces of Canada (what is now Quebec and Ontario) in the period 1841–67. Although not required by law, most ministries were constructed by putting an English (Protestant) and a French (Catholic) minister jointly in charge of each department; and if the prime minister was English (Protestant), then a deputy or co–prime minister had to be French (Catholic). The awkwardness and instability of this system of 'dual ministries' was one of the motives for Confederation; and it showed that an informal system (however well intentioned) could only work if trust was widespread, which is of course not common. The principal amending formula in the Canadian Constitution Act, 1982, the so-called '7 and 50' rule, requires that two-thirds (7) of the provinces which contain at least 50 per cent of the population must approve constitutional amendments, thus ensuring a double majority of people and provinces.

A final example of an alternative which can protect various kinds of minorities – whether or not 'a people' – involves electoral systems. Jean A. Laponce has catalogued and analysed scores of ways in which aspects of electoral systems have been manipulated to try to reassure minorities about their 'welcome' or security in a country where they clearly could not aspire to majority status.[21] I wish to focus briefly on only a couple of options.

There are several ways to arrange reserved seats in a legislature. One may restrict the candidates to members of a particular group – low caste or tribal groups in India, for example – and ensure their representation even if members of all groups living in the constituency are allowed to vote. Alternatively, one may restrict the eligible voters in a territorial or non-territorial constituency to a particular group – such as aboriginals or francophones – and let the parties pick the candidates; to have a chance of winning, each party will almost certainly pick a candidate sharing the status of the voters in the restricted electorate.

Multi-member constituencies combined with proportioned representation, especially if 'at large' for a province or country, serve to protect minorities of all kinds (unless minuscule in number). If the minimum percentage of vote needed to elect a member (the 'quota') is very low – say, 5–8 per cent in a large constituency – one may be able to protect several minorities and still allow 'mainstream' candidates and parties to achieve fair representation. One may cite the Australian Senate as an instance, since with twelve members per state the quota is quite low; and in fact the range of partisan, ideological, and minority views exceeds that of the House of Representatives, which relies on single-member districts with transferable votes.

No electoral system or other 'gimmicks' like double-majorities can guarantee that a minority will be able to hold its own against the majority. That would in any case be profoundly undemocratic unless restricted to a few very specific circumstances such as minority language rights. The crucial point of electoral arrangements – and to some extent the others mentioned in this section – concerns their guarantee that key minorities are not under-represented or ignored completely. Whether such arrangements magnify minority powers or simply give them a modest 'voice' depends crucially on many other conditions, including relative size of the 'majority' (40, 50, 90 per cent, etc.); whether there is a minority government or a coalition government; whether a single majority party confronts several small parties; whether the legislature is unicameral or bicameral; and whether the system is federal and thus allows at least the possibility of provincial governments which speak for or give 'voice' to different interests than the national government.

This chapter cannot explore all of these combinations, nor should it. The purpose of the chapter has been to demonstrate that some minorities can be protected only by their controlling a government, that some governments can be accountable as non-territorial political authorities, and thus that the range of options for minorities is much greater than we usually recognize. This section has tried to point out that some mechanisms less potent than a government may still offer protection, benefit, and hope to minorities who feel threatened or fear permanent marginalization. These purposes having been accomplished, the remainder of the chapter will explore some implications of these observations.

CORPORATISM AND UNBUNDLING

Robert Dahl has argued that 'corporate pluralism,' or 'corporatism' as it is usually called, may involve a transformation of governing institutions 'as fundamental and lasting as the change from the institutions of popular government in the city-state to the institutions of polyarchy in the nation-state.'[22] His reasons for this conclusion include the new concept of representation implied by occupational organizations (labour unions, business) sharing power with governments. He also sees the corporate 'peak organizations' which jointly agree on policies as, in effect, an unelected parliament. Corporatism has many of the characteristics of Arendt Lijphart's concept of 'consociational democracy,' except that the former creates 'pillars' based on occupation or class and the latter's pillars reflect cultural communities.[23]

Corporatism in their discussions refers to the 'tripartite' version found in Western Europe. It is distinct in some respects from the 'Iberian' or Latin American kind of corporatism. The latter may involve many more than three groups; and the latter has usually been fostered by a more authoritarian or *dirigiste* state. Both forms of corporatism, by contrast to federalism as usually practised, may be characterized as non-territorial. By that I mean that within a territorial nation-state, no group (such as business, labour, the church, or others) can be said to have exclusive control of any particular territory; instead they all share a national territory, which is why they must collaborate.

Corporatism shares several features with my concept of unbundling, and indeed they are mutually supportive. Most crucial among the similarities is that both are inherently non-territorial forms of organization. The three pillars of government, business, and labour obviously coexist in the same territory; none of the three can claim exclusive control, even though the government acts as the executive arm for the state, which does claim exclusive sovereignty. The fact of power-sharing, however, undercuts any claim by the government to sovereignty in the degree asserted a century ago. Furthermore, the state and its government have been reduced by this power-sharing to a less inclusive, overarching, or all-purpose institution. As I have stated repeatedly, the nation-state is in no danger of extinction, but its functions have become less ubiquitous or all-encompassing.

Another feature shared by these forms of political organization derives from voluntary membership. As chapter 6 demonstrated, many communities in the unbundled world will be voluntary or achievement-oriented, and fewer will be based on ascriptive characteristics. This also seems to be the case with business and labour, exclusive categories but ones with highly permeable boundaries. As more 'peak organizations' form, if they do in countries with corporate-style governance, they will undoubtedly also be voluntary – for example, consumer associations or environmental preservation groups. Ascriptive communities will not disappear any more than nations will, but we can predict their downgrading in the hierarchy of identities for many people. As that occurs, it may become even more urgent that the remaining ascriptive groups, especially cultural minorities who constitute 'a people,' are not oppressed by the majority for whom such ascriptive characteristics have become nearly invisible because of their focus on voluntary communities.

Important features of the worlds of corporatism and unbundling will still be distinct. Perhaps the sharpest difference lies in the degree of concentration of power or authority in the peak organizations. The diverse and myriad communities of the unbundled world could never, I have argued, be coordinated or represented by the hierarchical organizations assumed essential by corporatism.

Yet one must insist that the issue is not which form of organization to choose, as though they were mutually contradictory. Both pose threats to the nation-state but in different ways. Even if every citizen became enmeshed in one or another peak organization – and thereby participated indirectly in setting industrial policy and perhaps fiscal or monetary policy – each citizen would have access to the unlimited number of communities analysed in chapter 6 as well as traditional cultural communities. Again we return to the conclusion that the world of correlated statuses and forced choice among groups or identities has been giving way to a world in which one may add almost indefinitely to one's identities by joining communities which emphasize specific aspects of value to the person.

MIGRATION AND APARTHEID

Citizenship and its attendant rights have become cherished possessions, and nowhere more than in the affluent societies. For most of Europe and North America and a few other outposts, affluence coexists with relatively low population densities, and thus these societies guard their borders so that only a fraction of the envious millions in poor countries may enter and remain as citizens. Ironically, it seems that for the vast majority of human beings, place of birth and citizenship have become ascriptive characteristics rather than achieved or 'earned.' Ironic because the dominant thrust of Western political thought for centuries has been an effort to shift emphasis from ascriptive characteristics to personal achievement as the basis of life chances. And yet during this period these same nations have been turning citizenship into a birthright rather than a human right. This is most obvious in cases like Germany and Israel, which have legislated a 'right of return.' The reunification of East and West Germany has, for example, brought back as instant citizens many former residents of Eastern Europe or the former Soviet Union who speak no German but derive from German ancestry. Obversely, 'guestworkers' from Turkey, Greece, and elsewhere may live in Germany for decades and speak German perfectly but are not eligible for citizenship.[24] These provisions make it apparent that citizenship can be an ascriptive characteristic. But they differ only in degree from the impediments and restrictions common in almost all countries today.

The most common defence of these restrictive powers, aside from selfish concern to maintain one's own affluence and lack of crowding, involves preservation of a culture.[25] That is, the majority in a society has relied on the argument we have been examining for protecting a minority way of life. Of course, on a world scale, the majority in any country is a minority. But having control of a state and territory puts each such apparent 'world minority' very much into the enviable position that engenders our concern about minority cultures. By forcibly keeping out the millions who wish to share what we have been born into, do we create a version of *apartheid*? Can one use this term of opprobrium for sovereign nations or only, as in South Africa, where a majority creates enclaves against the will of the minority or minorities so segregated? In other words, is there a significant difference between, on the one hand, creating segregated living by 'inventing' nations and imposing them on the rest of the world and, on the other hand, creating 'homelands' which are not fully sovereign or which do not reflect the political will of the minority to occupy that particular piece of turf?

My attention to assumptions about territoriality has repeatedly led to questions about non-territorial ways of achieving goals which in recent centuries were thought to be dependent on territorial political units. If we can convert some territorial political units into non-territorial affiliation, do we reduce the need for migration? For the non-territorial communities in chapter 6, participation or 'citizenship' depends not at all on migration in a physical sense. Likewise the non-territorial provinces of Aboriginal Peoples Province and La Francophonie were conceptualized to minimize the need for migration as a defence for the minority's way of life.

If I have uncovered a formula for turning at least some kinds of territorial minorities into non-territorial majorities, is this just another version of *apartheid*? Or does *apartheid* apply only to territorial segregation? Since a comprehensive answer to these questions would require more than one section of a chapter, only an incomplete sketch will be given here. The aim, as before, will be to outline a scenario and not to offer precise predictions. Without knowledge of the outcome of the processes examined in this book, one cannot provide proper evaluations. For example, will non-territorial provinces protect the minorities who become majorities, and will they be felt by citizens to be equal in value to the existing territorial provinces? Until we can answer 'yes' to these queries, it is virtually impossible to make the case that non-territorial separatism is quite different from *apartheid*. I believe it is worth considering these options, but I recognize that they leave open many important and frustrating questions. But if we do not think through such scenarios, we are unlikely to realize any benefits they might offer.

'Separate but equal' and 'different but equal' are expressions which have been used to justify racial and gender inequities. But they can be true of certain kinds of comparisons, if both 'sides' or groups feel the same way. For example, Afro-Americans in the South during the century after the Civil War were not the ones who believed that their schools and white schools were 'separate but equal.' If views about equality are reciprocated – as seems to be the case between most sovereign nations – then they may not be primarily a mask for oppression and exploitation. So again we come up against an empirical question about the mutuality of perceptions and respect between territorial and non-territorial political units, and our answers are speculations about scenarios. All one can say is that mutual respect seems possible, but it may depend on the specific history of exploitation between the groups. Bosnia in the 1990s does not seem a prime candidate for this suggestion, whereas La Francophonie and Aboriginal Peoples Province have greater plausibility.

'A room of one's own' was the phrase Virginia Woolf used to describe the basis of empowerment for women (especially women writers).[26] In her eyes, that room would not be a ghetto or a form of *apartheid*. But recall that she also recommended a reasonable income independent of the husband's. Thus, one may speculate that some kinds of 'contiguous solitudes' have potential to heal some wounds, but only when the majority or the dominant group (or husband) accepts the solution as a form of genuine equality.

Let us return to 'exit,' 'voice,' and 'loyalty.' These are often viewed as three distinct and independent courses of action for an individual or group. Hirschman's analysis suggests that the interconnections among the three are more important than any one avenue alone. For example, loyalty has much more meaning when exit is a live option. Likewise failing to reward loyalty and to allow voice will lead with near certainty to exit, or at least attempted exit. Hence, for a majority to accept a non-territorial entity in which the minority has some of the privileges of a majority, at least on some key policies, should engender some degree of trust and loyalty in the very act of 'exit.'

The examples and arguments just given assume some degree of respect and mutuality. These limit the applicability of non-territorial as well as territorial solutions. But even when the majority really intends to help the minority feel secure, we come up against the issue of international migration. 'Exit' implies 'entrance.' Can we avoid hypocrisy in letting minorities become majorities (whether in a territorial or non-territorial space) by 'exiting' while refusing to allow immigration? It seems contradictory to allow one but not the other; however, immigration may create minorities afresh or increase present minorities to majority status and thus challenge the current majority's security. Have we earned our status as affluent majority here, or were we just the lucky inheritors of an accidental privilege? I will offer only one more possible defence at this point.

Let us recall that Europe during the period of transition to nation-states was, on average, no more affluent than many other parts of the world.[27] The life expectancies, technical achievements, and artistic wonders of Europeans may even have been below those of China, India, the Aztecs, Incas, some Muslim polities, and perhaps others. Thus, one needs to explain why 'the West' is now so enormously more affluent than the areas which once surpassed it in opulence. Of course, conquest, plunder, and colonialism may have aided Europe; that these events fully account for the difference seems unlikely when one turns to the rise of capitalism in parallel with the creation of nation-states in Europe.[28]

In chapter 3, I speculated whether the creation of nation-states and the invention of capitalism were separate processes or two sides of the same coin. Either way, they both grew to 'maturity' in Europe and only later were transplanted elsewhere. Thus, whatever the extra boost from conquest or imperial links, Europeans stumbled on a device (or two devices) for creating wealth.

That device clearly is exportable. Japan is the most striking example, but many others can be offered. How can one best share this 'secret' to wealth? I speculated in chapter 3 that networks of corporations may allow wealth to be generated across great distances via electronic and other networks of cooperation. The communities of chapter 6 may also play a useful role. Whether this will prove to be an entirely benign process cannot be known until many groups have tried it, but I must point out one implication which suggests that its success might undermine the intent of this chapter, which is to create zones or spaces in which minority ways of life may be preserved or made to feel secure.

The wealth-sharing networks postulated in previous chapters will, at least in the first instance, engage the participation of those people in poor countries who might otherwise be most likely to 'exit' and try to migrate to wealthier places. If so, will these individuals and families remain within their natal nation-states but become, in effect, 'citizens' of here? If so, how much of their culture, way of life, and rootedness there must be sacrificed to achieve what citizens of affluent countries were born to? How much does it matter? And will they then become a dispossessed 'people' in their country and seek to form a non-territorial political unit there which allows them to exercise majority control?

DEMOCRACY, VOICE, AND LOYALTY

Two views of democracy have coexisted for a long time. In one view, the danger inherent in democracy derives from the difficulty we have in disciplining government, in making it enact the will of the people. This view prevails at the present time and accounts, at least in part, for the cynicism of the public and their negative views of most politicians. In the other view, the danger is perceived as the likelihood that governments will be tempted to 'buy' votes or to 'sell out' to large vote blocs by offering expensive or superficially attractive policies. If so, the majority can all too easily encourage its government to retain power by catering to its wishes or whims, and thus the minorities (whether cultural or elitist or whatever) can be overwhelmed and frozen out.

Our view of remote or unresponsive governments contrasts sharply with the second view, which was at its peak in the English-speaking world during the French Revolution and continued through the nineteenth century. Ironically, the other great revolution of that era – the American – brought to dominance a generation of politicians who wrote into the United States Constitution the view that institutional arrangements were needed to insulate the government from the fickle moods of mobocracy. These arrangements, of course, included federalism, the separation of powers (in contrast to the concentration of executive power in parliamentary systems), and checks and balances. Later they added the Bill of Rights. In taking for granted the value of these inhibiters of 'democracy run wild,' the American founding fathers agreed with this premise of the French revolutionaries but evaluated the consequences differently.

One need not – indeed should not – assume that one of these views is correct and the other false or misleading. The contradictory nature of these perspectives and their correctness in specific situations does no more than highlight the fundamental nature of politics. Political life centres around the need to resolve contradictory, incompatible, independent, and incommensurate views. If disputes can be resolved by reference to rules, we call that bureaucracy. When rules conflict or when rules fail us, we resort to politics. Sometimes we can 'trade off' positions or compromise our positions ('split the difference') or redefine the problem so that there are no clear winners or losers. But sometimes we cannot. Then we are tempted to retreat to first principles, but they are as often as not the underlying source of the dispute. And so at some point, we rise above our principles and ask that the majority should prevail after a free and fair vote.

Majority rule explicitly assumes that all principles and views are equal, and it implicitly assumes that 'the chips' will fall at random. Hence, all citizens have one vote and thereby 'voice.' The opportunity to 'have one's say' should, in this scenario, be coupled with 'loyalty' in Hirschman's sense. Loyalty means that losers do not automatically 'exit' or 'take their marbles and go home,' wherever 'home' may be. Why should one express loyalty in this way? What incentives do losers have to be loyal? As noted at the beginning of this chapter, the incentive consists in the expectation that one will sometimes be in the majority and not always in the minority. We have seen that this expectation is not reasonable for all types of minorities. And yet the majority generally acts as though their 'voice' leading to their 'loyalty' should be paralleled by the 'voice' of the minority leading to its 'loyalty.'

'Let's all dance together,' said the elephant to the chickens. Let Canadians take a vote on whether they should all speak English or all speak French. Let Canadians or Americans or Australians take a vote on whether to give the land back to the aboriginals. Few people would argue that justice would be served for minorities in such votes. Certainly it would be hard to find chickens, French speakers, or aboriginals who thought these examples of majority vote were fair and just. And yet, astonishingly, there are a great many members of minorities who do not 'exit.' They may or may not have loud voices, but they remain loyal in many unpromising situations. Part of the reason they do not take their marbles and go home is that the land, the territory itself, constitutes the marbles and home; and they must share the land with others or lose it. Thus, my concern to find a way to secure a majority in a non-territorial framework.

This discussion of non-territorial alternatives to majority rule can offer no certainties. I cannot assure either the majority or the minority that these suggestions will work to everyone's advantage. But I am quite certain that territorial nation-states and their territorial sub-units cannot always do the trick. Majority peoples want to harness the energy and enthusiasm of their fellow citizens, and minority peoples want to feel secure, so that their energy and enthusiasm can be directed to positive goals and not just to survival. For each 'people' to get what they want, they must say 'yes' to each other. They must affirm their mutual respect for the other's fears or concerns. Reciprocity is a form of equality.

Whatever the future holds, history teaches that the political arena operates on power, authority, and rules and only slightly on trust. That is one reason many people find politics a distasteful or 'shady' endeavour. And yet we persist in asking minorities to trust the majority. As more and more provisions are added to human rights codes and the like, we create new spaces for trust because we create places or domains where the majority – through its government – may not intrude. We thereby offer some security to individuals, but the cultural minorities, the minority 'ways of life,' and the 'permanent minorities' inherent in majority rule require separate protections. Sometimes these are referred to as 'collective rights,' and in one sense they are that. But whether they are 'really' rights or not, there must be enforcement mechanisms. In the end, enforcement depends on trust to the extent that it depends on some majority; or else it depends on some external force.

Most discussions of majority rule endeavour to answer the question of *when* the majority rules. In this context, the answers usually given include constitutional changes, basic freedoms or liberties, conscription for military service, or other matters which can be considered 'fundamental' or 'priority-setting' or matters of 'life-and-death.' In this chapter, I have in addition tried to pose questions about *where* the majority should rule. 'Where' has usually meant 'in which territorial units,' but I have opened the possibility that non-territorial political authorities may be necessary or preferable in some cases. I have tried to specify some criteria for identifying such cases. The crucial point does not concern whether I have postulated criteria which everyone can support; more fundamental than that, we can agree that not all minorities can have exclusive, continuous, and contiguous territories and thus there must be some criteria which signify that some non-territorial minorities need to have their own majority rule. If we can agree on that, we have moved to some degree 'beyond nations' and 'beyond sovereignty' into the unbundled world of the twenty-first century.

8

A Menu for the Twenty-First Century

A large part of this book involves the different meanings of choice. Some choices are liberating, others are constricting, some are Hobson's choices, and some are illusory. I have envisioned situations in the twenty-first century that are full of choice: choices about economic and political regimes, choices about communities to be involved in, choices about citizenship. Some of my friends, upon hearing a summary of the arguments, have queried whether most people have the capacity to make informed choices about so many important matters. My initial reaction was to note that people *must* make choices whether ready or not. (Of course, one choice is apathy, withdrawal, or denial; but for now let us focus on substantial choices.) My later reaction was that people learn by doing, and choices which appear hopelessly confusing at one point may later be seen as routine or at least can be taken in stride. Then they become habits.

FORCED TO CHOOSE?

Consider a historical analogy. Think of a bishop, a lord, a peasant, and a craftsman in Europe sometime during 1400–1500 (depending on which area of Europe). Suppose one were to pose this choice to them: you must each choose one and only one community to which all loyalty will be owed and whose identity will be the central concept around which a hierarchy of your identities will coalesce. How puzzled they would have been! What could one mean by this? Why would you have to exalt one community and degrade the others? If you cannot choose what type of clothing you wear or what jobs your children may aspire to perform, in what sense might you have a choice about these matters of community?

236 Beyond Sovereignty

For us, the singularity of an overarching community focused on the nation-state seems as natural as the multiplicity of communities did to those very real but hypothetical Europeans at the dawn of the 'modern' world. We cannot conceive of tolerating a world in which one could observe multiple, independent communities and yet have little or no choice among them. They could not conceive how all people could be equally part of a single community which also allows no choice, except for rare cases of migration and 'naturalized' citizenship. Both views of the world offered stability, albeit of quite different types. Stability can seem like comfort, but it can also be a prison.

Their puzzlement at a choice which seemed pointless if not meaningless would, I suspect, have turned into fear if they took my question seriously. They would have had little basis for choice. How would they envision the alternatives? How could they calculate the benefits and costs of choosing one nation-state over another? They might be able to evaluate what they were giving up, but how could they weigh the alternatives which constituted the new and singular communities?

This book has argued, to put it crudely, that a period of plural authorities among which people had little choice was followed by a period of sovereign territorial states among which people had little choice. As that period of the hegemonic nation-state draws to a close, people may encounter a greater pluralism of political authorities, including nation-states but transnational authorities too, and the question arises whether choice will be denied again or whether people in the future will have greater choices. If they do, one must also query who will choose and among what range of options.

Readers of this book probably began it in puzzlement and may now have a growing sense of fear, although the obverse of our fifteenth-century characters. Where is the stability in the unbundled world?[1] What holds all these myriad communities together? Does not 'all that is solid melt into air'?[2] Why should one be forced to choose when the world already comes neatly packaged in the form of nation-states which have bundled together a wondrous variety of places, traditions, communities, heroes, and myths?

The new or unknown is always puzzling and often provokes fear. Eventually it becomes familiar, manipulable, and chooseable, and then later it is taken for granted as 'given' or 'natural.' Ever since our hypothetical fifteenth-century types of people, the territorial nation-state has been based on assumptions so deep and tectonic that few people have seen them. They do not see them any more than they see the eyeglasses they wear, because they are the means by which one sees the political world that one has created or inherited. My eyes hurt for awhile when I get eyeglasses with a new prescription – especially when I first chose to use bifocals – but the unease passes, and the world comes into sharper focus.

RESTAURANTS AND NATIONS

Perhaps an analogy involving restaurants may make the points more plainly. What choice remains if a restaurant offers 'table d'hôte'? Of course, one may choose the restaurant to patronize according to the posted menu. Or one may, as some of my friends do, make a very different kind of choice: they never look at the menu, even if it is 'à la carte,' but choose to let the chef decide what is appropriate that day. A restaurant with only an *à la carte* menu poses a different kind of choice; indeed it *forces* a different degree of choice. This is good if you like choice or do not like the 'blue plate special,' but choice can be painful because it means excluding all of those other items which may be equally delicious.

The unbundled world of the twenty-first century may be more like an *à la carte* menu, even as regards political authorities, than the *table d'hôte* menu of nation-states. I have tried to describe or envision the possibilities in several areas of political, economic, administrative, and social life. My vision entails that one will in the future more often be able to choose one's networks, communities, and identities than has been the case up to now. I believe firmly and sincerely that such will be the case, but there is something much deeper at work here. Choice in itself is not the goal. Among what will people be able to choose? Who will be able to choose?

Before turning to some speculations which aim to draw together many of the themes in the book, let me explore some assumptions lurking behind the example of these two types of menu. There are many – such as monetization of economic life, widespread literacy, and low risk of poisoning – that I wish to leave aside. Instead I want to point out how narrow and recent is the concept of restaurant, regardless of its type of menu. To oversimplify only a bit, there were almost no restaurants before the creation of nation-states.

Throughout human history, travellers have confronted the difficulty of feeding themselves. Several common patterns emerged in many times and places. For one, soldiers pillaged and confiscated food stores. Another involved customs of hospitality, of inviting strangers to one's home under codes of non-violence and reciprocity. Eventually inns and hostels were invented, and religious sanctuaries offered accommodation to those who made donations. In these and related examples, someone was in charge, and little choice existed. Of course, some people in some times and places simply brought their own food and cooks as part of a large entourage, but this has always been rare and somewhat impractical.

By the early modern period, elite and wealthy individuals invited others of their ilk to visit for a few days or for extended periods. Again, someone was in charge, but there were great selections of food and drink. Reciprocity probably was an essential part of the system, and no money changed hands.

The great travellers of the nineteenth century could rely on hotels, resorts, guides, steam and sail boats, and many features we find familiar. But prepared food was probably still less familiar. Eventually, however, Europeans invented the concept of the restaurant. Even aside from such prerequisites as monetization of the economy, restaurants presumed some fairly amazing things which we now take for granted. One did not need an invitation. People would serve you, but they were not your servants. No *one* was in charge, in the sense that *everyone* was in charge: the owner and chef gave orders to staff and focused the ambiance; each diner chose to attend or not; and customers could give directions (more wine or whatever) because they were paying.

Restaurants work but have no 'sovereign.' They offer choice between and within restaurants. If they fail to satisfy, they go out of business or transform themselves to a new or more appealing style. People who frequent a restaurant regularly may come to know each other or at least the manager or chef, but unknown people are welcome so long as they desire the style of food and hospitality on offer. *Habitués* may know each other's tastes in food and clothing but little about backgrounds or opinions on a whole range of other matters. Anonymity rests comfortably with familiarity.

Sounds a lot like the unbundled world of the twenty-first century, doesn't it? That should not be surprising since the unnoticed evolution of nation-states has seen parallel changes in restaurants. The difference between the stages of nation-states mentioned in earlier chapters raised the question of whether one should invent words to mark the differences. Likewise, should an *à la carte* restaurant bear the same designation as a *table d'hôte* establishment of a century or two ago? How different is different enough for us to cease using labels like 'nation' or 'restaurant'?

The other analogy between nations and restaurants brings us back to the feasibility of the unbundled world. We draw moderately sharp lines among establishments like restaurant, diner, bar, nightclub, strip joint, and theatre, even though at various times and places any or all of these elements or functions may have been combined. We draw lines among political, military, economic, and technological functions but still find it peculiar to envision their embodiment in distinct institutions without an overarching all-purpose territorial sovereign. Unbundling nations poses more challenges than inventing restaurants, but then all analogies break down at some point. That is why they are analogies rather than identities. But analogies can help us to unblock our concepts, and that is often harder than changing the world. Indeed, by the time we have changed our concepts, we may find that the world has long since beat us to that conclusion.

It has been my argument in this book that there may be some value in updating contemporary concepts as we go along. Once the unbundled world is in full flood, global citizens will have less chance of channelling the direction of the flow. Maybe they cannot influence these global forces at all, but they can think about them. Or try. A hundred years from now, historians will note that I have *failed to foresee precisely* the contours of the unbundled world. I accept that. As noted before, exact prediction is not my game. But those same historians will note that I have failed to foresee precisely the contours of *the unbundled world*. There is no doubt in my mind that the unbundled nature of that world will be its key feature; the details seem less central to me. So what have I shown or envisioned? What will be the menu in the next century or millennium? Will the menu be the crucial point, or should we examine the nature of the restaurant in which we study the menu?

METAPHORS AND THE LIMITS OF CHOICE

Phrases like 'à la carte' or 'table d'hôte' are entirely metaphoric. I do not intend to conclude that every person or group will eventually have the degree of choice about political authorities that a reasonably affluent person in an affluent society today has in regard to meals in restaurants. Metaphors serve several purposes. In this case, their primary purpose is to shock or provoke or raise doubts about matters seldom brought to consciousness for inspection. A further purpose was captured by Susanne Langer half a century ago:

Really new concepts, having no name in a current language, always make their earliest appearance in metaphorical statements; therefore the beginning of any theoretical structure is inevitably marked by fantastic inventions.[3]

Finally, I have used these metaphors as Archibald MacLeish suggested: 'A world ends when its metaphor has died.'[4] However exaggerated, there is some truth in the view that 'table d'hôte' is now being replaced by an age of 'government à la carte.'

Bundling has assumed many forms in different eras or places. Each form of bundling involves some degree of limitation on social choice. Some forms of bundling may limit choice more than others; and territorial bundling is very constraining, the more so when it involves sovereign, all-purpose political units. Relaxing some or all assumptions about territoriality (exclusivity, contiguity, and continuity, and thereby congruent territories) makes the bundle less constraining. Single-purpose, non-territorial units – that is, hardly bundled at all – yield maximum scope for choice. Not every political function can be organized as single-purpose, non-territorial units. Thus, designers of future political forms must endeavour to strike the optimum balance or mix among units bundled in different ways, among degrees or number of functions bundled together, among territorial and non-territorial forms of bundling. In that way, 'à la carte' will eventually take on more concrete and less metaphoric meanings, and it will become apparent that 'à la carte' involves *relatively* greater choice than the national 'table d'hôte' offered now, but not absolutely unlimited choice.

If there will be greater choice, who will be allowed to choose what? Let me outline very briefly two choice situations, with very different answers to this question. First, one may postulate that whoever helps to create or participates in 'constructing' more *types* of political forms (non-territorial ones being of special interest here) will have made choices. The key 'choosers' should be existing nation-states who set up international regimes and agencies, transnational corporations, transnational 'watch-dog' groups, and only rarely individuals. But if individuals play a secondary role in this process, the outcomes should realize a more flexible and less fully bundled set of institutions with some of the consequences for individual choice mentioned throughout the book.

After a period of creating more such unbundled units, the second type of situation will likely involve a period of stability among more units and more types of units. Individuals will then not have complete *à la carte* choices, but some will have considerably more choice than now. A great many people should have an indefinite expansion of choice regarding the 'virtual communities' described in chapters 2 and 6. Ever greater numbers (but never the vast majority?) should find greater choices of consumer goods, in the sense of goods tailored or customized to their tastes, and through their choices they could exercise influence on the balance between local and transnational corporations. Except for small proportions of people, choice among citizenships in nation-states will probably remain very limited. But physical location in a territorial state will constrain the above forms of choice less than now, especially in liberal, open, or democratic states and for affluent citizens even in relatively poor or authoritarian territorial units. There will, in short, be a greater range of options and combinations of options for a significant proportion of human populations; fewer eggs in one basket might be a better metaphor than 'à la carte,' but both accurately portray the possibility of somewhat more choice among somewhat more types of political authorities.

Readers will recall from chapters 1 and 3 that *pluralism* in legal systems and in bases of political authority played a significant role in the medieval period. For several centuries the church, feudalities, cities, and kingdoms struggled for supremacy. Even after the territorial state achieved hegemony in the form of absolutist monarchies, no single state was able to subdue the others, so that a *state system* characterized Europe. Competition among territorial states in the framework of Christianity meant that cultural differences were small enough (compared to Islam, for example) that learning or imitation could occur. As Berman demonstrates so clearly, even after the dominance of the state system was established, multiple legal traditions (church, royal, municipal, commercial) ensured that no single body of law could be fully hegemonic, thus lending dynamism to the laws and fostering a degree of balance and tolerance.[5] Although true more in some times and places than others, the general point is valid. The unbundling at the heart of my analysis evokes the structural pluralism of those distant times, even though the reasons for pluralism and their exact lines are different now. Whether for individuals or societies, some degree of 'à la carte' has crept back into the options for the twenty-first century.

BEYOND NATIONS

To move beyond nations does not entail replacing nations. Most nation-states of our familiar twentieth-century world will survive the twenty-first century, although some will not. What, then, will grow up alongside of nations, share functions with them, and provide some of the order and meaning in the unbundled world? What institutions will provide structure in the unbundled world? One must not allow current presumptions to blind us to new possibilities. National citizens have become so habituated to thinking of political authority as deriving from one single sovereign national centre that they can easily jump to the conclusion that some one institution will eventually supplant the nation-state as the sovereign. Of course, that eventuality is logically possible, and some groups might welcome it. In this book, however, I am exploring a radically different possibility – many sovereigns, and thus no sovereigns in the usual sense.[6] And this new structure will rely less and less on territoriality. As I stated in chapter 1, I wish above all to corrode the presumptiveness of territoriality.

Previous chapters have mentioned a number of institutions or communities which might gain prominence in the unbundled world. Besides ever more nations, I will discuss supra-national communities, supra-national and sub-national functional organizations, city-regions, city-states, transnational corporations, voluntary organizations, religious groups, and states decoupled from nations. These forms may never replace the nation-state, but they will very likely come to share the global stage with nations. Indeed, they are already doing so and show signs of gaining in power and functional jurisdiction. Which will be more and which less crucial a century hence cannot be foreseen. Instead, I envision a world in which many of these entities – and perhaps others – jostle and cooperate in non-territorial arenas and handle functions which territorial nation-states have juggled awkwardly and with less and less success. Territorial functions – including certain kinds of taxation and social infrastructure – will remain within the purview of the more focused realms of nation-states. And, of course, nations will probably retain some, if not all, of their military capabilities, although these too may be shared with the United Nations or other bodies.

The most certain scenario or prediction 'beyond nations' is that there will be more of them. Some will perhaps arise from the breakup of larger nations, such as India or Nigeria or Canada. Some may represent the coalescence of ethnic nations now fragmented among several jurisdictions, such as Kurds or Mayas. Many seem likely to grow out of regional groupings in particular nations, as a result of the general loosening of authority in the unbundled world of cross-cutting and overlapping non-territorial institutions. Examples include the Basque and Catalan regions of Spain, Scotland and Wales in Great Britain, Quebec in Canada, and perhaps Hawaii or other regions of the United States.

Parallel with more nations will be broader groupings of nations. Some may, like the European Community, move far along the path of political integration and may even become, in one sense, nations themselves. But if so, they will be a new (or older) kind of nation: a state ruling several nations, an empire but one without absolute sovereignty. Others may be trading blocs, security alliances, or scientific and technological cooperatives. Whatever the form and whatever the scale, their existence will not require complete dismantling of nation-states like France or Japan. They will instead reflect the hard fact that some jurisdictions need to encompass territories beyond the scope of any existing nations, just as local organizations will be required but will not *ipso facto* sound the death knell of national and supra-national communities.

It is worth distinguishing between supra-national communities which may look quite like nations in many respects and supra-national organizations with specialized functions. Recall the discussion in chapter 3 about ostensibly economic organizations like GATT, IATA, the World Bank, and the Bank for European Reconstruction and Development. Although created to regulate economic or financial matters, these organizations are *de facto* governments, albeit with highly focused functional jurisdictions. They also share another important feature – they were created by nation-states to serve their interests. The question for the next century concerns whether these or similar organizations will continue to serve national interests or will become more autonomous. Indeed, it may turn out that they can only serve national interests by achieving greater autonomy. I will return to this issue in a later section about unintended consequences of our deliberate actions.

Such organizations share many features with police. As I noted in earlier chapters, 'policing' has become more specialized and often non-territorial. It also involves much more than earlier ideas about criminal violations or 'law and order.' Several of the supra-national regulatory bodies – along with national and sub-national 'police' – are inherently non-territorial. Their 'logic' does not generally reinforce the hegemony of territorial nation-states. This is an important point in its own right but will arise as well in regard to consequences unanticipated by creators of particular organizations or institutions. It seems that unbundled police flow from and feed back on unbundled nations.

CITY-STATES

In keeping with the remarks above about more nations, one should consider carefully suggestions by Jane Jacobs about the role of cities as engines of economic vitality.[7] She argues that certain kinds of cities – 'import-replacing' cities analogous to Michael Porter's 'clusters' of industries[8] – are more important than any other organization for economic development. Nations, she argues, often harm their cities, or at least inhibit their economic dynamism, because nations must have uniform currency exchange rates, as we noted in chapter 3 above. Hence, some cities receive inappropriate feedback about economic performance or incentives. For that and other reasons, it is difficult to have more than one really dynamic city-region per nation for extended periods. As one replaces another (e.g., southern California and Arizona replacing New England in the United States), change rather than development occurs. Of course, some nations – such as Denmark, Singapore, and Taiwan – may be no more than city-states or city-regions; but most countries have several city-regions, and they do not all prosper simultaneously.

Jacobs argues from these premises that separatism may be a reasonable alternative in some cases.[9] By giving all regions a jolt, it shakes up routines and helps get people and organizations out of their ruts.[10] It avoids the subsidization of one region or city by another, and thus it may (after a transition period) enhance economic productivity. The multiplicity of currencies which would normally grow out of the breakup of a nation into several city-states would yield much more precise and timely feedback than occurs under a regime with a single currency.[11]

One may speculate, therefore, that unbundling of nations should allow more leeway for cities, even short of outright separation. If separation occurred, this reinforces my earlier point about more nations being what we expect to find beyond the nation-state. Without separation, one would still expect that city-regions would have greater autonomy because of the sharing of sovereignty among nations, localities, and supra-national entities. To some extent this has already happened in Canada and elsewhere: Vancouver and Montreal have special legislative powers as international financial centres, for example, so that designated institutions may provide clearing-houses for off-shore investments without incurring local taxes. One of several intended consequences concerns increased numbers of 'high-tech' jobs locally. Another closely related result is the diffusion of expertise and, following on that, a more 'international' (i.e., non-national) outlook among sectors of the business and financial communities.

Would city-states be territorial? Probably in most respects, they would. And this is another reason why they might be subsumed under the general trend of 'more nations.' However, several qualifications should be noted. For one, the hinterlands of each city-state might overlap those of other city-states, 'violating' the assumption of exclusivity. Some hinterlands might, on the contrary, be quite distant, as they are now for specialized natural resources or certain technological components. In addition, city-states currently in each existing nation would likely share a language and culture, as would be true of most regions in the United States, except for Hispanic influence in Florida, the Southwest, and perhaps Texas. By contrast, Canadian cities – if allowed to become city-states – would be more varied, mainly because of the French language in Quebec, but also as a result of other features which sharply divide the Maritimes and British Columbia from Central Canada.

Recall the arguments in earlier chapters that sovereignty will be less meaningful because shared more fully and that unbundling allows solutions which can be fitted more precisely to the problem. The greater latitude Jacobs envisions for city-states would obviously involve rearrangements of sovereignty, and differentiated exchange rates would be an example of fitting a solution to a problem. Furthermore, once one moves a certain distance down the road of unbundling, the next step may seem less threatening than it looks from the vantage point of national hegemony. Even short of separatism, there may be forms and degrees of autonomy for city-regions that serve as economic benefits, and yet would not engender the hysteria which usually attends any mention of separation or national breakup.

While useful as a basis of speculation, the city-regions or city-states advocated by Jacobs should not be considered in isolation. They are now – and would be more so in almost any plausible future scenario – supplemented by another institution which takes us 'beyond nations.' I refer, of course, to transnational corporations, which exist already and which are most prominent in precisely those city-regions Jacobs uses as frequent examples.

THE ERA OF ORGANIZATION

Peter Drucker has been the most cogent chronicler of the idea that the future rests with organizations and in particular with specialized organizations. The most visible and remarked upon of these organizations is the corporation. In the 1950s, books were sold by denouncing the conformity and uniformity imposed on (and by) 'organization men' or 'men in grey flannel suits.' Later attacks were directed more at multinational corporations, especially American multinationals, which were said to be exploiting Third World or developing countries.

Recently the terminology has changed, and attitudes may be changing as well. The key phrase currently is *transnational* corporations, and they are touted (and equally often denounced) because they are beyond national control. 'Multinational' meant that whereas a business had its headquarters in a particular country, it conducted business elsewhere in the sense of marketing its products in several other countries. Central control of a web of influence seemed to define this organization. 'Transnational,' on the contrary, has been taken to mean that there is no single national headquarters, no web emanating from a single place, no single spider at the centre of the web. Instead, each function (research, banking, advertising, manufacturing, assembly) has a location based on cost factors, convenience, or opportunity, and most lines of influence could go directly between units without all going back through 'headquarters.' To the extent that there is always some kind of headquarters (such as where the board of directors meets most often), the people located there might carry passports of many countries and have had experience of operations in many localities.

As Drucker has shown, the evolution of the business corporation entails many momentous changes and reflects broad trends in the world economy. But Drucker's analysis goes far beyond these corporations. He has argued convincingly that we live already in the twenty-first-century era of organizations in several senses in addition to transnational corporations.[12] One of his most intriguing points is that small businesses are just as likely to be transnationals as large ones, whereas virtually all multinationals were huge conglomerates. I will return to some unintended consequences of this feature, but for the moment I want to outline his vision of organizational futures in non-business arenas.

Drucker focuses on what he calls 'the third force.' This category consists of organizations which are non-governmental but also non-profit. It includes, among others, private hospitals and schools, most colleges and universities, philanthropic and charitable organizations (ranging from the International Red Cross to local Meals on Wheels), advocacy groups (environmental, health, civil rights, etc.), community service groups (Girl Scouts, Salvation Army), many churches and church-related groups, and a plethora of cultural enterprises (symphony orchestras, museums, film cooperatives, festivals, troops of street performers, etc.). This third force has reached its most luxuriant growth in the United

States, but it is evident in all societies of any size. Drucker argues that the volunteer (non-paid) nature of much of the work done in this sector accounts in large part for the substantially lower taxes in the United States than in European countries, where many more groups are funded directly by governments (e.g., symphony orchestras). Canada apparently falls, in this as in many things, somewhere between Europe and the United States.

Although not emphasized by Drucker, there are 'cultural' groups in a sense different than those he discusses. These are the community-based groups of people sharing a common language or culture. Sometimes they receive funding or tax advantages from governments, but often not. They also may overlap his 'high culture' groups in the degree that libraries, reading rooms, galleries, museums, research institutes, and the like come under the umbrella of local or national ethnic organizations. Regardless of funding or overlap, immigrant societies like Canada and the United States harbour growing numbers of organizations which serve to maintain a sense of community among groups of people who wish to live in a country but not lose touch with the language and culture of their ancestral country. Of course, many countries have not welcomed immigrants (such as Japan), and the proportion varies enormously from country to country. On a world scale, however, Drucker correctly notes the role of volunteer or self-starting organizations; and ethnic groups, I allege, are an important addition to his 'third force' category.

It is only fair to note that aboriginal groups – especially in countries now dominated by 'settler societies' – have increasingly seen the value of organization. Some accept funds from national governments; some have access to natural resources, casinos, small businesses, and the like and can be self-sustaining; and some are actually 'peak' organizations which bring together internationally – or, more exactly, transnationally – the myriad of tribal, community, or national organizations. Whatever the specifics, and they are extremely varied types of organizations, many aboriginal groups meet Drucker's definition of non-governmental and non-profit organizations and thus may be part of his third force.

I dwell at some length on the examples Drucker uses as well as the ones I have added in order to lead up to a specific point which brings us back to the question of 'beyond nations.' In chapter 6, I outlined my vision of a world – a globe – in which people who wish to share an interest may form a community. Some of these will be highly transient and consist of little more than electronic bulletin boards. Many of them, however, will be global versions of the organizations Drucker calls the third force. They will be formally constituted, with officers, boards, and staff (paid and unpaid); and they will last beyond the life or interest of any particular member. Drucker refers to these groups as organizations because of his own concern with management theory, while I call them communities of interest. In either case, they represent *choice* because they are voluntary and because one may join an indefinite number of them. They also represent *identities* for the reasons I gave in chapter 6. Most importantly, they represent a way to provide *structure* and *stability* in a world in which territory and national states play a much less prominent role than hitherto.

Among the most significant institutional forms which take us 'beyond nations,' therefore, are organizations, networks, and communities which lie somewhere between the purely public and purely private domains. Each in its own way should 'usurp' to some degree the roles played (or believed to have been played) by families in earlier eras (socialization, continuity of culture and language, emotional support, and so on) and those of sovereign governments in a limited territory. These global communities of choice already exist here and there, and the spread of literacy and telecommunications technology should ensure their proliferation.

Some obvious consequences should follow from this proliferation of non-territorial communities, whether local or global. Most obvious will be their irrelevance to national borders. They will thus be among the many forces working against the logic of territorial nation-states, although not against them in any traitorous sense. Instead of nations fearing groups who consciously aimed to overthrow them, the danger posed by these communities and organizations will be that national governments cannot control them. Indeed, they will be largely invisible to surveillance; and even more ominous, their members will over time come to find national borders quite irrelevant as far as the specific interests of their own community are concerned. Nations will, at least in regard to certain matters, be 'put in their place' by growing indifference rather than by opposition, insurrection, or revolution. But the long-term consequences may well be, nonetheless, as revolutionary as any organized protest. As I have emphasized, however, that does not necessarily mean the end of nation-states, but it will almost certainly mean they will be curtailed in authority and sovereignty as more and more interests pass beyond the reach of territorial states into the hands of voluntary organizations, communities, and corporations.

RELIGION AND SPIRITUALITY

There are two other candidates for what lies 'beyond nations.' In this section, I discuss religion and spirituality, and in the next I offer some thoughts on mass migrations. Religion and mass migrations, of course, are hardly new actors or events, but the twenty-first century may see new forms of religion and increased scale of migration.

Religion has come to mean, for most people, organized churches, and of course these institutional forms have been important for centuries and may in certain countries be regaining some of their lagging vitality. I believe that one should be mindful, in addition, of the texts, symbols, and moral codes which underly the organized churches, since they may be of more lasting influence. After all, schisms occur, ecumenical movements ebb and flow, and social forms vary as technology opens new possibilities. Thus, in discussing the religious dimension which may come to prominence 'beyond nations,' I use the phrase 'religion and spirituality' to remind readers that this category goes beyond mere churches. Indeed, it seems likely that the spirituality aspect may be growing faster than the overt signs of religion such as church attendance, although evidence for this must be impressionistic.

The most visible signs of renewed or revitalized religion and spirituality may be found in the areas of 'revivalism' or fundamentalism. Islamic fundamentalism has captured many headlines, as has the religious right and Moral Majority in the United States. One may also suggest that the efforts by Pope John Paul II to entrench and reaffirm certain Catholic doctrines (such as celibacy, non-ordination of women, prohibition of contraceptives) which have come under intense opposition constitute a form of fundamentalism in the sense of 'back to basics' in the tradition of the church.

Whatever the exact boundaries one wishes to place around the concept and phenomena of fundamentalism, it appears to enjoy enhanced vitality and wider acceptance. Forecasting its continued spread and growth is hazardous, but in conjunction with other observations, that may be quite plausible. Regardless of accuracy of prediction, my main points here concern the likelihood that religion and/or spirituality are prime candidates as structuring frameworks in the world beyond nations and the certainty that these phenomena are inherently non-territorial and thus congruent with many other elements which I have argued constitute the unbundled world. Of course, some particular religious movements have nationalist connotations – such as the Shiite version of Islam in Iran – but that is not their primary intent; the national governments are convenient vehicles.

If one accepts the hypothesis that organized religions are not dying out, as some had feared or hoped, and may even be rebuilding, then one might speculate that the explanation lies in a greatly enhanced respect for spirituality. In other words, I am suggesting that the rise of fundamentalism and of mainline church attendance stems less from the management skills of religious leaders and much more from the search for meaning in life through spiritual values and experiences. Nationalism was a religion[13] and reflected spiritual values for many of its adherents in the nineteenth century and certainly for many Europeans in the period between the two world wars, as well as for many colonial peoples in the period since the Second World War.[14] However, nationalism no longer satisfies as many people, perhaps because of its prior excesses, and religious or spiritual experiences of non-national sorts seem more promising as motives and structures beyond nations.

To the extent these speculations make sense of uncertain trends, they should lead us to look upon some phenomena as religious or spiritual even though we usually apply other labels like ecology, environmentalism, and aboriginality. I do not intend to mock or limit these phenomena by referring to them as religious. Rather the point to affirm concerns the motives of many people in the environmental and ecology movements, and even more their sense of wonder, awe, grandeur, interconnectness of life, and reverence for everything living. These splendid feelings can be turned to idolatry or bigotry or used to justify harmful actions, but all religions have those dark sides. Instead the parallels between 'standard' religions and those aspects of the ecology and environmental movements which have deep spiritual meaning are twofold. For one, they share an emphasis on the need to fit one's actions into a wider framework which is so vast as to be almost beyond comprehension. Second is the energy, the powerful motivational force, of these beliefs to engender action, sacrifice, exaltation, and wonderment. All of these expressions of spirituality provide deep meaning and an avenue of understanding in a complex and frightening world.[15]

Aboriginal spirituality needs no defence as a form of religion, despite what the European conquerors and settlers may have believed five centuries ago. If anything, it is a bridge between the more 'standard' church-based religions and the spirituality of the ecologists and environmentalists. A faith and way of life which has survived centuries of brutal and thoughtless efforts at national acculturation and assimilation – and without turning violent or bitter very often – should serve as a worthy example of a framework which lies beyond nations in the unbundled world.

The Enlightenment in the eighteenth century cemented in the Western world-view the dogma that feelings, emotions, and spirituality are suspect and that reason and rationality must reign supreme. The tide has turned in this century. Not only have irrationalities like Naziism and fascism and Stalinism figured prominently – even while claiming scientific status – but the reactions against them have not been sufficient to dam up the flow of true spiritual feelings, as noted above. The questioning of reason and science as unalloyed goods has been accepted by many observers as a healthy recognition of the need for balance among the forces of reason and spiritual meaning. If spirituality meant blind faith in some eras, and thus constituted a threat to science, our own age may be able to see that they do not pose a zero-sum choice.

Even eminent scientists – or maybe especially eminent ones – speak and write as though scientific theories were works of art. The intricate 'simple complexity' of physical nature inspires awe and wonderment in lay observers as well as Nobel Prize winners.[16] I must hasten to clarify the point at issue, lest readers be misled about how these aspects of spirituality may be different in the world beyond nations compared to earlier historical periods. Newton and many of the greatest scientific minds of the early modern world were deeply spiritual, but in an older fashion. Newton's motives for his work were not disinterested science as we have come to understand it. He sought to demonstrate the existence and rationality of the Christian God by exhibiting the perfection and symmetry of His creation. I am suggesting that no major scientist today shares that view or motive. Instead, doing science and probing to the extremes of elementary particles and cosmology has led a great many scientists to invest their theories – and, by extension, the world as observed – with deeper meanings and a form of spirituality. But it is a spirituality not confined merely to worship of a divine being; the worship or wonderment is for the world of which they are part.

MIGRATIONS AND HIDDEN ASSUMPTIONS

How does one justify saying 'no' to the people who wish to immigrate to Canada or other affluent, underpopulated nations? The justifications usually take two forms – national sovereignty and national ways of life.[17] The arguments based on sovereignty are essentially circular: we can keep you out because we have the power to keep you out. Sovereignty has been deemed its own justification, especially by those who exercise it on behalf of the nation. Perhaps that worked when nothing seemed able to resist, but sovereignty has been questioned in recent times and this book documents many ways in which sovereignty no longer remains unchallenged. As sovereignty comes to be shared – and thus loses some of its allure if not its meaning – power to stop immigration will be less easily equated with the right to do so.

That leaves the defence of a coherent national culture as the bulwark against immigration, at least against types of people who would not 'fit' and might undermine the national culture. The first problem with this defence concerns the evident fact that coherence of a culture is a variable; some cultures seem homogeneous and coherent, while others may be less so. Which members of the United Nations have a coherent national culture? Japan? China? Korea? France? Iceland? Certainly the list could not be extended much beyond these possibilities. One could not grant that India, Nigeria, Brazil, Indonesia, Russia, or Great Britain exhibited the degree of coherence of language and culture found in France, let alone China or Japan. And other countries are ruled out because the ideal of a coherent national culture consists of multiculturalism (Switzerland, Belgium) or of relative openness to immigrants from all cultures (United States, Canada, Australia). Thus, defence of national cultures, while carrying more weight than sovereignty as a justification, cannot in most cases account for how tightly the borders are sealed.

The reaction against immigration must be put in perspective. To Canadians, 200,000–250,000 immigrants (including refugees) seems a lot to admit each year. Likewise with the larger numbers (although lower proportion) in the United States. Various international agencies place the current numbers of refugees or would-be refugees prevented from crossing borders at between 50 and 100 million. Every agency studying the matter assumes that the numbers will grow. In part the future trends depend on the degree of repression in the home country, which can increase or decrease; prediction is difficult. Regardless of the absolute level of repression, the relative level will, in all future scenarios, find less repression in the currently 'open' societies where immigrants have settled. The affluence in those countries – and in some 'closed' societies like Switzerland, Germany, and Japan – will serve as magnets for people who want to escape hopeless economic conditions as well as repression.

Thus, the twenty-first century must be imagined as a time of immense population pressures.[18] Population growth is greatest in Third World countries, and it is lowest (or even negative except for immigration) in the affluent countries, including most of Europe and not just the G-7. India's population will soon surpass one billion; Nigeria's will surpass that of the United States soon; and China's (although its rate is declining) will continue to grow well into the twenty-first century. If even 5–10 per cent of the populations of these and similarly poor countries wished to migrate, the numbers would dwarf the current scale of refugees, and exceed by several orders of magnitude the numbers of immigrants now welcomed in the few open, affluent countries.

So what? Is it the fault of Canadians that Nigerians are poor, that Somalia suffers from drought and civil war, and that some Mexicans see little opportunity at home? Of course not in any direct sense, but there is another perspective – a historical perspective – which I believe demonstrates that this is the wrong question, or at least not the only relevant question. This perspective points to the fact that place of birth is now the last remaining ascriptive category to which Western liberal individualists yield. They no longer – especially in the affluent societies who claim to honour human rights – accept the idea that people should be judged on ascriptive criteria (race, gender, wealth of one's parents) and insist that achievement and merit should count for more, if not for everything. Yet they accept uncritically the idea that birth in a benign and affluent place entitles them to exclude people who did not so prudently choose where their parents would live when they were born.

In earlier chapters, I have mentioned examples of ascriptive criteria which fell before the technological, economic, and ideological changes of the past few centuries. These included hereditary obligations of fealty, feudal ties to land, classes of nobility, and sumptuary laws. Enlightened moderns look with disdain on such matters and pride themselves on the opportunities provided to citizens: universal public education, non-discrimination on the basis of race or culture, a chance to be judged by what one does more than by what one is or whom one knows. And still we citizens of the affluent West act as though the greatest ascriptor – birthplace – were an achievement we had planned and can take credit for. How many readers of this book have felt humbled to realize that they could just as well have been born in a Third World barrio of parents who were poor, illiterate, and short-lived? Of those who have been thus humbled to realize their *luck*, how many have campaigned for an open immigration policy?

This is not the place to condemn my fellow citizens, especially since I am a beneficiary of migration, but it is worth putting the issue in strong language so that one cannot easily evade the issue. In the unbundled world of the next century, there will be more pressure of population growth and movement than ever before. If territorial nations share sovereignty with non-territorial governments and communities, who will control the migrants? How? Why?[19]

One response growing out of the arguments about territoriality seems promising, but cuts two ways. If we devise new global communities – including better jobs and opportunities – perhaps there will be less pressure to migrate. If firms draw employees from everywhere, there may be less incentive to go from one place to another. In short, if territory no longer defines so fully one's identity and one's life chances, why migrate? Of course, one can devise scenarios along these lines, and I have tried to sketch a few of them in earlier chapters.

But if territory matters less, why stop migrants? If I am already connected by employment or by any of the voluntary communities described in chapter 6 to people who share my interests but live elsewhere, why would I seek to prevent their migration to wherever I live? Rationally, this perspective should carry as much weight as that in the previous paragraph. Emotionally, however, it runs against self-interest, at least when generalized beyond one's own communities to open the borders for everyone else's communities. Of course, one may reasonably point out that some people may emigrate from Canada or other blessed countries under the same conditions that lead so many to want to immigrate here. Any plausible estimate of numbers going each way still leaves the dilemma about saying 'no' because the medium-term future will find Canada and other countries enormously more affluent and pleasant than most Third World countries (and even Eastern European countries).

Thus, it behooves us to think that beyond nations there will be mass migration unless we devise ways to share the wealth. This is correct, I believe, even if there is also some truth in the view that many countries have contributed to their own misfortunes.[20] I am trying not to be too judgmental, and so I am trying to envision a future which may happen whether it is fair or not. As I noted in earlier chapters, the future is not automatic; if readers imagine a better future, they can work toward it, and if they foresee distasteful possibilities, they can work to prevent them. To the extent that these scenarios involve massive migration, however, the values which have undermined ascriptiveness in the past should give us pause in saying 'no' to migrants in the future.

UNINTENDED CONSEQUENCES

An argument can be made on historical grounds that the unintended consequences of our actions and ideas have at least as much lasting influence as those we intend and work toward in a deliberate way. Within the perspective of this book, they may be vastly more important because they are largely unconscious and unnoticed. If I am right that each person's concepts and each society's culture become less available to conscious reflection as people become more dependent on them and more comfortable with them, then participants in a culture must make an extra effort to examine their concepts and assumptions and their unintended consequences from time to time. Now, I have argued, is the time to do so because assumptions about territoriality have been increasingly at odds with the 'logic' of the unbundled world being constructed by inadvertence.

Consider just one example of how we as global citizens got to where we are now. Lords of the manor found it clever and expedient to commute some feudal obligations, as I outlined in chapter 3, in order to gain rents in cash so that they could purchase goods from cities near or far. They never dreamed that this simple act was a giant step toward the creation of capitalism and nation-states and thus away from the world they ruled. Had they known – or even envisioned the possibility – that such self-serving and 'rational' actions would end the feudal system and bring in the age of absolute monarchs to whom they would pay tribute, would they have hesitated? Perhaps, but regardless of that possibility they took what seemed sensible steps to shore up their way of life; and those steps complemented other independent events involving people also unaware of the consequences of their own actions. No one envisioned the hegemony of the state system; no one orchestrated these actions; no one even noticed more than a few of these steps. Looking back, those steps, which led to the nation-state and now beyond it, seem inexorable. But they were contingent on many actions by actors unaware of their meaning or consequences.

An exhaustive examination of deterministic and voluntaristic perspectives on historical change would be a useless digression. Whether the twenty-first century will unfold deterministically, regardless of our conscious actions, it seems worthwhile to lay out some of the unintended consequences likely to follow from the trends and incipient institutions just outlined in the world I envision 'beyond nations.' Ironically, much of the force dragging us beyond nations has been generated by national governments in order to bolster themselves on the changing world stage. Be that as it may, the transnational forces I have examined in this chapter share several features which are obvious when enumerated, but they are unintended, I believe, by virtually all participants in the global drama. I will review them only briefly in most cases, as they have been discussed or at least alluded to at several points in the book. A couple deserve somewhat more expansive treatment.

First, let us remember that the unbundling to which I refer so often is part of two parallel processes – bundling and unbundling. The balance between them shifts, one predominant in the centuries leading to the absolutist monarchies and on to the modern state, another predominant for the twenty-first century and perhaps beyond. But bundling still continues even in the unbundled world; and this is most clear perhaps in the creation of more and more nations. Likewise rebundling some of the strands of the unbundling nations may take the form of religious movements, voluntary organizations or communities, and networks of transnational corporations. Unbundled does not mean chaotic or unstructured but multifocused rather than focused on one overarching and sovereign community. In seeking structure in new bundles, we unintentionally further the unbundling of the currently hegemonic structure, the nation-state.

Second, this changing balance between bundling and unbundling finds a parallel in the evolving relationships between individual and community, whether these are conceived as rights, duties, or simply conditions. Individuals find succour in communities, but unlike the nation, these will increasingly be communities they create or join and exit voluntarily. Communities will be sustained, not by who happens to be compelled to live within national borders, but by individuals with shared interests wherever they live. If each individual is, as I argued in chapter 6, a community of communities, or a community of relationships, those communities may claim a part – but only a part – of each individual. Communities will share individuals just as, in another sense, individuals will share communities.[21] If modernity created the autonomous individual, the postmodern condition will take us 'beyond individuals' as well as 'beyond nations' as units of analysis.

Third, the complementarity of individual and community contrasts with the usual zero-sum view of individuals smothered by communities, or communities weakened by individuals unwilling or unable to make the commitment implied by older notions of community. The complementarity is made possible by the proliferation of specialized, focused groups, communities, and organizations rather than the all-purpose nation-state or the correlated statuses of the medieval world. One is able now – and will be more so in the next century – to *add* communities to one's repertoire rather than being forced to choose which community will define one's identity at the expense of other communities.

Fourth, related to the greater specialization of the organizational environment is the transformation of the market-place. Reference to 'the global' market-place leaves a misleading impression of a vast, amorphous, out-of-control monster which swallows firms and nations. Perhaps there once was 'a market-place' in the sense of the periodic market which brought many goods and services together in one place, such as the village square. Perhaps the giant malls of our era are versions of this concept. At the global level of business and finance, it is extremely misleading to conceive of 'the market' as some analogy to these retail examples. Instead of 'global market,' there has been an increase in the number of specialized markets; their scope (range of goods or services) has shrunk as their geographical scale has expanded.

Fifth, the specialization of organizations and markets has called forth more and more specialized 'police' in the sense expounded earlier. Regulation of specialized but transnational markets follows a 'logic' clearly different from the 'logic' of territorial police, the nation-state, and the state system. Even the specialized forms of international governance set up by nation-states to serve their interests – the United Nations, GATT, and so on – must follow a logic detached to a significant degree from the exclusiveness of territorial nation-states. Unless these supra-national agencies achieve a degree of autonomy, they cannot effectively achieve or implement their intended purposes; to the degree they become autonomous, however, their unintended consequence will be to supplement, to circumvent, to undermine, or to replace some of the functions of the nations which created them. Likewise the international cooperation so evident in technologies of communication and travel foster the specialized and voluntary communities discussed above; they were not designed to create such communities, and few of the communities have the intention of helping to make nations less relevant. Unintentionally, that is exactly what they do.

Sixth, I noted above that small businesses often succeed as transnational corporations whereas only very large firms ever operated as multinational corporations. This seemingly small item may represent a momentous, unanticipated, and unintended consequence of many other changes. Although there are inherent limits to the number of large multinationals (since the total market is limited), there may be no effective limit to the number of transnationals (since small size is not a significant constraint). Indeed, if 'flat' organizations which are adaptable to sudden changes in their market are mandated by globalization, small transnationals should have an advantage over large ones. Financial institutions may be an exception, but that will not be certain for some time. 'Think globally, act locally' might be as fine a motto for transnationals as it is for the ecology movement. In both cases, the slogan may also be understood as an injunction to fit the solution (product) more precisely to the problem (consumer demand) wherever they may be, instead of working for global economies of scale and then 'dumping' excess production elsewhere. A final interpretation of this deceptively simple epithet could be its echo of the discussion of the first point above, that one can eschew zero-sum thinking and should focus instead on the balance between bundling and unbundling.

Seventh, earlier chapters have distinguished between globalization and globalism, between an enhanced awareness of differences among regions, nations, cultures, and societies and the greater scale of organizations or markets. One may note that the distinction helps in making sense of some of the developments anticipated to lie beyond nations. For example, this chapter has sketched out reasons to expect that there should be more nations not larger ones, that more specialized organizations will syphon off functions from nation-states without becoming global behemoths, and that more rather than fewer religions and forms of spirituality may be expected. Instead of the homogeneity and loss of local identity many prognosticators have feared, the unbundled world should find many lasting differences – that is, globalization and not just globalism. Of course, we should endeavour to remove or diminish certain types of difference, such as the vast disparities of wealth between North and South and the worst instances of repressive government. But I am confident that homogeneity of culture, language, and identity is unlikely on a global scale in the foreseeable future, if ever.

Eighth, having said that diversity will not be eliminated, I should qualify that by noting that English may become even more widely used than at present. I do not expect, however, a unilingual world of English-speakers. Rather more likely is the increasing use of English as the *lingua franca* of business, travel, and scholarship. As English becomes the language of international relations, trade, science, and art, it loses its exclusive ties to particular pieces of territory. Hence, it may be less threatening (even in Quebec) than it has been, just as Latin was not a threat to local languages in the medieval world. Whereas language has been closely linked to territory in Europe for a millennium, and for perhaps four millennia in China, English may rise above territoriality, although other languages may still remain mostly territorial. Furthermore, the languages which really are in competition with each other are the languages of the unbundling; computer software incompatibilities may prove more of a threat to science, networking, financial transactions, and trade than any of the territorial languages. This may be one case in which globalization (awareness of differences) leads to the ultimate globalism of one computer language, of a single cyberspace, with terrifying as well as beneficial consequences which would require another book to explore.

Each of the entities which may lie beyond nations is implicated to a varying degree in these eight possible consequences of the evolution of forms. None of the entities discussed could plausibly be said to exist for the purpose of bringing about these eight consequences. Important as more nations, more religions, more organizations, and more communities may be, their unintended and unanticipated consequences should loom as large as these institutions themselves in the global world of the twenty-first century. There are two additional consequences – or ways of conceptualizing the consequences – to which I now turn. They require more extended comment than the cursory remarks in this section.

DECOUPLING STATE AND NATION

What lies 'beyond the nation-state'? Besides all that has been said up to this point, the most significant consequence involves the decoupling of 'the state' from 'the nation.'[22] One may think of this as another unintended consequence of many other events, actions, and processes; and it surely is unintended. But I will address it instead as a way of understanding how the unbundling I have described may represent an incipient structure of great flexibility and power, with its own consequences which I cannot fully anticipate.

At several places in this book, I have alluded to the possibility that the state may wither, even if not quite disappear. Of course, this withering, if it occurs, would not be a fulfilment of Marx's hope and prediction, but an unintended consequence of the process of unbundling. Technology has enabled more non-territorial forms of organization, administration, and regulation or 'policing.' If governments as we know them excel at territorial functions, while the private sector operates better in non-territorial ways, will technology lead to a withering of the state? The answer is almost certainly 'yes' if we persist in thinking of government as the ultimate coercive force ruling the territorial nation-state. Even then, good reasons may be offered for why the state will continue to perform useful functions, even though fewer and fewer functions. Perhaps it will end up, as Reich and Ohmae urge, that national (and sub-national) territorial governments should leave the economy alone and focus on physical infrastructure and even more on social policies to enhance human resources.

We do not have to be limited to this narrow conception of government or the state. Many supra-national and transnational organizations and institutions already exist, and more are likely. As I have repeatedly stated, they are forms of governance; they are the state; they are 'politics by other means,' to paraphrase von Clausewitz. 'The state' or 'the conduct of public life' so that collective action may occur is a very capacious concept, and we should not overlook the variety of its manifestations just because they have not yet been generally seen as 'government.' No doubt lords of the manor doubted the value of taking functions away from themselves by creating specialized institutions like notaries and sheriffs. But the state as we know it was created by the accumulation of such incremental steps.

Furthermore, one cannot foresee a world in which there will be no public goods and hence no need to regulate access to them or to collect taxes and fees to support them. Some public goods, as we have seen, are territorial, and some are not; but 'government' or 'the state' is implicated in both types. That is the irreducible minimum level of state function, even if citizens choose to add more functions to the role of the state for other reasons. Whoever collects the taxes *is* the state, whether territorially based or not.

In discussing what lies beyond nations, we concluded that nations will continue to exist; the issue involved a shifting balance between nations and other structures. Likewise, the state will not wither away or disappear; it will instead cloak itself in new garbs and forms to fulfil its essential public roles. Some of the new forms of the state will involve some of the structures which take us beyond nations. The transfer of state functions from the territorial nation-state to non-territorial institutions, even though done in part at the behest of territorial nation-states, unintentionally serves to decouple the state from the territorial nation. Not completely, and perhaps not irrevocably, but enough that political science as a discipline will probably devise new terms for the several distinct entities lumped together as 'the nation-state.' I do not care what those terms may be, but I do care to demonstrate that a substantial portion of the trends and institutional adjustments outlined in this book will make it virtually impossible to equate 'the state' and 'the nation.'[23]

If this perspective has any validity, one may envision some substantial consequences. These are, in one sense, other descriptions of the eight listed in a previous section, but some deserve to be mentioned in different language. For one, if state functions are to a significant degree decoupled from the nation, then perhaps one can imagine that the nation itself could be decoupled from territory. 'Nation' would have a different meaning then than we have been accustomed to giving it, and it would be closer perhaps to earlier concepts, like tribe, 'folk,' 'a people,' and ethnicity.[24] Whether that constitutes a step forward or the first step on the slippery slope to universal racism depends on what citizens make of it, and it depends on the functions of governance which remain with this new 'nation' compared to the powers of the non-territorial (or partially non-territorial) state. In seeking to corrode the presumptiveness of unconscious assumptions — whether about territoriality, the state, or personal identities — I am content to paint plausible portraits since I cannot predict how the movie will end.

A second and perhaps related outcrop of a tectonic change in assumption involved in decoupling state and nation concerns the shifting boundaries of public and private spheres.[25] These have always been culturally diverse and historically transient. Since they change slowly, we come to accept the boundaries and the balance as 'given,' but they are not fixed. Just as I have shown that the opposition of individual and community is yielding to complementarity between individual and community, unbundling must lead to a redefinition of public and private.[26] Again, however, I cannot foretell the details of the new boundaries; but 'nation' may become a more private concept analogous to family on a grander scale, while the state will be essentially public.[27] The complication in such a hypothesis, of course, is that it seems likely that some of the state functions now assumed to be governmental may be performed by institutions (like transnationals, voluntary communities, and specialized 'police') which look more like the private sector to our current way of thinking. By working through some of the apparent paradoxes of these changing boundaries, our conception of citizenship will, as I have argued, necessarily change too, being less close to patriotism and integrating a wider range of settings for political participation.

Can we choose our concepts? Do we live in Alice's Wonderland, where words will mean what we stipulate, or must they lag behind the world as we construct and deconstruct it? I doubt if any of the lords, nobles, or kings involved in the Peace of Westphalia in the seventeenth century sat around asking about the best terminology or the appropriate definition of 'the state' or 'sovereignty.' Instead they acted, and the (largely unintentional) by-products of those actions were the rise to dominance of the absolutist monarchy with its incipient bureaucratic state apparatus and eventually the nation-state as we have lived with it for over a century. Scholars consciously define their terms, but the meanings which carry weight in daily life are the ones people construct by doing things, usually without intending any particular meaning.

BENEFITS OF UNBUNDLING

What would the world gain by giving up long standing assumptions about the territorial imperative of politics? What are the advantages of 'unbundled' nations? I would suggest three main types of benefits, without implying these exhaust the possibilities. In brief, they are: peace, freedom, and good government.

Unbundled nations might be less prone to warlike behaviour. One reason why nation-territories were created concerned their superiority to other forms of organization as war machines.[28] Once 'the nation' has been decoupled from the state and becomes only one of many identities or loyalties, war mobilization of citizens by a nation should be more difficult. Once citizenship is no longer exclusive to a nation – but might include membership in overlapping and cross-cutting entities – more citizens will presumably find themselves in 'conflict of interest' situations, and thus reluctant to take up arms or support policies hostile to their interests as embodied in transnational communities.

It would require great naïvety to conclude that unbundling would eliminate all wars or other forms of anti-social behaviour. All I mean to suggest at this point is that unbundling appears to favour conditions which make war less likely, less extensive, or of shorter duration. These conditions are matters of degree, not all-or-nothing; and the rate of unbundling will no doubt vary in different parts of the world. On balance, one might expect that it tends more away from war and toward peace than the reverse.

Freedom would be enhanced by the absence of war, but unbundling would facilitate greater personal freedom as well. To the extent that all aspects of one's identity come to have salience, rather than the dominance of territorial identities, facets of some personalities could blossom more easily. Currently, for example, Kurds or other groups, scattered among several countries, may be suppressed in some or all of these places; and thus place or location has a determinative force for their well-being. If political boundaries are no longer defined solely in territorial terms, such groups have greater scope for dignity, self-help, and self-expression. Similarly, people who share interests but are widely separated in distance could be brought together in electronic communities or travel without the current restrictions imposed by national borders or regulations.

The most significant practical consequences of unbundling should be in public administration. Instead of an all-purpose organization of a fixed territorial size, one can more easily create types and sizes of organizations suited to the particular nature of the problem. As in the case of local government, there are good reasons to believe that some problems are best addressed by territorial and others by non-territorial organizations. Even if some problems require a territorial form of organization, there is ample evidence that they need not all have exactly the same borders or boundaries. In fact, that is the logic behind federalism too: general powers for the national government and local powers for provincial governments. Why not extend the logic to include small local units and regional organizations? If that makes sense, then why not admit that territory is at best a convenient basis for public administration but not a necessary basis? Why not, in other words, fit the solution to the problem?

GLOBALIZATION, FINALLY

The final perspective I offer on the questions of what lies beyond nations and whether intentions count for more or less than unintended consequences of our concepts and actions leads back to globalization. Recall that globalization is distinct from globalism. One of the crucial differences consists of the ways in which awareness of variety elsewhere need not lead to homogeneity, even when conscious efforts are made to emulate features admired in other places. One may sketch the interaction in several ways, but it will be convenient to do so from the perspective of transnational corporations.

Consider an oversimplified diagram like the one below. It summarizes a vast amount of detail in a way which highlights the processes of most interest here.

264 Beyond Sovereignty

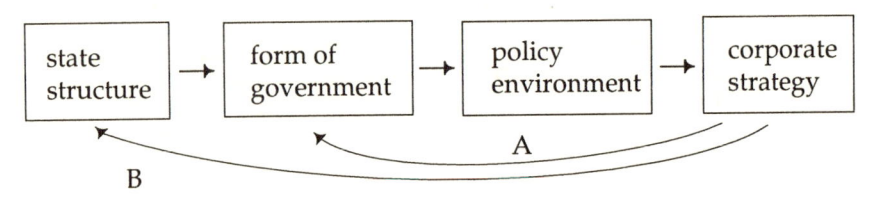

```
[state structure] → [form of government] → [policy environment] → [corporate strategy]
                                      ← A ←
        ← B ←
```

In brief, the historically specific state structure is taken as 'given' at any one time (nation-state now), and that sets severe constraints on types of government. Each type of government – and each 'regime' whether elected or self-chosen – creates somewhat different policy environments which constrain or offer opportunities to particular transnational corporations (and environmental groups, religions, and other entities ignored here). Transnationals by definition know what is going on in lots of places around the world, which is part of what I mean by 'globalization.' When they come across forms of government and/or policy environments which they believe favour their enterprise, they try to reinforce those forms and to modify the governments and policies elsewhere. That is shown as feedback loop 'A,' which may actually constitute numerous loops to specific departments, cabinet ministers, public opinion, or whatever; but one path can stand for all of them in this case. The first crucial point is that 'A' amounts to conscious, deliberate, and intentional efforts to evoke responses in government which improve the policy environment. In trying to get one government to implement policy learned in another political system, the result may be different even if everyone conscientiously works to implement the policy. This follows from the obvious fact that circumstances differ in small and large ways, and our knowledge is insufficient to compensate for the differences. These complexities alone are enough to suggest that emulation on a global scale, as a result of globalization of information, need not lead inexorably to globalism as worldwide homogeneity.

Let us turn now to feedback loop 'B.' Occasionally there are politicians or observers who consciously try to think through the likely consequences for the state system and state structure of the lobbying efforts of transnationals and of the policy environment and government structural adaptations. This book may be seen in that light, although it has other purposes as well. Such conscious reflection on state structure seems to be quite rare, and thus 'B' may be conceptualized as a largely unconscious, inadvertent, or unintended set of consequences for the state structure when the participants thought their 'target' was the government or the policy environment. Much of what I have called unintended consequences in this chapter consists of the contents of feedback loop 'B,' and much of what I envision as lying beyond nations consists of feedback's unanticipated effects on state structure. Of course, the picture is enormously richer and more complicated than this diagram can convey because transnationals are only one type of organization which generates feedbacks like 'A' or 'B.'

Theoretical understanding and the successful conduct of everyday life require that details be ignored. The world buzzes with 'facts' and complexities and mysteries. Understanding grows out of finding a 'logic' for at least some of what is happening. Thus, I do not apologize for an oversimplified diagram or for the brevity of most of the major points in this book. Of course, I believe that I have uncovered the 'logic' behind the flux so evident in the world. At the least I have set forth many hypotheses about that logic. Central to this logic is the increasing role of non-territorial forces, technologies, groups, and governments (or 'police'). From this premise, I have tried to question the appropriateness of many assumptions and institutions. I have also endeavoured, especially in this chapter, to provide a sense of the structures and points of leverage or stability which may lie ahead in the unbundled world, which looks so much more mobile, complex, and chaotic than the apparently tidy world of the territorial nation-state.

Some observers have looked ahead, but not far enough, and perceived only the chaos, as I suggested in the Introduction. I hope that I have seen farther and thus may have seen structures that lie beyond the transition to a new historic era. Readers must decide for themselves whether chaos has a structure. In doing so, we should all be cautious in assessing the connotations or unintended meanings of our words and concepts. Zbigniew Brzezinski, former national security adviser to the president of the United States, has written a book entitled *Out of Control: Global Turmoil on the Eve of the Twenty-First Century*.[29] While I sympathize with the frustrations he so evidently feels about the suffering and potential dangers in global politics, I am shocked at how narrow and short-sighted are his conceptions of control or structure. In his book, 'out of control' means primarily 'out of American control.' Even if one leaves aside the fears that America may lose its grip, 'out of control' is a loaded phrase.

One may evaluate some of the issues Brzezinski raises in a different light by using other words: 'decentralized,' 'autonomous,' and 'non-tyrranical control,' among others. There is always the danger that the words I choose – for my own arguments or for Brzezinski's – convey a sense of benign calm. That is not my intent. I have tried to choose words which are less 'loaded'; and by contrast to the words often used by observers of our world, they may seem to play down the ominous portents and dangerous possibilities the unbundled world brings with it. Words may be chosen because they express precisely what one intends, but it is difficult to find such words about a future world which looks to be radically different than our own. Thus, I have consciously chosen words because they may shock readers into examining the flip side of common sense and because they challenge assumptions so deeply ingrained that they float below our conscious awareness. Nothing is certain, and nothing should be exempt from challenge, especially the beliefs and assumptions we are most loathe to question.

EXPLAINING THE UNPREDICTABLE

Prediction is easy, and its worth is proportional to its difficulty. Correct prediction is impossible, if one wishes to be certain in advance which prediction is correct, and thus it is worthless too. Therefore, I have repeatedly urged that prediction was not the aim of this book. Although I look into the future, my goal is explanation rather than prediction. Is there a logic to what is happening in the world, or at least to some significant part of the world? If we can discern some logic, some pattern, some theoretical framework, then prediction might be improved; but more importantly, when something happens we can say whether it should be watched closely and why it occurred. The logic, pattern, or theory gives meaning to our observations. It is a common cliché, but facts do not speak for themselves. They have very different meanings and significance in alterative frameworks.

The aim of theory should be to multiply the number of plausible explanations and only secondarily to extrapolate or to predict the future. By this I mean that as one works through the complexities of unintended consequences, the theory will suggest more explanations than will one's common sense. If prediction is your game, you will often be surprised. If theory is your game, surprises may be used to gain a deeper understanding of the theory. One can accept a surprise as one of the possibilities, and then conclude, 'So that is why it happened!' I hope that this book provides a framework or perspective that will, when the future unfolds, allow readers to explain why it happened that way rather than another. In that sense and that alone, one may explain unpredictable events.

I noted at the beginning of the book that concepts constitute implicit predictions. When we use words like 'nation' or 'state' or 'corporation' or 'federalism,' we implicitly assume that the way those terms have up to now captured reality has some continuing relevance. If so, they aid our understanding. At some point, however, we find ourselves devising explicit definitions, or subdividing categories, and for good reason. Those are signs – not infallible predictions but hints and portents – that the world has been changing faster than our ways of describing it. If there is one message more than any which I hope this book will demonstrate – and I do hope more than one message comes through – it is that the time has come to question the common assumption that 'nation,' 'state,' and 'political authority' necessarily involve territoriality. That was a good working assumption for two or three centuries, but it serves us ill as we enter the twenty-first century.

For decades, most philosophers of science believed that explanations and predictions were two sides of the same coin. Explanations were predictions that came true, or at least anything which one could explain 'after the fact' could, in principle, have been predicted if one had only had all the relevant facts. I do not know what the balance of opinion would be today among self-identified philosophers of science about this controversy. And I must confess it to be more complicated than what I have summarized; for example, the phrase 'in principle' when used about predictions may be a tautology, and on that hangs as well the view one holds about whether the world is predestined or open to modification by informed actions. There may never be proof one way or the other – at least in the way mathematicians can prove Pythagoras's Theorem. So it may be only fair to reveal to readers that I am an optimist: I believe that our actions make a difference, especially when they reflect careful thought. Of course, I have just expounded at length the view that unintended consequences may be as crucial as those we intend; that is part of why I believe in a non-deterministic world and why I believe that the 'in principle' above has no meaning.

My optimism may have biased this book. If so, it may counterbalance the pessimism which biases other books. Several times I have cautioned the reader that now is the time to take action to bring about or to head off the future I have expounded. Only an optimist offers that kind of advice.

Stephen Toulmin – physicist, philosopher of science, and historian – has written a book which overlaps my own in some ways, although his sweep is even more audacious than mine. He justifies his attempt to 'look ahead' in terms I am happy to apply to this book:

The most that we can hope to foresee is the limits within which 'available' human futures lie. Available futures are not just those that we can possibly forecast, but those that we can actively create: for these de Jouvenal coined a new name – 'futuribles.' They are futures which do not simply happen *of themselves*, but can be *made* to happen, if we meanwhile adopt wise attitudes and policies.[30]

Although our 'wise attitudes and policies' have unintended consequences, sometimes of great magnitude, we still need to take actions, and we will always need to look for the underlying 'logic' of events, situations, and trends rather than merely extrapolating from the past to the future. The relaxation of assumptions about territoriality broadens 'the limit within which "available" human futures lie.'

Thomas Kuhn – another philosopher of science and historian – gained fame primarily for his analysis of how scientific revolutions occur and how they differ from 'normal science.' Interesting as his insights were about these matters, I have always found one other aspect of his work more profound. At the end of *The Structure of Scientific Revolutions*, he interjects a brief discussion of what realistic progress means in science.[31] Progress consists, he states, not in moving toward truth but in moving away from known errors. That counsel of humility has been in my zone of awareness for almost thirty years, and it has never been more valuable to me than in writing this book. We can never know for sure where we are going, but we may be able to discern the errors or misleading conceptions or outdated assumptions we should try to leave behind. That is such a limited goal, but that is also everything if we do it often enough.

Step by step, we move into the future. But the future is not a 'thing.' It is not like a train which pulls into the station at a particular hour, and that's it, complete and ready. The future is part of the present, albeit different enough to be confusing, frustrating, surprising, novel, and exhilarating. Although the future is not a simple tunnel which the flashlight of our theories may illumine, it may be a stage on which we can construct or modify some sets. Whatever the metaphor, it falls short; just as this book was inspired by other books' failures, perhaps it will sufficiently upset or inspire other people to envision one of the 'available' futures, in de Jouvenal's phrase.

Although I disclaim the ability to predict the future, I aspire to envision a future. The word 'envision' has been used frequently in this book, and I will not attempt a rigorous definition at this point. Drucker writes of the difference between predicting the weather and predicting the climate. If I have envisioned the 'climate' of political authority in the twenty-first century, my achievement will be welcome. If not, that will be one less vision other writers need to consider. Of course, this book concerns the past as much as the future. As Toulmin stated, 'This is a book about the past, and about the future: about the terms in which we make sense of the past, and the ways in which our view of the past affects our posture in dealing with the future.'[32]

Notes

INTRODUCTION

1 Quoted in David Osborne and Ted Gaebler, *Reinventing Government: How the Entrepreneurial Spirit Is Transforming the Public Sector* (New York: Penguin, 1993), p. xxii.
2 Sir G.N. Clark, *The Seventeenth Century*, 2d ed. (Oxford: Clarendon Press, 1947), p. 155.
3 E.L. Jones, *The European Miracle* (Cambridge: Cambridge University Press, 1981), p. 123.
4 Hegel, as quoted by John H. Herz, 'Rise and Demise of the Territorial State,' in W.A. Douglas Jackson, ed., *Politics and Geographic Relationships* (Englewood Cliffs, N.J.: Prentice-Hall, 1964), p. 411.

CHAPTER 1 Is Territory Imperative?

1 'State sovereignty may be regarded as the counterpart in doctrine to the modern territorial division of the world into legally separate jurisdictions ... The twin attributes of sovereignty became a monopoly of force and a monopoly of the coinage' (Christopher Brewin, 'Sovereignty,' in James Mayall, ed., *The Community of States: A Study in International Political Theory* [London: George Allen and Unwin, 1982], pp. 34, 40).
2 The contrast between religious and territorial assumptions has been nicely put by Joseph R. Strayer: 'A man can lead a reasonably full life without a family, a fixed local address, or a religious affiliation, but if he is stateless he is nothing ... This was not always so ... In those times it was the man without a family or a lord, without membership in a local community or a dominant religious group, who had no security and no opportunity ...' (*On the Medieval Origins of the Modern State* [Princeton: Princeton University Press, 1970], p. 3).

272 Notes to pages 14–22

3 Indeed, federalism does not require territory at all; but if territorial in organization, it does not involve exclusivity. See Jean A. Laponce, 'L'Heure du fédéralisme personnel est-elle arrivée?' in Jean Lafontant, ed., *L'Etat et les minorités* (Saint-Boniface: Les Editions du blé / Presses universitaires de Saint-Boniface, 1993), pp. 55–65.
4 William H. McNeill, *The Pursuit of Power: Technology, Armed Force, and Society since A.D. 1000* (Chicago: University of Chicago Press, 1982).
5 Charles E. Lindblom, *Markets and Politics* (New York: Basic Books, 1977).
6 David J. Elkins and Richard Simeon, 'A Cause in Search of Its Effect, or What Does Political Culture Explain?' *Comparative Politics* 11 (1979), 127–45.
7 For example, there are radically new assumptions underlying 'development' as it has become known as 'sustainable development.' A nice summary has been provided by Keith A. Bezanson, 'A Changing World of the Strong and Weak,' *Globe and Mail*, 26 Oct. 1992, p. A25.
8 John A. Armstrong, *Nations before Nationalism* (Chapel Hill: University of North Carolina Press, 1982).
9 Some very helpful overviews of the 'construction' of nation-states include: Strayer, *On the Medieval Origins of the Modern State*; Perry Anderson, *Lineages of the Absolutist State* (London: N.L.B., 1974); Jean Gottman, *The Significance of Territory* (Charlottesville: University Press of Virginia, 1973), ch. 2; William H. McNeill, *Polyethnicity and National Unity in World History* (Toronto: University of Toronto Press, 1986); Charles Tilly, *Coercion, Capital, and European States, A.D. 990–1992*, rev. ed. (Oxford: Blackwell, 1992); and Bruce D. Porter, *War and the Rise of the State: The Military Foundations of Modern Politics* (New York: Free Press, 1994).
10 Pierre Elliott Trudeau, *Federalism and the French Canadians* (Toronto: Macmillan, 1968), pp. 183, 185.
11 Ernst H. Kantorowicz, in *The King's Two Bodies* (Princeton: Princeton University Press, 1957), argues that loyalty to place developed later than loyalty to king or other persons; 'community' only gradually (around the fifteenth century?) became primarily territorial rather than personal. Harold J. Berman, in *Law and Revolution: The Formation of the Western Legal Tradition* (Cambridge: Harvard University Press, 1983), argues convincingly that the *plurality* of political and legal forms coexisting in Western Europe from the eleventh century was a crucial element in what later became 'the modern world.' That is, no form had exclusive control of a group or territory in the early centuries he examines.
12 For a brief summary of the Thirty Years' War and the significance of the Peace of Westphalia in 1648, see Kalevi J. Holsti, *Peace and War: Armed Conflicts and International Order 1648–1989* (Cambridge: Cambridge University Press,

1991). For a perspective on the changing significance of these events, see Mark W. Zacher, 'The Decaying Pillars of the Westphalian Temple: Implications for International Order and Governance,' in James N. Rosenau and E.-O. Czempiel, eds, *Governance without Government: Order and Change in World Politics* (Cambridge: Cambridge University Press, 1992).

13 One must be careful with words like 'border' or 'place,' since only recently have they had the meanings of sharp line or precise location that we attribute to them. For example, Sir G.N. Clark in *The Seventeenth Century*, 2d ed. (Oxford: Clarendon Press, 1947), notes that 'I have not been able to discover a case of a frontier fixed literally on the map until the year 1718' (p. 244); and that 'we may say that a frontier was ceasing to be an area and tending to become a line' (p. 143).

14 Porter (*War and the Rise of the State*, p. 135) notes that passports were used extensively in France during the Napoleanic period, but these were internal documents designed primarily to help identify spies. Thus, they were not intended for the purposes now taken for granted in the twentieth century.

15 Indeed, as Professor John Helliwell has reminded me, the period 1890–1910 may have been more global and people more mobile than even today.

16 The transition may be helped along by its own internal (il)logic, as Trudeau noted: '... the very idea of the nation-state is absurb. To insist that a particular nationality must have complete sovereign power is to pursue a self-destructive end. Because every national minority will find, at the very moment of liberation, a new minority within its bosom which in turn must be allowed the right to demand its freedom' (*Federalism and the French Canadians*, p. 158).

17 Although no author has approached this issue in precisely the way I have in this book, I should mention several suggestive and forceful presentations of relevant information and interpretations, including Friedrich Kratochwil, 'Of Systems, Boundaries, and Territoriality: An Inquiry into the Formation of the State System,' *World Politics* 39 (Oct. 1986), 27–52; John Gerald Ruggie, 'Territoriality and Beyond: Problematizing Modernity in International Relations,' *International Organization* 47 (Winter 1993), 139–74; John H. Herz, 'Rise and Demise of the Territorial State,' *World Politics* 9 (1957), 473–93 (some parts of which were 'recanted' in his 'The Territorial State Revisited: Reflections on the Future of the Nation-State,' in James N. Rosenau, ed., *International Politics and Foreign Policy: A Reader in Research and Theory* [New York: Free Press, 1969], pp. 76–89); and Richard Falk, 'A New Paradigm for International Legal Studies: Prospects and Proposals,' in Richard Falk et al., eds, *International Law: A Contemporary Perspective* (Boulder: Westview Press, 1985), pp. 651–702.

18 James Mayall, *Nationalism and International Society* (Cambridge: Cambridge University Press, 1990), especially chapters 2 and 3; Michael Ignatieff, *Blood*

and Belonging: Journeys into the New Nationalism (Toronto: Viking/Penguin, 1993).
19 Benedict Anderson, *Imagined Communities: Reflections on the Origin and Spread of Nationalism*, rev. ed. (London: Verso, 1991).
20 Robert H. Jackson, *Quasi-States: Sovereignty, International Relations, and the Third World* (Cambridge: Cambridge University Press, 1990).
21 Andrew F. Cooper, 'Questions of Sovereignty: Canada and the Widening International Agenda,' *Behind the Headlines* 50 (Spring 1993), 1–16. Ignatieff (*Blood and Belonging*, pp. 138–9) notes: 'With the creation of the Kurdish enclave [in Iraq], it [the international community] endorsed the idea that the duty of humanitarian intervention overrode the principle of the inviolability and integrity of sovereign states.'
22 Professor Michael Goldberg has suggested to me that centralization and decentralization in the state system may be cyclical rather than linear, just as corporate structures seem to go through cycles of acquisition or merger and divestiture or decentralization.
23 Recall that the title of Adam Smith's famous book was *The Wealth of Nations*, not the wealth of people or firms or sectors.
24 David J. Elkins, 'Canada in the Twenty-First-Century,' *Australian-Canadian Studies* 8 (1991), 3–15.
25 Bundling and unbundling may also be cyclical, as was noted above in regard to centralization and decentralization of corporate structures and the state system.
26 David J. Elkins, 'The Sense of Place,' in David J. Elkins and Richard Simeon, *Small Worlds: Provinces and Parties in Canadian Political Life* (Toronto: Methuen, 1980), pp. 1–30.
27 While writing this book, I was startled to discover two other scholars who have used the concept of 'unbundling' in ways very similar to my usage here (see note 17 above for citations of articles by Kratochwil and by Ruggie). This independent convergence on the same processes reassures me that my analysis is not entirely idiosyncratic.
28 Multiple identities may also be conceptualized as a 'postmodern' phenomenon of multiple perspectives and 'embedded selves' as trenchantly described by Kenneth J. Gergen, *The Saturated Self: Dilemmas of Identity in Contemporary Life* (New York: Basic Books, 1991). Whatever one calls the phenomenon, people seem to handle identities differently than they did a few centuries ago. This theme will be developed more fully in several later chapters.
29 Kenichi Ohmae, *The Borderless World: Power and Strategy in the Interlinked Economy* (New York: Harper Perennial, 1991); and Robert Reich, *The Work of*

Nations: Preparing Ourselves for Twenty-First-Century Capitalism (New York: Alfred A. Knopf, 1991).
30 I am indebted to Professor Avigail Eisenberg for clarifying my thoughts about citizenship and entitlement.
31 Peter F. Drucker, *The New Realities* (New York: Harper and Row, 1989); and his *Post-Capitalist Society* (New York: Harper Business, 1993).
32 One should not overstate the contrast between nations and private organizations, as we are reminded by Albert O. Hirschman, *Exit, Voice, and Loyalty: Responses to Decline in Firms, Organizations, and States* (Cambridge: Harvard University Press, 1970).
33 One could, in principle, sort activities rather than people, but the fundamental issue regarding territorialtiy remains the same.
34 Luke McNamara, 'Aboriginal Self-Government and Justice Reform in Canada: The Impact of the Charter of Rights and Freedoms,' *Australian-Canadian Studies* 11 (1993), 43–75.
35 David Osborne and Ted Gaebler, *Reinventing Government: How the Entrepreneurial Spirit Is Transforming the Public Sector* (New York: Penguin, 1993).

CHAPTER 2 Technology and Territory

1 Several authors provide valuable overviews of the process summarized here, including Charles Tilly, *Coercion, Capital, and European States, A.D. 990–1992*, rev. ed. (Oxford: Blackwell, 1992); William H. McNeill, *The Pursuit of Power: Technology, Armed Force, and Society since A.D. 1000* (Chicago: University of Chicago Press, 1982); Carlo M. Cipolla, *Before the Industrial Revolution: European Society and Economy, 1000–1700* (New York: W.W. Norton, 1976); and Stephen Toulmin, *Cosmopolis: The Hidden Agenda of Modernity* (New York: Free Press, 1990), especially chapter 3.
2 Carlo M. Cipolla, *Guns and Sails in the Early Phase of European Expansion 1400–1700* (London: Collins, 1965); and Bruce D. Porter, *War and the Rise of the State: The Military Foundations of Modern Politics* (New York: Free Press, 1994).
3 For a nice summary of transnational forces on the nation-state, although interpreted differently than I have, see Paul Kennedy, *Preparing for the Twenty-First Century* (New York: Harper Collins, 1993), chapter 7.
4 Alfred W. Crosby, *Ecological Imperialism: The Biological Expansion of Europe, 900–1900* (Cambridge: Cambridge University Press, 1986; Canto edition, 1993) contains a fascinating analysis of some of the very complex interactions among colonists and the technology they bring to a new environment.
5 Ursula Franklin, *The Real World of Technology*, CBC Massey Lectures (Concord, Ont.: Anansi, 1990).

276 Notes to pages 41–7

6 'All too often we tend to identify technology with mechanics, because our civilization is essentially mechanical. Political and administrative organization, military organization, architecture and road construction, even artistic products such as frescoes, bear the mark of technology ...' (Cipolla, *Before the Industrial Revolution*, p. 159).

7 William H. McNeill, *Plagues and Peoples* (Garden City, N.Y.: Anchor/Doubleday, 1976) offers the perspective that civilization or modernity consists of exposure to all major diseases so that they are endemic rather than epidemic.

8 Bernard Lewis, *The Muslim Discovery of Europe* (New York: W.W. Norton, 1982) reveals how little each 'side' knew of the other and why Europeans seem to have learned more about 'the Orient' than vice versa until recently.

9 Apparently Europeans were also capable of appropriating ideas, technology, food staples, and medicines from natives in North and South America while forgetting their sources. See Jack Weatherford's two books, *Indian Givers: The Continuing Impact of the Discovered Americas on the World* (New York: Crown, 1988) and *Native Roots: How the Indians Enriched America* (New York: Crown, 1991).

10 Cipolla, *Before the Industrial Revolution*, especially p. 160; David Landes, *Revolution in Time: Clocks and the Making of the Modern World* (Cambridge: The Belknap Press of Harvard University Press, 1983); and E.L. Jones, *The European Miracle: Environments, Economies, and Geopolitics in the History of Europe and Asia* (Cambridge: Cambridge University Press, 1981). Harold J. Berman, *Law and Revolution: The Formation of the Western Legal Tradition* (Cambridge: Harvard University Press, 1983), has also emphasized the multiple sources of Western law (royal, manorial, civic or commercial, and church), which had the unintended effect of making rulers and legal scholars more tolerant in the special sense of willing to incorporate elements from one of these systems into others.

11 Jacques Ellul, *The Technological Society* (New York: Alfred A. Knopf, 1964).

12 Jerry Mander, *In the Absence of the Sacred: The Failure of Technology and the Survival of the Indian Nations* (San Francisco: Sierra Club Books, 1991).

13 Of course, some negative consequences may show up quickly, as the case of Thalidomide demonstrates.

14 I will explore these networks in more detail in chapter 6. For a very amusing account of Internet – one of the electronic 'cyberspaces' – see Robert Wright, 'Voice of America: Overhearing the Internet,' *New Republic*, 13 Sept. 1993, pp. 20–7.

15 Canals and rivers share 'fixedness' with railroads, while oceans are more similar to airlines in their flexibility.

16 Colin Cherry, *The Age of Access: Information Technology and Social Revolution*

(London: Croom Helm, 1985), makes an interesting distinction between types of sharing – 'sharing by division (sharing *between*)' and 'sharing by participation (sharing *with*)' (p. 43) – and hypothesizes that information technologies thereby represent a different social 'logic' than exchange of goods because they may be shared with people rather than divided between them. Despite this helpful perspective, he surprisingly concludes that there is no information revolution comparable to the earlier industrial revolution.

17 Porter, *War and the Rise of the State*, develops this idea in considerable detail.
18 Kennedy, *Preparing for the Twenty-First Century*, suggests that there may be such threats although he offers these views very tentatively.
19 Alvin and Heidi Toffler, *War and Anti-War: Survival at the Dawn of the Twenty-First Century* (Toronto: Little, Brown, 1993), offer an alternative but not contradictory interpretation of evolving military technology.
20 Jones, *European Miracle*, especially chapter 7, offers a succinct summary of a series of very complex events and interactions; see also Porter, *War and the Rise of the State*.
21 Jane Jacobs, *The Economy of Cities* (New York: Vintage Books, 1970); Jane Jacobs, *Cities and the Wealth of Nations: Principles of Economic Life* (New York: Random House, 1984); and Engin F. Isin, *Cities without Citizens: The Modernity of the City as a Corporation* (Montreal: Black Rose Books, 1992).
22 Michel Foucault, *Discipline and Punish: The Birth of the Prison* (New York: Vintage Books, 1979).
23 Jean A. Laponce, *Languages and Their Territories* (Toronto: University of Toronto Press, 1987).
24 Benedict Anderson, *Imagined Communities: Reflections on the Origin and Spread of Nationalism* (London: Verso, 1991), especially chapter 3; Lucien Febvre and H.-J. Martin, *The Coming of the Book: The Impact of Printing, 1450–1800* (London: New Left Books, 1976); and Elizabeth Eisenstein, 'Some Conjectures about the Impact of Printing on Western Society and Thought: A Preliminary Report,' *Journal of Modern History* 40 (March 1968), 1–56.
25 In one of those ironies that history offers, incredibly expensive paper and cheap labour coexisted for centuries, to be followed by very cheap paper and ever more expensive labour costs. This was documented on The Learning Channel in the spring of 1993, although I cannot locate the exact date of broadcast.
26 Gilbert Ryle, *The Concept of Mind* (New York: Barnes and Noble, 1949), p. 27, presents the intriguing view that people had to learn to 'read to themselves' only after printed copies became widely available. This contributed, as chapter 3 will show, to the 'construction' of individuals and 'subjectivism' and thus to the Protestant Reformation's emphasis on personal piety.

27 Ithiel de Sola Pool, *Technologies of Freedom: On Free Speech in an Electronic Age* (Cambridge: The Belknap Press of Harvard University Press, 1983).
28 Russell Neuman, *The Future of the Mass Audience* (Cambridge: Cambridge University Press, 1991).
29 One of the first steps in this process has recently taken place in the United States, as reported in 'U.S. Phone Firms Allowed into TV,' *Globe and Mail*, 24 Aug. 1993, p. B13.
30 It is salutary to recall that the transition to the 'information age' will likely encounter many moral and social, and not just technological, hurdles. See the cautious report by Ronald D. Doctor, 'Information Technologies and Social Equity: Confronting the Revolution,' *Journal of the American Society for Information Science* 42 (1991), 216–28.
31 Karl Deutsch, *Nationalism and Social Communication: An Inquiry into the Foundations of Nationality* (New York: John Wiley and Sons and the Technology Press of MIT, 1953).
32 I noted in chapter 1 that there may be cyclical processes in corporate structure and the state system. This may also be what occurs in the balance between territorial and non-territorial forces, even though I am emphasizing one part of that process (unbundling) more than the other (bundling).
33 Of course, some saints in the Christian tradition have been associated with specific places. This qualification reminds us that territorial and non-territorial are matters of degree, and different religious traditions do fall predominantly toward one or the other end of the continuum.
34 Harvey Cox, *The Secular City: Secularization and Urbanization in Theological Perspective* (New York: Macmillan, 1965), especially pp. 18, 54–5.
35 Maurice Ashley, *The Golden Century, Europe 1598–1715* (London: Cardinal, 1975), chapter 7, has a nice summary of the issues and the drama of this momentous change.
36 The Roman Catholic Church may be conceived of as a form of mass medium which belies these conclusions, as Alvin Toffler, *Powershift* (New York: Bantam Books, 1991), p. 346, points out. The same may be said of Islam, and both are thus well positioned to take advantage of a world more fully non-territorial than the present. I will return to this theme in chapter 8.
37 Richard Carlson and Bruce Goldman, *2020 Visions: Long View of a Changing World* (Stanford: The Portable Stanford, 1991), p. 4.
38 Kenichi Ohmae, *The Borderless World* (New York: Harper Perrenial, 1991).
39 For a review of the technology and some warnings about options, see David Ellis, *Split Screen: Home Entertainment and the New Technologies* (Toronto: Friends of Canadian Broadcasting, 1992).

40 Charles Taylor, *The Malaise of Modernity*, CBC Massey Lectures (Concord, Ont.: Anansi, 1991).
41 Arthur Kornhauser, *The Politics of Mass Society* (n.p.: Free Press of Glencoe, 1959).
42 Neuman, *The Future of the Mass Audience*.
43 William Gibson, in a series of fascinating science fiction novels and short stories, has painted a picture of another kind of threat in 'cyberspace.' His vision involves a combination of violent and ruthless gangs vying for control, and anarchy. The 'police' are not at all like the uniformed 'cops' or 'brown shirts' of the twentieth century. See especially his first novel, *Neuromancer* (New York: Ace Books, 1984), and his collection of short stories, *Burning Chrome* (New York: Ace Books, 1986).
44 One should note, however, that the Canadian public has evinced considerable concern in recent years about the potential abuses of SIN (Social Insurance Number) as a tool for centralizing information about individuals.
45 Professor John Helliwell has reminded me that CNN were present primarily because of Gorbachev's state visit, which was of course part of the reason the students chose that moment to demonstrate so openly.
46 Professor Stephen Milne has reminded me that many massacres occur, especially in Third World countries, with virtual impunity because there are regularly few cameras or reporters in many such regions.
47 Cipolla, *Before the Industrial Revolution*, places quite a bit of emphasis on diffusion of the water mill in the Middle Ages as a source of long-term productivity in Europe.
48 As noted above, Gibson's dark vision of cyberspace also assumes very little 'control' and much 'policing,' with the consequence that, for many activities, 'might makes right.'
49 Robert Heilbroner, *Twenty-First-Century Capitalism*, CBC Massey Lectures, (Concord, Ont.: Anansi, 1992).
50 David Gelernter, *Mirror Worlds: Or the Day Software Puts the Universe in a Shoebox ... How It Will Happen and What It Will Mean* (New York: Oxford University Press, 1992).
51 I confess that there are many obstacles to overcome, including viruses, security of files, lose of records as a result of software incompatibilities, and others. But the potentials are there as well.
52 Obviously, realization of these possibilities will require good software in order to take advantage of the flexibility and robustness of massively parallel processing.

53 John A. Armstrong, *Nations before Nationalism* (Chapel Hill: University of North Carolina Press, 1982).
54 Robert H. Jackson, *Quasi-States: Sovereignty, International Relations, and the Third World* (Cambridge: Cambridge University Press, 1990).
55 William H. McNeill, *Polyethnicity and National Unity in World History* (Toronto: University of Toronto Press, 1986); and Barry Buzan, 'The Idea of International System: Theory Meets History,' unpublished paper delivered at the Convention of the Japanese Association for International Business, Kita-Kyushu, October 1993.

CHAPTER 3 Economics and Territory

1 Some books have been especially helpful in clarifying my thinking about these matters, including the following: Kenichi Ohmae, *The Borderless World* (New York: Harper Perrenial, 1991); Robert Reich, *The Work of Nations* (New York: Alfred A. Knopf, 1991); Peter F. Drucker, *Post-Capitalist Society* (New York: Harper Business, 1993); Peter F. Drucker, *The New Realities* (New York: Harper and Row, 1990); Robert Heilbroner, *Twenty-First-Century Capitalism*, CBC Massey Lectures (Concord, Ont.: Anansi, 1992); Nuala Beck, *Shifting Gears: Thriving in the New Economy* (Toronto: Harper Collins, 1992); Paul Kennedy, *Preparing for the Twenty-First Century* (New York: Harper Collins, 1993), especially chapters 3–5.
2 Some theories of economic growth do include technology, but none includes as wide a range of phenomena in the concept of technology as I do here.
3 Carlo M. Cipolla, *Before the Industrial Revolution* (New York: W.W. Norton, 1976), especially chapters 4–5. Harold J. Berman, in *Law and Revolution: The Formation of the Western Legal Tradition* (Cambridge: Harvard University Press, 1983), estimates that at least a thousand new towns and cities were founded in the eleventh and twelfth centuries; and they served (among other things) to reinforce the growing pluralism of legal traditions because the cities had charters and harboured their independence and because the growth of commerce paralleled new laws governing commerce.
4 E.L. Jones, *The European Miracle: Environments, Economies, and Geopolitics in the History of Europe and Asia* (Cambridge: Cambridge University Press, 1981).
5 Douglass C. North and Robert Paul Thomas, *The Rise of the Western World* (Cambridge: Cambridge University Press, 1973), especially chapter 2.
6 Charles Tilly, *Coercion, Capital, and European States, A.D. 990–1992*, rev. ed. (Oxford: Blackwell, 1992).
7 Jack Weatherford, *Indian Givers: The Continuing Impact of the Discovered Americas on the World* (New York: Crown, 1988).

8 This is part of what Stephen Toulmin calls the 'hidden agenda of modernity,' involving rationalistic, analytic, and 'atomistic' conceptions of reality. See *Cosmopolis* (New York: Free Press, 1990). Professor Michael Goldberg has reminded me that interdisciplinary scholarship and experiential learning, among others, are examples of ways in which the intellectual world is moving 'beyond modernity.'
9 Albert O. Hirschman, *The Passions and the Interests: Political Arguments for Capitalism before Its Triumph* (Princeton: Princeton University Press, 1977).
10 Readers should recall from the first two chapters and above that pluralism of legal traditions, a lack of hierarchy among incipient states, and rivalries among the church, cities, feudalities, and monarchies laid a groundwork for innovation and growth of institutions which was apparently unique to Europe. See Berman, *Law and Revolution*; Jones, *The European Miracle*; and Tilly, *Coercion, Capital, and European States*.
11 The existence of an incipient form of bureaucracy in monastic orders should probably be included in any comprehensive analysis of these institutional developments.
12 Jones, *The European Miracle*, chapter 6.
13 It is also worth noting another type of pluralism. After 1648 the pope, the Catholic Church, and the Holy Roman Empire could never again aspire to dominance. Thus, these non-territorial political forces were kept separate from nation-states, assuring that pluralism encompassed many types of political units, even though analysts focused more and more on the state system itself.
14 Michael Porter has so thoroughly captured the attention of business elites and analysts with his concept of 'competitive advantage' that it takes an act of will to remember that the original idea involved complementarity based on a specialized division of labour. Porter seems to argue that one should focus instead on 'winning' a competition for market share, a notion with ruthless overtones of a zero-sum game. See Michael Porter, *The Competitive Advantage of Nations* (New York: Free Press, 1990).
15 Leonard Tivey, 'States, Nations and Economies,' in Leonard Tivey, ed., *The Nation-State: The Formation of Modern Politics* (New York: St Martin's, 1981), chapter 3.
16 Professor Michael Goldberg has reminded me that this ability to dispose of property varies widely among cultures. Ownership is most absolute in the United States, for example, but less so in Britain and many parts of the Commonwealth where, strictly speaking, land is owned by the Crown and held in fee simple by individuals or other legal entities.
17 Hirschman, *The Passions and the Interests*. One may see the contrast in quite

dramatic form by comparing Machiavelli's views of politics with those of John Locke or other early liberals.
18 Indeed, women were almost like property themselves, if married. For a detailed history of changing property laws in Britain, which varied of course in other countries, see Lee Holcombe, *Wives and Property: Reform of the Married Women's Property Act in Nineteenth-Century England* (Toronto: University of Toronto Press, 1983).
19 North and Thomas, *The Rise of the Western World*.
20 Charles E. Lindblom, *Politics and Markets: The World's Political-Economic Systems* (New York: Basic Books, 1977), especially Part V, where he argues that business occupies a 'privileged position' because investment decisions are so crucial in job creation.
21 Morris Cohen, 'Property and Sovereignty,' in C.B. Macpherson, ed., *Property: Mainstream and Critical Positions* (Toronto: University of Toronto Press, 1978), chapter 10. This is a reprint of a lecture which Cohen had published in 1927.
22 Nuala Beck, in *Shifting Gears*, has much useful material on components of the service economy.
23 Drucker, in *The New Realities*, has an extensive discussion of 'the third force,' which he defines as those organizations and productive activities which are neither governmental ('public affairs') nor done for profit ('private' or 'entrepreneurial'). They include a vast array of very important and often 'advanced' organizations ranging from universities and symphony orchestras to the Girl Scouts and the Red Cross. Virtually all would be part of the service sector.
24 For a nice overview, see Kimon Valaskakis, 'A Prescription for Canada Inc.,' *Globe and Mail*, 31 Oct. 1992, p. B4.
25 Beck, *Shifting Gears*, chapter 5.
26 Recall the distinction made in chapter 2, following Colin Cherry, *The Age of Access* (London: Croom Helm, 1985), p. 43. Cherry contrasts 'sharing between' (dividing up something) and 'sharing with' (holding in common). Different types of property are shared in different ways.
27 It may be impractical or even impossible to measure these hypothetical costs and benefits, but the logical exercise helps to point out that our current measures do not give a complete or transparent accounting of social costs or benefits.
28 If the office or position is a sinecure, then it is a source of income and probably should be counted. If it amounts to a sale of an asset, it would not have shown up in GDP in the first place. How we view these offices may be more 'economic' than they were viewed at the time, which is another way of making the same point.

29 As a non-expert, I am unsure whether these anti-pollution activities would show up as additional components of GDP, as changed patterns of constant GDP, or as a combination of both.
30 As North and Thomas note: 'For as trade was expanding a need was created for larger political units to define, protect, and enforce property rights over greater areas (thus internalizing some of the costs of long-distance commerce)' (*The Rise of the Western World*, p. 94).
31 Arlene W. Saxonbouse, *Fear of Diversity: The Birth of Political Science in Ancient Greek Thought* (Chicago: University of Chicago Press, 1992).
32 Some helpful summaries of the vast literature relevant to this topic include the following: Louis Dumont, 'The Modern Conception of the Individual: Notes on Its Genesis and That of Concomitant Institutions,' *Contributions to Indian Sociology* 8 (1965), 13–61; Louis Dumont, *From Mandeville to Marx: The Genesis and Triumph of Economic Ideology* (Chicago: University of Chicago Press, 1977); Jones, *The European Miracle*; Christopher Brewin, 'Sovereignty,' in James Mayall, ed., *The Community of States* (London: George Allen and Unwin, 1982); and Richard Falk, 'A New Paradigm for International Legal Studies: Prospects and Proposals,' in Richard Falk et al., eds, *International Law* (Boulder: Westview, 1985), especially pp. 660ff.
33 Charles Taylor, *The Malaise of Modernity*, CBC Massey Lectures (Concord, Ont.: Anansi, 1991).
34 See also Paul Krugman, 'Why the Global Race Is a Non-Starter,' *Globe and Mail*, 23 March 1993, p. B22.
35 For a stimulating debate about the extent to which economic theory concerns 'economic man' in the sense of males, and how it might be different if its concepts 'brought women in,' see Marianne A. Ferber and Julie A. Nelson, eds, *Beyond Economic Man: Feminist Theory and Economics* (Chicago: University of Chicago Press, 1993).
36 Indeed, the development of a notion of interior space seems to be a necessary step in hypothesizing the so-called 'mind-body' problem, which preoccupied Descartes and many other philosophers during the period that also saw the establishment of territorial nation-states. See Gilbert Ryle, *The Concept of Mind* (New York: Barnes and Noble, 1949).
37 Some people restrict the concept of 'rights' solely to those which inhere in individuals, whereas 'rights' of a position or group would be 'privileges.' I do not make such a distinction, for historical reasons such as those outlined in Engin Isin, *Cities without Citizens: The Modernity of the City as a Corporation* (Montreal: Black Rose Books, 1992).
38 Frank Scott has characterized this set of rights as 'liberty against government'

in order to contrast them with various sources of group or collective security which take the form of 'liberty through government.' See his *Essays on the Constitution* (Toronto: Universitiy of Toronto Press, 1977), especially pp. 356–61.
39 See the interesting observations by Brewin, 'Sovereignty,' cited above, especially pp. 34–7.
40 Cohen, in Macpherson, ed., *Property*, pp. 172–3.
41 Although interesting, the idea of specialized regulators for specialized markets is too complex for the present discussion.
42 Ohmae, *The Borderless World*.
43 Ohmae, *The Borderless World*; Reich, *The Work of Nations*; and Reich, 'The REAL Economy,' *Atlantic Monthly*, Feb. 1991, pp. 35–52.
44 For an amusing example of the revised view of market size, see Michael Kay, 'Why Yogurt Flows Better in Short Runs,' *Globe and Mail*, 6 April 1993, p. B24.
45 Jane Jacobs, in *Cities and the Wealth of Nations: Principles of Economic Life* (New York: Random House, 1984), chapter 11, argues that large and diverse countries with more than one city-region impose a faulty feedback mechanism by having a single currency with one exchange rate. Smaller countries like those mentioned in the text, she argues, have an advantage because the exchange rate does not affect different city-regions differently. Some regions might cross national boundaries, as noted by Kenichi Ohmae, 'The Rise of the Region State,' *Foreign Affairs* 72 (Spring 1992), 78–87.
46 Jacobs, *Cities and the Wealth of Nations*, especially chapters 3, 4, and 10, describes the process in detail.
47 As noted in chapter 1, smaller firms than could previously operate as multinationals can now operate as transnational corporations. Another indicator of structural change is the dramatic increase in trade/GDP ratios. It is not just that trade has gone up, it has done so many times faster than the increases in GDP in any country.
48 Professor Stephen Milne has reminded me that Bismarck favoured universal literacy so that workers and soldiers in Germany could read instruction manuals. Recall the comments above about how globalized the late nineteenth century was, and thus how we share features with that period more than with the intervening century. See, for example, the column by Peter Cook, 'Toward the Unfettered Capitalism of 1914,' *Globe and Mail*, 9 Aug. 1993, p. B2.
49 Globally competitive firms have already discovered that 'command and control' types of organization work less well than ones patterned on teams, cooperation, and complementarity. Likewise, there has been increased inter-

50 Note in this regard the significance of the name change from the earlier European Economic Community (EEC) to the current European Community (EC). The latter signals that the community now goes beyond economic matters.
51 Cities, of course, have always expanded in this way. Recall that local governments have not been territorial in the way nations have, and they may (as I argued in chapter 1) reveal some of the features of the unbundled world.
52 Jock A. Finlayson and Mark W. Zacher, *Managing International Markets: Developing Countries and the Commodity Trade Regime* (New York: Columbia University Press, 1988).
53 For an interesting and rigorous analysis of the provision of public goods at the level of the international system, even when some key nations fail to cooperate, see Duncan Snidal, 'The Limits of Hegemonic Stability Theory,' *International Organization* 39 (Autumn 1985), 579–614.
54 William H. McNeill, *Plagues and Peoples* (Garden City, N.Y.: Anchor/Doubleday, 1976) is the classic statement of the case. See also the accounts of European diseases when first introduced to North and South America in Ronald Wright, *Stolen Continents: The 'New World' through Indian Eyes since 1492* (Toronto: Viking, 1992); and Alfred W. Crosby, *Ecological Imperialism: The Biological Expansion of Europe, 900–1900* (Cambridge: Cambridge University Press, 1986; Canto edition, 1993).
55 Kennedy, *Preparing for the Twenty-First Century*, chapter 2, has an exhaustive summary of current trends.
56 Despite the economic costs and benefits, the main motive of many U.S. politicians in pushing for NAFTA would seem to be its potential to reduce illegal immigration.
57 The phrase 'liberties of action' was coined by Colin Cherry, *The Age of Access*.
58 In technical terms, the emphasis will shift from zero-sum games to increasing-sum (or positive-sum) games.
59 I do not mean this strictly in the sense of 'guest-workers.' The issue will be raised again in chapters 6 and 8.
60 See the suggestive studies by Charles Hampden-Turner and Alfons Trompenaars, *The Seven Cultures of Capitalism* (New York: Currency/Doubleday, 1993).
61 The experiences of Singapore, South Korea, and other 'tigers' suggest not, but it is too early to generalize about these matters.

est in flexible organizations with work forces which are able to adapt to new circumstances because of higher education and regular training. Chapter 4 explores several of these conclusions.

CHAPTER 4 Functions and Administration

1 Note the contrary argument by Vincent Ostrom, *The Intellectual Crisis in American Public Administration*, rev. ed. (University: University of Alabama Press, 1974): 'Based upon a theory of public goods, these political economists are developing a theory of collective action which assumes that the principles of organization required for the efficient conduct of *public* enterprises will be different from the principles of organization for private enterises' (p. 29).
2 'When the central problem in public administration is viewed as the provision of public goods and services, alternative forms of organization may be available for the performance of these functions apart from an extension and perfection of bureaucratic structures' (Ostrom, *Intellectual Crisis*, p. 19).
3 Elinor Ostrom, *Governing the Commons: The Evolution of Institutions for Collective Action* (Cambridge: Cambridge University Press, 1990) is one of the most trenchant expositions of this view and of several detailed case studies which exemplify this perspective.
4 Alvin and Heidi Toffler, *War and Anti-War* (Boston: Little, Brown, 1993), especially chapter 24.
5 Electronic mail is currently available only to a very small proportion of individuals and organizations. However, in a few years every television set in almost every affluent country in the world (currently over 800 million sets) will be a two-way communication device useful for electronic mail. This will follow from the removal of the artificial separation of regulatory regimes for telephones and for radio and television. Current court battles suggest that the regulatory regimes will be merged in three to five years.
6 For a more extensive discussion of some practical issues related to this topic, see David J. Elkins, 'Aboriginal Citizenship and Federalism: Exploring Non-Territorial Models,' a report sponsored by the Royal Commission on Aboriginal Peoples, 1994.
7 For arguments about the need to assume low information costs or large numbers of well-informed citizen-consumers, see Paul Teske et al., 'Establishing the Micro Foundations of a Macro Theory: Information, Movers, and the Competitive Local Market for Public Goods,' *American Political Science Review* 87 (Sept. 1993), 702–13.
8 Existing political elites have vested interests in these assumptions, but my ques-tion concerns whether they are necessary or required rather than expedient.
9 Sovereignty is a matter of degree, although it is often portrayed as all or nothing. Furthermore, it may be helpful to refer to older concepts like suzerainty as distinct from sovereignty.

10 Peter Drucker, in *The New Realities* (New York: Harper and Row, 1990), chapter 7, analyses what he calls the 'new pluralisms' in society and polity. They are characterized mainly by their narrow focus on a single purpose, and they include 'single-interest groups' or 'mass movements of small but highly disciplined minorities' (p. 76). He explicitly contrasts these groups to the attempts by sovereign states to concentrate control in a territorial government.
11 Globalization, especially in the sense of trading areas like the European Community, does not eliminate bundling, but it does change the num- ber of bundles and some of the new bundles are non-territorial. Note that I have defined 'globalization' differently for my purposes, and that the large units mentioned here should be called 'globalism' in my terms.
12 Tom Peters, 'Enter Clusters, Exit Hierarchy,' *Inside Guide* 5 (Sept. 1991), 16–17.
13 Margot Gibb-Clark, 'Coping When the Only Constant Is Change,' *Globe and Mail*, 28 Oct. 1991, p. B4.
14 David Osborne and Ted Gaebler, *Reinventing Government: How the Entrepreneurial Spirit Is Transforming the Public Sector* (New York: Penguin, 1993) contains many case studies of organizations which have or have not redefined goals and measures of achievement, and describes some consequences of such redefinition.
15 Harvey Gellman, 'Re-Engineer or Bust,' *Inside Guide* 5 (June 1991), 23–4.
16 Of course, governments do not currently coordinate the job descriptions in linear form, but most public servants do so in their own minds. As it gets more difficult to see one's pattern, it may be incumbent on unions, employers, or professional associations to think more creatively about appropriate ways of conceptualizing career progress, at least until employees come to think it less important.
17 Drucker, *The New Realities*, chapters 7 and 13, has several useful observations about these changes in what he calls 'knowledge workers.'
18 Gellmann ('Re-Engineer or Bust') notes the creation of 'case managers' who handle a file from beginning to end, rather than passing it on to someone in another department so that both perform more specialized roles.
19 Under the label of 'matrix management,' some of these features may already be gaining in prominence, although it is often difficult to tell how much change consists of talk and how much involves new activities or patterns of activities.
20 Under present hierarchical systems, the 'solution' occurs automatically and somewhat arbitrarily by assigning responsibility at a particular level in the hierarchy, even if this does not correspond to 'authorship.' There are perverse consequences in at least some cases. See, for example, Sharon Sutherland,

'The Al-Mashat Affair: Administrative Responsibility in Parliamentary Institutions,' *Canadian Public Administration* 34 (1991), 573–603.
21 Henry Mintzberg, *Mintzberg on Management* (New York: Free Press, 1989), especially chapter 10; Drucker (*The New Reality*) also discusses universities as models.
22 Drucker, *The New Realities*, chapter 13.

CHAPTER 5 Non-Territorial Federalism

1 Unlike most chapters in this book, the present one focuses almost completely on Canada. This partly reflects my greater familiarity with Canada than with most other countries. Even more, however, it stems from a recognition that the degree of territoriality of populations is very different in each country and the degree to which that poses a problem is quite variable even though territorial 'solutions' to non-territorial problems may be a general issue.
2 John George Lambton, Earl of Durham, *Lord Durham's Report: An Abridgement of the Report on the Affairs of North America*, ed. Gerald M. Craig, Carleton Library no. 1 (Toronto: McClelland and Stewart, 1963).
3 For a good description of the period after Lord Durham's report and leading up to Confederation, see J.M.S. Careless, *The Union of the Canadas: The Growth of Canadian Institutions, 1841–1857* (Toronto: McClelland and Stewart, 1967), and W.L. Morton, *The Critical Years: The Union of British North America, 1857–1873* (Toronto: McClelland and Stewart, 1964).
4 Dual ministries is the usual term for the practice in the United Province of Canada of having two people in charge of each department of government (one French-Catholic and the other English-Protestant); the practice usually involved implicit vetoes by either group in regard to relevant legislation.
5 Thus, the British North America Act, 1867 – now the Constitution Act, 1867 – lists the powers and jurisdictions of the federal or general government in s. 91 and those of the provinces in s. 92. Of course, today many Canadians think of education, health, and other matters as worthy of national concern, but in the nineteenth century they were viewed as matters of 'local' concern because Quebec insisted on certain jurisdictions in order to protect 'the French fact' and the Catholic faith.
6 Protection of the way of life of Quebeckers, thus, served as a very different motive for accepting federalism in Canada than its origin in the United States, where the principal argument seems to have been that it divided power and authority so that no one group (or 'faction') could tyrannize over another. For Americans, federalism was akin to the separation of powers and

checks and balances as means of dispersing power widely. This point can be most clearly seen when arguments about the ratification of the American constitution are formulated in general terms, as in Vincent Ostrom, *The Political Theory of a Compound Republic: Designing the American Experiment*, 2d ed. (Lincoln: University of Nebraska Press, 1987).
7 Nunavut comprises a vast area in the eastern half of the Northwest Territories, almost entirely populated by Inuit.
8 Some will object to La Francophonie because it is the name of an international organization of French-language countries, analogous to the British Commonwealth. The name is not the main point of my discussion, but it serves to highlight a dominant characteristic of the non-territorial province.
9 As with La Francophonie, there may be objections to this name. Its use is purely a convenience. In either province, I assume the residents will choose their own name.
10 After an aboriginal province or third order of government has been established, it will have to decide on residence requirements. I assume that in the first instance, as with La Francophonie, residence will be based on self-selection. Once a government has been constituted and elected, it might establish various criteria and restrictions, depending on popular opinion, whether the Charter of Rights and Freedoms applied, and other concerns.
11 David J. Elkins, 'Aboriginal Citizenship and Federalism: Exploring Non-Territorial Models,' a report sponsored by the Royal Commission on Aboriginal Peoples, 1994, explores many aspects of Aboriginal Peoples Province in greater depth than is possible in this chapter.
12 One should note that the issue really concerns a third order of government, the federal and provincial governments comprising the other two orders. I refer to a 'province' because Canadians understand what that is, and because provinces are sovereign within their heads of power enumerated in s. 92 (and elsewhere) in the Constitution Act, 1867. Perhaps the third order will develop a label other than 'province,' but for now I need a convenient way to refer to it.
13 Some analysts draw a sharp distinction between federation and confederation. I do not. Thus, readers should not assume that it will involve any particular degree of centralization.
14 One should also note that federalism serves as a means of sharing power; otherwise one would have independent countries instead of provinces or states. Several federal systems, of course, do not try to demarcate exclusive jurisdictions in the way Canada does, but rely much more on concurrent powers; the United States and Australia are two prominent examples.

15 Royal Commission on Aboriginal Peoples, *Aboriginal Peoples in Urban Centres* (Ottawa: Supply and Services Canada, 1993) reports testimony suggesting that daycare for children may be a special concern in urban areas. See also Luke McNamara, 'Aboriginal Self-Government and Justice Reform in Canada: The Impact of the Charter of Rights and Freedoms,' *Australian-Canadian Studies* 11 (1993), 43–75.
16 W.R. Lederman, *Continuing Canadian Constitutional Dilemmas* (Toronto: Butterworths, 1981).
17 Former prime minister Trudeau has consistently put forward this view for decades. See his discussion in *Federalism and the French Canadians* (Toronto: Macmillan, 1968), p. xxv, among other references.
18 Elinor Ostrom, *Governing the Commons* (Cambridge: Cambridge University Press, 1990) is the most thorough presentation of why different mixes best serve different situations.
19 Parti Libéral du Québec, *Un Québec libre de ses choix: rapport du comité constitutionnel (pour dépôt au 25e congrès des membres)*, 28 jan. 1991.
20 Robert A. Dahl, 'The City in the Future of Democracy,' *American Political Science Review* 61 (Dec. 1967), 953–70. See also Robert A. Dahl and Edward R. Tufte, *Size and Democracy* (Stanford: Stanford University Press, 1973).

CHAPTER 6 A Community of Communities

1 It seems that Althusius – that great but now largely forgotten writer of the early seventeenth century – originated the concept of 'a community of communities.' 'From Althusius we can learn that the centralized territorial state is indeed only one of two alternative traditions of political organization which have both accompanied the evolution of western civilization. The other one is a federalized plurality of rule, and this is in fact not only the older tradition, but also the dominant one during most of the course of that evolution' (Thomas O. Hueglin, 'Re-Reading Althusius for the Twenty-First Century,' a paper prepared for the Althusius Symposium, Philadelphia, 11–12 November 1990, p. 21). I cannot say if former prime minister Joe Clark knew of Althusius's phrase when he used it in the Canadian general election in 1979, but his usage did echo that of Althusius and harkened to a tradition more ancient and supple than that advocated by his rival and critic, and also former prime minister, Pierre Trudeau.
2 The 'construction' of nation-states in the seventeenth century coincided with social contract theories by Hobbes, Locke, and others; those theories emphasized that consent to authority was individualistic, not communal or collec-

tive, and they were thus an important part of the intellectual paternity of liberal individualism.
3 Ferdinand Tönnies, *Fundamental Concepts of Sociology (Gemeinschaft und Gesellschaft)* (New York: American Book Co., 1940).
4 Robert Bellah et al., *Habits of the Heart: Individualism and Commitment in American Life*, Perennial Library ed. (New York: Harper and Row, 1986).
5 Among many useful references on these points, see especially Carol Tavris, *The Mismeasure of Woman: Why Women Are Not the Better Sex, the Inferior Sex, or the Opposite Sex* (New York: Simon and Schuster, 1992), and Lillian Faderman, *Surpassing the Love of Men: Romantic Friendship and Love between Women from the Renaissance to the Present* (New York: William Morrow/Quill, 1981).
6 Michael Walzer, in *Spheres of Justice: A Defense of Pluralism and Equality* (New York: Basic Books, 1983), argues that a moral community is based on shared understanding. Such understandings may be facilitated by the unbundled voluntary communities but do not replace overarching communities of meaning. See also the interesting critiques of Walzer and 'shared meanings' in Susan Moller Okin, *Justice, Gender, and the Family* (New York: Basic Books, 1989), chapters 3 and 6.
7 See the interesting speculations and impressions in Kenneth J. Gergen, *The Saturated Self: Dilemmas of Identity in Contemporary Life* (New York: Basic Books, 1991).
8 Paul F. Lazarsfeld, Bernard Berelson, and Hazel Gaudet, *The People's Choice* (New York: Columbia University Press, 1948), introduced the concept as an explanatory variable in their path-breaking study of the 1940 presidential election. For an extensive and insightful review of the concept and evidence about its usefulness, see Peter W. Sperlich, *Conflict and Harmony in Human Affairs: A Study of Cross-Pressures and Political Behaviour* (Chicago: Rand McNally, 1971).
9 See especially Jennifer Nedelsky, 'Reconceiving Rights as Relationship,' *Review of Constitutional Studies* 1 (1993), 1–26; she states: 'What makes autonomy possible is not separation, but relationship ... Further, autonomy is not a static quality that is simply achieved one day. It is a capacity that requires ongoing relationships that help it flourish ... The whole conception of the relation between the individual and the collective shifts: we recognize that the collective is a source of autonomy as well as a threat to it' (p. 8).
10 See, for example, Howard M. Leichter, *Free to Be Foolish: Politics and Health Protection in the United States and Britain* (Princeton: Princeton University Press, 1991).
11 As the product cycle accelerates, more of the product cost is 'up front' in research and development costs. Thus the societies which succeed in global

competition may be those which can socialize more of the risk or uncertainty in R & D.
12 Bellah et al., *Habits of the Heart*, pp. 207ff.
13 Perry Anderson, *Lineages of the Absolutist State* (London: Verso, 1979); Simon Schama, *Citizens: A Chronicle of the French Revolution* (New York: Alfred A. Knopf, 1989); and Engin Isin, *Cities without Citizens: The Modernity of the City as a Corporation* (Montreal: Black Rose Books, 1992). Of course, Harold J. Berman, in *Law and Revolution: The Formation of the Western Legal Tradition* (Cambridge: Harvard University Press, 1983), reminds us that vestiges of these distinctions lingered on, at least in some places, and have played a crucial role in the dynamic and more 'tolerant' nature of Western legal thought.
14 Edwin M. Borchard, *The Diplomatic Protection of Citizens Abroad, or the Law of International Claims* (New York: Bank Law Publishing, 1916); and George Armstrong Kelly, 'Who Needs a Theory of Citizenship?' *Daedalus* 108 (Fall 1979), 21–36.
15 Albert Weale, 'Citizenship beyond Borders,' and Geraint Perry, 'Conclusion: Paths to Citizenship,' in Ursula Vogel and Michael Moran, eds, *The Frontiers of Citizenship* (London: Macmillan, 1991).
16 Michael Ignatieff, 'The Myth of Citizenship,' *Queen's Quarterly* 94 (Winter 1987), 966–85.
17 Borchard, *The Diplomatic Protection of Citizens Abroad*.
18 *Sparrow v R.* (1990), 70 D.L.R. 385 (S.C.C.) and *A.G. Quebec v Sioui* (1990), 1 S.C.R. 1025 seem to address the issue of 'portability' of treaty rights, a serious concern of urban aboriginals as well as reserve-based aboriginals like Sparrow and Sioui. These cases may point the way to a definition of citizenship in an aboriginal third order of government which is based on treaty rights and aboriginal rights rather than on residence or band membership.
19 Alan Cairns, *Charter versus Federalism: The Dilemmas of Constitutional Reform* (Montreal and Kingston: McGill-Queen's University Press, 1992).
20 Isin, *Cities without Citizens*; and Berman, *Law and Revolution*.
21 Gergen, *The Saturated Self*, p. 146. It is worth quoting at length another of Gergen's major points: 'We have an impoverished language of relatedness. We cannot ask whether a *relationship* hopes, fears, or wishes, nor can we understand how it is that a relationship could determine Bob's feeling and Sarah's thoughts rather than vice versa. It is as if we have thousands of terms to describe the individual pieces in a game of chess, and virtually none by which we can articulate the game itself. Relationships cannot become the reality by which life is lived until there is a vocabulary through which they are realized' (p. 160).
22 Nedelsky, 'Reconceiving Rights as Relationship.'

23 Benedict Anderson, *Imagined Communities: Reflections on the Origin and Spread of Nationalism*, rev. ed. (London: Verso, 1991).
24 Gergen, *The Saturated Self*, pp. 242-3.
25 Roger Chartier, ed., *A History of Private Life: III – Passions of the Renaissance* (Cambridge: The Belknap Press of Harvard University Press, 1989); Louis Dumont, 'The Modern Conception of the Individual: Notes on Its Genesis and That of Concomitant Institutions,' *Contributions to Indian Sociology* 8 (1965), 13-61; Louis Dumont, *From Mandeville to Marx: The Genesis and Triumph of Economic Ideology* (Chicago: University of Chicago Press, 1977); and Gergen, *The Saturated Self*, chapter 2.
26 'Virtual community' is a label used for the multitude of potential communities discussed in chapter 2 and earlier in this chapter. So far as I know, the term was coined by Howard Rheingold, *The Virtual Community: Homesteading on the Electronic Frontier* (Reading, Mass.: Addison-Wesley, 1993).
27 William Gibson, *Neuromancer* (New York: Ace Books, 1984); *Burning Chrome* (New York: Ace Books, 1987); *Count Zero* (New York: Ace Books, 1986); *Mona Lisa Overdrive* (New York: Bantam Books, 1988); and *Virtual Light* (Toronto: Seal Books, 1993).
28 Vincent Ostrom, *The Political Theory of a Compound Republic: Designing the American Experiment*, 2d ed. (Lincoln: University of Nebraska Press, 1987).

CHAPTER 7 Majority Rules

1 Robert Dahl, *Dilemmas of Pluralist Democracy: Autonomy vs. Control* (New Haven: Yale University Press, 1982), pp. 80ff.
2 Pierre Elliott Trudeau, *Federalism and the French Canadians* (Toronto: Macmillan, 1968), pp. 114-15.
3 See, for example, *International Covenant on Economic, Social and Cultural Rights* (adopted by the General Assembly of the United Nations on 16 December 1966), Part I, Article 1: 'All peoples have the right to self-determination. By virtue of that right they freely determine their political status and freely pursue their economic, social and cultural development.'
4 For a detailed analysis of overlap, non-overlap, and lack of consensus, see David J. Elkins, *Manipulation and Consent: How Voters and Leaders Manage Complexity* (Vancouver: University of British Columbia Press, 1993).
5 Vincent Ostrom, *The Political Theory of a Compound Republic: Designing the American Experiment*, 2d ed. (Lincoln: University of Nebraska Press, 1987).
6 David J. Elkins, 'Democracy and Political Culture in Australia and Canada,' a paper delivered at the annual meetings of the Canadian Political Science Association, Charlottetown, P.E.I., 31 May – 2 June 1992.

7 *The Tremblay Report: Report of the Royal Commission of Inquiry on Constitutional Problems*, ed. David Kwavnick (Toronto: McClelland and Stewart, 1964), pp. 37, 110.
8 Section 15 (1) of the Charter of Rights and Freedoms lists a number of defining attributes of groups which are protected from discrimination. These attributes include race, national or ethnic origin, colour, religion, sex, age, and mental or physical disability. This list, the language makes clear, is not exhaustive, but may be enlarged over time. Section 15 (2) indicates that affirmative action is warranted for these same groups.
9 Herschel Hardin, *A Nation Unaware: The Canadian Economic Culture* (Vancouver: J.J. Douglas, 1974).
10 Frank R. Scott, 'Expanding Concepts of Human Rights,' in his *Essays on the Constitution* (Toronto: University of Toronto Press, 1977), especially pp. 357–8.
11 Christian Dufour, *The Canadian Challenge / Le Défi Québecois* (Halifax and Lantzville, B.C.: The Institute for Research on Public Policy and Oolichan Books, 1990), p. 108.
12 Note the intriguing comments by (then) Madame Justice Bertha Wilson in her dissenting opinion in the case of *McKinney v U. of Guelph* (1990): 'It is, in my view, untenable to suggest that freedom is coextensive with the absence of government. Experience shows the contrary, that freedom has often required the intervention and protection of government against private action' (p. 47).
13 David J. Elkins, 'Facing Our Destiny: Rights and Canadian Distinctiveness,' *Canadian Journal of Political Science* 22 (Dec. 1989), 699–716.
14 William Coleman and Grace Skogstad, eds, *Policy Communities and Public Policy in Canada: A Structural Approach* (Mississauga, Ont.: Copp Clark Pitman, 1990), especially pp. 8–11.
15 Kayyam Paltiel, 'Group Rights in the Canadian Constitution and Aboriginal Claims to Self-Determination,' in Robert Jackson et al., eds, *Contemporary Canadian Politics: Readings and Notes* (Scarborough, Ont.: Prentice-Hall, 1987); and William Janzen, *Limits on Liberty: The Experience of Mennonite, Hutterite, and Doukhobor Communities in Canada* (Toronto: University of Toronto Press, 1990).
16 Janzen, *Limits to Liberty*.
17 For a recent and very moving account of part of this process, see Boyce Richardson, *People of Terra Nullius: Betrayal and Rebirth in Aboriginal Canada* (Vancouver: Douglas and McIntyre, 1993).
18 Albert O. Hirschman, *Exit, Voice, and Loyalty: Responses to Decline in Firms, Organizations, and States* (Cambridge: Harvard University Press, 1970).
19 For an elaboration of these points, see A.I. Silver, *The French-Canadian Idea of Confederation, 1864–1900* (Toronto: University of Toronto Press, 1982).

20 André Siegfried, *The Race Question in Canada*, Carleton Library, no. 29 (Toronto: McClelland and Stewart, 1966).
21 Jean A. Laponce, *The Protection of Minorities* (Berkeley: University of California Press, 1960).
22 Dahl, *Dilemmas of Pluralist Democracy*, p. 80.
23 Arendt Lijphart, *Democracy in Plural Societies: A Comparative Exploration* (New Haven: Yale University Press, 1977).
24 Michael Ignatieff, *Blood and Belonging: Journeys into the New Nationalism* (Toronto: Viking/Penguin, 1993), chapter 2.
25 The most trenchant analysis of arguments about open borders may be found in several publications by Joseph Carens, including 'Aliens and Citizens: The Case for Open Borders,' *Review of Politics* 49 (Spring 1987), 251–73; and 'Migration and Morality: A Liberal Egalitarian Perspective,' in Brian Barry and Robert E. Goodin, eds, *Free Movement: Ethical Issues in the Transnational Migration of People and of Money* (University Park: Pennsylvania State University Press, 1992).
26 Virginia Woolf, *A Room of One's Own and Three Guineas* (London: Chatto and Windus / The Hogarth Press, 1984); originally published in 1929 and 1938 respectively.
27 Carlo M. Cipolla, *Before the Industrial Revolution: European Society and Economy, 1000–1700* (New York: W.W. Norton, 1976), chapter 9.
28 For an argument that precious metals from the New World were crucial in European commercialization, industrialization, and economic development, see Jack Weatherford, *Indian Givers: The Continuing Impact of the Discovered Americas on the World* (New York: Crown, 1988).

CHAPTER 8 A Menu for the Twenty-First Century

1 See the concerned musings of Neil Bissoondath, 'A Question of Belonging,' *Globe and Mail*, 28 Jan. 1993, p. A17.
2 Marshall Berman, *All That Is Solid Melts into Air: The Experience of Modernity* (New York: Simon and Schuster, 1982).
3 Susanne Langer, *Philosophy in a New Key*, New Library of World Literature (New York: Mentor Books, 1948), as quoted in Vincent Ostrom, *The Political Theory of a Compound Republic*, 2d ed. (Lincoln: University of Nebraska Press, 1987), p. 11.
4 Archibald MacLeish, as quoted in Harold J. Berman, *Law and Revolution* (Cambridge: Harvard University Press, 1983), p. v.
5 Berman, *Law and Revolution*.
6 Assumptions lurk everywhere. Note that 'in the usual sense' is correct only

for the past three hundred or so years; before that there was no notion of a single sovereign political authority.
7 Jane Jacobs, *Cities and the Wealth of Nations* (New York: Random House, 1984), especially chapter 2. A similar argument may be found in rough outline in Kenichi Ohmae, 'The Rise of the Region State,' *Foreign Affairs* 72 (Spring 1993), 79–87.
8 Michael Porter, in *The Competitive Advantage of Nations* (New York: Free Press, 1990), describes many of the clusters in ways which sound like 'city-regions' in Jacobs's terms.
9 Jacobs, *Cities and the Wealth of Nations*, pp. 214–20.
10 Mancur Olsen, *The Rise and Decline of Nations: Economic Growth, Stagflation, and Social Rigidities* (New Haven: Yale University Press, 1982).
11 If this line of reasoning has any validity, it makes all the more puzzling the insistence by Quebec sovereigntists that an independent Quebec would continue to use the Canadian dollar as its currency even if Canada objected.
12 Peter Drucker, *The New Realities* (New York: Harper and Row, 1989), especially chapters 6 and 13; and Drucker, *Post-Capitalist Society* (New York: Harper Business, 1993), especially chapters 2 and 5.
13 E.J. Hobsbaum, *Nations and Nationalism since 1780: Programme, Myth, Reality*, Canto ed. (Cambridge: Cambridge University Press, 1991).
14 Benedict Anderson, *Imagined Communities: Reflections on the Origin and Spread of Nationalism*, rev. ed. (London: Verso, 1991); and George L. Mosse, *Nationalism and Sexuality: Respectability and Abnormal Sexuality in Modern Europe* (New York: H. Fertig, 1985).
15 That people might feel a need for meaning makes more sense when one recalls the dismal scenarios for the future which I summarized in the Introduction.
16 For popular examples, see Kenneth Brower, *The Starship and the Canoe* (New York: Holt, Rinehart and Winston, 1978); and Freeman Dyson, *Infinite in All Directions*, Perennial Library (New York: Harper and Row, 1988).
17 For clarifying my thoughts about migration, I am indebted to Professor Joe Carens; see the references cited in chapter 7 above.
18 Paul Kennedy, *Preparing for the Twenty-First Century* (New York: Harper Collins, 1993), especially chapters 2, 4, and 10.
19 Jacques Attali, *Millennium: Winners and Losers in the Coming World Order* (New York: Random House / Times Books, 1991), chapter 4, has some interesting observations about 'nomadic man' today.
20 One should recall that during the period leading up to the 'construction' of the nation-state (A.D. 1300–1500, or thereabouts), Europe was certainly no

more prosperous – and arguably less so – than many other parts of the world, including China, India, the Incan Empire, and the Islamic areas around the Mediterranean. See Douglass North and Robert Paul Thomas, *The Rise of the Western World: A New Economic History* (Cambridge: Cambridge University Press, 1973), and E.L. Jones, *The European Miracle: Environments, Economies, and Geopolitics in the History of Europe and Asia* (Cambridge: Cambridge University Press, 1981).

21 Kenneth J. Gergen, *The Saturated Self* (New York: Basic Books, 1991), chapter 6.
22 Bernard Nietschmann, 'The Third World War,' *Cultural Survival Quarterly* 11 (1987), 1–16, contains extensive examples of nations (mainly indigenous peoples) which are already decoupled from states; indeed, in many cases, a state has declared war on their nation.
23 For a complementary perspective on this topic, see the major book by James N. Rosenau, *Turbulence in World Politics: A Theory of Change and Continuity* (Princeton: Princeton University Press, 1990).
24 John A. Armstrong, *Nations before Nationalism* (Chapel Hill: University of North Carolina Press, 1982).
25 Charles S. Maier, ed., *Changing Boundaries of the Political: Essays on the Evolving Balance between the State and Society, Public and Private in Europe* (Cambridge: Cambridge University Press, 1987).
26 As noted in chapter 3, one should perhaps distinguish between 'private' and 'personal.' 'Private' has in recent decades come to bear a particular meaning in political theory because of the efforts of many scholars to resurrect the tradition of 'civic republicanism.' Thus, private refers to what might more commonly be called 'civil society' (as opposed to military and governmental, etc.). 'Personal' has been given a special cast by feminist theorists, particularly in the slogan 'The personal is political.' I offer these examples to show that there is less certainty than in some earlier periods about where to draw the line between public and private, or indeed for what purposes one would draw the line in a particular way.
27 For suggestive arguments along these lines, see N. Bar-Yaacov, *Dual Nationality* (London: Stevens and Sons, 1961).
28 Charles Tilly, ed., *The Formation of National States in Western Europe* (Princeton: Princeton University Press, 1975); Charles Tilly, *Coercion, Capital, and European States, A.D. 990–1992*, rev. ed. (Oxford: Blackwell, 1992); and Bruce D. Porter, *War and the Rise of the State: The Military Foundations of Modern Politics* (New York: Free Press, 1994).
29 Zbigniew Brzezinski, *Out of Control: Global Turmoil on the Eve of the Twenty-First Century* (New York: A Robert Stewart Book, 1993).

30 Stephen Toulmin, *Cosmopolis: The Hidden Agenda of Modernity* (New York: Free Press, 1990), p. 2 (his emphasis).
31 Thomas Kuhn, *The Structure of Scientific Revolutions* (Chicago: University of Chicago Press, 1962), chapter 13.
32 Toulmin, *Cosmopolis*, p. 1.

Index

Aboriginal Peoples Province, 152–64
aboriginals: as minority, 206, 207; as non-voluntary citizens of Canada, 221, 222; organizations, 247; and reserves, 13; and self-government, 208, 211, 222; spiritual revival, 250–1
Acadians, 148
accountability: in unbundled organizations, 143–4. *See also* responsibility
administration: benefits of unbundling nation-states, 263; definition, 122; and development of bureaucracy, 85–6; non-territorial, 137–46, 259–60; pluralistic authorities as check on tyranny, 201; territorial, 133–7, 259–60; and territory, 122–3, 126–33, 242
Africa: quasi-states, 73
airlines: and territorial organization, 45, 46
alimony and child support payments, 135–6
Allaire Report, 163
American Revolution, 232
Amnesty International, 25, 188
apartheid: and migration, 227–31
audience: fragmentation of, 53–4, 61–3; mass, decline of, 54–5, 61, 63, 65
Australia, 19, 30

Baha'i: as religion not linked to territory, 57
Basques: as ethnic nation, 73; possible future of, 242
Bill of Rights (U.S.), 232
biogenetic engineering: possible future of, 5–6
broadcasting media: changes in, 9–10; evolution of, 52–6; as public good, 124; and territoriality, 53. *See also* communication; computers; information industry; telecommunications
bundling: definition, 29. *See also* unbundling
bureaucracy: and conflict resolution, 232; development of, 85–6
business. *See* corporations; service industry

Canada: and 'bundling' of citizens' identities, 30, 31; as federation, 207–8, 220; health insurance, 136, 182; as hybrid nation-state, 73–4; as nation created by constitution, 19; possible future of, 242; problems associated with uneven social distribution, 147-9; proposals for non-territorial provinces, 149-64; social services, 104

Canada-U.S. Free Trade Agreement: as example of globalization, 26; as non-territorial government, 112

Canadian Charter of Rights and Freedoms. *See* Charter of Rights and Freedoms (Canada)

Canadian Security and Intelligence Service (CSIS), 69

capitalism: capital markets, 12; and growth of cities and towns, 81; and printing, 52; and property ownership, 89-91; and territorial nation-states, 80, 83, 231; and unbundling of nation-states, 70; variations on, 119

Catalans: as ethnic nation, 73; possible future of, 242

centralization: of administration, 50-1; and technology, 44

Charter of Rights and Freedoms (Canada), 148, 194, 212

China: lack of control of information boundaries, 66; population growth, 253

choice: and community, 235-7; and 'third force' groups, 248

Christianity: as religion not linked to territory, 57-60

cities and towns: and capitalism, 81; and citizenship, 194-5; and individualism, 99-100; as possible organizations for economic development, 243-5; and territoriality, 49-50

citizenship: as birthright, 228, 253; and community, 192-7; identity and territory, 29-32; and immigrants, 228; and inhabitants of Aboriginal Peoples Province, 153; non-territorial, 38-9; and passports, 33-4; possible changes in, 261; and territory, 23, 36-7, 167

'City in the Future of Democracy, The' (Dahl), 164

colonialism: decline of, 25; and economic history, 87; and territory, 14

communication: globalization of, 15; mass, 52-6, 61; non-territorial, 61-3; personal, 60, 61. *See also* broadcasting media; computers; information industry; telecommunications

communism: and 'unbundling' of citizens' identities, 30-1

communities: ascriptive, 227; based on common interest, 63; and citizenship, 192-7; congruent, 189-90; and decentralization, 173; definition, 168; and individuals, 170-1, 180-1, 197-200, 256; moral, 186-9; natural versus constructed, 169; non-territorial, 174-89, 237, 246-8; possible future of, 192; and responsibility, 186-9; and shared values, 177, 178, 187; and socialization of risk, 181-6, 187; and technology, 172-4; and territory, 167, 170-89, 189-201; in unbundled world, 242; virtual, 201

computer networks. *See* telecommunications

computers: and global information sharing, 55; and personal communication, 61; supercomputers, as decentralizing agents, 70-2; and surveillance, 69; and territoriality, 71-2. *See also* broadcasting media; com-

munication; information industry; technology; telecommunications
congruency: of communities, 189–90; of territory, 14–15
consociationalism, 166, 226
Constitution (U.S.), 232
Constitution Act (Canada, 1982), 224
contiguity: of territory, 14
continuity: of territory, 14
contracting out, 143–4
corporations, transnational: and currency, 128; definition, 246; and infrastructure, 110–11; and labour force, 116–18; as non-territorial, 264–5; organization of, 110; possible future of, 257–8; and unbundling, 34–6, 174–5
corporatism: definition, 166; and sovereignty, 226; and unbundling, 226–7
criminal codes: and territory, 37
'cross pressures': definition, 32; in non-territorial communities, 191; and special-purpose communities, 179–80
crossroads: and territorial organization, 45–6
Crusades: and globalization, 41–2
CSIS (Canadian Security and Intelligence Service), 69
culture: definition, 16–17
currency: and European Union, 128; and exchange rates, 10–11, 12; as territorial function, 127–8; and transnational corporations, 128
cyberspace: as non-territorial, 72

day care: as negative externality, 94–5; as territorial function, 126
decentralization: and community, 173; and supercomputers, 70–2
democracy: and majority rule, 231–2; and technology, 44. *See also* majority
Denmark: as city-state, 244
Drucker, Peter, 102, 145, 245, 268–9

economics: depression, as future possibility, 5; and externalities, 94–7; globalization of relations, 15; history of, and political organization, 79–83; markets, 107–10; regulation by non-territorial political organizations, 28–9; regulation of global economy, 112–14; service sector, 91–4; systems, and technology, 80; and telecommunications, 118–21
economies of scale: and markets, 108
education: and Aboriginal Peoples Province, 155; and La Francophonie, 152; organization on territorial basis, 32; as public good, 131–3; voucher systems, 132–3
electoral systems: and protection of minorities, 224–5
employees: and contracting out, 143–4; of unbundled organizations, 140, 141–3. *See also* labour market; unions
English: as language of international relations, 258–9
entitlement: and identification of authorized holders, 37; and public goods, 134–5; and territory, 32–4
environment: and aboriginal concepts of property ownership, 88; concerns about, as negative externality, 94, 95; possible future of, 5; as spiritual movement, 60, 250. *See also* pollution
espionage: possible future of, 5

Europe: exploration and economic history, 82
European Community: and currency, 128; as example of globalization, 26; as non-territorial government, 112–13; possible future of, 243; and protectionism, possible future of, 4–5; and sub-national territorial units, 74
European Union. *See* European Community
exchange rates: and currency trading, 10–11, 12
'exit' criterion: for non-territorial majority, 221–2, 230
exploration: and economic history, 82
externalities, 94–7

family: changes in meaning of, 19
federalism: asymmetric, 159–64; in Canada, 207–8; and sharing of territory between levels of government, 14
France: and 'bundling' of citizens' identities, 30; French Revolution, 22, 48, 232; as nation-state, 19, 73
francophones: and 'loyalty' to Canada, 222; as non-voluntary citizens of Canada, 221, 222. *See also* Quebeckers
Francophonie, La, 149–53, 155–66, 216–17, 223. *See also* Quebec
free riders: definition, 123–4; and entitlement to public goods, 135; and mass transit, 126; and public goods, 186
free trade. *See* Canada-U.S. Free Trade Agreement; European Community; NAFTA (North American Free Trade Agreement)

French Revolution, 22, 48, 232
future: explaining, 266–9

G-7: as non-territorial government, 112
GATT (General Agreement on Tariffs and Trade): as non-territorial government, 28, 112, 243, 257; possible future of, 5
Gemeinschaft, 168, 174
General Agreement on Tariffs and Trade. *See* GATT
genetic engineering: possible future of, 5–6
geography: and territory, 16
Germany: and 'bundling' of citizens' identities, 30; as hybrid nation-state, 73
Gesellschaft, 168
globalization: definition, 26–7, 41; as distinct from globalism, 26, 258, 263; and economics, 15, 82; effect on differences between cultures, 27; and homogeneity, 119, 120; and individualism, 99; and interdependence of institutions, 86–7; and migration, 115–17; of political organizations, 15; possible future of, 258; and service industries, 92–4; and specialized markets, 109, 119, 120
Globe and Mail, 53
Goods and Services Tax (GST), 129
government: à la carte, 29; and administration of territorial functions, 259–60; constrained by state structure, 264; expenditures, and externalities, 96; and infrastructure, 111; local, and sharing of common territory, 23–4; and majority rule, 210–15; and minority rights, 211–12; by non-territorial organizations,

28–9, 112–14, 257; and public goods, 125; 'public' versus 'private' organizations, 214; scope of, 164–6; and social equality, 102–7; table d'hôte, 29
Greenpeace, 25

Hamlet, 9
Hawaii: possible future of, 242
health services: insurance, 135–6, 182, 183; in non-territorial Canadian provinces, 155–8; as territorial function, 32, 126
Herald Tribune, 53
homogeneity: and globalization, 119, 120
House of Representatives (U.S.), 224, 225
housework, 95
human resources. *See* labour force
human rights: and immigration, 253–4; and individualism, 103; and non-territorial governments, 114
Hutterites, 219–20

IATA (International Air Transportation Association): as non-territorial government, 28, 112, 243
identities, of citizens: and citizenship, 197; hierarchy of, 29, 31, 34; multiple, 32, 63; and territory, 29–32
IMF (International Monetary Fund): as non-territorial government, 112
immigrants: as minorities, 219, 222; organizations, 247; reaction against, 251–4. *See also* migration
income taxes, 129–30
India: and bundling of citizens' identities, 29, 30; as hybrid nation-state, 73; population growth, 253; possible future of, 242
Indians, North American. *See* aboriginals
individual: and citizenship, 192–3; and community, 180–1, 190, 191, 197–200, 256; creation of, 98–101; and human rights, 103; and property ownership, 88, 89–90
individualism, 170–1, 195–6
information: access to, in non-territorial world, 56; industry, 93; movement of, in non-territorial world, 47. *See also* broadcasting media; communication; computers; telecommunications
information superhighway, 10
infrastructure: and global economy, 111–12; proposed, for non-territorial Canadian provinces, 158–9
insurance. *See* socialization of risk
intellectual property, 92
'invisible hand' theory, 100
Islam: fundamentalist revival, 250; as non-territorial religion, 34, 57, 58, 59
Italy: as hybrid nation-state, 73

Japan: balance of trade with United States, 11–12; and bundling of citizens' identities, 29–30; and capitalism, 231; and globalization of economic relations, 15, 26; as natural nation-state, 73
Jewish religion: as non-territorial, 57, 58, 59
journals: electronic, 55
justice: development of concept of, 86

kings. *See* monarchs

Kurds: as ethnic nation, 73; possible future of, 242

labour force: investment in, 111; and transnational corporations, 116–18
labour market: and capitalism, 82; people as assets, 92–3. *See also* employees; unions
labour unions. *See* unions
land. *See* property
languages: English as language of international relations, 258–9; minority rights, 225; and television channel specialization, 54; and territoriality, 36, 51; vernacular, and importance of printing, 51–2
literacy: and individualism, 100–1
loyalties of citizens: multiple, 32, 197
'loyalty' criterion: for non-territorial majority, 222, 230

magazines: and territoriality, 53
majority: and democracy, 202, 204–5, 231–2; as distinct from 'majorities,' 203, 204; double, 224; and loyalty, 232; and minority rights, 208–10, 223–4; non-territorial, 210–15, 221–3, 233–4; rule, conditions for, 215–16
markets: capital, 12; and economies of scale, 108; global, 257; local mass, 108, 109; specialized, 108–9
Marx, Karl, 90
mass audience. *See* audience
mass communication. *See* broadcast media; communication; television
Mayas: possible future of, 242
McLuhan, Marshall, 119–20
Mennonites, 219–20
Métis, 153
migration: and *apartheid*, 227–31; control of, 32–3; and the global economy, 115–17; and human rights, 253–4; and territory, 254. *See also* immigrants
military: citizen armies, 50; defence, and socialization of risk, 133–4; defence, as territorial function, 126; as insurance, 182; possible future of, 242; technology, and territoriality, 48–9; technology, as non-territorial, 44–5
minorities: classifying, 218–21; and democracy, 223–4, 231–2; as distinct from 'minority,' 203, 204; language rights, 225; and loyalty, 232; non-territorial, 216–17; permanent, 202–3, 215; protection of, 205–10; rights, 208–11, 211–12; visible, 217–18
monarchs: and bureaucracy, 85–6
Montreal: as financial centre, 244
moral communities, 186–9
moral majority: as fundamentalist revival, 250; and unbundling, 34

NAFTA (North American Free Trade Agreement), 74, 116
nation-state, territorial: and bureaucracy, 86; and capitalism, 80, 82, 93; and citizenship, 23, 167; compared with 'table d'hôte' menu, 237; decline of, 24–6; and ethnic states, 73; hybrid, 73; natural, 73, 74; and non-territorial political organizations, 248; origins, 18–20, 21–2, 48, 52, 75–8; possible future of, 6–7, 254–69; and type of government, 264; unbundling, 75–6, 259, 262–3
nationalism: and hierarchy of citizens' identities, 29; and membership of United Nations, 24; in Quebec, 196;

and religion, 57–60, 250; and territoriality, 56–7; weakness of, as an organizational form, 26
nations: as apart from state, 260–1; ethnic, 25, 73; possible future of, 241–2; and unbundling of citizens' identities, 32
native North Americans. *See* aboriginals
newspapers: and territoriality, 52–3
Nigeria: population growth, 253; possible future of, 242
nuclear war, 4
Nunavut, Territory of, 149, 208, 222

OPEC (Organization of Petroleum-Exporting Countries): as non-territorial government, 28, 112
organizations: non-territorial, 15, 28–9; peak, 227; unbundled, 139–46
outcomes: and unbundled organizations, 140–1
outputs: and unbundled organizations, 140–1
ownership: and individualism, 100; of information, 93; and property, 87–91

Pakistan, 36
Palestinians: as ethnic nation, 73
Parti Québécois, 223
passports: and entitlements, 37; issuance on territorial basis, 32, 33; origins of, 22; unbundling, 33–4
Peace of Westphalia: and the modern nation-state, 48, 52
peak organizations, 227
PEN (International Association of Poets, Playwrights, Editors, Essayists and Novelists), 25, 188
'people' versus 'a people,' 203, 218–21

pessimism: of futurist predictions, 7–8
police: as insurance, 182; non-territorial, 243; and socialization of risk, 133–4; unbundling of, 68–9
politics: and conflict resolution, 232; and economic history, 79–83; identification of target groups, 62–3; and new technologies, 64–78; possible future of, 6–7
pollution: as negative externality, 94, 95, 96. *See also* environment
population growth: and pressure on developed countries, 252–3
postal services: as territorial function, 126–7
Powershift, 6
predictions, futurist, 3–9
printing: and diffusion of ideas, 100; and rise of capitalism, 52; and territoriality, 53; in vernacular languages, 51–2
productivity: in unbundled organizations, 140–1
property: changing concepts of, 91; collective ownership of, 88; concepts of ownership, 87–91
protectionism: possible future of, 4–5
Protestantism: Reformation, and printing in vernacular languages, 100; and territory, 58–9
public goods: definition, 123; disappearance of, 260; education, 131–3; and entitlement, 134–5; and excludability, 124; and government, 125; and socialization of risk, 133–7; and taxes, 129–30; and territory, 125; weights and measures, 130–1
'public' versus 'private': cultural changes, 97–102, 261; organizations, 214

'quasi-states', 25, 73
Quebec: conflicts with Canadian Confederation, 147–9; as ethnic nation, 73; nationalism, 196; possible future of, 242; and territoriality, 73. *See also* Francophonie, La
Quebeckers: and government, 211; as minority, 207; relations with non-Quebec francophones, 222–3. *See also* francophones

radio: and territoriality, 53
railroads: and territorial organization, 45, 46
RCMP (Royal Canadian Mounted Police), 69
Red Cross: as moral community, 188
refugees: and immigration, 252; possible future of, 5
religion: and 'bundling' of citizens' identities, 30; fundamentalist revival, 249–50; non-denominational spiritual movements, 250–1; as public activity, 98; and science, 84–5; and sovereignty, 59–60; and territory, 57–60; and unbundling, 34
research and development, 185
reserves (aboriginal): as non-contiguous territory, 13
responsibility: and community, 186–9; and non-territorial administration, 143–4. *See also* accountability
restaurant menus: as analogy for political organizations, 237–41
retail taxes, 129, 150–2
revolution: economic, 19, 22, 48, 83; political, 19, 22, 48, 83
risk, socialization of, 133–7, 181–6
Roman Catholic Church: and territory, 58; and unbundling, 34

Rosencrantz and Guildenstern Are Dead, 9

satellite transmission, 46, 53–4
science: evolution of, 84–5; as separate from religion, 101; and spirituality, 251
Scots: as ethnic nation, 73; possible future of, 242
Senate: Canada, 207, 208, 220; U.S., 224
service industry, 91–4
Singapore: as city-state, 244
small businesses: as transnational corporations, 246, 257
social services: and global economy, 111–12; and territoriality, 32, 102–7
South Africa, 14
sovereignty: and bureaucracy, 86; and centralization of administration, 50–1; and corporatism, 226; and decline of territoriality, 63; and non-territorial organizations, 114; and religion, 59–60; and rise of 'third force' organizations, 248; and territory, 139
specialization: of communities, 178–81; of goods, for global markets, 109; of institutions, 86–7; of products, and global markets, 119, 120; in social groups, 257
Star Trek: The Next Generation, 47
state: disappearance of, 259–60, 261
subjectivism, 98
surveillance: and new technologies, 68–9
Switzerland, 30, 51

Taiwan: as city-state, 244
taxation, 129–30, 150–2
technology: and centralization, 44; and community, 172–4; and democ-

racy, 44; logic of, 43–4; military, as non-territorial, 44–5; negative consequences, 42–5; and political organization, 64–78; possible future of, 6–7; and territoriality, 36–7, 40, 48–9, 65–6; and totalitarianism, 64; and unbundling, 40–2, 63. *See also* broadcast media; computers; military technology; satellite transmission; telecommunications; television

tectonic change: definition, 17; in meaning of public and private activities, 97, 261; and territoriality, 17

telecommunications: amalgamation of television cable and telephone systems, 55–6; and community, 173–4; and education, 132; and the global economy, 118–21; and labour force, 117; as non-territorial, 28, 45, 46–8, 55, 56. *See also* broadcasting media; communication; computers; information industry; technology

teleconferencing, 47

telephone systems: amalgamation with television cable systems, 55–6

television: amalgamation with telephone systems, 55–6; cable systems, 46, 53–4, 124; channel specialization, 53–4, 64; and territoriality, 9–10. *See also* broadcast media; mass communication; technology

territorial nation-state. *See* nation-state, territorial

territoriality: as basis for political authority, 9, 13–14, 20–3; and cities and towns, 49–50; and computers, 71–2; decline of, 15, 63; and globalization, 15–16; and government functions, 105, 106; and media of communication, 52–6; and nationalism, 56–7; and printing, 53; and social services, 32; tectonic changes in, 17–18; and television, 9–10; and vernacular languages, 51

territory: and administrative functions, 122–3, 126–33, 242; and *apartheid*, 229; and bundling of citizens' identities, 29–32; and citizenship, 36–7, 38–9; and community, 167, 170–89, 189–201; and criminal codes, 37; decline in significance of, 28–9; and defence, 49; and entitlements, 32–4, 134–5; exclusivity, 13–14; and externalities, 96–7; and geography, 16; historical assumptions about, 13–15; and immigration, 254; and language, 36; and property ownership, 88; and public goods, 125; and sovereignty, 139; and taxation, 129–30; and transportation crossroads, 45–6; unbundling, 262–3. *See also* nation-state, territorial

Texas Instruments, 11

'third force' organizations, 102, 145, 246–8

Thirty Years' War: and religious nationalism, 59; and rise of nation-states, 22, 48, 52

Tiananmen Square demonstrations: and information technology, 66

totalitarianism: and technology, 64. *See also* tyranny

towns. *See* cities and towns

trade: definition, 11; wars, as future possibility, 4–5

transnational corporations. *See* corporations, transnational

transportation: mass transit, as territo-

rial function, 126; routes, and territorial organization, 45–6
Tremblay Report, 207–8
tyranny: checking by pluralistic authorities, 201. *See also* totalitarianism

unbundling: in corporations, 34–6; and corporatism, 226–7; definition, 30–1, 32; of nation-states, 256, 262–3; of organizations, 139–46; of religions, 34; of social institutions, 84–7. *See also* bundling
unemployment insurance, 135
unions: opposition to NAFTA, 116–17; in unbundled organizations, 140, 141–3. *See also* employees; labour market
United Nations: membership criteria, 20; membership growth, 24; as moral community, 188; as non-territorial government, 112, 257
United States: balance of trade with Japan, 11–12; and bundling of citizens' identities, 30, 31; as created nation, 19; dollar, status of, 12; and globalization of economic relations, 15; and health insurance, 136, 182; as hybrid nation-state, 73; and territory, 14
Universal Declaration of Human Rights, 114

universities: as models of unbundled communities, 144–5, 174, 175–6
USSR (former): role of information technology in failed *coup d'état*, 66–7

Vancouver: as financial centre, 244
VAT (Value-Added Tax), 129
victim assistance programs, 135, 136
'voice' criterion: for non-territorial majority, 222–3, 225, 230
voters: and majority rule, 203; and territorial residence, 33

Wales: possible future of, 242
wars: possible causes, in future, 4; of redistribution, 4; and unbundling of nation-states, 262
weights and measures: as public goods, 130–1
welfare state, 103, 104
workforce. *See* employees; labour market
World Bank: as non-territorial government, 25, 28, 112, 243
World Council of Churches: as moral community, 188
World Health Organization: as non-territorial government, 112
World Watch: as moral community, 188